New Cultural Studies

'*New Cultural Studies* is a rousing call to reinvigorate cultural studies. Presenting and interrogating a range of new theoretical discourses, the book provides a generous and informative look at a new generation of theorists whose work is crucial to understanding the agency of politics within cultural studies. *New Cultural Studies* is a must read for anyone concerned not just about the future of cultural studies but also about theory's presence in constructing such a future.'

Henry Giroux, McMaster University

'This is a wonderful book about emergent possibilities within cultural studies. The contributors valuably deconstruct and rearticulate the too-often taken for granted theoretical discourses of cultural studies. Rather than a declaration of generational independence as the title might suggest, it is an important reminder of the need for cultural studies to go on theorizing, in ever-changing contexts of political demands.'

Lawrence Grossberg, University of North Carolina at Chapel Hill

'Hall and Birchall, along with the writers they have included in this volume, breathe fresh intellectual life in the field of Cultural Studies by looking to strands in contemporary philosophy and showing how an animated conversation between Cultural Studies and Philosophy, especially in relation to world events, ethics, war, multi-culturalism, technology and the body, is long overdue. The chapters in this collection are erudite and lucid, they are also lively and engaged, and they are highly effective insofar as they bring Cultural Studies into a new era.'

Angela McRobbie, Goldsmiths College London

New Cultural Studies: Adventures in Theory

Edited by Gary Hall and Clare Birchall

The University of Georgia Press
Athens

For Pat and John, Chris and Roger
(we'll be quizzing you later)

Published in the United States
by The University of Georgia Press
Athens, Georgia 30602
by arrangement with Edinburgh University Press Ltd
22 George Square, Edinburgh

© Edinburgh University Press, 2006
Copyright in the individual contributions is retained by the authors
All rights reserved

Typeset in 11/13 Ehrhardt
by Servis Filmsetting Ltd, Manchester, and
printed and bound in Great Britain by
MPG Books Ltd, Bodmin, Cornwall

06 07 08 09 10 C 5 4 3 2 1
06 07 08 09 10 P 5 4 3 2 1

Library of Congress Cataloging-in-Publication Data available upon request

ISBN-13 978-0-8203-2959-8 (hardcover)
ISBN-13 978-0-8203-2960-4 (paperback)
ISBN-10 0-8203-2959-2 (hardcover)
ISBN-10 0-8203-2960-6 (paperback)

Contents

1 New Cultural Studies: Adventures in Theory (Some Comments, Clarifications, Explanations, Observations, Recommendations, Remarks, Statements and Suggestions) 1
Gary Hall and Clare Birchall

Part I   New Adventures in Theory 29

2 Cultural Studies and Deconstruction 31
Gary Hall

3 Cultural Studies and Post-Marxism 54
Jeremy Valentine

4 Cultural Studies and Ethics 71
Joanna Zylinska

5 Cultural Studies and German Media Theory 88
Geoffrey Winthrop-Young

Part II   New Theorists 105

6 Cultural Studies and Gilles Deleuze 107
Gregory J. Seigworth

7 Cultural Studies and Giorgio Agamben 128
Brett Neilson

8 Cultural Studies and Alain Badiou 147
Julian Murphet

9 Cultural Studies and Slavoj Žižek 162
Paul Bowman

Part III   New Transformations   **179**

10 Cultural Studies and Anti-Capitalism   181
Jeremy Gilbert

11 Cultural Studies and the Transnational   200
Imre Szeman

12 Cultural Studies and New Media   220
Caroline Bassett

Part IV   New Adventures in Cultural Studies   **239**

13 Cultural Studies and Rem Koolhaas' Project on the City   241
J. Macgregor Wise

14 Cultural Studies and the Posthumanities   260
Neil Badmington

15 Cultural Studies and the Extreme   274
Dave Boothroyd

16 Cultural Studies and the Secret   293
Clare Birchall

Bonus Section: Free with Every Copy of this Book   **311**

New Cultural Studies Questionnaire   313

Contributors   316

Index   319

Adventure *n* dangerous enterprise; a novel or exciting experience; commercial or financial speculations . . . a. playground where children devise their own games equipment out of waste materials ~ adventure *v/t* risk, set at stake; dare, incur risk

The Penguin English Dictionary

With each new birth something uniquely new comes into the world. With respect to this somebody who is unique it can be truly said that nobody was there before.

Hannah Arendt

CHAPTER 1

New Cultural Studies: Adventures in Theory (Some Comments, Clarifications, Explanations, Observations, Recommendations, Remarks, Statements and Suggestions)

Gary Hall and Clare Birchall

The editors would like to use this space, traditionally reserved for what is known as the 'Introduction', to draw your attention to one or two things worth bearing in mind while reading this book.

❖ **The continuing importance of theory – to cultural studies, and to 'new cultural studies' in particular . . .**

First and foremost, we would like to begin by apologising to some of our readers for, in effect, pointing out the shark fin of theory just when you were beginning to think it was safe to go back into the surf of cultural debate. We realise that, while few would deny the impact of structuralism, Marxism, post-Marxism, deconstruction, psychoanalysis, French feminist theory, postcolonial theory and so forth on cultural studies since at least the 1970s, when Stuart Hall taught a cultural theory course on the Centre for Contemporary Cultural Studies (CCCS) MA programme at Birmingham, the role and status of 'theory' within cultural studies has changed in recent years; so much so that the 'aura' of theory as 'contemporary and "cutting edge"' is for many now very much in retreat (Gibson 2004: 1), as conferences, journals, courses and schools which were once hotbeds of Foucauldian, Derridean and Lacanian 'high theory' increasingly (re)turn to a more humanist ethos and what are regarded as more politically or instrumentally 'useful' modes of research and analysis, such as those associated with sociology, social policy and political economy. What's more, we know that (for reasons we'll deal with shortly) a lot of people in cultural studies consider this to be no bad thing.

But if for some the so-called 'theory revolution' has now more or less come to an end, recent years have also seen the emergence from the long shadow cast by the Birmingham School of a new generation of cultural studies writers, scholars and postgraduate students.[1] It is a generation that can be described, at least in part, as being a product (albeit an indirect one) of those theorists who strove so hard to introduce European thought into the English-speaking academy in the 1970s, 1980s and early 1990s, and whose work had itself developed out of an engagement with literary studies, Frankfurt School-style critical theory and continental philosophy (in the UK they're associated with postgraduate courses at universities such as Essex, Sussex and Warwick in particular). In other words, it is a generation whose whole university education has been shaped by theory, who have never known a time *before theory*, and who continue to see in it a means of testing and thinking through some of the most important issues and problems in contemporary culture and society – and, indeed, cultural studies.

Perhaps the easiest and quickest way for us to illustrate just how important theory is to this new generation is by taking, as an example, the current sense of 'crisis' over cultural studies' politics, and in particular cultural studies' ability (or rather lack of it) to align itself with political forces and movements *outside* the academy.

One of the defining features that is often given of cultural studies, on which it is proposed that everyone in cultural studies will agree, is that it is a politically committed field.[2] It was certainly in political terms that Stuart Hall positioned his own activities as a teacher, writer and academic. Speaking at the landmark 1990 conference 'Cultural Studies Now and In the Future' of his time at the Birmingham Centre in the 1970s, Hall remarked that 'Gramsci's account still seems to me to come closest to expressing what it is I think we were trying to do . . . we were trying to find an institutional practice in cultural studies that might produce an organic intellectual'. And this is so even though, as Hall admits, the 'problem about the concept of an organic intellectual is that it appears to align intellectuals with an emerging historic movement and we couldn't tell then, and can hardly tell now, where that emerging historical movement was to be found' (Hall 1992a: 281). Anyone attempting to translate this kind of politically committed role into the present historical conjuncture, however, is immediately confronted by some rather difficult and challenging questions. Does the hope, for instance, that, in Hall's words, 'there *could* be, sometime, a movement which would be larger than the movement of petit-bourgeois intellectuals' continue to be one we *can* actually carrying on 'living with', given that we now occupy a period in which the victory of capitalism's free-market economy and defeat of any political alternatives to neo-liberalism seem somewhat assured (1992a: 288)? Even if the rise of such a movement *is* still considered to be a possibility, is any historical alliance of progressive forces today really going to be discernible as the kind of radical political project with which cultural studies, and the work of Hall and the Birmingham School in particular, has traditionally been associated: that of the British New Left and the 'new social movements' (feminism, anti-racism, anti-imperialism, gay liberation and so on)? Or is it more likely to adopt the kind of 'disorganised', decentralised, multitudinous form that appears to characterise the new wave of large-scale, 'anti-capitalist' and anti-war protests that have emerged over the course of the 1990s and early 2000s? In which case, is the development of a *new* form of politics and a *new* political project not required if cultural studies is to retain its sense of political engagement in the twenty-first century – something perhaps more along the lines of that conceived by Agamben (1993), Derrida (1994) and Hardt and Negri (2004) in terms of the 'coming community', the 'new international' and the 'multitude' respectively? And is cultural studies something that *can* connect with or otherwise assist such a 'movement of movements' anyway? It certainly doesn't seem to have had much success in this respect so far (as Jeremy Gilbert's chapter in this volume makes clear).

Now, for many, the raising of such questions is no doubt challenging enough given the importance of Birmingham School, New Left, new social movements-style politics to cultural studies' sense of its own identity. Yet difficult though they may be, these questions still all have their basis in a fundamental premise which underpins cultural studies but which, despite (or more likely because of) this, too often remains unaddressed. This is the assumption that historical and social movements of some kind, whether organised or disorganised, recognisable by cultural studies as traditionally conceived or not, *do indeed continue to be possible or at least desirable*. In fact, we would go so far as to argue that the continuing resort on the part of much of the left in general, and cultural studies in particular, to such progressive historical narratives (even as, like Hall, they often simultaneously express certain reservations about the wisdom of doing so) is actually part of a far larger problem. It is a situation summed up most incisively by Wendy Brown, when she draws attention to the way in which, while many on the left have:

> lost confidence in a historiography bound to a notion of progress or to any other purpose, we have coined no political substitute for progressive

understandings of where we have come from and where we are going. Similarly, while both sovereignty and right have suffered severe erosions of their naturalistic epistemological and ontological bases in modernity, we have not replaced them as sources of political agency and sites of justice claims. Personal conviction and political truth have lost their moorings in firm and level epistemological ground, but we have not jettisoned them as sources of political motivation or as sites of collective fealty. So we have ceased to believe in many of the constitutive premises undergirding modern personhood, statehood, and constitutions, yet we continue to operate politically as if these premises still held, and as if the political-cultural narratives based on them were intact. (Brown 2001: 3–4)

It is consequently crucial, for Brown, that those of us who still consider ourselves as being *of the left* think about how we might 'develop historical political consciousness in terms other than progress, articulate our political investments without notions of teleology and naturalized desire, and affirm political judgement in terms that depart from moralism and conviction' (2001: 4). Brown gets right to the heart of the problem when she asks:

> If the legitimacy of liberal democracy depends on certain narratives and foundational presuppositions, including progress, rights, and sovereignty, what happens when those narratives and assumptions are challenged, or indeed simply exposed in their legitimating function? What kinds of political cultures are produced by this destabilization of founding narratives and signal terms? . . . How do we live in these broken narratives, when nothing has taken their place? (2001: 14)

It is with questions of this kind, concerning some of cultural studies' fundamental and, indeed, founding premises, assumptions and presuppositions, that many members of this new generation of cultural studies writers and practitioners are currently engaged in speculating upon and experimenting with.[3] And, significantly, at a time when it often seems theory is being increasingly marginalised, within cultural studies, the institution of the university and society in general,[4] it is theory that they are drawing on for help in doing so.

❖ That whole 'here's a new generation' thing we just slipped in back there . . .

We'll come back to say more about why this new generation is so heavily invested in theory in a moment. Before we do so we'd just like to make it clear, once and for all, right from the start, so there can be no misunderstanding, that we are in no way trying to position either ourselves or our contributors as leaders of any such 'new generation'. In one respect at least, *New Cultural Studies* is simply an attempt on our part to draw attention to what appear, to us anyway, to be some interesting things that are happening in cultural studies at the moment, but which are often marginalised or otherwise overlooked, or at any rate don't get the attention we think they deserve.

In fact, as far as we're concerned this 'new generation' is not really a generation at all, at least if you understand this to imply that they're all of approximately similar age. Although they perhaps share a common set of (often philosophically orientated) theoretical languages, they do not have a common approach or methodology: say, poststructuralist, post-Marxist, postfeminist, philosophical, literary, aesthetic or 'textualist' (whatever that last one is). They don't constitute a group, movement or school in the way the Birmingham School is or was. We're not trying to name or establish a new school in that sense – partly because if it was recognisable as a new school it would be much the same as the old school. If anything, what's different about this 'generation' is that *it is not recognisable as a school*, but is rather more mobile: this 'new generation' is fluid, flexible and spatially diffuse, involving a multiplicity of often conflicting, contradictory and incommensurable theories, approaches, objects, pedagogies and styles. Hence the multiple-edited and -authored nature of this book. The various contributors to *New Cultural Studies* do not all say the same thing: about cultural studies; or about what in shorthand we are here calling 'theory', for that matter. Some of them would no doubt disagree with much of what we have said (about them) in this 'introduction' (the narrative of which is itself 'broken' and made up of multiple parts).

Nor do the different members of this 'generation' all necessarily identify themselves primarily or even substantially with cultural studies. In fact, and as one participant in a recent online discussion on the state of cultural studies in Australia acknowledged, restricting any such account of cultural studies merely to what is explicitly called or calls itself (or aligns and identifies with) 'cultural studies' risks completely missing, among other things:

> a new generation of [in this case] students . . . who don't identify themselves as 'Cultural Studies' and probably don't subscribe to this list, cos it is too passe. They effortlessly do publishing, poetry, new media, 'ficto-criticism' (awful word), and from within a very theoretically informed perspective, but with the theory worn lightly and perhaps even treated in a magpie fashion. There's a huge world of that out there . . . This new terrain has not been mapped as a whole, probably because it is too diverse and ever-changing. (Jacka 2004)

Indeed, if we want to explore some of the most interesting developments that are taking place 'in' cultural studies today, it seems to us that we do often find these being forged by people operating at the margins and even 'outside' of 'cultural studies' spaces and institutions, at least as they are traditionally and most narrowly defined. And we're not *just* thinking of people associated with so-called 'high theory' either. One notable example is provided by the architect Rem Koolhaas' Project on the City. In the words of Fredric Jameson: 'These extraordinary volumes are utterly unlike anything else one can find in the print media; neither picture books nor illustrated text, they are in movement, like a CD Rom' (Jameson 2003: 65). However, with their formal innovations and 'performance' of the built space, the first two volumes of this project are perhaps 'closest to cultural studies' (2003: 65), in Jameson's view – albeit an experimental and creatively reimagined cultural studies, we would suggest. (J. Macgregor Wise's chapter in this volume is concerned precisely with the extent to which Koolhaas' Project on the City provides a possible signpost to thinking 'cultural studies differently'.)

Having said that, we did admittedly gather our contributors on the basis that they were identifiable as part of certain global, national and regional networks of communication, including many which are explicitly associated with 'cultural studies' (institutions, associations, journals, publications, conferences, email lists and so on). No doubt this mode of composition and assembly would suggest, at least to some, that 'the network', the organisational model which is supposedly most characteristic of the postindustrial 'information' or 'new economy', might indeed have been a more a useful way of conceiving this 'new generation'.[5] Given that we have actually met only a few of our contributors face to face, and have relied almost entirely on electronic modes of communication to put this book together, *New Cultural Studies* could certainly be said to have depended on a degree of *'abstract cooperation'* in its production (Hardt and Negri 2000: 296). Yet while the network, or the multitude for that matter (Hardt and Negri 2004), might both in their different ways have provided us with rival, and potentially extremely productive, ways of thinking about the relation between the people whose work is contained here (ways it would certainly have been interesting to have explored and experimented with further and more rigorously), we have for the most part preferred to privilege a generational model. We have done so for a variety of reasons, including those concerned with strategy (some of which will hopefully become clear in a moment), but also because it seems to us that this model, for all its problems and simplifications, perhaps comes closest to capturing something of the phenomenon we are endeavouring to describe.

Still, we want to make it clear that, as far as we're concerned, to use *any* of these terms in this context – 'new generation', 'network', 'multitude' – is, as J. Hillis Miller observes with regard to attempts to understand the Internet as a net, web, mosaic, galaxy or superhighway, also:

> to reduce to familiar and comprehensible patterns . . . what does not exist like that at all . . .
>
> The rhetorical name for such figures is 'catachresis'. 'Catachresis' means 'against usage' in Greek. 'Catachresis' names the 'abusive' transfer of what names something known . . . to something unnamed and not an 'identifiable entity', something unknown. (Miller and Asensi 1989: 117)

❖ The somewhat disingenuous nature of our apology for theory . . .

Of course we realise that in apologising for drawing attention to the continued presence of theory within cultural studies, as we did earlier, we have in fact merely created more opportunities to discuss it. Continuing with this theme, we'd now like to turn our attention to saying a little more about the apparent waning of theory's influence, and why some people in cultural studies do indeed consider this to be no bad thing.

Various different explanations have been given for the decline of theory, all of which have their own local and regional variations. Some of these we've already raised questions for with our comments on left and liberal founding narratives of politics, progress, history and so forth; for others we'll proceed to do so throughout the course of this chapter. But here are ten reasons why some people at least have suggested that the time is right to move 'beyond theory':

1. **The crisis of the left** – the current crisis in Marxist and more widely leftist politics – evident in the fall of the Berlin Wall, the challenge to the authorities in the People's Republic of China and the massacre in Tiananmen Square, the collapse of the Soviet Union and the declaration of independence of the former Soviet Republics, the reshaping of Eastern Europe, the weakening of the unions and so on – has meant that the kind of radical 'far left' thinking often associated with theory is now regarded as being somewhat out of sync with the times.

2. **The marketisation of the university** – successive neo-liberal governments have sought to compete in the international marketplace by cutting state budget deficits through decreases in public spending, not least

on education. The ensuing drastic reduction in funding has led to profound changes in the institution of the university. Among them is the ever-growing pressure placed on universities to attract financial support from 'external' sources other than government. As Brett Neilson points out in this volume, this has meant paying 'increased attention to practical questions and applied outcomes' of a kind that a philosophically orientated theory is often held as being either unwilling or unable to provide, as academics endeavour to deliver research that is deemed economically and socially 'productive', and hence potentially fundable by grant-awarding bodies, research councils, business, entrepreneurs, industry and the like. One reason a humanist ethos and more sociological modes of analysis are today often prioritised over theory, then, is because, as Neilson puts it, they are quite simply perceived as being 'more amenable to funding bodies'.

3. **The rise of the 'new economy'** – Neilson is not alone in identifying a link between changes in the economy, the corporate transformation of the university and the decline of theory. Writing in a recent issue of the journal *Continuum*, Mark Gibson locates a 'surprising enthusiasm for humanist themes', as opposed to the 'anti-humanism' of theory, 'in business management and the educational programmes associated with it', in particular, 'with management gurus extolling the virtues of "creativity" and urging greater attention to subjectivity, intuition and emotion'. And a major factor behind this, for Gibson, 'has been the complex of developments summed up in the idea of the "new economy", with the premium they have placed on intellectual property and "ideas" as material assets' (Gibson 2004: 1–2).

4. **The creation of the 'creative industries'** – if neo-liberal cuts to funding for both universities and their students have led to a greater demand for courses with a more or less direct outcome in the job market, this has not resulted merely in the privileging of those areas of study most closely associated with the new 'information economy': business, management, science, technology, IT and so on. There has been a related effect within the arts and humanities, too, as academics specialising in humanist discourses and practices to do with creativity, subjectivity and emotion also now find themselves in favour with research councils, university managers and students-as-paying-customers alike. ('Anti-humanist' theory, by contrast, is not generally regarded as being particularly useful or profitable in this respect – and this despite the fact that theory actually has quite a lot to say about creativity, inventiveness and emotion.)[6] Nor is this a one-way street, whereby those aspects of the arts and humanities deemed important and useful in the global 'knowledge economy' are extracted and

incorporated into more commercially profitable areas of study. Terry Flew, in the same issue of *Continuum*, describes something of:

> a feedback loop in operation, where discourses identified as having their origins in the arts have filtered through to business, and now returned to artistic and cultural practice through the concept of the 'creative industries', where artists are increasingly expected to view themselves as *cultural entrepreneurs*, managing their creative talents, personal lives and professional identities in ways that maximise their capacity to achieve financial gain, personal satisfaction and have fun. (Flew 2004: 2)

So we're all supposed to be entrepreneurs now, whether we're in business (studies) or not.

5. The celebration of the public intellectual – one interesting manifestation of the feedback loop between the arts and humanities and business is the current celebration of the figure of the 'public intellectual', who is able to write reader-friendly pieces for the press and generally get themselves featured in the media and who, by becoming a 'cultural entrepreneur' in this way, is praised for having escaped the restrictive and rarefied atmosphere of the university. It is a desire to make links with the 'outside' of the university that has a certain correspondence both with the attempt of many within cultural studies to seek authentication and validation for what they do in terms of their ability to connect with some 'real world', 'out there'; and with the subsequent emphasis often placed on avoiding the difficult 'jargon' associated with theory, precisely in order to communicate better – whether as public or organic intellectuals – with 'ordinary people'. Indeed, could this belief that, as a field of practice, cultural studies is only really important to the extent to which it is able to ally itself to social and political forces and movements external to the academy not be at least one reason why ideas concerning the 'creative industries', 'cultural entrepreneurship' and the 'public intellectual' appear to have found such a happy home within cultural studies at the moment, and have in some places even become dominant?[7]

6. Lack of time – theory can often be extremely demanding in terms of the time and effort one is required to spend on it: not just thinking about it, but also reading, learning and even understanding it. Thanks to many of the above changes in the institution of the university, however, gone are the days when a scholar could take years, say, to research thoroughly and write the definitive monograph on a given subject. The current emphasis on productivity, efficiency, league tables, measurable 'outputs' and so forth has placed the majority of academics in a position where they are now under pressure to squeeze out far more research in far less time than was generally the case previously, especially given everything else they have to do nowadays (like securing external funding, delivering excellent teaching and learning that external reviewers and students rate highly, and dealing with the increased administrative load the contemporary university's 'audit culture' has also produced). The resulting sense of haste and urgency has left many researchers feeling that they just can't afford to spend too long reading and writing difficult texts that frequently require them to slow down, take their time and think, and thus threaten to make them appear unproductive and inefficient in the eyes of colleagues, departmental heads, university managers and funding bodies.

7. **Changes to the academic publishing industry** – decreases in the level of funding that institutions receive from government sources and the associated corporatisation of the university have also had a marked effect on the academic publishing industry. As both institutions and their students have found it harder and harder to purchase texts, the traditional market for the academic monograph has experienced something of a decline. The response on the part of many academic presses has been to prune their lists, and to focus on publishing accessible Introductions and Readers designed to appeal to the relatively large undergraduate student market instead. Granted, the number of new journals that are regularly being established, in part to meet the need of academics for 'research impact', Research-Assessment-Exercise-submittable publishing opportunities, has compensated for such developments to a certain extent. However, the high and ever increasing prices charged by many publishers of medical, scientific and technical periodicals has meant that a lot of institutional libraries are unable to maintain their current holdings, let alone take out further journal subscriptions. The upshot is that, even if academics *can* still find the time to write theory-led texts, because theory is seen as 'difficult' and thus not necessarily suitable for undergraduates, it is becoming harder, for less established members of the profession especially, to get such work published and disseminated, in print form at least, and thus read, reviewed, discussed etc.

8. **Fashion** – no doubt partly for some of the reasons supplied above, theory, at least of the literary/philosophical/critical/cultural kind we are referring to here (there are many other types of theory being produced in places other than the university: by the media, the military, government think-tanks, policy institutes, management consultancies and so on), is not

nearly as fashionable or sexy as it once was. When we first presented some of these ideas at an academic conference in the US, a conference very much concerned with the politics of cultural studies in relation to the second Gulf War, one review (in a tongue-in-cheek manner which we actually quite like) put it as follows:

> A cadre from the UK bordered on heresy by arguing that theory might be our best hope, the last refuge for experimentation and possibility in an age that seeks to make everything function, to turn meandering into instruments, and surrender speculation to financial markets . . . From the perspective of the new economic turn, these Brits looked like they were auditioning for 'I Love the 80s, Francophile style' when the only nostalgia show allowed in town is the 'I Love the 70s, Birmingham edition'. (Anonymous 2004)

9. The many deaths of theory – there is a feeling that an era has ended: that, especially with the death of Jacques Derrida in 2004, the golden generation of Althusser, Barthes, de Man, Deleuze, Lacan, Lyotard, Foucault et al. has finally come to a close (although one's tempted to ask 'What about the women: Kristeva, Cixous, Irigaray and so on?'); and that, for all the efforts to champion Agamben, Badiou, Nancy, Stiegler or whoever as the 'next big thing', a new generation truly capable of replacing them has yet to emerge.

Such attitudes to theory are of course inflected differently in different cultural analyses. At one end of the spectrum, they amount to the idea that the 'theory moment' was something we had to go through at the time, but it was just a fashion, a craze. Now it's over, now that we've *done* theory, we can put it back where it belongs in the box of tools labelled 'useful approaches to culture' and get on with the kind of teaching and research we should really have been doing all along, perhaps a little bit altered by the experience, perhaps not.

Towards the other end of this continuum is the view that presents theory as having once been radical, innovative and challenging, but as having now been accepted into the mainstream of teaching and research. From this perspective the 'theory wars' are over, the last battle having long since been won. So much so that theory doesn't even need stand-alone courses anymore – one reason it perhaps seems less visible nowadays. In fact, such is the extent of theory's integration that for some it has become almost a new orthodoxy or canon, concerned for the most part merely with the continued application of an unquestioned set of techniques, practices, approaches and strategies. The result is a seemingly endless series of readings producing more or less the same predetermined 'discoveries' of assemblages, aporias, becomings, decentrings, deterritorialisations, flows, immanences, intensities, hauntings, hybridities, networks, nomadic practices, phallocentrisms and spectres as previous generations of theorists. Consequently, most of the really interesting stuff, the cutting edge of intellectual work and thought, is now regarded as taking place elsewhere.

Somewhere in between is a position often adopted by those cultural analysts who have at times been willing to employ theory where necessary, at least to the extent that it doesn't create problems for their fundamental conceptions concerning politics, progress, morality, the socio-cultural, what it means to do cultural studies and so forth. This is a view which regards theory as having been useful and important, but which sees its declining influence as a sign that an intellectual reassessment is now taking place; that what is happening is a working through of many of the ideas and arguments that have been so influential since the 1970s, in order to decide what needs to be kept and what discarded, so that we can 'come out the other side' of theory (Gibson 2004: 3), 'after theory', as it were (Eagleton 2003).[8]

10. 9/11 and all that – there is also a sense of 'post-theoretical' political urgency apparent within cultural studies at the moment; an urgency which, especially after 9/11 and the wars in Afghanistan and Iraq, is seen as leaving little time for the supposedly elitist, Eurocentric, text-based concerns of Derrida, Lacan, Lyotard, Irigaray, Kristeva, Butler, Bhabha, Spivak et al.

Having outlined some of the reasons that are often given for the apparent waning of theory's influence within cultural studies, we'd like to come back, as promised, to the question of why this 'new' cultural studies 'generation' continues to be so interested in theory.

There are a number of responses we could give to this question, but we're going to restrict ourselves here to privileging three in particular:

1. The first reason is that theory is frequently concerned with examining and testing the kind of founding ideas, narratives and systems of thought that (as we saw previously with the example of Marxist-inspired left-historical progressive politics) cultural studies all too often relies upon.

What's more, we would argue that a lot of the narratives and explanations that have been constructed around theory's supposed demise – the '"decline" of the political left' (McQuillan et al. 1999: p. xi), the marketisation of the university, the rise of the new economy and so forth – can and should be included in this. For the waning of theory's influence can no more be simply read off economic, cultural and political changes in history and society, for example, than its rise in the 1960s and 1970s can be attributed to the society of *that* period. Indeed, as far as we're concerned, if theory is about anything at all, it is about interrogating (which is different from rejecting) such narratives, such easy explanations (especially for what they may marginalise or ignore in their own drive for closure and will to power–knowledge), and acknowledging what remains unknowable and unreadable, and thus resistant to any exhaustive or systematising interpretation; and which, in doing so, draws attention to the limits of our own theory and thinking, too.[9]

It is important to emphasise that such interrogation of founding ideas and narratives is not for its own sake but can rather (and among other things) help us to avoid slipping into what Wendy Brown calls an 'anti-political moralism'. Brown uses this term to refer to a certain 'resistance' to thinking through the conditions and assumptions of one's own discipline; and, in particular, to the consequences for both leftists and liberals of not being able to give up their devotion to previously held notions of politics, progress, morality, sovereignty and so forth. Significantly, theory has been a regular target for moralists, Brown observes, frequently being chastised for its 'failure' to tell the left what to struggle for and how to act (2001: 29). Indeed, Brown asserts that 'moralism so loathes overt manifestations of power . . . that the moralist inevitably feels antipathy toward politics as a domain of open contestation for power and hegemony'; and that 'the identity of the moralist is', in fact, actually 'staked against intellectual questioning that might dismantle the foundations of its own premises; its survival is imperiled by the very practice of open-ended intellectual enquiry' (2001: 30).

Now part of what we want to argue here is that an anti-political moralism is also identifiable in cultural studies. It can be recognised in much of the work that has been done around identity and cultural politics, as Brown shows. But an anti-political moralism is also apparent in many of the calls that were made over the course of the 1990s and early 2000s for cultural studies to move away from the 'self-reflexivity' of theory and return to a concern with 'real politics': be it in the guise of 'concrete' forms of political activity; or modes of social, historical and economic research and analysis (political economy, social policy etc.) regarded as being more directly connected to 'real-world' issues. Of course, for many, the moral righteousness of such calls to action has been amply borne out by recent events, not least among them the post-September 11 foreign policies of the UK and US governments, which, besides the invasion of Iraq, also include the torture of prisoners in Abu Ghraib, the deployment of white phosphorous bombs during the attack on Fallujah, and the use of 'enhanced interrogation techniques' – slapping, freezing, sleep deprivation, near-drowning – by the

CIA in secret prisons established outside the protection of US law. Nevertheless, for us, clinging *unquestioningly* to 'left-political' conceptual frameworks and methods of analysis like this – as if things are basically the same now as they were even just pre-September 11, pre-George W. Bush or pre-Tony Blair and New Labour, at least to the extent it can be simply *assumed* that positions and practices forged in an earlier era continue to be relevant and applicable today – leads to the kind of anti-political moralism outlined by Brown. The problem is that such moralising occupies the place of and in fact replaces genuine critical interrogation. Indeed, Brown goes so far as to argue that:

> Despite its righteous insistence on knowing what is True, Valuable, or Important, moralism as a hegemonic form of political expression, a dominant political sensibility, actually marks both analytic impotence and political aimlessness – a misrecognition of the political logics now organizing the world, a concomitant failure to discern any direction for action, and the loss of a clear object of political desire. In particular, the moralizing injunction to act, the contemporary academic formulation of political action as an imperative, might be read as a symptom of political paralysis in the face of radical political disorientation and as a kind of hysterical mask for the despair that attends such paralysis. (2001: 29)

It is no doubt worth stressing that none of this is to suggest that left politics or left forms of political practice and analysis (including those associated with sociology, political economy and so on) should necessarily be abandoned; that all this collapses into some moral relativism on our part and that we are actually arguing *against* taking a position and maintaining particular political or ethical values when it comes to issues of social justice; or that we ourselves do not identify as being 'of the left'. What it does mean is that we cannot take our 'politicality' for granted. In fact, as Brown makes clear, to have certain political 'convictions' fixed and defined in advance is not to be especially *political*:

> We do no favour, I think, to politics or to intellectual life by eliminating a productive tension . . . in order to consolidate certain political claims as the premise of a program of intellectual enquiry. . . . If consolidated representations of identity and truth are the necessary premise of certain democratic political claims, they also necessarily destroy the openness which the intellectual life required by rich formulations of democracy depends. (2001: 41)

For us, as for Brown, then, we have to be able to 'live with this paradox' (2001: 41). In particular, we have to be able to place our political convictions in question and, in doing so, be open to the specific and contingent demands of each singular conjunction of the 'here' and 'now'. And as part of this, we have to face the possibility that the 'here' and 'now' may change us; that we may indeed have to change if we are to be capable of recognising each such singular conjuncture and respond to it responsibly. (Which is why we would argue that much of theory, while often appearing to be *less political* than political moralism, is actually capable of being *more political*: because it *does not* simply decide what constitutes politics and the political *in advance* but instead remains open to the complexities of a situation, including the 'real', practical, empirical, experiential, concrete, political or historical complexities.)[10] In short, we have to be able to imagine and invent new forms of politics.

One way to think of the new cultural studies we are describing here, then, is as the invention of a cultural studies without the mourning, moralism or melancholia Brown sees as symptomatic of much of the left.[11] From this point of view theory is regarded by this new generation of cultural studies writers and practitioners as presenting rigorous, if risky, ways to think cultural studies without necessarily having to resort to teleological or historical narratives of progress, or depend on epistemological or ontological systems which have their basis in 'nature, fetishized reason, the dialectic, or the divine' (Brown 2001: 42).

2. The second reason this 'new generation' continues to draw so heavily on theory is that, with its concern for what is ambivalent, complicated, marginalised, remaindered and repressed, theory offers cultural studies means of understanding and thinking through – rather than merely repeating – many of the ambiguities and anxieties, confusions and contradictions, urgencies and uncertainties that radically disrupt and even paralyse cultural studies, but which it has a tendency to deny, disavow, exclude or otherwise downplay in order to maintain its identity *as cultural studies*. Not least among these, as far as this book is concerned, are the difficult, multiplicitous and often paradoxical relations between politics and theory (see Jeremy Gilbert, 'Cultural Studies and Anti-Capitalism'), modernity and postmodernity, old and new (Gary Hall, 'Cultural Studies and Deconstruction'), humanism and anti-humanism (Neil Badmington, 'Cultural Studies and the Posthumanities'), the human and the machine (Geoffrey Winthrop-Young, 'Cultural Studies and German Media Theory'), culturalism and structuralism, knowledge and experience (Gregory J. Seigworth, 'Cultural Studies and Gilles Deleuze'), immanence and transcendence, agency and application (Brett Neilson, 'Cultural Studies and Giorgio Agamben').

3. Additionally, by opening cultural studies to forms of knowledge and analysis it can comprehend only by reconceiving its identity, theory provides this generation with ways of thinking cultural studies beyond some of the limits the latter has set to its own powerful and important thinking. To put it another way, this time using the words of Paul Bowman from his chapter in this book: if, as Slavoj Žižek says, cultural studies functions 'as a discourse which pretends to be critically self-reflexive, revealing predominant power relations, while in reality it obfuscates its own mode of participating in them', theory can help cultural studies appreciate and understand this, and even 'to apply some of its own stock insights *to itself*'. What's more, this is the case not just with regard to questions of politics (see Jeremy Valentine, 'Cultural Studies and Post-Marxism'; Brett Neilson, 'Cultural Studies and Giorgio Agamben'; Gary Hall, 'Cultural Studies and Deconstruction'; and Jeremy Gilbert, 'Cultural Studies and Anti-Capitalism'), but also those of ethics (see Joanna Zylinska, 'Cultural Studies and Ethics'), knowledge (see Clare Birchall, 'Cultural Studies and the Secret'), nationality (see Imre Szeman, 'Cultural Studies and the Transnational') and even the human (see Neil Badmington, 'Cultural Studies and the Posthumanities').

❖ Our insistence on using terms we have yet to define . . .

You may have noticed that we have not attempted to provide a closed definition of that broad range of discourses which are often, but not exclusively, 'associated on the one hand with philosophy, or rather with a critical response to the systematic, totalizing claims of philosophy; and on the other, with the study of literature and of language as the medium to which that critical response appealed' – a range of discourses it is actually quite 'difficult to classify or to name univocally, for one of the things they share is precisely the radical questioning of all such univocity' (Weber 2000), but which, first in the US, and later elsewhere, have regularly been placed under the heading of 'theory'. Nor have we sought to provide a tight definition of cultural studies here – assuming that cultural studies and theory can be so easily distinguished in the first place, which is actually by no means certain (see Hall forthcoming) – other than to say that the version with which we are most concerned is that associated with and derived from the work of the Birmingham School; or attempted to account for the differences between, say, British, American and Australian cultural studies (these being the countries perhaps most influenced by the Birmingham School and in which its versions of cultural studies have been most dominant – see Bowman's chapter in this volume; Hall forthcoming). We have instead, for the most part, preferred to leave such questions (relatively) open, and to let the different contributors to *New Cultural Studies* address the relation between 'theory' and 'cultural studies' in their own specific contexts, in their own singular ways.

Our only condition in this respect has been to insist contributors to *New Cultural Studies* treat cultural studies with the same degree of care and rigour as any of the theorists or theories they're dealing with. Too often people associated with theory have lamented the way theoretical work has been condemned almost out of hand by people (journalists, the media, academics in other fields and so forth) who don't appear to have read it particularly carefully, if at all, only for the same theorists then to treat cultural studies in a similarly off-hand way. It is a trap we wanted to try to ensure wherever possible that *New Cultural Studies* did not fall into. We love cultural studies – even if ours is a complicated relationship – and so we've tried to include contributors who love it too.

❖ A summary (of sorts) . . .

Having so far (conspicuously) failed to provide one of those condensed summaries or orientating overviews that can be helpful when reading a book of this kind, we would now like to go some way towards rectifying this omission. Basically, *New Cultural Studies: Adventures in Theory* addresses the question: whither theory's place, position and future with regard to cultural studies now?

It does so, first, by introducing some of the most interesting members of this new 'post-Birmingham-School' generation of cultural studies writers and practitioners: Neil Badmington, Caroline Bassett, Dave Boothroyd, Paul Bowman, Jeremy Gilbert, Julian Murphet, Brett Neilson, Gregory J. Seigworth, Imre Szeman, Jeremy Valentine, Geoffrey Winthrop-Young, J. Macgregor Wise and Joanna Zylinska.

Second, it does so by providing a guide to the main theories and thinkers that influence and inform their work: Jacques Derrida and deconstruction; the philosophy of Gilles Deleuze; the radical, democratic post-Marxism of Ernesto Laclau and Chantal Mouffe; Donna Haraway on techno-science; Giorgio Agamben on biopolitics; the Hegelian Lacanianism of Slavoj Žižek; the ethical philosophies of Emmanuel Levinas and Alan Badiou; Georges Bataille's general economics of expenditure; and the German media theory of Friedrich Kittler and Niklas Luhmann – all of which are for the most part still largely marginal in mainstream cultural studies, certainly in the UK, although perhaps slightly less so in the United States and Australia.

Having said that, if *New Cultural Studies* provides a guide to these different theories, it is one that does not simply introduce and explain them; instead it tries to *engage* readers with such theories *head on*. In this respect *New Cultural Studies* is not a book that is uncritical of theory: it is not, for instance, concerned merely with the kind of continued application and enactment (for which one could also read banal and clichéd repetition) of a pre-given set of theories that have been inherited from previous generations of theorists. Far from it. If there is a certain dissatisfaction with cultural studies among this new generation, something similar is recognisable with regard to this kind of easy 'theoretical fluency', which, as Paul Bowman notes, also 'indicates institutional comfort and political complacency'.

In one attempt on our part to avoid slipping into such institutional comfort here, as well as looking at instances where there is already a recognised relation between cultural studies and certain theorists – Deleuze, Haraway, Laclau and Mouffe, Žižek and so on – *New Cultural Studies* also examines the work of a number of thinkers who are relatively new even to the arena of theory, and whose work has to date been somewhat underappreciated and underutilised within the English-speaking academy (and certainly within cultural studies). Agamben, Badiou, Kittler and Luhmann could all perhaps be included in this latter category, albeit to varying degrees and extents.

Third, this book approaches the question of the place, position and future of theory by exploring some of the new directions and territories currently being mapped out across, and at the intersections of, cultural studies and theory – often, as we say, by people operating outside 'cultural studies' spaces and institutions as they are traditionally and most narrowly defined. So, again, *New Cultural Studies* is concerned with politics, with post-Marxism and with anti-capitalism, of course (and with them Seattle, the 'war on terror', the attack on Iraq, Guantánamo Bay, the re-election of Bush and Blair, the killing of Jean Charles de Menezes in the aftermath of the 7/7 bombings in London . . .). But it also looks at recent developments in fields as diverse as architecture, science and new media technology (see Caroline Bassett, 'Cultural Studies and New Media'), not to mention a number of other themes and topics which might initially appear to be somewhat marginal to the cultural studies project, such as the secret and the extreme.

In this way, *New Cultural Studies* endeavours to provide a guide to theory's past, present and possibly future role in cultural studies, from a perspective that is sympathetic to, but not uncritical of, theory and theoretical ways of thinking.

❖ That pesky term 'new' in our title . . .

In our title, and indeed throughout this book, we use the word 'new' to refer to the particular kind of cultural studies we are describing here. No doubt some of you will be thinking that:

1. Strictly speaking this is incorrect, and is in fact somewhat contradictory. 'The *new* proclaims a break, the emergence of something unprecedented, different, and forward looking', James Donald (2004: 2) writes with regard to the 'New Humanism' of Gibson and Flew (2004). Yet the idea of producing something *new* within cultural studies is of course not new at all, and is actually quite old. The term 'new' itself provides a case in point, as it is by now quite a well used one, having already been adopted within cultural studies to refer to the 'New Left', 'New Times' (Hall and Jacques 1990), 'new ethnicities' (Hall 1992b) and indeed 'New Humanism', to name but a few.
2. This is somewhat disrespectful to those who have been doing cultural studies much longer than us and really do know better. We would like to take this opportunity to apologise for any offence we may have caused. We're really very sorry. Honestly, we are. To those committed to the development of cultural studies, we hope that this 'new' will excite rather than offend.

Rather than using 'new' blindly, then, we are using it provocatively, while being aware of the contradictions and tensions it carries. We understand that positioning something as 'new' looks as if we are saying that existing cultural studies work is 'old' and somehow 'out of date'. But we're not making a point about fashion. We're not interested in fuelling a passing fad or trend. This is the future of cultural studies we're talking about, after all, which is something extremely important to both of us. As far as we're concerned, many of the questions that cultural studies has hitherto asked can and must still be asked – it's just that there might be ways of thinking those questions *and* the answers to them differently. At the same time there also needs to be room in cultural studies for 'new' questions and answers. It is these possibilities that we are endeavouring to explore and experiment with here.

This is perhaps the place to point out that we did actually have a number of alternative titles we were considering, including:

- *Experiments in Cultural Studies* – this would definitely have captured something of the experimental, inventive, alchemical, provisional feel

we wanted. But to be honest, it just seemed a little too a 'hard' science or avant-garde in some of its connotations.
- *Adventures in Cultural Studies* – we liked this. A lot. Not least because it seemed less dialectic, more provisional and speculative than *New Cultural Studies*. The reason we didn't go for it in the end is because it also conjured up images of 'boy's own annuals' and men in pith helmets colonising new lands and territories (an obvious 'no no' as far as cultural studies is concerned).

❖ The mysterious 'missing' chapters . . .

A reluctance to decide on our politics in advance, and keenness to avoid resorting to 'moralism as anti-politics' especially, is one reason we haven't adhered to a 'checklist formula' when deciding on themes, subjects, contributors and contributions for this volume. You know the kind of thing: 'Have we got a chapter on gender? Check! Race? Check! Sexuality? Check! . . .'

Among other reasons for passing on such chapters are these:

- We didn't want to succumb to the pressure to be 'politically correct' – nor, at the same time, to resort to knee-jerk, stereotypical condemnations of 'political correctness'. Both responses would have represented a kind of moralistic 'righteousness' and 'defensiveness' on our part, and would in effect have constituted an 'anti-political' 'refusal of the very intellectual and political agonism that one expects to find celebrated in left and liberal thinking' (Brown 2001: 37).
- The assumption that often underpins this 'checklist' approach – that the ultimate aim of all examination and enquiry is to arrive at the politics of a given subject, be it seen in terms of class, race, gender, ethnicity, sexuality or whatever – marginalises and excludes other possible readings: readings which do not place politics, moralistically, in a position where it is always already known and decided upon in advance; and which make allowances both for a text's singularity and its performative possibilities.
- There is no guarantee that someone from, say, India or Korea or Chile will not harbour 'Western' or 'Northern' ideas. To think otherwise is to essentialise such identities. To quote Wendy Brown one last time (and if we have referred to her more than most in this chapter, it's because Brown's work is one of the places in which the relation between cultural theory and politics has been addressed most interestingly and productively in recent years), including a diversity of perspectives is too often simply 'equated with populating a panel or a syllabus or an anthology

with those who are formally – or, more precisely, phenotypically, physiologically, or behaviourally – marked as "diverse"' (2001: 38).
- Let's face it, there are already a lot of books in cultural studies and cultural theory which deal directly and explicitly with class, race, gender and sexuality.
- Besides, we *are* still dealing with these issues, albeit often in less direct or obvious ways. The chapter by Neil Badmington on 'Cultural Studies and the Posthumanities', to take just one example, engages with the way in which theory has reconceived identity politics. In doing so this chapter prompts us to think through developments in postfeminism and sexuality as well as ethnicity.

❖ Talking about new cultural studies before it happens . . .

It's important to realise that our earlier claim to be *merely* describing the work of this 'new generation' of cultural studies writers and practitioners is not entirely accurate, and perhaps even a little disingenuous.

OK, for ease of access we have divided the book up into four parts. First, there are the chapters that position the concerns of cultural studies in relation to another more or less coherent and distinct form of thought: deconstruction, post-Marxism, ethics and German media theory. A second group of chapters does something similar with the work of a single author: Deleuze, Agamben, Badiou, Žižek. A third confronts cultural studies with sites of recent social, political or technological transformation: anticapitalist movements, the transnational, and new media. Four final chapters, on Koolhass' Project on the City, the posthumanities, the extreme and the secret respectively, bid to rethink cultural studies from the point of view of a particular theme, approach or concept that is actually incredibly important to it, but that cultural studies has, to date, otherwise tended to marginalise, exclude, delimit or ignore.

However, we're not just introducing this 'new cultural studies' and describing some ready-made end product here. We're also inventing it, in the sense that this book may play a part in transforming and so creating the context and environment in which this new cultural studies can be read and understood. In other words, as well as plotting the development of previous and existing traditions of cultural studies, *New Cultural Studies* is gesturing towards the forging of its own – a cultural studies which (at least in the case of the contributors to this book) is conceived and thought through the work of Gilles Deleuze, Henri Bergson, Jacques Derrida, Slavoj Žižek, Michael Hardt and Antonio Negri, Giorgio Agamben, Friedrich Kittler, Donna Haraway, Alain Badiou, Emmanuel Levinas, and/or Georges

Bataille et al. *as well as* that of Richard Hoggart, Raymond Williams, Stuart Hall, Lawrence Grossberg, Kuan-Hsing Chen, Tony Bennett, bell hooks, Angela McRobbie, Meaghan Morris, Tricia Rose, Henry Giroux, Paul Gilroy or the Birmingham School. Indeed, diverse though they may be, a feature we *would* suggest most of the contributors to this book can perhaps be said to share or have in common in one way or another is precisely a willingness to rethink and reinvent cultural studies – to question what the possibilities of doing cultural research can be and to explore and experiment with thinking them differently and otherwise, and thus, by remaining open to the irruption of otherness or alterity, to imagine a new cultural studies – and to draw on theory in some shape or form for help in doing so. In other words, this book and its account of new cultural studies and this new generation are performative, in that the book is producing the very thing of which it speaks: it is inventing this new cultural studies, and also the new generation that is creating it. (Since one of the things that links writers as diverse as Agamben, Deleuze, Derrida and even Koolhaas is the emphasis they place on the performative aspect of their work – the way their texts function as catachresis, producing the things of which they write, as well as the norms and laws which validate and legitimise them, thus constituting singular, active, 'practical' events, gestures and interventions into the here-and-now space and functioning of culture and the institution – responding to a cultural studies that is being thought through theory in this way seems to us quite appropriate.) As J. Macgregor Wise (quoting Elizabeth Grosz) contends with regard to Koolhaas' Project on the City, then, the chapters in this book:

> could, more in keeping with the thinking of Gilles Deleuze, be read and used more productively as little bombs that, when they do not explode in one's face (as bombs are inclined to do), scatter thoughts and images into different linkages or new alignments without necessarily destroying them. Ideally, they produce unexpected intensities, peculiar sites of indifference, new connections with other objects, and thus generate affective and conceptual transformations that problematize, challenge, and move beyond existing intellectual and pragmatic frameworks. (Grosz 2001: 58)

❖ Producing a 'little bomb' of our own . . .

With this performative aspect in mind, we wanted to experiment to some extent with making this opening chapter slightly different in its form, too. Sure, for the most part *New Cultural Studies* adopts the familiar guise of a cultural studies collection or 'critical reader', consisting of a number of essays devoted to introducing a specific aspect of cultural studies' relation to theory. In line with our commitment to what we might hesitatingly call a 'performative' cultural studies, however, we have supplemented this traditional book format with an experimental, playful, provocative 'introduction' intended to disrupt the reader's expectations a little. In this way, *New Cultural Studies* not only provides a guide to some of the most interesting new ways currently available of thinking about culture, but also endeavours to (keep) open a future for cultural studies, and for theory, that is somewhat different from many of those currently on offer. In short, this book is at once catering to an existing audience *and* trying to encourage that audience to reinvent itself, to think cultural studies differently and otherwise, and create a 'new cultural studies'. In this sense, this opening chapter, and with it this book, could indeed be seen as cultural studies 'stuttering, trembling, trying out new resonances, new rhythms', to quote J. Macgregor Wise once again.

❖ On not copping out . . .

It's perhaps just worth stressing that by turning to these self-reflexive questions and to theory, we are not seeking shelter from the 'global uncertainty' about politics (as the mandate of the 2004 'Crossroads in Cultural Studies' conference put it). Nor are we advocating political silence or moral indifference. Rather, *New Cultural Studies* is endeavouring to reposition cultural theory and reaffirm its continuing intellectual, and indeed 'political' (and 'ethical'), relevance to cultural studies, and to culture and society at large. By so doing *New Cultural Studies* is attempting to invent a cultural studies which comes *after* Gramsci, Hall, the Birmingham School and so on in all senses of the word *after*: not just as in *following on from*, *coming afterwards* and *in reaction to*, but also *in the footsteps* and *in the tradition of*. A cultural studies, in other words, which neither abandons nor simply affirms the cultural studies tradition, but which rather repeats the difference and the inventiveness of that tradition, along with its disruptive force and performative affect, in order to explore and experiment with some of the possibilities for doing cultural studies *after Birmingham*, but *after theory*, too.

❖ Our reticence to summarise our contributors' arguments before they do . . .

To summarise the different ways in which each member of this 'new generation' featured here engages with such questions would not only take too long, it would lack the 'performative' aspect we are saying is for us a crucial feature of this 'new' cultural studies (in the sense that we would be trying to describe and explain it rather than enacting it and making it happen). So the editors would like to move the proceedings on and let the contributors to this book perform this new cultural studies each in their own singular way . . .

. . . But not before noting that, as we hope the reader has by now realised, this list of what one could almost call 'errata' is intended to flag up the risks that any investment in the 'new' entails. What may to some appear like 'errors' are exciting to us; we feel that cultural studies is robust enough to experiment with what Lyotard would call 'paralogic moves' (Lyotard 1984). Cultural studies can face the challenges of a future we do not yet, or perhaps cannot ever, know, not by assimilating the 'new', but by opening itself to it.

Notes

1   As Johan Fornäs writes, 'Cultural studies has widely diverse roots and routes in different world regions, and though globally dominant, the one that goes through the Birmingham CCCS is only one of several trajectories' (Fornäs 2005: 4–5). There are many other important and interesting versions of cultural studies – and of theory – associated with other times, countries and regions throughout the world. Indeed, a strong feature of cultural studies is its inter- and transdisciplinarity, intellectual diversity and geographical dispersion. Any rigorous and responsible engagement on our part here with the whole of cultural studies – even presuming such a thing were conceivable, which it's not, not least because, for us (as with culture for Derrida), what is proper to cultural studies is to not be identical to itself – is thus clearly impossible. Consequently, it is the version of cultural studies that was developed in the 1950s, 1960s and 1970s, and which is most closely associated with Britain and Birmingham, that we have for the most part chosen to focus upon and engage with in this book: not least because, for many, this is where cultural studies first emerged; but also because this is the version that still tends to dominate (see Fornäs 2005: 3).

For more on the history of cultural studies at Birmingham, see: Grossberg (1997); Hall (1980, 1990, 1992a); Hoggart (1992); Johnson (1983); Webster (2004). For a recent attempt to capture something of the flavour of cultural studies internationally, see Abbas and Erni (2005), as well as Szeman in this volume.

2   Different attempts to encapsulate or otherwise define cultural studies occur throughout this book. Julian Murphet's chapter on Badiou, for instance, cites both Nick Couldry's description of cultural studies as a quest for a 'common culture' (2000: 142), and Simon During's grouping of the 'panoply of cultural studies trajectories under three modalities: Cultural studies "takes into

3 It's important to point out that not all of this new generation would entirely agree with Brown's reading of history here (or with every aspect of our interrogation of cultural studies' politics, for that matter). After all, is Brown's own analysis not itself underpinned by a resort to a legitimating grand narrative: the idea that something has changed historically; that where certain narratives and foundational presuppositions concerning politics, progress, rights, sovereignty and so forth once held, now they have been eroded; that the epistemological and ontological bases of sovereignty and rights have recently been 'challenged' or 'exposed' where once they weren't?

4 For an interesting recent exception that introduces and explains the importance to cultural studies of a number of cultural theorists, including Judith Butler, Fredric Jameson and Homi K. Bhabha, see McRobbie (2005).

5 See Castells (1996) for what is merely one of the best-known instances. A more recent example is provided by Rossiter's research on 'organised networks'. See Lovink and Rossiter (2005).

6 For two recent examples drawn from the field of literary studies, see Attridge (2004) and Clark (2005). For more on the revived emphasis on creativity, imagination, experience and so on within contemporary cultural studies, see Gregory J. Seigworth's chapter on 'Cultural Studies and Gilles Deleuze' in this volume.

7 With respect to cultural studies in Australia, for example, Simon During writes:

> Nowadays Australian cultural studies is increasingly normalised, concentrating on cultural policy studies and, often uncritically, on popular culture and the media. Indeed it is in Australia that the celebration of popular culture as a liberating force . . . first took off through Fiske and Hartley's contributions. The young populists of the seventies now hold senior posts and what was pathbreaking is becoming a norm. The readiness of a succession of Australian governments to encourage enterprise universities has empowered the old tertiary technical training departments in such areas as communications, allowing them to have an impact on more abstract and theorised cultural studies in ways that appear to have deprived the latter of critical force. Furthermore, the structure of research funding, which asks even young academics to apply for grants, has had a conformist effect. Perhaps Australian cultural studies offers us a glimpse of what the discipline would be like were it to become relatively hegemonic in the humanities. (During 2005: 26; cited by Gregg 2005; see also the ensuing discussion on the csaa forum, www.csaa.asn.au/discussion/emaillists.php)

8 Gibson gives the example of Paul Gilroy's 'turn from his anti-humanist past' to talk in recent books such as *Between Camps* (2000) and *After Empire* (2004) of a 'planetary humanism' (Gibson 2004: 3). Yet *can* theory simply be added to

ideas and concepts – of politics, progress and so forth – it is frequently concerned with placing in question? And what is the other side of theory anyway? Can modes of thought as taken up with interrogating ideas of identity and difference as psychoanalysis or deconstruction be said to have an 'other' side in any such simple sense? Is theory – or even French feminism, say, or post-Marxism – so self-identical a body of thought as to enable it to be treated in this way?

It's also worth remembering that announcements of the death of theory are almost as old as theory itself. As Derrida put it with regard to deconstruction:

> from the very beginning . . . people have been saying . . . it's waning, it's on the wane. I've heard this for at least twenty-five years: it is finished, it is dying. Why do I say dying? It is dead! I tell you it's dead! . . . I'm totally convinced that deconstruction started dying from the very first day. (Derrida 1996: 224–5)

In a strange kind of way nothing could be said to provide more evidence of the continued life of theory than the regular pronouncements of its death – as the fact that it is felt necessary to keep on repeating at regular intervals that something is dead or dying only testifies to its continuing survival.

9 For more on the limits of theory, see Dave Boothroyd's chapter in this volume and Hall (forthcoming).
10 For instance, given that, as we saw earlier, the current tendency in cultural studies to move away from theory and towards politics is in many ways motivated by neo-liberalism and the 'new economy', we would argue that this is not necessarily nearly as radical a 'political' thing to do as many on the left seem to think. In fact, it is often quite conservative.
11 For more on cultural studies as moralism, see Birchall (2006) as well as Zylinska (2005) and in this volume.

Bibliography

Abbas, Ackbar and Erni, John Nguyet (eds) (2005), *Internationalizing Cultural Studies: An Anthology*, Oxford: Blackwell.

Agamben, Giorgio (1993), *The Coming Community*, Minnesota: University of Minnesota Press.

Anonymous (2004), 'Double Crossing Back: A Review Essay of the 2004 Crossroads in Cultural Studies Conference', *InterActivist Info Exchange*, posted October, http://info.interactivist.net/article.pl?sid=04/ 10/02/2021233.

Attridge, Derek (2004), *The Singularity of Literature*, London: Routledge.

Birchall, Clare (2006), *Knowledge Goes Pop: From Conspiracy Theory to Gossip*, Oxford: Berg.

Brown, Wendy (2001), *Politics Out of History*, London and Princeton, NJ: Princeton University Press.

Castells, Manuel (1996), *The Rise of the Network Society*, Oxford: Blackwell.

Clark, Timothy (2005), *The Poetics of Singularity: The Counter-Culturalist Turn in Heidegger, Derrida, Blanchot and the Later Gaddamer*, Edinburgh: Edinburgh University Press.

Couldry, Nick (2000), *Inside Culture: Reimagining the Method of Cultural Studies*, London: Sage.

Derrida, Jacques (1994), *Specters of Marx: The State of the Debt, the Work of Mourning, and the New International*, London: Routledge.

Derrida, Jacques (1996), 'As If I Were Dead: An Interview with Jacques Derrida', in John Brannigan, Ruth Robbins and Julian Wolfreys (eds), *Applying: To Derrida*, London: Macmillan, pp. 212–27.

Donald, James (2004), 'What's New? A Letter to Terry Flew', *Continuum: Journal of Media and Cultural Studies*, 18: 2, June, pp. 235–46.

During, Simon (2005), *Cultural Studies: A Critical Introduction*, London: Routledge.

Eagleton, Terry (2003), *After Theory*, London: Allen Lane.

Flew, Terry (2004), 'Creativity, the "New Humanism" and Cultural Studies', *Continuum: Journal of Media and Cultural Studies*, 18:2, June, pp. 161–78.

Fornäs, Johan (2005), 'Editorial', *Cultural Currents: Newsletter of the International Association of Cultural Studies*, 1, September, pp. 3–6.

Gibson, Mark (2004), 'Introduction – The New Humanism', *Continuum: Journal of Media and Cultural Studies*, 18:2, June.

Gibson, Mark and Flew, Terry (eds) (2004), *Continuum: Journal of Media and Cultural Studies*, 18:2, June.

Gilroy, Paul (2000), *Between Camps: Race, Identity and Nationalism at the End of the Colour Line*, London: Allen Lane.

Gilroy, Paul (2004), *After Empire: Melancholia or Convivial Culture?*, London: Routledge.

Gregg, Melissa (2005), 'Conformist and Lacking Critical Force', posting on the csaa-forum forum Friday 26 August, csaa-forum@lists.cdu.edu.au.

Grossberg, Lawrence (1997), 'Introduction: "Birmingham" in America?', in *Bringing It All Back Home: Essays on Cultural Studies*, Durham, NC, and London: Duke University Press.

Grosz, Elizabeth (2001), *Architecture from the Outside: Essays on Virtual and Real Space*, Cambridge, MA: MIT Press.

Hall, Gary (forthcoming), 'British Cultural Studies – It's the Real Thing', *Oxford Literary Review*, 21.

Hall, Stuart (1980), 'Cultural Studies and the Centre: Some Problematics and Problems', in Stuart Hall, Dorothy Hobson, Andrew Lowe and Paul Willis (eds), *Culture, Media, Language*, London: Hutchinson, pp. 15–47.

Hall, Stuart (1990), 'The Emergence of Cultural Studies and the Crisis of the Humanities', *October*, 53, pp. 11–23.

Hall, Stuart (1992a), 'Cultural Studies and its Theoretical Legacies', in Lawrence Grossberg, Cary Nelson and Paula Treichler (eds), *Cultural Studies*, New York: Routledge, pp. 277–94.

Hall, Stuart (1992b), 'New Ethnicities', in James Donald and Ali Rattansi, *'Race', Culture and Difference*, London: Sage, pp. 252–60.

Hall, Stuart and Jacques, Martin (1990), *New Times*, London: Lawrence and Wishart.
Hardt, Michael and Negri, Antonio (2000), *Empire*, London: Harvard University Press.
Hardt, Michael and Negri, Antonio (2004), *Multitude: War and Democracy in the Age of Empire*, Harmondsworth: Penguin.
Hoggart, Richard (1992), *An Imagined Life. Life and Times, Vol. III, 1959–1991*, London: Chatto and Windus;
Jacka, Liz (2004), 're: Magpie studies', CSAA discussion list, Wednesday 27 October, csaa-forum@lists.cdu.edu.au.
Jameson, Fredric (2003), 'Future City', *New Left Review*, 21, May/June, pp. 65–79.
Johnson, Richard (1983), *What Is Cultural Studies Anyway?*, Birmingham: University of Birmingham Centre for Contemporary Cultural Studies.
Lovink, Gert and Rossiter, Ned (2005), 'Dawn of the Organised Networks', *Fibreculture Journal*, 5, http://journal.fibreculture.org/ issue5/index.html.
Lyotard, Jean-François (1984), *The Postmodern Condition: A Report on Knowledge*, trans. Brian Massumi and Geoff Bennington, Manchester: Manchester University Press.
McQuillan, Martin, Macdonald, Graeme, Purves, Robin and Thomson, Stephen (1999), 'The Joy of Theory', in *Post-Theory: New Directions in Criticism*, Edinburgh: Edinburgh University Press, pp. ix–xx.
McRobbie, Angela (2005), *The Uses of Cultural Studies*, London: Sage.
Miller, J. Hillis and Asensi, Manuel (1989), *Black Holes: J. Hillis Miller; or, Boustrophedonic Reading*, Stanford, CA: University of Stanford Press.
Weber, Samuel (2000), 'The Future of the Humanities: Experimenting', *Culture Machine* 2, http://culturemachine.tees.ac.uk/Backissues/j002/Articles/art_webe.htm.
Webster, Frank (2004), 'Cultural Studies and Sociology At, and After, the Closure of the Birmingham School 1', *Cultural Studies*, 18:6, November, pp. 847–62.
Zylinska, Joanna (2005), *The Ethics of Cultural Studies*, London: Continuum.

Part I: New Adventures in Theory

BIRMINGHAM IS DEAD — LONG LIVE BIRMINGHAM

CHAPTER 2

Cultural Studies and Deconstruction

Gary Hall

Deconstruction is . . . on the one hand, a movement of overturning or reversal of the asymmetrical binary hierarchies of metaphysical thought (one/many, same/other . . . center/periphery . . .), in such a way as to register the constitutive dependence of the major on the minor term; on the other, a movement beyond the framework delimited by these terms . . . to an always provisional suspension of their force. This suspension operates by means of new, provisional concepts . . . (*différence*, *pharmakon*, *hymen*, *archiécriture*) and 'which can no longer be included within philosophical (binary) opposition but which, however, inhabit philosophical opposition, resisting and disorganizing it, *without ever* constituting a third term, without ever leaving room for a solution in the form of speculative dialectics'. (Frow 2005: 71; citing Derrida 1981: 43)

Deconstruction – it's just *so* September the 10th!

Although I work and teach in a media, communications and cultural studies department, speak at cultural studies conferences, and publish in cultural studies books and journals, what I'm really interested in and what I think I'm doing a lot of the time is deconstruction. If I've sometimes found it necessary to keep this to myself, it's partly because, well, let's face it, there aren't too many jobs around for people who 'do' deconstruction these days – at least not in cultural studies in the UK. But it's also because cultural studies tends to have a rather negative and even hostile attitude to deconstruction, at the moment anyway. You know how the argument goes: deconstruction is too theoretical, too self-reflexive, too concerned with producing texts about other texts rather than real-life empirical, ethnographic or experiential issues, while the language it uses is too complicated and too full of jargon to be understood by anyone other than a university-closeted elite. Indeed, the 'post-theoretical' sense of political urgency that has permeated cultural studies over the course of the 1990s and early 2000s, and which has only increased in intensity in the wake of the protests for global social justice in Seattle and the events of September 11, has led to some serious doubts being expressed regarding the relevance of deconstruction to cultural studies full stop. Deconstruction has frequently been censured for failing to provide an alternative left politics – in fact, for lacking any obvious political agenda whatsoever. What's needed today, it's maintained, is not more theory but more social, political and economic analysis.

Now it seems to me that this is a shame. It's a shame because for cultural studies to attempt to be *more political* in this way is not necessarily for cultural studies to be particularly political at all. Indeed, one of the things I want to convey with this chapter is that, while cultural studies habitually perceives (re)turning to politics and the 'real' as a political thing to do, it's frequently not (and paradoxically enough, it is precisely the kind of emphasis that's currently being placed on a certain understanding of what it is for cultural studies *to be political* that's largely responsible for this). But it's also a shame because this is something deconstruction can help cultural studies to understand. Deconstruction can be of great assistance to cultural studies when it comes to thinking through some of the problems and paradoxes in its complicated relationship to politics and the political. That said, I have to admit the situation hasn't exactly been helped by the way in which the majority of those associated with deconstruction have, in turn, tended to condemn cultural studies almost out of hand, because of both what they see as its lack of intellectual rigour and its rather simplistic ideas around deconstruction – with the result that cultural studies gets to keep on regurgitating more or less the same clichés about deconstruction without ever really being challenged. So let me try to go some way towards addressing this state of affairs with a quick discussion of a few cultural studies myths about deconstruction.

❖ **Deconstruction fails to provide a positive alternative politics and is therefore conservative.**

It's certainly fair to say deconstruction *does not* provide a politics, a political programme or even a political theory as such. That's because these concepts are all part of the metaphysical tradition deconstruction is trying to understand. For deconstruction to satisfy the demand to *be political* in a way those who make such a demand could recognise, it would have to adhere to the kind of metaphysical thinking deconstruction wants to interrogate and exceed. Granted, this might finally result in deconstruction being perceived by many of its supposedly more political critics as *political enough*. Yet this would be the case *only* to the extent that deconstruction *did* adhere to metaphysical concepts of the political (of action, activism, revolution, social justice and so on), and *did not* challenge, question or otherwise say anything radical about them.

Deconstruction – even if I restrict myself to that version which is associated with the name 'Jacques Derrida' (there are many others) – has nevertheless addressed any number of clearly recognisable political subjects, although for reasons which will become clear, Derrida has often done so by means of 'marginal themes' such as friendship, spectrality and secrecy. Here is a list of just some of the *obviously* political topics Derrida has written and spoken on: social justice; democracy; globalisation; institutions (particularly the university); the law; the death penalty; the refugee and asylum issue; the question of European identity; the question of Jewish identity (not least in connection with the Israel/Palestine conflict); political thinkers (Hobbes, Rousseau, Schmitt, Marx . . .); political documents (e.g. the American Declaration of Independence); political movements (including that for racial emancipation in South Africa); political resistance (in Algeria, for example).

❖ Deconstruction is concerned too much with theory and texts, and not enough with practical political issues.

A similar point can be made regarding the idea that we can, if not entirely forget about them, then at least keep 'theoretical' issues (including those concerned with self-reflexively interrogating what it means to *do cultural studies*) within certain limits in order to proceed all the quicker to more urgent matters in the real world of concrete materiality. What would such realist or pragmatic discourses actually do or achieve, asks Derrida?

> Let us answer: they could do very little, almost nothing. They would miss the hardest, the most resistant, the most irreducible, the othermost of the 'thing itself'. Such a political history or philosophy would deck itself out in 'realism' just in time to fall short of the thing – and to repeat, repeat and repeat again, with neither consciousness nor memory of its compulsive droning. (Derrida 1997: 81)

Practical 'real-world' issues can only be engaged if careful thought has been given over to the question of *how* they can be engaged.

❖ **Deconstruction is just a mode of negative literary or philosophical critique.**

Perhaps the quickest way to deal with this is with reference to Derrida's work on the institution of the university. I'm thinking of his claim that 'an event of foundation can never be comprehended merely within the logic that it founds . . . The foundation of a university institution is not a university event' (Derrida 1992: 30). What Derrida means by this is that an institution cannot simply found itself, because that would require it to be already in existence and to possess the authority to do so *before* it was actually founded. In this way, Derrida is able to demonstrate: (1) that there is an aporia, an insoluble difficulty or paradox of authority at the origin of the institution; (2) that the foundation of the university is both inherently unstable and irreducibly violent since it cannot by definition rest on anything but itself, in that it is a *performative* act which produces the very thing of which it speaks. Now the important thing to note here is that this reading of the institution is not a negative *destruction*; it's not connected to some naive idea that the revelation of this aporia will bring the university crashing down. Derrida's deconstruction is rather positive and affirmative, in that it shows that the impossibility of any such foundation is also constitutive for the university, and highlights the chance this situation presents to rethink the manner in which the university 'lives on'. As he puts it in a text very much concerned with the pragmatics of deconstruction:

> once it is granted that violence is *in fact* irreducible, it becomes necessary – and this is the moment of politics – to have rules, conventions and stabilizations of power. All that a deconstructive point of view tries to show, is that since convention, institutions and consensus are stabilizations, . . . they are stabilizations of something essentially unstable and chaotic. Thus, it becomes necessary to stabilize precisely because stability is not natural; it is because there is instability that stabilization becomes necessary; it is because there is chaos that there is need for stability. Now, this chaos and instability, which is fundamental, founding and irreducible, is at once naturally the worst against which we struggle with laws, rules, conventions, politics and provisional hegemony, but at the same time it is a chance, a chance to change, to destabilize. If there were continual stability, there would be no need for politics, and it is to the extent that stability is not natural, essential or substantial, that politics exists and ethics is possible. Chaos is at once a risk and a chance, and it is here that the possible and the impossible cross each other. (Derrida 1996: 83–4)

Hence Derrida's involvement in founding and supporting numerous 'real-life' (counter-)institutions such as the Greph, the Etats généraux de la philosophie and the Collège international de philosophie.

That's probably enough demythologizing for now. I don't want to give the impression Derrida's writings contain a secret, including a secret politics, that can be uncovered if only one devotes enough time and trouble to actually *reading* them. Even though part of the idea behind this chapter is to (re)introduce the relevance of deconstruction to cultural studies, I'm not going to be decoding Derrida's thought here into a more accessible language or otherwise excavating its 'politics'. As Derrida himself acknowledged when speaking on the intelligibility or otherwise of his writing, it is important that his texts hold something back:

> there is a certain 'I hope that not everyone understands everything about this text', because if such transparency of intelligibility were ensured it would destroy the text, it would show that the text has no future, that it does not overflow the present, that it is consumed immediately. . . . If everyone can understand immediately what I mean to say – all the world all at once – then I have created no context, I have mechanically fulfilled an expectation and then it's over, even if people applaud and read with pleasure; for then they close the book and it's all over.
> . . .There has to be the possibility of someone's still arriving; there has to be an *arrivant*, and consequently the table – the table of contents or the table of the community – has to mark an empty place for someone absolutely indeterminate, for an *arrivant*. . . .
> But this is also a way of giving to be read. If something is given to be read that is totally intelligible . . . it is not given to the other to be read. Giving to the other to be read is also a *leaving to be desired*, or a leaving the other room for an intervention by which she will be able to write her own intervention: the other will have to be able to sign in my text. And it is here that the desire not to be understood means, simply, hospitableness to the reading of the other, not the rejection of the other. (Derrida 2001: 30–2)

And all this despite (and as well as) the fact that Derrida really does 'try to be clear', and that it's all there, in his writings, as a reading of almost any one of his texts indicates (p. 31). (Let's take as an example 'I Have a Taste for the Secret'.)

For me to provide an 'easy' introduction to deconstruction here would not therefore be a very 'deconstructive' thing to do, at least as the latter is performed in Derrida's writings. Which is why I've so far resisted schematising the 'general strategy of deconstruction' as a 'double gesture' – you know, the kind of thing that's usually taken from the third interview in *Positions*. (John Frow's (2005) *New Keywords* entry on deconstruction, cited in my epigraph, provides a recent example.) To 'do' deconstruction I need rather to respond to Derrida's inventive and at times difficult interventions in the texts of Plato, Freud, Joyce and so on – inventive in the sense that Derrida's writings 'performatively' transform and so 'create' the 'context' in which they can be read and perhaps eventually understood (2001: 14, 30) – by producing inventive and, yes, at times difficult interventions of my own, signed with my own name, in the texts of Derrida and others.

From this perspective, the kind of critique of cultural studies I've provided so far, although quite common among those associated with deconstruction, is not a particularly appropriate way of handling the situation. Given the concerns of this chapter and book, a more hospitable response to cultural studies' rather inhospitable treatment of deconstruction, it seems to me, is not to chastise it but to show how cultural studies, too, as a community (of academics, intellectuals and practitioners), is open to the possibility of 'someone absolutely indeterminate' still arriving, and thus to 'the reading of the other, not the rejection of the other'. So let me start again, and try to provide at least the beginnings of something of this kind, taking as my point of departure precisely the sense of urgency around cultural studies' politics at the moment that has led it, like deconstruction, to be often criticised for 'paying too much attention to culture and not enough to the state and economics, too much to cultural differences and not enough to social commonalities, too much to popular resistance and not enough to political domination' (Grossberg n.d.).

Cultural studies after Gramsci, hegemony theory and the Birmingham School

For many people cultural studies is currently experiencing something of a 'crisis' around its ability to understand and intervene in the societies of the North Atlantic capitalist industrial nation-states. Speaking in 1998 of the change in the political landscape represented by the then new New Labour government, Stuart Hall put it like this:

> Old left positions don't seem to have any purchase . . . because those positions are not really engaged with the modern world, with the problems currently facing us. Cultural studies has a lot of analytic work to do . . . in terms of trying to interpret how a society is changing in ways that are not amenable to the immediate political language. Blair will formulate those changes in certain ways, but there's a deeper level of shifts to be included in such analyses, shifts in the popular. (Hall 1998: 193–4)

Repeating Hall's claim that it is 'a highly transitional moment, a very Gramscian conjuncture that we are in – between the old state that we can neither fully occupy or fully leave, and some new state toward which we may be going, but of which we're ignorant . . . [we are] living in the moment of the post' (Grossberg n.d., quoting Hall 1998), Lawrence Grossberg agrees that such changes in society require cultural studies to change, too. For Gramsci, the popular was a key site at which ongoing political struggle took place – which of course is why Hall was so interested in 'deconstructing' popular culture: 'Popular culture is one of the sites where . . . socialism might be constituted. That is why "popular culture" matters. Otherwise, to tell you the truth, I don't give a damn about it' (Hall 1981; cited by Grossberg n.d.). But once it's no longer the site of such hegemonic struggle, then cultural studies' attention needs to move on. Significantly, for Grossberg, this now involves shifting away from an emphasis on what he calls 'textual or aesthetic culture', since culture, in the 'textual (media and popular)' sense, 'does not appear to be playing the same central role . . . It is not where change is being organized and experienced, and it is certainly not where resistance is being viably organized.' Instead, he hypothesises that 'people are experiencing politics and economics as the primary field of change, and as the primary experience of change itself'. Consequently, what is required, according to Grossberg in some of his most recent writings, is a (re)turn to a more classical British cultural studies emphasis on 'political economy', albeit a 'new' or significantly rethought political economy in which politics, the state, and economies are thought of as 'inescapably cultural' (Grossberg n.d.).

Now, while Grossberg's argument seems to me incredibly interesting and important – there has certainly been something of a '(re)turn' in cultural studies to what's been termed 'cultural economy' recently (Du Gay 1997; Du Gay and Pryke 2002; Amin and Thrift 2004; Merck 2004) – is it just a shift in cultural studies' location of political struggle from 'textual and aesthetic' culture to the more explicitly political and economic that is required? Or does cultural studies need to change in more fundamental ways? The reason I ask is because this is somewhat ambiguous in Grossberg's account. Writing in another recent essay he asserts that, on the one hand, British cultural studies, the Birmingham School, '*Policing the Crisis* and the work that circulated around it and followed in its path . . . offered a unique and productive reading of Gramsci's notion of hegemony' that is still incredibly useful (Grossberg 2005: 356). On the other, he draws attention to the way 'too often, people ignore the specific theory of hegemony offered here, as a particular kind of political struggle, not a universal one' (p. 357). The 'presence of a hegemonic struggle is not guaranteed', for Grossberg: it can't be assumed that the contemporary conjuncture *can* be understood as a hegemonic struggle (p. 357). In fact, he sees it rather in terms of 'a struggle between those (liberals and to some extent, leftists) who think they are waging a hegemonic struggle, and those (significant fractions of the new right) who are trying to invent, not only a new social formation, but a new political culture as well, one built not on compromise but on fanaticism', and in which the settlement is often 'accomplished behind the back of those struggling over the field of the social formation' (p. 358).

So, to provide an example of my own from the UK, whereas Thatcher sought to win consent to lead through a hegemonic strategy of constant (re)negotiation, the modernising of the Blair government operates rather differently. Close to two million people can protest on the streets of London against attacking Iraq, but Tony Blair is still prepared to 'ignore the public will' and take his country to war on the grounds that he and George W. Bush consider the use of such force and power *the right thing to do* – and what's more he doesn't need to hide it. Hegemony is thus 'inadequate', according to Grossberg, 'to either analyse or respond to the complexly changing balance in the field of forces or, more conventionally, to the vectors and restructurings that are potentially changing the very fabric of power and experience' (p. 358). But if the current conjuncture is not necessarily hegemonic, or not *just* hegemonic, to what extent *can* cultural studies continue to use the classic, mainstream, British formation of the project with its emphasis on Gramsci and hegemony (and politics and economics) to analyse it? If Grossberg and Hall are right, and we are in a period of transition, is the 'old left' cultural studies tradition associated with the old political culture appropriate to analyse and fight against what Grossberg regards as the 'production of a new modernity' (p. 365)? Or does cultural studies need to embark on the transition to a new, post-Gramscian, post-hegemony theory, post-Birmingham School cultural studies, too?

Cultural studies and Hardt and Negri

Although the above questions can be formulated by following the logic of Grossberg's argument, these are not issues he explicitly addresses himself. For help in answering these questions I therefore want to turn to one of the places in contemporary cultural and political theory where, if 'there is a growing disparity between the apparent vectors and effects of "culture" and the leading edge of political transformation and historical change' (Grossberg n.d.), this leading edge is seen as having been analysed most powerfully in recent years.

Michael Hardt and Antonio Negri's *Empire* (2000) is a book people in cultural studies are increasingly drawing on, whether as part of the general move towards politics and economics, or in an attempt to understand politics in what appears to be a period of transition.[1] Hardt's and Negri's thesis is this: a new era is emerging, what they call Empire, for which the current methods of analysis are no longer adequate. They are inadequate because 'they remain fixated on attacking an old form of power and propose a strategy of liberation that could be effective only on that old terrain . . . What is missing here is a recognition of the novelty of the structures and logics of power that order the contemporary world. Empire is not a weak echo of modern imperialisms but a fundamentally new form of rule' (p. 146), one which replaces the sovereignty of nation-states with a '*decentered* and *deterritorializing* apparatus of rule that progressively incorporates the entire global realm within its open, expanding frontiers' (p. xii).[2] However, it's not my intention to deal with all the various ins and outs of Hardt and Negri's thesis. I want to concentrate merely on an intriguing paradox, one that has significant consequences, it seems to me, both for their analysis of Empire and for cultural studies' relation to politics.

This concerns their claim, in the section entitled 'The Mole and the Snake', that 'we need to recognize that the very subject of labour and revolt has changed profoundly. The composition of the proletariat has transformed and thus our understanding of it must too' (p. 52). Insisting that by proletariat we should now understand '*all* those exploited by and subject to capitalist domination' (p. 53), they proceed to identify, in the 'most radical and powerful struggles of the final years of the twentieth century: the Tiananmen Square events in 1989, the Intifada against Israeli state authority, the May 1992 revolt in Los Angeles, the uprising in Chiapas that began in 1994' (p. 54), signs of a 'new kind of proletarian solidarity and militancy' (p. 54). In contrast to the proletarian internationalism of the past, however, 'none of these events inspired a cycle of struggles, because the desires and needs they expressed could not be translated into different contexts. In other words, (potential) revolutionaries in other parts of the world did not hear of the events in Beijing, Nablus, Los Angeles, Chiapas . . . and immediately recognise them as their own struggles' (p. 54). For Hardt and Negri this is one of the 'central and most urgent political paradoxes of our time': the fact that 'in our much celebrated age of communication, *struggles have become all but incommunicable*' (p. 54) – and this 'despite their being hypermediatized, on television, the Internet, and every other imaginable medium' (p. 56).

Two tasks are thus urgent: (1) to recognise a common enemy against which these struggles are directed – 'the situations all seem utterly particular, but in fact they all directly attack the global order of Empire and seek a real alternative' (pp. 56–7); (2) to construct a new common language of struggles that 'facilitates communication, as the languages of anti-imperialism and proletarian internationalism did for the struggles of a previous era' (p. 57). These tasks are urgent because, as far as Hardt and Negri are concerned, 'the power of Empire and the mechanisms of imperial sovereignty can be understood only when confronted on the most general scale, in their globality' (p. 206). However, the reason I'm so interested in this particular section is because, as well as being one of the places where they repeat their main thesis, it's also where they most clearly raise questions for it. For, intriguingly, their 'intuition' (p. 57) also tells them that recognising a common enemy and constructing a new common language of struggles would be to miss the point, and would be to retain a model of analysis that is no longer adequate to the new social and political context. It would be to fail to grasp the 'real potential' presented by these struggles (p. 57): that this incommunicability is not a weakness but a strength; and that the 'movement of movements' is not a new cycle of the old type of internationalist struggles, but evidence of a new cycle in itself. This new, new cycle is 'defined not by the communicative extension of the struggles but rather by their singular emergence, by the intensity that characterizes them one by one. In short, this new phase is defined by the fact that these struggles do not link horizontally, but each one leaps vertically, directly to the virtual center of Empire' (p. 58).

Hardt and Negri consequently appear to be caught in something of a contradictory tension in *Empire*: between, on the one hand, the desire for things to conform to the old political vocabularies and conceptual frameworks; and on the other, their suspicion that something has changed profoundly, and that our understanding of contemporary struggle needs to change profoundly too. Indeed, although it's not always as clearly acknowledged as it is in 'The Mole and the Snake', this tension – between old and new, horizontal and vertical, commonality and singularity – occurs throughout the book. The problem is that when it comes to understanding the new era of Empire, rather than consciously maintain or think through this tension, Hardt and Negri tend to privilege the old ways of doing so that they themselves suspect are outmoded. Witness their account of this new era predominantly in the language of the old, modern, grand narratives. Witness, too, their quite traditional (and somewhat messianic) telos of revolutionary change whereby a large group is going to arrive that will effect global transformation. This is evident in Hardt and Negri's insistence towards the end of *Empire* that for the actions of the 'multitude' to become political they *must* communicate and cohere horizontally:

> it is a matter of crossing and breaking down the limits and segmentations that are imposed on the new collective labour power; it is a matter of gathering

together these experiences of resistance and welding them together in concert against the nerve centers of imperial command. (p. 399)

Yet don't Hardt and Negri also suggest that it is precisely the 'new' nature of 'these experiences of resistance' that *prevent* them from being welded 'together in concert'?

So these struggles *cannot* be understood using the 'old' political language and frameworks; but neither can they necessarily be regarded as absolutely new – for, like *Empire* itself, these struggles still have something of the old about them. As Hardt and Negri acknowledge, 'all these struggles, which pose really new elements, appear from the beginning to be already old and outdated' (p. 57). In fact, these struggles are *old* for Hardt and Negri precisely because they *don't* communicate horizontally as the old cycle of international proletarian struggles did; which, paradoxically, is also what is new and different about these struggles: the way they don't communicate horizontally, they don't communicate what is new about them (but attack vertically at the heart of Empire), and so often *appear* like old calls for peace and democracy. There is thus an unresolved tension in *Empire* which points to the very issue Hardt and Negri are wrestling with, but which they themselves appear unable to provide a solution to or even think through in a particularly rigorous manner: how are the struggles of the Zapatistas in Mexico, the International Solidarity Movement in Palestine, the *sans-papiers* in France, the 'Argentinazo' and Mocase in Argentina, Otpor! in Serbia, Mjaft! in Albania, those fighting in Bolivia against the privatisation of natural resources, the WTO and G8 demonstrations in Seattle, Prague, Genoa and Edinburgh, the Indymedia campaigns against the Woomera detention centre in South Australia, the Stop the War Coalition, Make Poverty History campaign and so forth to be understood? In terms of the old type of politics or the new?

Community without community

What interests me here is precisely the apparently contradictory nature of Hardt and Negri's attempt to think the new *and* the old, verticality *and* horizontality, singularity *and* commonality of such struggles in *Empire*. And what I want to suggest is that it is in their conflicting claims that a kernel of a deconstructive gesture can be found regarding contemporary politics – despite the fact that it is partly Hardt and Negri's attempt to delimit deconstruction that gets them into this mess. I don't mean by this that they reject deconstruction. Far from it. They in fact assign it an important place in their methodology:

> our reasoning here is based on two methodological approaches that are intended to be nondialectical and absolutely immanent: the first is *critical and deconstructive*, aiming to subvert the hegemonic languages and social structures and thereby reveal an alternative ontological basis that resides in the creative and productive practices of the multitude; the second is *constructive and ethico-political*, seeking to lead the process of the production of subjectivity toward the constitution of an effective social, political alternative, a new constituent of power. (pp. 47–8)

Nevertheless, here too their argument is somewhat contradictory. Sure, they employ what they describe as a deconstructive methodology for critical purposes. Yet for all its 'enormous contribution' they restrict it to a critical role, making it clear that this is not enough, that deconstruction (on this basis) can only go so far, and that eventually it must be left behind as the baton is passed to a second, more 'constructive' approach. Once again, then, Hardt and Negri get caught up in attempting to analyse the new in old and, it has to be said, dialectical terms – and this despite explicitly stating their methodology is 'intended to be nondialectical'.

I say their restriction of deconstruction is partly responsible for the contradictory nature of their analysis in *Empire*, because it is only by portraying deconstruction as critical and confining it to this role that they can continue to operate in this manner. A more rigorous engagement with deconstruction would have helped Hardt and Negri avoid the mistake of trying to oppose the old 'deconstructive phase of critical thought' with a new, non-dialectical alternative (p. 217). To attempt to do so is to remain caught in the dialectic, which is why Derrida insists he has 'never *opposed* the dialectic. Be it opposition to the dialectic or war against the dialectic, it's a losing battle. What it really comes down to is thinking a dialecticity of dialectics that is itself fundamentally not dialectical' (Derrida 2001: 33). Derrida does this, not by negating Hegel's dialectical system in an attempt to leave it behind and replace it with a system of his own, but by adhering to the logic of Hegel's argument as closely and rigorously as possible – to the point where Derrida is able to agree with Hegel *against himself*. By reading Hegel according to a radically non-oppositional notion of difference in this way, Derrida is able to demonstrate how Hegel's system already contains a thinking of the dialecticity of dialectics that is not dialectical:

> I have constantly attempted to single out that element which would not allow itself to be integrated in a series or a group, in order to show that *there is* a non-oppositional difference that transcends the dialectic, which is itself always oppositional. There is a supplement, or a *pharmakon* – I could give many more examples – that does not let itself be dialectized. Precisely that

which, not being dialectical, makes dialectic impossible, is necessarily retaken by the dialectic that it relaunches. At this point, we have to remark that the dialectic consists precisely in dialecticizing the non-dialectizable. What we have, then, is a concept of dialectic that is no longer the conventional one of synthesis, conciliation, reconciliation, totalization, identification with itself; now, on the contrary, we have a negative or an infinite dialectic that is the movement of synthesizing without synthesis.

... basically, we are dealing with two concepts or figures of the dialectic – the conventional one, of totalization, reconciliation and reappropriation through the work of the negative etc.; and then a non-conventional figure, which I have just indicated. (pp. 32–3)

Now hopefully this goes some way toward explaining why, in *Culture in Bits* (2002) and elsewhere, I have tried to demonstrate that 'deconstruction is/in cultural studies' already (Hall et al. 2004); and why I would likewise not want to be regarded here as somehow contrasting Hardt and Negri (or cultural studies) negatively to Derrida and deconstruction. Is it not apparent, even from the little I've already said, that a different reading of *Empire* is available too? Would it not be possible to show through a careful and patient analysis that Derrida's 'non-dialectical' thinking of Hegel's dialectic is already at work 'in' *Empire*; that *Empire* – and Empire – is 'in deconstruction', as it were, and already contains 'two concepts or figures of the dialectic':

1. 'the conventional one, of totalization, reconciliation and reappropriation through the work of the negative etc.', evident most obviously in Hardt and Negri's presentation of Empire as the emergence of a new, non-dialectical era (albeit, paradoxically, in old, dialectical terms) and desire to move towards some messianic or teleological political end-goal;
2. a 'non-conventional figure' which presents Empire as both old *and* new, dialectical *and* non-dialectical, and which holds both the old (commonality, 'totalization, reconciliation and reappropriation') and the new (singularity, difference, dissensus) together at the same time in 'a concept of dialectic that is no longer the conventional one of synthesis, conciliation, reconciliation, totalization, identification with itself; now, on the contrary, we have a negative or an infinite dialectic that is the movement of synthesizing without synthesis'.

Such a reading, had I space for it, would suggest that what's interesting about *Empire* is, in a sense, precisely its 'failure'. Sure, in places Hardt and Negri want to move toward a global, horizontally unified alternative to the contemporary world order of Empire, and to this extent display something of a liberatory revolutionary telos characteristic of many 'old left positions'. Nevertheless, they are conspicuously unable to answer the question in *Empire* as to how any such synthesis between commonality and singularity can be achieved: how the multitude, which is made up of groups as diverse as labour unions, environmentalists and those protesting immigration policies and gender inequalities, and which is characterised precisely by its 'mobility, flexibility and perpetual differentiation' (p. 344), can be gathered together in a 'new experience of resistance' and welded together 'in concert' as a political subject. Far from this being a deficiency in their analysis, however – as many critics have claimed (see Swiboda and Hurtler 2001; Brown and Szeman 2002, 2005; Poster 2005) – I believe this *inability* is part of what makes *Empire* so interesting and powerful. For if what the 'moment of politics' does is try to stabilise the movement of this 'infinite dialectic', what *Empire* reveals in its 'poetic', 'indefinite' (Hardt and Negri in Brown and Szeman 2002) conception of the multitude is that:

- This is indeed an irreducibly violent stabilisation of something 'essentially unstable'. (The identity of the multitude is not already given but, as we'll see, a political construction, something that is 'invented' by means of a 'decision' (Negri 2004: 68, 143).)
- This stablisation can never be fully or finally achieved. There is always something that escapes, something different, heterogeneous, other, an excess, 'a supplement . . . that does not let itself be dialecticized'.
- This is not just the case with regard to Empire and the multitude, but to politics in general. Hence the way in which even the 'old' 'horizontal' struggles weren't 'organised' or welded together for Hardt and Negri, but constituted merely a 'potential or virtual unity of the international proletariat' that 'was never fully actualised' (p. 262).

This is not to say the multitude is incapable of coming together and acting in common. The potential for solidarity and communality is part of the 'movement' in this reading. What makes achieving integration and consensus impossible is also what makes coming together and cooperating possible; 'and it is here that the possible and the impossible cross each other', for if the process of forming a community wasn't irreducibly violent, there wouldn't be a need for politics. The disparate, indefinite, open nature of collective struggle in *Empire* is what gives politics its 'chance', as well as 'a chance to change'. It just *is* caught in this infinite dialectic between singularity and commonality, the one and the many, the individual and the collective.

Although it is composed of singularities, then, the multitude does not consist of absolute heterogeneity, difference and dissension – not least because (as we know from reading Hegel and Derrida) absolute difference falls back dialectically into identity. It's a process of 'synthesizing without synthesis', unification without unity, 'community without community'.[3] In fact, it's possible to locate an infinite dialectical movement or non-oppositional difference between the singular and the common in the very concept of singularity. A singularity must escape recognition as a singularity, as something that relates to the common understanding of what a singularity is, otherwise it's not singular – it's just an example of a general type 'singularity', the singular being by definition that which resists being described in general categories. Yet a singularity also has to be capable of being recognised as an instance of the general type 'singularity', since if it were *absolutely different and singular* no one would ever be able to understand it *as a singularity*. In this sense, Hardt and Negri can in their own way be seen to be sharing in *Empire* what for Derrida is:

> the sharing of what is not shared: we know in common that we have nothing in common. There may be an unlimited consensus on the subject, but the consensus is of no use, since it is a consensus on the fact that the singular is singular, that the other is other, that *tout autre est tout autre*. (Derrida 2001: 58)

Inventing a new cultural studies?

We can thus see how a careful 'deconstructive' reading of the kind I'm suggesting could help us think through and articulate the difficult, paradoxical relation between commonality and singularity, old *and* new, dialectical and non-dialectical that Hardt and Negri set out in *Empire*. From this perspective, the point is to acknowledge that the inherent instability and irreducible violence of this relation cannot be resolved, eliminated or escaped; instead, it constitutes the potential for collectivity and community at the same time as providing its essential limits. In this way, far from being merely an intellectual exercise, as many of its critics have claimed, deconstruction can provide a means of exploring forms of social and political organisation which avoid fusional and totalising (and totalitarian) fantasies of arriving at the One, at total unity and unification, while nevertheless being compatible with some form of gathering together of a multiplicity of singularities. (And what could be more important, or more political, than that?)

Yet this would really be only the beginning of any such reading. Had I the space, I would have liked to have taken the logic of Hardt and Negri's thought even further beyond their own explicit claims, to address the question of 'the role of the decision' (Negri 2004: 143) that enables us to 'reunite the multitude' (p. 70), to 'invent a politics of the multitude' (p. 68) – a theme Negri accepts 'is so noticeably missing from [his] work, yet upon which everything in it converges' (p. 143). This, too, is something deconstruction could help with, for if deconstruction is anything at all, it is a thinking of the decision. In particular, deconstruction would be able to demonstrate that it is precisely between the irreconcilable but indissociable poles of old *and* new, commonality *and* singularity, that any such act of invention or decision would have to take place. And, perhaps most importantly, that such a decision cannot be calculated in advance:

> A decision has to be prepared by reflection and knowledge, but the moment of the decision, and thus the moment of responsibility, supposes a rupture with knowledge, and therefore an opening to the incalculable . . . In other words, one cannot rationally distribute the part that is calculable and the part that is incalculable. One has to calculate as far as possible, but the incalculable happens: it is the other, and singularity, and chance. (Derrida 2001: 61)

As far as any 'practical' politics is concerned, then, the decision as to the socially just thing to do can't be left completely open and incalculable. If it's not going to be subject merely to the particular demands of the specific conjuncture, the decision regarding political action cannot simply be taken afresh each time, in a singular way, but has to be based on rationally calculated *universal* values of infinite justice and responsibility. That's why a decision, for Derrida, 'has to be prepared by reflection and knowledge'. At the same time, any such decision can't be made in advance on the basis of a pre-decided political agenda or theory (say that of Marx, the 'old left', Gramsci or hegemony) which is both beyond question and unconditionally and universally applicable. As Hardt and Negri show, that would be to risk failing to 'recognize adequately the contemporary object of critique', its possible novelty and difference (2000: 137). It would be to take too little account of the complexity and specificity of a given situation – particularly those elements that do not fit the 'old', pre-given conceptual framework and vocabulary – and would thus not be hospitable to the incalculable, 'the other, and singularity and chance'. A responsible political decision rather requires respect for both poles of this (non-oppositional) relation between the old and new, common and singular, calculable and incalculable. While not in itself a politics, this is very different from an avoidance of politics. Indeed, far from the difficult, uncertain nature of this situation having a depoliticising affect, a just and responsible political act, for Derrida, *has* to go through the ordeal of taking a decision in an incalculable and undecidable space.

Political decisions, such as that enabling the reuniting of the multitude, the forging of a politics of the multitude, are acts of invention, then: both in the sense that they can't simply be calculated in advance; but also in that, like Derrida's texts, and *Empire*, too, they 'performatively' transform and so 'create' the 'context' in which they can be read and perhaps eventually understood. Still, as I say, all this is nothing more than the speculative beginnings of an analysis of Hardt and Negri's book. Since a more rigorous and patient engagement is impossible here for reasons of space, I want to conclude by emphasising some of the implications of this inventive intervention in *Empire* with four points concerning the relation between cultural studies and deconstruction.

1. We can now see what I meant when I said earlier that cultural studies' attempts at closing down the question of what it is to be political by deciding on the answer to this question in advance (e.g. that today, in the wake of 9/11 and the attack on Iraq, and now 7/7, it involves shifting away from theory and deconstruction towards politics and the 'real') is precisely *not political*. Interestingly, this can be concluded from reading one of the very texts it is suggested cultural studies turn to in order to be more political: *Empire*. (This is not to say a responsible decision cannot be taken to the effect that political economy, or whatever, *is* the political thing to do in a particular situation; just that a decision has to be *taken* on each singular occasion for it to be responsible, and not made in advance.)

2. Far from failing to help with pragmatic political decisions, deconstruction provides one of the most rigorous and responsible means of doing so – precisely because deconstruction *does not* simply decide what constitutes politics and the political *in advance of the moment of decision*. In this way, by means of a calculation that is open to the complexities of a social or cultural situation, to the incalculable, to what cannot be predicted or foreseen, deconstruction can help cultural studies take just and responsible political decisions; decisions which are sensitive to the specific demands – including 'real', practical, empirical, experiential, concrete demands – of each singular conjunction of the 'here' and 'now'.

3. The necessity of keeping the question of the political open, and of not deciding in advance what is political (that it *obviously is* to be concerned with left politics, the economic, hegemonic struggle, but *obviously not* so much with theory, deconstruction, the extreme, the animal, the secret and

so forth), has a direct relation to the difficulty of Derrida's works, and especially the difficulty of identifying in them an obvious politics, at least of the kind many people in cultural studies would recognise.

4. The questioning of the political space is also one of the most *cultural studies thing to do* of all. (I'm returning here once more to Derrida's strategy of reading based on the notion of non-oppositional difference.) Hence the way it's previously been possible for me to produce careful readings of certain privileged texts in the cultural studies tradition which, by following their logic as closely and rigorously as possible, reveal these texts to challenge and disrupt that tradition – including its ideas of politics and what it is to be political – as much as they uphold and maintain it. Such inventive interventions in the cultural studies tradition – which are *more than* cultural studies while still being cultural studies – are readable:

- in the early work of Williams and the Adult Education Association (Hall 2002a);
- in the 'experimental character of [Stuart] Hall's pedagogy and his practice as an academic . . . evident in books like *Resistance Thorough Rituals* and *Policing the Crisis*' (McRobbie 2000: 215; cited in Hall 2004);
- in Angela McRobbie's accounts of 'feminist cultural studies' (Hall 2002b).

In this sense cultural studies has the right to analyse and criticise everything, including itself and its politics – even the idea that cultural studies is inherently left-wing (Flew 2005). Which is not to say cultural studies *doesn't* entail certain values and commitments, including political commitments, which mark the limits and boundaries of this self-critical attitude. Its right to analyse and criticise everything, including its politics, is something cultural studies has often marginalised or at least kept within certain limits in recent years: no doubt as a result of its desire to become a 'legitimate' academic discipline and to be accepted within the institution; but also in an attempt to maintain and reinforce its own boundaries and politically committed identity *as cultural studies*. Yet, as we've seen, to close down the space of the political is precisely what it means for cultural studies *not to be political*. Once again, cultural studies is caught in a difficult (non-oppositional) relation between two equally undecidable positions. In a way cultural studies *just is* this aporia, what Stuart Hall calls this 'irresolvable but permanent tension' (Hall 1992: 284), between theory and politics – but also, I would add, between openness and closure, singularity and commonality.

As far as the questions I raised earlier are concerned, what this means is that if, as Hall and Grossberg seem to suggest, cultural studies can't merely apply the 'old left positions' associated with Gramsci, hegemony theory and the Birmingham School to the contemporary conjuncture, neither can it simply devise a new, post-Gramscian, post-hegemonic, post-Birmingham cultural studies. As Hardt and Negri illustrate with their own analysis, which is itself a complex mix of 'old' and 'new', there is nothing that is absolutely new. In fact, if the current situation were absolutely new, it would be unrecognisable, since (as we know from Derrida's 1988 analysis of iterability), in order to be able to *cognise* something, we already have to be able to *re-cognise* it, to be able to compare and assimilate this 'new' object to that which is already known and understood. Besides, any attempt to invent an absolutely new politics just risks unknowingly repeating the old anyway, as *Empire* amply demonstrates. Instead, a decision based on a calculation that is open to the incalculable, to the other, to singularity and to chance has to be made as to what it is for cultural studies to be political in each *singular* situation.

Let me just stress: none of this is to say that the 'old' cultural studies tradition associated with Gramsci, the theory of hegemony and the Birmingham School (and indeed Hall and Grossberg) is no longer useful; nor that this (politically committed) tradition must now be abandoned in favour of the development of a 'new (apolitical) cultural studies'. This kind of responsible questioning of the cultural studies tradition may be in excess of that tradition, but it is also a fundamental part of it (and if I had space I could say more about how this is the case with regard to Stuart Hall, the Birmingham School, and Grossberg's work on politics and economics). *What it is to suggest* is that we have to remain open to the possibility that such a responsible cultural studies might not be recognisable as cultural studies, at least as it is currently and most obviously understood. It won't necessarily be a *Policing the Crisis*, a *New Times* or a *We Gotta Get Out of This Place* for our times, and may instead be something unpredictably and incalculably different from the work of the Birmingham School, Stuart Hall and Lawrence Grossberg, since it involves not so much reproducing what it is to do cultural studies as performatively inventing it, each time, *without any guarantees*.

Postscript

What might such a cultural studies look like? What forms might it take? What language and conceptual frameworks could it use? It is these questions that the contributors to this volume are all exploring and experimenting with in their different and singular ways (and I'd include my own chapter in this). Given what I've just said about the relation between the old and the new, however, it seems fitting to give the last word to Stuart Hall, for now at least. For in 1998 Hall had already gone some way towards answering the question regarding the possibility of a new cultural studies after Gramsci, hegemony theory and the Birmingham School. Nowhere is this more evident than in his designation of the 'highly transitional moment . . . we are in', not as a 'Gramscian' conjuncture, as Grossberg claims (Grossberg n.d.), but as a 'deconstructive' one. 'We are in the deconstructive moment', Hall says:

> That's what deconstruction means to me: that's what I understand Derrida to be saying: we have no other language in which philosophy has been conducted, and it no longer works; but we're not yet in some other language, and we may never be . . . That is exactly what the notion *post* means for me. So, *postcolonial* is not the end of colonialism. It *is* after a certain *kind* of colonialism, after a certain moment of high imperialism and colonial occupation – in the wake of it, in the shadow of it, inflected by it – it is what it is because something else has happened before, but it is also something new. (1998: 189)

Notes

1 See Gilbert in this volume. I'm focusing on *Empire* rather than their more recent *Multitude* (2004b) because the former has had more impact on cultural studies – indeed, it was recently described in *Cultural Studies* as 'one of the most influential and controversial academic books of our young century' (Brown and Szeman 2005: 372) – whereas the latter is still too recent to be able to tell what its effect is going to be.
2 Since *Empire* was written (1997) and published (2000), Hardt and Negri have been at pains to emphasise that events following 9/11 have not contradicted their thesis but confirmed it: 'Most obvious is the failure of the unilateralist military strategies pursued by the US government particularly in the past two years' (Hardt and Negri 2004a).
3 The phrase 'unification without unity' comes from Negri: 'It is important to distinguish between unity seen as a process of unification and unity conceived as an abstract bloc, that is, as "One"' (Negri 2004: 166). 'Community without community' is a version of Blanchot's 'community of those without community' (Derrida 1997). In 'I Have a Taste for the Secret' and elsewhere (Derrida 1978), Derrida is hesitant to follow Blanchot and Nancy in using the word 'community': because too often it 'resounds with the "common", the as-one' (2001: 25); and because it runs the risk of sliding into 'a question of identity (individual, subjective, ethnic, national, state, etc.)' (1997: 299). However, as long as one speaks of community in the sense of 'an alliance that not only does

not cancel out the singularity of the allies but, on the contrary, accentuates it', then Derrida has no objections (2001: 24). That said, if Derrida is suspicious of certain connotations of the word 'community', so, too, is Negri: 'community – what a horrible word' (2004: 88), he says in *Negri on Negri*. Interestingly, community is repeatedly described here as a 'process', as a '*constructing*-with', a '*constituting*-with' (p. 88).

Bibliography

Amin, Ash and Thrift, Nigel (eds) (2004), *The Cultural Economy Reader*, Oxford: Blackwell.

Brown, Nicholas and Szeman, Imre (2002), 'The Global Coliseum: On *Empire*', *Cultural Studies*, 16:2, March, pp. 177–92.

Brown, Nicholas and Szeman, Imre (2005), 'What is the Multitude? Questions For Michael Hardt and Antonio Negri', *Cultural Studies*, 19:3, May, pp. 372–87.

Derrida, Jacques (1978), 'Violence and Metaphysics: An Essay on the Thought of Emmanuel Levinas', in *Writing and Difference*, London: Routledge and Kegan Paul, pp. 79–153.

Derrida, Jacques (1981), *Positions*, Chicago: University of Chicago Press.

Derrida, Jacques (1988), *Limited Inc*, Evanston, IL: Northwestern University Press.

Derrida, Jacques (1992), 'Mochlos; or, The Conflict of the Faculties', in Richard Rand (ed.), *Logomachia: The Conflict of the Faculties*, Lincoln, NE, and London: University of Nebraska, pp. 1–34.

Derrida, Jacques (1996), 'Remarks on Deconstruction and Pragmatism', in Chantal Mouffe (ed.), *Deconstruction and Pragmatism*, London: Routledge, pp. 77–88.

Derrida, Jacques (1997), *Politics of Friendship*, London: Verso.

Derrida, Jacques (2001), 'I Have a Taste for the Secret', in Jacques Derrida and Maurizio Ferraris, *A Taste for the Secret*, Cambridge: Polity, pp. 77–88.

Du Gay, Paul (1997), 'Introduction', in Paul Du Gay (ed.), *Production of Culture/Cultures of Production*, London: Sage, pp. 1–10.

Du Gay, Paul and Pryke, Michael (2002), *Cultural Economy*, London: Sage.

Flew, Terry (2005), 'Is Cultural Studies Inherently Left-Wing?', posting to the CSAA discussion list, 5 January, http://lists.cdu.edu.au/mailman/listinfo/csaa-forum.

Frow, John (2005), 'Deconstruction', in Tony Bennett, Lawrence Grossberg and Meaghan Morris (eds), *New Keywords: A Revised Vocabulary of Culture and Society*, Oxford: Blackwell, pp. 347–9.

Grossberg, Lawrence (2005), 'Cultural Studies, the War against Kids, and the Re-becoming of U.S. Modernity', in Cameron McCarthy, Warren Crichlow, Greg Dimitriadis and Nadine Dolby (eds), *Race, Identity and Representation in Education*, 2nd edn, New York: Routledge, pp. 349–67.

Grossberg, Lawrence (n.d.), 'The Lives and Times of Culture' (as yet unpublished paper).

Hall, Gary (2002a), 'The (Monstrous) Future of Cultural Studies', in *Culture in Bits: The Monstrous Future of Theory*, London: Continuum, pp. 65–94.

Hall, Gary (2002b), '"*Something Else Besides*": The Third Way of Angela McRobbie', in *Culture in Bits: The Monstrous Future of Theory*, London: Continuum, pp. 41–64.

Hall, Gary (2004), 'Why You Can't Do Cultural Studies *and* Be a Derridean: Cultural Studies After Birmingham, the New Social Movements and the New Left', *Culture Machine*, 6, http://culturemachine.tees.ac.uk/Cmach/Backissues/j006/Articles/hall.htm.

Hall, Gary, Boothroyd, Dave and Zylinska, Joanna (eds) (2004), 'Deconstruction is/in Cultural Studies', *Culture Machine*, 6, http://culturemachine.tees.ac.uk/Cmach/Backissues/j006/journal.htm.

Hall, Stuart (1981), 'Notes on Deconstructing "the Popular"', in Raphael Samuel (ed.), *People's History and Socialist Theory*, London: Routledge and Kegan Paul, pp. 227–39.

Hall, Stuart (1992), 'Cultural Studies and its Theoretical Legacies', in Lawrence Grossberg, Cary Nelson and Paula Treichler (eds), *Cultural Studies*, New York: Routledge, pp. 277–94.

Hall, Stuart (1998), 'Cultural Composition: Stuart Hall on Ethnicity and the Discursive Turn', *Journal of Composition Theory*, 18:2, pp. 171–96.

Hardt, Michael and Negri, Antonio (2000), *Empire*, London: Harvard University Press.

Hardt, Michael and Negri, Antonio (2004a), 'Why We Need a Multilateral Magna Carta', *Global Agenda*, www.globalagendamagazine.com/2004/antonionegri.asp.

Hardt, Michael and Negri, Antonio (2004b), *Multitude: War and Democracy in the Age of Empire*, Harmondsworth: Penguin.

McRobbie, Angela (2000), 'Stuart Hall: The Universities and the "Hurly Burly"', in Paul Gilroy, Lawrence Grossberg and Angela McRobbie (eds), *Without Guarantees: In Honour of Stuart Hall*, London: Verso, pp. 212–24.

Merck, Mandy (ed.) (2004), 'Cultures and Economies', *New Formations*, 52.

Negri, Antonio (2004), *Negri on Negri: Antonio Negri in Conversation with Anne Dufourmantelle*, London: Routledge.

Poster, Mark (2005), 'Hardt and Negri's Information Empire: A Critical Response', *Cultural Politics*, 1:1, pp. 101–18.

Swiboda, Marcel and Hurtler, Kurt (2001), 'A Multitude of Possibilities', *parallax* 21, 7:4, October–December, pp. 138–41.

ALWAYS SPECULATE

CHAPTER 3

Cultural Studies and Post-Marxism

Jeremy Valentine

'Purity' itself would be the exception, I agree, but I know of no example to refer to. (Althusser 1982a: 106)

Shouting at post-Marxism

The nature of the relation between cultural studies and post-Marxism is suggested by Stuart Hall's claim that cultural studies has never been submerged within Marxism but remains 'within shouting distance' of it (Hall 1996a: 265). If that is the case, then it is important to bear in mind that the Marxism which cultural studies shouts at is not a stable and unified object which could simply be applied to the study of culture. This caution is especially relevant as Marxism is a critical materialist analysis which takes social change as its object, and which is therefore formed by and within social change. Materialism means there is simply nothing more than the material world (and anyone who claims otherwise is either confused or wants to confuse you for their own advantage). Marxism is materialist because the accounts of social formations it develops are rooted in the principle that the social world is produced, and that production is socially organised. Marxism is critical because its materialist assumptions undermine the view that social formations are natural or are given by a god. This critical approach is also aimed at Marxism itself. 'Post-Marxism' is simply a term with which to categorise this process. The term is needed in order to differentiate a critical materialist approach from a dogmatic approach which tends to regard Marxism as canonical.

There is not sufficient space here to examine the various components of post-Marxism, or to demonstrate the different ways in which these are derived from the writings of Marx and Engels. Instead, this chapter will focus on a direction within post-Marxism which is within shouting distance, as Hall puts it, of cultural studies. In doing so, it will take the distinguishing characteristic of cultural studies to be its engagement with a post-Marxian approach which emphasises the analysis of the relations between culture and politics within determinate historical conditions ultimately derived from capitalism.

At its simplest, capitalism refers to a system of production based on human labour in which the power of labour is commodified and exchanged for other commodities. For capitalism to work, the value of the commodities which the labourer receives for labour power has to be less than the value of labour power itself, even though these commodities are produced by labour power. The difference between the two values is a surplus from which are derived both profit and additional capital which is invested in the production of more commodities. Thus capitalism is based on an inequality within production which is not recognised as such by systems of justice within capitalist social formations. Indeed, as each labourer is technically free to sell his or her own labour power as a commodity, as far as capitalism is concerned there is no inequality and the system is morally justified. Marx and Engels maintained that the solution to this problem would arise from the organisation of society into two opposed social classes derived from their relation to production; the bourgeoisie, who benefited from the inequality, and the proletariat, who were impoverished by it. The expectation was that the proletariat would confront the bourgeoisie from a majority position and eliminate the economic system on which they depended. Unfortunately, thus far, things have not turned out like that. As distinct from the original positions of Marx and Engels, post-Marxism is concerned with developing a materialist understanding of the increasing complexity of social relations and the place of production within them. The significance of the political dimension of culture emerges from the analysis of such complex relations.

Culture and politics in post-Marxism

The analysis of the relations between culture and politics within cultural studies is dependent upon a direction within post-Marxism that has sought to develop the political dimension of Marxism and which, for the sake of argument, can be said to refer primarily to the work of Ernesto Laclau and Chantal Mouffe (1985, 1990), which is in turn derived from that of Antonio Gramsci (1971) and Louis Althusser (1971, 1982b, 1982c; Althusser and Balibar 1975). Although none of these writers is particularly concerned with culture directly, whether as artefact or form of life, they are united to a certain extent by a common emphasis on the ways in which culture is constitutive of relations of power which may become political, in the sense that they may become contested or opposed, or may be connected to the exercise of rule and authority, and which are seen as the conditions of any relations between power and the organisation of a social formation.

Yet culture acquires a specific and abstract theoretical value in the work of these writers, in that it refers to the systematic and organised social production of meaning and understanding. In that respect they are post-Marxist, in that they recognise the relative autonomy of culture from politics and the economy as part of the increasing complexity of capitalism, and thus in addition to the question concerning the extent to which culture is formed by politics and the economy, also pose the question of the extent to which politics and the economy are formed by culture. The significance of doing so stems from the gulf this latter question opens with respect to the dogmatic insistence on economic reductionism within traditional Marxism, the argument that anything and everything can be explained by reference to the organisation of the economy narrowly conceived as the moment of production, rather than the systematic relations which condition and sustain such a moment. From the point of view of post-Marxism, there is no reason to exclude culture from the economic, and from capitalism in particular, because these phenomena are meaningful and are understood, albeit in different and often opposed ways. One could thus summarise the main elements of the contribution of post-Marxism to cultural studies as follows, beginning with the oldest.

This is Gramsci's realisation that the success of Fascism in Italy after World War I could not entirely be explained with reference to the economy, especially as it drew on the support of both significant sectors of the working class and industrial capitalism, as well as other, more diverse social elements, such as the church and the peasantry. Rather, Fascism's success was better explained as a project to produce social and economic unity through the political category of the nation – or what Gramsci called the 'national-popular' in order to emphasise the ability of Fascism to attract the support of diverse social forces. The clue was in the name. In Italian *fascis* means bundle. Not only was the existence of the nation independent of the economy, in that nations pre-date capitalism, but the ability to lead it was political in the sense that doing so relied on the ability to establish and maintain relations of coercion and consent, or what Gramsci called 'hegemony'.

In turn, 'hegemony' is dependent on two other forces. First is the level of political development within an existing social formation. In the Italian context Gramsci noted the conflict between a small official level of limited liberal parliamentary democracy locked in disputes with the residues of pre-capitalism such as the aristocracy, the military and the church, and a larger but less specific 'people' generally uninvolved in and unrepresented by the former but linked 'organically' to the latter. The genius of Fascism lay in its ability to shape the people by focusing its resentments on the political elites, a relation which Gramsci called 'people versus power-bloc'. Second is the extent to which leadership is felt as a subjective property of the people, rather than as something imposed from outside; that is to say, the degree to which leadership becomes an organic part of 'common sense', the vague and contradictory terrain of superstition, prejudice and pragmatic rules of thumb which allow people to get on from one day to the next and which constitute a culture. In itself 'common sense' is uncontrollable and ultimately unpredictable. Yet leadership must engage with it in order to build consent through what Gramsci called 'moral and intellectual leadership'. Fascism was excellent at doing that by mobilising popular resentment against the perceived privileges of the power-bloc, something which allowed the constraints of the political system to be circumvented. In this respect the identity of 'the people' was primarily derived from what it was not, the 'power-bloc'. On that basis it was a relatively straightforward matter for Fascism to add its own peculiar 'culture' to that of 'the people' in order to lead it, such as the cult of the machine, the theatrics of blood and sacrifice, and the opportunity to settle long-standing feuds and vendettas through state-backed coercive violence at the level of ordinary life. By stimulating the powers and passions of the imagination Fascism neutralised and displaced the political force of class struggle, the conflict between bourgeois and proletarian social classes which Marxism had expected to dominate social relations as a consequence of capitalist development. Under such circumstances Marxism could hardly complain that it was not fair that Fascism had circumvented economic causes.

Next among the main elements of the contribution of post-Marxism to cultural studies is the more theoretically reflective work of Althusser and his colleagues, including Etienne Balibar, Pierre Macherey and, initially, Jacques Rancière. There are two concepts in Althusser's work which are particularly relevant. First, there is the notion of 'overdetermination', which was adopted, with reservations, from Freudian psychoanalysis, where it describes the non-literal nature of the content of dreams and its relations with both the unconscious and other processes encountered in ordinary life, such as traumatic events (Althusser 1982b, 1982c). Thus 'overdetermination' both establishes distinct analytical objects and shows that they are related on the basis of the presence of each within the other, or their impurity, condensed in a specific object or experience. Althusser simply applies the concept to the categories of Marxism in order to show

how the elements of a social formation can be thought of as related. In fact, Althusser claimed that the concept of 'overdetermination' summarises Marx's argument in his '1857 Introduction to the critique of political economy' (Marx 1973), and Lenin's concept of 'combined and uneven development', which was invented to explain the need for a Communist revolution in industrially backward countries, contrary to the orthodox expectations of Marxism (Lenin 1916). In doing so, Althusser rejected the idea that the economy is an element that always determines everything else 'in the last instance', precisely because in reality the last instance never comes. Each element of a social formation is, to a greater or lesser extent, present in the other. The purpose of 'overdetermination' was to show that the elements of a social formation and their relations could only be established through the analysis of their concrete existence, rather than through reference to an ultimate cause such as a god or the economy. Capitalism was not a thing, then, but a complex structure of 'overdetermined' relations with no cause exterior to itself.

Ironically, Althusser's view of capitalism is very similar to the view of the god of monotheism advocated by the heretic seventeenth-century philosopher Spinoza, where it is the same thing as nature (Spinoza 2002). There is no distinction between the essence of capitalism or God or nature and its existence, in that it is a cause of itself and not of the effect of something exterior to it. Althusser's commitment to the immanence of capitalism, the idea that capitalism grows out of itself, might suggest a rather pessimistic view of the chances of change. Yet Althusser included the political moment of revolutionary transformation within overdetermined social relations in order to get away from the idea that one should wait for economic change in order for political change to occur, a view also proposed by Gramsci. In doing so Althusser included a moment of incompletion, of contingent action and unexpected event expressed as division and conflict, within the totality of social relations. Hence any overdetermined totality fails or reaches a limit which is internal to itself. In Marxism, such a moment corresponds to the non-equivalence between labour as a commodity and commodities in general within production. It is the gap within capitalism, the bit which does not make sense with respect to capitalism's self-understanding as a system of perfect equilibrium in which all values are freely exchanged for each other and everything adds up in the economy. Althusser generalises such a moment to the level of the incompletion of overdetermination itself. However, for Althusser, incompletion does not mean that nothing happens. Just as Marx and Engels thought that the agency of revolution would emerge from the gap in the commodity economy constituted by the exploitation of labour, so Althusser generalises the agency of revolution across the terrain of a social formation as its incompletion, albeit with the element of prediction and probability removed. Hence revolution was understood as a paradoxical moment of 'ruptural unity' in which one complex of social relations is transformed into another. The gap in the economy is no longer privileged in this process. Although Althusser did not go so far as to do so, it is possible to argue that culture is a causal moment of such a complex structure, and that the other elements of the structure are present within culture, including both political transformation and opposition to it.[1]

There is an additional aspect of Althusser's thought which establishes a closer relation with culture and is consistent with the elimination of the simplicity of the economic entailed by the concept of 'overdetermination'. Althusser argued that as capitalism exists in time it has to reproduce itself across each temporal moment (1971). For Althusser, this occurs largely 'outside the firm', within the wider social formation where the mechanism of reproduction is 'ideology', located in social institutions such as education, the family and the media. Participation in such institutions, or 'ideological state apparatuses', entails that individuals adopt modes of conduct which allow them to be subjected to forms of rule, rather than simply doing as they are told as a response to the threat of violent force exercised by 'repressive state apparatuses'. Although the distinction is similar to that between coercion and consent in Gramsci, Althusser goes further by proposing that the relation between ideology and individuals is explained by the category of 'interpellation', or form of address, in which individuals mis-recognise themselves as the source of meaning and understanding, rather than the recipient, something which includes their self-understanding of themselves as the agents of their existence. For Althusser, subjects are subjects because they are subjected, and not because they are identical to the first person form of the grammatical subject of sentences, e.g. as if I correspond to the word 'I' when I say it or write it or in general refer to it.[2] This means both that the idea that individuals are the source of the meaning of themselves and the cause of what happens in the world is a fantasy of god-like proportions; and that believing this to be the case is the basis on which individuals are reconciled with their part in the reproduction of capitalism as true, natural 'common sense' and the way things are, and thus as self-caused, rather than the contingent effects of processes beyond their control. In this way Althusser also effectively provides a definition of ideology as that which claims an ultimate grasp of existence, whether this be through knowledge or action.

Although it is an unfashionable position now, Althusser maintained that science escaped the illusions of ideology through its commitment to the falsification of knowledge (Althusser and Balibar 1975). In an indirect way Althusser is consistent with science in that his work does not provide a positive ultimate account of what capitalism is. There is always more to know and capitalism itself changes. Yet the specificity of capitalism becomes a problem as through 'overdetermination' it is released from its narrow economic definition and generalised across the social formation and, more remarkably, the eternity of time. One can only refer to capitalism within the relations which constitute specific concrete situations. All that can be done is to analyse the different concrete formations and their divisions or the incompletion in which capitalism exists, and which, like psychoanalysis, is interminable. There is no ultimate cure, as it were, because there is no ultimate cause. As with Freud's view of human subjects, capitalism is not perfect and self-sufficient. However, capitalism continues to be understood in terms of the presence of a stable structure to which contingent and unpredictable things happen, including its revolutionary transformation. If that is the case, then a more complete Marxism would have to think the material dimension of time as an element of the overdetermined complex of social relations. It is not sufficient to replace the strict determination of economic reductionism with a general expectation that something will happen by chance, like the tantrums of a cruel and capricious god. Although Althusser's work points to such a task it does not completely succeed in getting to grips with it, possibly because of the headache which usually occurs when people try to think about what time is. However, that does not mean that it is not worth trying to do it.

The last element of the contribution of post-Marxism to cultural studies this chapter is going to summarise concerns the way in which Laclau and Mouffe formalise the work of Gramsci and Althusser and build upon it. Laclau's early work sought to demonstrate that the Fascism which Gramsci analysed was more prevalent than had otherwise been thought, especially in Latin America (Laclau 1979). For Laclau, 'populism' is a more general category with which to understand the phenomenon and is characterised by the absence of any essential content. In principle, anything can be 'populist' as long as it is organised by the form of the 'people versus power-bloc' relation, although Laclau was less successful in showing that 'populism' could be compatible with democratic socialism (see Beasely-Murray 1998). Indeed, much of the discussion is concerned to demonstrate that there is no necessary link between the economy and a social formation within Marxism, in order to propose a specifically Marxist theory of the political. This dimension was developed in conjunction with Mouffe in order to subordinate the narrow Marxist understanding of politics as a class struggle determined by economic phenomena to a broader radical democratic notion of politics (1985). It was done by generalising the Marxist logic of conflict across the social formation without the requirement of a reference to class struggle as the necessary content of conflict. Instead, the logic of conflict is subordinated to the logic of 'populism', which boils down to the view that the identity of any entity, including that of social agents, is given by that which opposes it, as in Gramsci's 'people versus power-bloc' opposition. It is important to remember that the 'populist' formula describes a structural relation, and not one of cause and effect or before and after. In essence, you are what threatens you. Moreover, unlike Althusser, Laclau weakens the negative and critical status of the concept of ideology in order to emphasise its positive presence as the decisive agent of a social formation, rather than the economic level. For Laclau, the illusions of subjectivity are a component of the material world and are constitutive of social relations. Ideology overcomes incompletion through the formation of the illusion of social unity based on the illusion of subjective self-sufficiency.

In addition to deepening Althusser's subversion of the idea that the individual subject is the cause of itself, as the identity of anything depends on what it is not, no matter how much it may seek to preserve its pride by denying that to be the case, Laclau and Mouffe also affirm the overdetermined character of the identity of any social subject: that is to say, the presence of what a subject is not within it. This is categorised as 'antagonism', which is the name of the general form of conflict in Laclau and Mouffe through which hegemonic social formations are both constituted and destroyed. 'Antagonism' is the presence of the fact that the existence of social subjects is contingent, in that they may or may not exist and thus have no grounds, or cause, or essence within themselves, within the subjective imagination through which subjects understand their existence. Antagonism is thus a subjective experience of being incomplete expressed as resentment towards the other on which the subject is dependent for completion, or that against which the subject defines itself. To try and make the point easier to understand, it is like those cases analysed by Freud when the memory of some traumatic experience which you do not even realise you had forgotten suddenly enters your thoughts, thus undermining your self-confidence. In Laclau and Mouffe, such moments are positive in that they are the only occurrences in which anything happens. Things happen, not because they are grounded and complete, but because they are not.

Yet unlike Althusser, Laclau and Mouffe dispense with a concern to differentiate the complex relations between distinct levels of a social formation, such as economy, politics, institutions and so on in favour of an exclusive concern with subjectivity. The reason for doing so is that the status of such levels is purely discursive. There is therefore no real difference in the manner of existence between economy, politics, institutions etc. and subjectivity, in that none of these entities can be derived from a pre-existing metaphysical essence, and that each presupposes a subjective dimension. That is to say, the notion of discourse refers to the historical and material nature of phenomena and their meaningfulness for the subjects which are constituted within them. Although the claim for the material existence of discourses is a realism in terms of a theory of knowledge, in the sense that discourses are an object in the world as much as the world they refer to, it is not a naturalism or a commitment to the proposition that discourse necessarily reflects or represents a world exterior to it (see Howarth 2000). Consequently, all discourses are equal with respect to their knowledge claims. The truth of discourse is established politically through the elimination of rival discourses or their hegemonic subordination to a dominant discourse. This allows Laclau and Mouffe to account for the existence of a social formation in terms of its 'articulation', the capacity of a subjective social agent to establish discursive unity over diverse elements by establishing an antagonistic relation to what they are not, and thus creating the illusion of necessity within what would otherwise be a random and arbitrary existence (see Slack 1996). In this respect 'populism' determines Laclau and Mouffe's theory of what knowledge is.

Moreover, the level of articulation is privileged in Laclau and Mouffe's account, in that it establishes the overdetermined character of a social formation, the presence of everything in everything else. Articulation is confined to a specific location as it takes place in the symbolic realm which stands above discourses as their conditions of existence. The symbolic is the mega-being, or Being in the upper case, of all beings. At the same time the fact of 'articulation' is purely contingent in that, like the unity of a social formation, it may or may not happen. Thus by the same token the notion of 'antagonism' is co-extensive with the generalisation of 'articulation'. 'Articulation' always fails to constitute a closed, overdetermined social formation. There is always a further 'not' to add. Consequently, Laclau and Mouffe's exclusive commitment to 'populism' constitutes a hegemonic model of hegemony: as the production of social formations through 'articulation', by which heterogeneous discursive failures are unified by an opposition to a more general or universal failure which threatens them, and thus constitutes them as a social formation organised as the effort to defeat and eliminate the cause of its failure. Hence 'hegemony' is always like Fascism in Gramsci's case, and probably requires a similar commitment to feud and vendetta.

Despite these conclusions Laclau and Mouffe are indifferent as far as the political value of 'hegemony' is concerned. It is simply a neutral, objective, political fact of social existence. One of the many difficulties with that position is that Laclau and Mouffe are then faced with the problem of accounting for an apparent proliferation of social, cultural and political subjectivities, such as ethnic minorities, alternative lifestylers and single mothers, within the social formation of modern, postindustrial, liberal democratic, capitalist societies, and their relatively harmonious co-existence with more traditional social subjectivities such as workers, civil servants, entrepreneurs and married mothers.[3] Although such subjectivities have existed through antagonistic relations with social forces which seek to eliminate or limit them, it is not clear if such phenomena depend on the articulation of hegemonic relations. This is because the notion of a proliferation and multiplicity of subjectivities is incompatible with the relative fixity which populist hegemonic relations seek to establish in relation to an exterior enemy which defines and limits them, as in the Fascist 'people versus power-bloc' formula. The problem is deepened as Laclau and Mouffe regard the unlimited proliferation of subjectivities as exemplary of radical democracy, which happens to be a political value they are enthusiastic about, seeing it as a better political option than Communism for post-Marxism. The radical dimension refers to the proliferation of subjectivities as a consequence of the contingency of democracy itself. In short, democracy is incompatible with hegemony.

Yet the alternative explanation for the proliferation of subjectivities, which presents it in terms of the unlimited capacity of subjects to create themselves out of nothing, or as the expression of a deep, inner, metaphysical essence, is incompatible with the materialist commitment of post-Marxism. Such subjects are as contingent and overdetermined as any other. There is nothing essential about them, as they are produced by forces beyond their control. However, the idea that one is free and self-determined may also be an ideological illusion which is particularly compatible with the self-image of capitalism as morally justified. Indeed, the emphasis on freedom and self-determination within liberal social formations discourages the idea that one is dependent on being hegemonically articulated with others for one's existence. The suggestion is experienced as an insult and cause of shame by most people. However, the question of the illusory nature of the proliferation of subjectivities hangs on the fact that overdetermination is not limited and is thus neither complete or incomplete. Complete overdetermination would eliminate any possibility of illusion. But it would also eliminate any possibility of making a distinction between illusion and reality, as on Laclau and Mouffe's account this can only be done from within hegemony.

So, if radical democracy refers to characteristics such as incompletion and unfixity with respect to both a social formation and the subjectivities which are present within it, then some sort of materialist explanation is required in order to make it consistent with post-Marxism. The consequences of doing so would have knock-on effects for the concept of hegemony as the presupposition that social formations can only exist as an attempt to fix and stabilise themselves, whether successful or not. It would mean adding the conceptualisation of something similar to time in Althusser's account so that the symbolic itself would be contingent – in the sense that it may or may not happen – and thus less essential. The next section will bring these problems in Laclau and Mouffe to bear on the 'shouting' within cultural studies.

Post-Marxism in cultural studies

The importance of post-Marxism within cultural studies can be seen by the approach to culture and politics that culminated in the development of the concept of Thatcherism (Hall 1980a), and which in turn depended on Gramsci's concept of hegemony and drew on Laclau's notion of 'populism'. For Thatcherism, the 'power-bloc' referred to the post-World War II social democratic consensus in Britain in favour of the existence of the welfare state. Resentment against it was mobilised as the content of 'the people'. At the same time, some people were excluded from 'the people' and included within the 'power-bloc'; primarily ethnic and sexual minorities, trade unionists, 'intellectuals' and the unemployed. Importantly, many of the working class, which Marxism was accustomed to regard as its natural constituency, were not. Thatcherism became a 'new common sense', through its ability to align itself with obvious truths like 'you can't spend more than you earn', as a means of reducing tax revenue support for welfare services and nationalised industries and the workers who work in them. In short, cultural studies demonstrated that Thatcherism constituted a particular style of 'interpellation' (O'Shea 1984). That is to say, through 'intellectual and moral leadership', Thatcherism established sufficient consent for its ability to rule over electorally significant working-class voters in the form of what Hall called 'authoritarian populism': authoritarian relations, in a democratic form, centred on the indeterminacy of 'the people' as a moral absolute, and which displaces political and economic issues (Hall 1980b: 179). Thatcherism constitutes an authoritarianism 'from below' which manages a new relation between the state, capital and 'the people'.

The success of cultural studies in demonstrating the relations between culture and politics through post-Marxism has been, like the curate's egg, good in parts. On the one hand it has entailed a commitment to what Hall called a Marxism 'without guarantees' (1996b). On the other hand, the collapse of the centrality of the economic in political explanation, and thus of class struggle as an expression of it, has created a vacuum within the question of agency and subjectivity which has been filled by the category of culture itself. Yet there has been less enthusiasm in adopting the consequences of the materialist critique of subjectivity. As Chen summarises these developments, cultural studies has sought to decentre politics and recentre culture, at the same time as promoting a total politicisation of culture as the site of continuous struggle 'where engagement is immediate and urgent' (1996: 312). In the enthusiasm culture is substituted for politics, subjectivity is substituted for culture, and the materialist logic of the political is disavowed. That is to say, overdetermination, which eliminated economic reductionism, has itself been eliminated from accounts of culture and politics which it has made possible. Consequently, culture has become the sort of automatic guarantee which used to be provided by the economy. Culture has acquired the value of a good in itself, which is then cashed in for the political value of the capacity for self-creation out of nothing, verified by morally wholesome assumptions about historical continuity embodied in criteria for judging types of subjectivity: 'identity politics', in other words. From the perspective of post-Marxism there are no best cases in these developments.

The problem becomes visible if we consider a representative example of the affirmation of cultural guarantees. Angela McRobbie claims that the critique of economic reductionism associated with post-Marxism warrants the rejection of the idea that a social formation can be understood as a totality (1992, 1996). On that basis political opposition to capitalism is replaced by the defence of social identity, which, for reasons that are never clear, is supposed to be emancipatory because it is the positive value of 'how people see themselves . . . as active agents whose sense of self is projected onto and expressed in an expansive range of cultural practices, including texts, images and commodities' which can be objectified through ethnography (1992: 730). Undoubtedly such self-perceptions enjoy material force, but this stems from the extent that their self-sufficiency is illusory. For its part, capitalism is excluded from any social formation, absolutely exterior to it, which is probably news for capitalism. Hence the illusion that social identities are fully autonomous and untainted by capitalism is reinforced. These so-called 'new subjectivities' are pure in heart and virginally innocent (McRobbie 1996: 247), a perfect coincidence of agency and autonomy outside of the illusory structure of ideology. Who would not like to think of themselves in that way?

In McRobbie's position, the Marxist project of emancipation is displaced from the working class and appropriated by the sociological category of identity, in which it is subsequently subsumed through an absolute subjectivism. That is to say, what I am is simply what I think I am. So, rather than deepening the critique of the automatic Marxist link between class and political emancipation, the privilege is preserved and generalised across the representation of the social by breaking the link between emancipation and capitalism through the power of positive thinking. It's as if social identities possess the same essentially oppositional characteristics that the working class was once thought to have (Gilbert 2001). In a sense, new subjectivities are always and already emancipated, and their struggles are reduced to squabbles to get others to see them as they see themselves in order to make their autonomy complete. Conflict is relegated to disputes over status, and identity is sucked back into the vacuum of sociology and spat out into the cesspit of community.

McRobbie grounds her argument in the claim that Laclau's work provides 'the theoretical underpinning for what has already happened in cultural studies' (1992: 724). That may be true. But if so, then it has happened by mistake. It would be hard to pin Laclau and Mouffe down to the position McRobbie advocates. In fact, Laclau and Mouffe attribute the decline of the political value of the classical working class and the emergence of new forms of social protest to the 'structural transformation of capitalism' (Laclau and Mouffe 1990: 97). As new forms of social protest are a good thing and are linked to radical democracy, then in this respect Laclau and Mouffe follow Marx and Engels's positive account of the destabilising effects of capitalism as it made its way from the urban squalor of Manchester to the rural squalor of India and back. Thus: 'All that is solid melts into air, and all that is holy is profaned' (Marx and Engels 1967: 83). Capitalism is not a ground but something which ungrounds the identities which constitute hegemony. It is therefore good for radical democracy, as the destabilising effects of capitalism destroy the illusion that 'the being of objects, which is a purely social construction, belongs to things themselves' (Laclau and Mouffe: 119), such that the world is 'an entirely social construction of human beings which is not grounded on any metaphysical "necessity" external to it – neither God, nor "essential forms", nor the "necessary laws of history"' (p. 129). Capitalism reveals this fact by its dislocation of social practices otherwise secured by repetition, thus making identity impossible; and Laclau and Mouffe propose a theory of discourse which is adequate to dislocation, insofar as it affirms the 'historicity of being' against the metaphysics of presence, and is therefore, along with its philosophical antecedents in the work of Heidegger, Wittgenstein and Derrida, 'internal to Marxism itself' (p. 119). As a result, capitalist dislocation of identity 'necessarily leads to new forms of collective imaginary which reconstruct those threatened identities in a fundamentally new way' (pp. 127–8). That is to say, the self-image of 'new subjectivities' is the effect of a capitalist dislocation in that they are constituted by it. Capitalism is internal to new subjectivities.[4]

For that reason, Laclau and Mouffe endorse the 'consolidation and democratic reform of the Liberal state' through the expansion of its values across the social in response to capitalist dislocation, which on reflection is a better option than more Fascist hegemonic bundling. In other words, capitalism is overdetermined by the level of political development of the state. Yet if that's so then two elements of the social formation have been reintroduced into the argument where they had previously been excluded; namely, economy and politics as levels of a social formation. Just because dislocatory capitalism and the state are external to the articulated space of hegemony, it does not follow that they are external to the existence of a social formation. In which case the limit of hegemony is a problem of knowledge, of knowing how the non-articulated is linked with the articulated, something which cannot be satisfied with reference to the concept of articulation itself, as the problem is larger than it. Articulation does not therefore determine the levels of a social formation. It is only one element within it. Which means that any further development of a materialist analysis of a social formation would have to begin from that which is not articulated. The task for cultural studies would be to conceive the political dimension of culture which is not articulated.

Notes

1 Often this presence is demonstrated through the practice of 'symptomatic reading', which focuses on the gaps and absences through which meaning both does and does not make sense.
2 For more on the problem of the subject, see Valentine (2002) and the references therein.
3 Of course, one must exclude the vendettas between Protestants and Catholics in Northern Ireland and similar phenomena, such as feuds between rival ethnic minorities in urban areas, from these generalisations.
4 Indeed, this consequence of Laclau and Mouffe's position is the basis of Smith's rejection of it in the name of how people see themselves (Smith 1998). See also Smith's contributions to an interview with Laclau in Laclau (1990).

Bibliography

Althusser, Louis (1971), 'Ideology and Ideological State Apparatuses', in *Lenin and Philosophy and Other Essays*, New York: Monthly Review Press, pp. 127–186.
Althusser, Louis [1965] (1982a), *For Marx*, London: Verso.
Althusser, Louis [1962] (1982b), 'Contradiction and Overdetermination', in *For Marx*, London: Verso, pp. 87–128.
Althusser, Louis [1963] (1982c), 'On the Materialist Dialectic', in *For Marx*, London: Verso, pp. 161–218.
Althusser, Louis and Balibar, Etienne [1968] (1975), *Reading Capital*, London: New Left Books.
Beasley-Murray, Jon (1998), 'Peronism and the Secret History of Cultural Studies', *Cultural Critique*, 39, pp. 189–223.
Chen, Kuan-Hsing (1996), 'Post-Marxism: Between/Beyond Critical Postmodernism and Cultural Studies', in David Morley and Kuan-Hsing Chen (eds), *Stuart Hall: Critical Dialogues in Cultural Studies*, London: Routledge, pp. 309–25.
Gilbert, Jeremy (2001), 'A Certain Ethics of Openness: Radical Democratic Cultural Studies', *Strategies: Journal of Theory, Culture and Politics*, 14:2, pp. 189–208.
Gramsci, Antonio (1971), *Selections from Prison Notebooks*, London: Lawrence and Wishart.
Hall, Stuart (1980a), 'Thatcherism: A New Stage?', *Marxism Today*, February, pp. 22–7.
Hall, Stuart (1980b), 'Popular-Democratic vs Authoritarian Populism: Two Ways of "Taking Democracy Seriously"', in Alan Hunt (ed.), *Marxism and Democracy*, London: Lawrence and Wishart, pp. 157–85.
Hall, Stuart (1996a), 'Cultural Studies and its Theoretical Legacies', in David Morley and Kuan-Hsing Chen (eds), *Stuart Hall: Critical Dialogues in Cultural Studies*, London: Routledge, pp. 262–75.
Hall, Stuart (1996b), 'The Problem of Ideology: Marxism Without Guarantees', in David Morley and Kuan-Hsing Chen (eds), *Stuart Hall: Critical Dialogues in Cultural Studies*, London: Routledge, pp. 25–46.
Howarth, David (2000), *Discourse*, Buckingham: Open University Press.
Laclau, Ernesto (1979), *Politics and Ideology in Marxist Theory*, London: Verso.
Laclau, Ernesto (1990), 'Theory, Democracy and Socialism', in *New Reflections on the Revolution of Our Time*, London: Verso, pp. 197–213.
Laclau, Ernesto and Mouffe, Chantal (1985), *Hegemony and Socialist Strategy*, London: Verso.
Laclau, Ernesto, and Mouffe, Chantal [1987] (1990), 'Post-Marxism Without Apologies', in *New Reflections on the Revolution of Our Time*, London: Verso, pp. 97–132.
Lenin, Vladimir Ilyich (1916), *Imperialism: The Highest Stage of Capitalism*, www.marxists.org/archive/lenin/works.

Marx, Karl [1857] (1973), *Introduction to the Critique of Political Economy*, in *The Grundrisse*, Harmondsworth: Penguin, pp. 81–112.

Marx, Karl and Engels, Friedrich [1848] (1967), *The Communist Manifesto*, Harmondsworth: Penguin.

McRobbie, Angela (1992), 'Post-Marxism and Cultural Studies: A Post-Script', in Lawrence Grossberg, Cary Nelson and Paula Treichler (eds), *Cultural Studies*, New York and London: Routledge, pp. 719–30.

McRobbie, Angela (1996), 'Looking Back at New Times and its Critics', in David Morley and Kuan-Hsing Chen (eds), *Stuart Hall: Critical Dialogues in Cultural Studies*, London: Routledge, pp. 238–61.

Morley, David and Chen, Kuan-Hsing (eds) (1996), *Stuart Hall: Critical Dialogues in Cultural Studies*, London: Routledge.

O'Shea, Alan (1984), 'Trusting the People', in Anonymous (ed.), *Formations of Nation and People*, London: Routledge and Kegan Paul, pp. 19–41.

Slack, Jennifer Daryl (1996), 'The Theory and Method of Articulation in Cultural Studies', in David Morley and Kuan-Hsing Chen (eds), *Stuart Hall: Critical Dialogues in Cultural Studies*, London: Routledge, pp. 112–27.

Smith, Anna Marie (1998), *Laclau and Mouffe: The Radical Democratic Imaginary*, London: Routledge.

Spinoza, Baruch [1647] (2002), 'Ethics', in Michael Morgan (ed.), *Spinoza: Complete Works*, Indianapolis: Hackett, pp. 213–382.

Valentine, Jeremy (2002), 'The Theoretical Link Between Politics and the Subject', in Alan Finalyson and Jeremy Valentine (eds), *Politics and Post-Structuralism: An Introduction*, Edinburgh: Edinburgh University Press, pp. 36–51.

MIND THE GAP

CHAPTER 4

Cultural Studies and Ethics

Joanna Zylinska

Political issues seem to be increasingly conceptualised in moral, religiously inflected terms – from formulations of international policies against the 'axis of evil' through to descriptions of DNA experimentation and cloning as attempts to 'play God'. What concerns me in this chapter is how members of society broadly associated with 'the left' can respond to this moralisation of politics without resorting to the same moral figures drawn on by their opponents. In other words, how can the left deal with the moralisation of politics from a sounder philosophical foundation than just its own 'natural' moral superiority, which manifests itself in deciding in advance that capitalism, globalisation or war are 'bad'? I want to suggest that the academic framework known as cultural studies provides a good starting point for developing responsible political thinking which both critiques political moralism and remains accountable for its own ethical investments.

The politicians of good and evil

One of the significant features of the contemporary conjuncture 'post-9/11' in both the United States and Britain is an explicit moralisation of the political agenda. In his address to the West Point Military Academy on 1 June 2002, nine months after the 9/11 attacks, George Bush declared: 'We are in a conflict between good and evil, and America will call evil by its name' (quoted in Singer 2004: 1). The religiously inflected tone of Bush's proclamation regarding North Korea, Iran and Iraq, which allegedly constitute an 'axis of evil', resonates with Tony Blair's moralistic stance towards international relations. BBC world affairs analyst Louise Tillin points out that Blair has brought a very personal morality, rooted in his own Christian beliefs, to the need to act against terror. In his speech to the Labour Party conference in October 2001 Blair talked of 'a moral duty to act if a conflict such as Rwanda happened again today. "Out of the shadow of this evil should emerge lasting good," he said.'[1] We can see from the above that in the US as well as the UK '9/11' has played a symbolic role in founding a new moral sensibility. This political moralism has underpinned the all-encompassing 'war on terror' unequivocally championed by Bush and Blair and fought against an invisible enemy, 'terror' itself.[2] And it is through recourse to moral rhetoric, a discourse of good and evil, that a difference between 'us' and 'them' has been established in this war. Morality has therefore been made to work in the service of politics; it has been used to justify and forge democratic (neo-)liberalism.

Positioning '9/11' as an extraordinary, apocalyptic event after which 'nothing will ever be the same' has been part of this moral agenda, which attempts to legitimate military intervention with references to transcendent concepts and values. In order to demystify some of this uniqueness of the 9/11 event, I want to suggest that the post-9/11 moral conjuncture actually presents itself as something of a *déjà vu* in our political history. As Wendy Brown makes clear in *Politics Out of History* (2001), polarised thinking tinted with strong moral undertones and a clear division between oppressors and victims had already structured the Western political universe in the second half of the twentieth century, up until 'the fall of the Iron Curtain' in 1989. The world was then seen as divided into the US and Soviet blocs, freedom fighters and Communists. However, the collapse of Communism eliminated the opposition against which democratic freedom could be figured, with 'Western liberalism' losing its moorings in anti-Communism (2001: 13). Also, the stark opposition between Communism and liberalism was revealed to be untenable because, as Brown points out, '[m]any of the least defensible elements of twentieth-century communist states . . . have lately made their appearance in ours: overgrown state size, power, and reach; groaning apparatuses of administration intermixed with a labyrinthine legal machinery; extensive . . . welfare systems that routinely fail their client populations; inefficient and uncontrolled economies; lack of felt sovereign individuality' (p. 13). This realisation that the Communist 'other' was not so wholly other put in doubt the appropriateness of moralism as a structuring device for politics, and, consequently, led to political melancholia for the not-quite-acknowledged loss amongst the citizens of many nations on both sides of the Iron Curtain.

However, it seems to me that the temporarily dismantled binary structure of power, rooted in the moralised 'us/them' opposition, re-emerged a mere decade or so later, through the interlocking of Islamophobia, the moral panic about terrorism, and the fear of asylum and immigration after the events of 9/11. Significantly, just as Communism could to some extent be seen as Cold War liberalism's alter ego, current democratic neo-liberalism entails many of the features it ascribes to its own 'constitutive others': 'rogue states', elements in the axis of evil – e.g. torture, violation of international law and suspension of human rights. In spite of this, 'the democratic West' levels accusations of the 'breach of human rights' against 'the enemies of democracy' such as Iraq, North Korea and (much more reticently) China in order to establish a moral distinction between itself and its others. What is nevertheless significantly different about the construction of this opposition between good and evil in the political conjuncture post-9/11 in comparison with the Cold War period is the creation of the 'zones of exception' *within* the ideological or even geographical space of neo-liberalism, where international, state and moral law can be legally and legitimately suspended. In spite of employing torture in the wars on Iraq and terrorism, suspending international law in prison camps such as Guantánamo Bay or in asylum detention centres such as Yarl's Wood in the UK (see Moore 2005), and proposing to withdraw citizen rights through the introduction of the Patriot Act or the Prevention of Terrorism Bill, the US and the UK can avoid accusations of immorality and the breach of human rights precisely thanks to confining their terror and violence to these zones of exception. Those special zones are inhabited by not-fully-human non-citizens, whose participation in the political community of the holders of human rights is denied a priori, and to whom sovereign law only applies negatively. As no *human* rights are thus being violated in those zones, the moral and political domination of the West is ultimately ensured. Through references to Samuel Huntington's 'clash of civilisations' thesis, which is used to justify an intrinsic difference between Christian and Muslim cultures, through appeals for a tighter control of immigrants who bring diseases and pollute the healthy body politic of democratic nation-states, and through calls for the development of terrorist camps and asylum detention centres as zones of indistinction where the law and life coincide,[3] the founding notions of liberalism such as progress, sovereignty and freedom are recuperated. In order to wish away the destabilisation of, and threats to, the founding narratives and signal terms of liberalism, morality is brought in by politicians and picked up on by the media as glue that will repair the national myths of origin and the economic myths of providence-ensured prosperity (e.g. 'They are attacking us because they envy us our freedom').

Just do it: ethical shopping

So much so expected, perhaps. This narrative concerning the (im)morality of neo-liberal capitalist democracies and their vexed political allegiances is by now a familiar one, at least among critics on the left. However, the problem of morality in politics is much more complex than that. I want to suggest that this moralisation of politics has been evident not only in the pronouncements of our political leaders but also in the humanitarian responses issued by non-governmental lobbying groups and charities, which are not affiliated with any political parties or even nations, to developments such as the allegations of torture by the US and British troops at Abu Ghraib prison outside Baghdad, the 2004 tsunami disaster, the increased presence of genetically modified foods in European supermarkets and the breeding and cloning of animals for research. What interests me even more is that morality seems to serve not only as a placeholder for the hopes and aspirations of unilateral politics in the 'global' world, and a legitimation for its actions, but also as a (frequently unacknowledged) driving force for many of the 'progressive', leftist forms of political activism that explicitly repudiate the moral certainties of their political adversaries. Indeed, moral tropes are drawn upon by various social movements, activist networks and overtly non-political bodies devoted to single-issue 'good causes' – from the makers of charity wristbands carrying such diverse messages as 'Cultivate Peace' (light blue), 'Honour' (smudgy black and white) or 'Save Street Children' (dark blue) through to Bob 'Live8' Geldof (who, incidentally, promoted his 2005 'Make Poverty History' initiative with a white wristband).

To focus a little more on just one example of such moralised left-wing activism, on 21 March 2005 the website for the Adbusters movement – a 'global network of artists, activists, writers, pranksters, students, educators and entrepreneurs' aiming to 'topple existing power structures and forge a major shift in the way we will live in the 21st century' – featured an article titled 'Is Bush Morally Perverse?' Its main premise was to oppose what the anonymous authors termed Bush's 'cafeteria morality' (by which they meant his deeply inconsistent views on 'life', which made him and his Republican allies fight for the survival of Terri Schiavo, a patient in a persistent vegetative state since 1990, against the wishes of her husband, while simultaneously accepting the deaths of 100,000 Iraqi civilians as part of inevitable 'collateral damage') against the presumably morally superior position of Adbusters themselves – producers of the first 'ethical shoe set to kick Nike's ass', the Blackspot sneaker 'made from organic, vegetarian, and recycled materials in a Portuguese union shop'.[4] However, the self-avowed 'ethical' manufacturers are not actually offering any *new ethics*; instead, it can be argued that they in fact reinforce the dominant capitalist ethos which sells individualism and social distinctiveness as a product (see Beckett 2005). Besides, this negative 'fetishization of the brand as cause and root of the ills of contemporary capitalism', which is evident in anti-consumer activist politics and performed most strongly in *No Logo*, Naomi Klein's 'activist bible', works so successfully at the expense of obscuring the complexity of the globalised late capitalist system, of which brands are only one component (Littler 2005: 234). Even if it manages to lead to effective and 'successful' action, 'brand-bashing' nevertheless denies or covers up the affective investments of its practitioners, and thus ends up both polarising and moralising politics.[5]

What I am therefore principally interested in exploring in this chapter is how members of society broadly associated with 'the left' can respond to this moralisation of politics without resorting to the same moral figures drawn on by their opponents. In other words, how can the left deal with the moralisation of politics from a sounder philosophical foundation than just its own 'natural' moral superiority, confirmed by branding capitalism or 'Bushism/Blairism' as 'bad' up front? To start answering this question, I want us to consider the proposition that *any* investments that drive political action, no matter what its actual orientation or relation to the dominant structures of power, are situated *between ethics and morality*. The conceptual opposition between ethics and morality deserves our closer attention, but for the sake of simplicity let us call these affective investments 'ethical' for the time being. These investments are both conscious and unconscious and emerge out of a combination of rational arguments and libidinal drives that get translated into normative positions informing politics. According to Ernesto Laclau, the normative ('this-is-the-way-things-are-or-should-be') character of the political stems from, and is underpinned by, ethical investments that members of a certain community (be it 'activists', 'shoppers', 'politicians', 'cultural studies practitioners' or 'anti-globalisation protesters') made at some point, and which by now may have receded into their unconscious (Laclau 1990: 125, 197–8). But, while this mechanism of affective ethical investments has arguably constituted an inextricable part of the constitution of the political as we know it, the overt recourse to moral rhetoric at the dawn of the twenty-first century has transformed politics into a terrain of moral struggle.

Between morality, moralism and ethics

In order to consider some possible ways of challenging this normative consensus on value and the ensuing right course of action in different forms of transnational and local politics it is important to make a distinction between morality and ethics – especially that the latter concept is often employed when the former would be more appropriate (for example, in phrases such as 'ethical shopping' or the above-mentioned 'ethical shoe'). I define ethics here as a secondary reflection on moral values, beliefs and practices, and thus, more specifically, on the appropriateness of a given political position or action. Morality, in turn, can be seen as a first-order set of beliefs and practices concerning values which have been developed, codified and accepted by a given society. Indeed, it serves as the very legitimation of the political position or action in question. Wendy Brown introduces a further distinction at work in contemporary political discourses – that between morality, which is understood as 'galvanising moral vision', and moralism, which stands for 'a reproachful moralising sensibility' (2001: 22). Brown writes:

> Morality stands in an uneasy relationship to the political insofar as it is always mistrustful of power; and it bears a slightly truncated relationship to the intellectual insofar as it is rarely willing to explore the seamy underside of righteousness or goodness in politics. Moralism is much less ambivalent: it tends to be intensely antagonistic toward a richly agonistic political or intellectual life. Moralism so loathes overt manifestations of power – its ontological and epistemological premises are so endangered by signs of action and agency that the moralist inevitably feels antipathy toward politics as a domain of open contestation for power and hegemony. But the identity of the moralist is also staked against intellectual questioning that might dismantle the foundations of its own premises; its survival is imperilled by the very practice of open-ended intellectual enquiry. It is thus in a moralistic mode that the most expansive revolutionary doctrines – liberalism, Maoism, or multiculturalism – so often transmogrify into their opposite, into brittle, defensive, and finally conservative institutions and practices. (pp. 30–1)

While both morality and moralism issue from unacknowledged attachments to a certain idea of truth and to identity conceptualised in terms of injury, the latter is particularly pernicious, as it replaces the passion of quasi-religious conviction which can nevertheless drive a liberatory movement with paranoia, mania and, ultimately, political stasis.

Taking these distinctions between morality, moralism and ethics into account, I want to suggest:

1. that it is precisely through recourse to what I term 'morality without ethics' that the consensus about values is currently being established – be it on the right, centre or left;
2. that this 'morality without ethics' co-exists in a zone of indistinction with what Brown terms 'moralism';
3. that morality needs an ethical supplement if it is not to turn into moralism, 'a kind of posture or pose taken up in the ruins of morality by its faithful adherents' (Brown 2001: 23);

4. that it is only via ethical reflection that a responsible response to the moralisation of political agendas can be developed.

I also want to propose that it is the interdisciplinary project known as cultural studies – rather than, as might seem more logical or appropriate, philosophy[6] – that can provide us with a propitious framework for not only thinking through the differences between morality, moralism and ethics but also proposing a responsible politics which will be capable of accounting for its ethical investments.

My interest in the moralisation of politics is thus not merely diagnostic: I also claim that the current convergence between politics and morality, often employed in different guises to support conservative, neo-liberal interests, calls for a responsible, ethical response from 'the left', while also recognising that the vision of a unified left fighting its crusade against the ills of capitalism is a symptom of the same moralising desire for totality and closure. Taking into account the dispersed character of the left and its politics, as well as the reformulation of its economics-focused agenda via an engagement with more 'culturalist issues' such as new social movements, cultural industries and identity politics, I postulate that cultural studies – for which culture is not a mere 'decorative addendum to the "hard world" of production and things' (Hall 1996b: 233) but rather a structuring, material element in the politico-economic landscape – can help us respond to the current 'moral conjuncture'. Cultural studies is able to provide us with tools to interpret and understand the meanings behind the 'moralising process' in contemporary politics and the way this moralisation is performed by governmental and media agencies. As an intellectual-political formation within academia which both reaches out to and draws on the events, practices and cultural forms outside it, cultural studies is a privileged discipline for interrogating relations of power in the world 'out there' (e.g. via Gramsci, Foucault and, more recently, Deleuze and Guattari, and Hardt and Negri), precisely because it is premised upon the interrogation of its own relationship to power (via its work on disciplinarity and its engagement with excluded or marginalised discourses and practices, such as race, gender or subcultural resistance). In this way it can perhaps avoid – or at least account for – the moralist drive of many forms of left politics.

The ethics of cultural studies

None of which is to say that cultural studies should be seen as more 'impartial' or 'unbiased'. To describe cultural studies, in Simon During's words, as a field which 'accepts that studying culture is rarely value-free, and so, embracing clearly articulated left-wing values, . . . seeks to extend and critique the relatively narrow range of norms, methods, and practices embedded in the traditional past-fixated, canon-forming humanities' (During 1999: 27), is to presuppose a certain value inherent in the idea of left-wing critique, in the transformation of the traditional model of education and in the concept of social justice which informs this transformation. Indeed, it is precisely cultural studies' declared 'politicality' that is often used to distinguish it from a number of allegedly more 'objective' disciplines. And it is the (broadly defined) Marxist legacy, with its interest in the material and its commitment to social justice, that has by and large informed cultural studies politics. While cultural studies may not have always relied on a unified theory of society or the kind of progressive notion of history that informs much of traditional Marxism, it has nevertheless retained the belief in the possibility of social and political change to be found in Marx and Engels's writings. As During explains, 'engaged cultural studies is academic work (teaching, research, dissemination, etc.) on contemporary culture from non-elite or counter-hegemonic perspectives ("from below") with an openness to the culture's reception and production in everyday life, or more generally, its impact on life trajectories' (1999: 25).[7]

However, this commitment to left-wing values, an engagement with non-hegemonic perspectives and openness to the alterity of culture and life itself will not automatically protect us against political moralism. Indeed, cultural studies itself has sometimes been guilty of adopting the holier-than-thou position against other disciplines and fields of enquiry and action. As Gary Hall argues in *Culture in Bits*, in its commitment to politics and to connecting with political forces outside the academy, cultural studies has at times tended to place politics 'in a transcendental position with respect to all other discourses' (2002: 9), as a safeguarded attachment that need not, or, indeed, must not be questioned. (Hall traces this 'protectionism' towards politics in the work of a number of key cultural studies thinkers, including Raymond Williams, Stuart Hall and Angela McRobbie.) And yet he also demonstrates, through the writings of the very same thinkers, how cultural studies needs to be understood as a permanent experiment playing off politics against different forms of theorisation that both threaten this politics and promise to take it into new territories. Hall thus concludes by painting a more optimistic – some might even say utopian – picture of the future of cultural studies and the possibilities it inheres:

> As Williams illustrates, there can be no pre-established programme or syllabus for such an experiment, no fixed and worked out agenda or set rules. Nor are the results of such an experiment foreseeable. The future of cultural

studies, if cultural studies is to have a future, cannot be predicted or predetermined – that would be just a repetition of the past. Each time, and in each context and 'singular instant', this 'tension' [between politics and theorisation] must take its own risks. And if this is what cultural studies is, it is also what threatens to carry cultural studies beyond itself – to the point where the identity of cultural studies becomes uncertain and is opened up to the future, the unpredictable, unforeseeable, 'monstrous' future. (p. 94)

It is precisely this ongoing theoretical reflection on politics – on canons, values, beliefs and practices (including its own values), and thus on the appropriateness of its political position or action – that allow me to position cultural studies as intrinsically ethical. And it is its openness to incalculable difference – to the unpredictable, the unforeseeable, the unknown – that allows cultural studies to enact this ethics (even if not guaranteeing that it will always *act ethically*). We should clarify that ethics, defined as a secondary reflection on moral values, beliefs and practices, does not contain a set of prescriptions for what to do. Rather this ethical reflection is enabled by an openness to the infinite alterity of the other, an alterity which poses a challenge to my own self-containedness and moral righteousness. (More on this non-foundational conceptualisation of ethics in the work of Emmanuel Levinas and Jacques Derrida later.)

Cultural studies can thus help us think through the workings of what we could tentatively describe as 'moralist culture' passed off as politics. As Angela McRobbie postulates in *The Uses of Cultural Studies* (2005), such a critical analysis of morality is more needed than ever, now that the emphasis in political and media debates has shifted from socio-economic factors to individual narratives, unique stories and dramatic case studies. And so, in popular TV programmes such as BBC's *What Not to Wear*, ABC's *Extreme Makeover* or Channel 4's *Wife Swap* issues concerning wealth, relationships and success in life are presented as isolated 'problem cases' which can be rectified with the help of singular interventions by 'makeover experts'. This logic also seems to have been embraced by the UK government in its all too willing dispensation of Anti-Social Behaviour Orders (ASBOs), which put physical restrictions on offenders' behaviour, including their removal from the community. ASBOs thus reduce the interlocking of poverty, crime, poor education, bad housing and other social and economic factors to individual behavioural problems that can be solved by the naming and shaming of the 'yobs' (defined as such against the 'normal' law-abiding citizens). It is the prevailing narrow logic of consensus between broadcasters and politicians of all ilks, in which there is 'very little, if any, questioning of the values upon which the basic structures of social and economic organisation are based' (2005: 20), that motivates McRobbie to propose cultural studies as a viable political and intellectual alternative for thinking our way out of this moralisation of political and social issues.

I agree with McRobbie that cultural studies is well placed to undertake this sort of interrogation. In my view an important point of entry for a critique of moralism in our politics and broader culture can be found in the Birmingham Centre for Contemporary Cultural Studies' (CCCS') early work on moral panics presented in *Policing the Crisis: Mugging, the State, and Law and Order* (1978). In this 'classic' text, Stuart Hall, Chas Critcher, Tony Jefferson, John Clarke and Brian Roberts set out to investigate why British society entered a state of moral panic about 'mugging' in the early 1970s, but also 'how the themes of *race, crime* and *youth* – condensed into the image of "mugging" – came to serve as the articulator of the crisis, its ideological conductor' (p. viii). Morality is seen there as a way of establishing and preserving a hegemonic political order. Challenging a number of accepted notions that are consolidated by this order, such as work, family, decency and respect, the authors outline an alternative to the dominant petty-bourgeois ethic of the day (1978: 161–4) – an ethic of responsibility for the victims of racialised discourse, rooted in a different colonial sensibility and different economics (see Zylinska 2005: 41–61). This critique of moralism in politics was given special focus in Stuart Hall's own later work, in particular the collection of essays *The Hard Road to Renewal* (1988b), devoted to the critique of Thatcherism. Describing it as another 'key' cultural studies text, McRobbie commends *The Hard Road to Renewal* for demonstrating how disparate elements such as popular opinions, prejudices and deeply held moral values had been rearticulated in the form of a conservative yet inclusive politics, the 'authoritarian populism' of Mrs Thatcher in 1980s Britain. According to Hall, capitalism conjoined with democratic populism became a moral force, which led to the positioning of the conservative politics of the 1980s as 'the strongest possible counter to the values and beliefs of the late 1960s, to the left-wing radicalism which developed through the 1970s, and which included new social movements and gay rights' (McRobbie 2005: 25).

Of course, as the forms and contents of 'morality' have changed today – the socio-political circumstances in the US and Europe post-9/11 are different from those of the 1970s or 1980s Britain; there is more recognition of the complexity, diversity and constructedness of race, gender and sexual identities; new forms of kinship have evolved due to developments in both queer politics and new technologies – we must recognise the need for a new modulation of the cultural studies analysis of dominant values.

Furthermore, as well as drawing on some 'classic' texts in the cultural studies tradition – the writings of Althusser, Gramsci or Stuart Hall – interrogations of morality by contemporary cultural studies scholars can also be developed (and indeed already are) via the more recent work on the multitude, biopolitics, performativity and 'life itself' inspired by such thinkers as Giorgio Agamben, Michel Foucault, Michael Hardt and Antonio Negri, Judith Butler and Paolo Virno. However, it seems to me that, if cultural studies is not to be just a neutral power analytics, its questioning of morality needs to be driven by – and, simultaneously, it needs to be able to outline (in a reflexive, performative way) – an ethics (see Zylinska 2005). The 'origin' of this 'ethics of cultural studies', I want to suggest, lies in infinite responsibility to the other, the way it has been conceptualised in the work of Emmanuel Levinas (and further developed by Jacques Derrida).[8]

I see Levinas' work as being particularly important for cultural studies because of his understanding of ethics outside, or beyond, the traditional discourse of moral philosophy, and because it focuses on the most ordinary events of everyday life. Levinas is concerned with workaday encounters with what he defines as 'the alterity of the other', encounters which challenge the familiar and the ordinary. His philosophy can thus be situated in close proximity to cultural studies' conceptualisation of culture as 'a whole way of life', and to its interest in the material, the quotidian and the ordinary. Ethics, for Levinas, is not something imposed from outside or above; instead, ethics is inevitable. An ethical event occurs in every encounter with difference, with the 'face' and discourse of the other that addresses me and makes me both responsible and accountable (even if I ultimately decide to turn my back on this difference or even annihilate it). I am thus always already a hostage of the other, of his or her ethical demand. As Levinas himself puts it in a poetic but also somewhat menacing way, our subjectivity 'does not have time to choose the Good and thus is penetrated with its rays unbeknownst to itself', because the Good 'has chosen me before I have chosen it' (1998: 11). It is through this encounter that I become aware of my place in the world, of my corporeal boundaries, of the language that comes to me as a gift. But it is also through this encounter that I may become a murderer, a destroyer of the difference that threatens my 'place in the sun' (even if I manage to persuade myself or others that this murder is 'only' an act of retaliation, that it is part of a 'just war', or that the other hates me and thus needs to be excluded from my world – through either being placed in a detention camp or being presented with an ASBO).

What I called earlier 'an ethics of cultural studies' manifests itself precisely in this response to the forms of alterity which have traditionally been marginalised in, or excluded from, our dominant structures of representation and political participation. Indeed, I would even go so far as to say that cultural studies, from its inception, has (unwittingly) been performing a form of Levinasian ethics, and that an openness to alterity, the contemporary forms of Levinas' 'stranger', 'widow' and 'orphan' (Levinas 1969: 77), has been its driving force (something that, incidentally, also accounts for cultural studies' somewhat problematic humanism).[9] We can think here of the aforementioned Birmingham CCCS' critique of 'moral panics' involving 'mugging' and young black youths; Dick Hebdige's pioneering work on 'subcultures' as forms of resistance against the hegemonic dominance of the 'parent culture' (1979); Erica Carter's analysis of women gaining political subjectivity via shopping (1984); Angela McRobbie's reading of 'young girls', with their apparently banal cultural practices such as bedroom poster culture and glossy magazines, as participants in 'cultural resistance' (1991); or Stuart Hall's recognition of 'new ethnicities' in Britain as a sign of the 'decline of the west' and the rethinking of the relations between the politico-cultural centre and its margins (1988a). All these familiar examples, often featuring in cultural studies' 'stories of origin' in introductory textbooks and courses on the subject, can be seen as embracing this very openness, or hospitality, not only to forms and practices which had previously been marginalised or dismissed under the all-encompassing label of 'popular culture' but also to those activities and conjunctures for which no name existed before.

Significantly, in his frequently cited essay, 'Cultural Studies and its Theoretical Legacies', Stuart Hall has described cultural studies as a 'project that is always open to that which it doesn't yet know, to that which it can't yet name' (Hall 1996a: 263), a view that can allow us to find in cultural studies a space for a non- or post-humanist ethics that will challenge both Levinas' and cultural studies' originary humanism. This description of the intellectual trajectories of the CCCS also creates a more complex picture than the 'view from outside', in which cultural studies either is reduced to 'bias studies' (Žižek in Butler et al. 2000: 230–3), an application of the readily available categories of injury and injustice to predefined social groups, or becomes a venue for the celebration of cultural populism (Garnham 1997), the already selected and despised forms of 'low culture'.

Cultural studies against the duplicity of impotence

This responsibility and openness of cultural studies I am talking about here would not be just a theoretical endeavour, nor would it amount to promoting an 'anything goes' politics, a warped liberalism which permanently keeps all options open while celebrating 'cultural differences' in a colourful but meaningless festival. A responsible politics that cultural studies could help us work out would need to spring from the recognition of antagonism and violence as constitutive to any form of identity or political belonging. However, it would also be underpinned by a double ethical injunction – to make a decision, always anew, about how to respond to alterity with the least amount of violence possible, and to live and think through the consequences of this decision.

To sum up the main points I have raised so far, cultural studies thus understood would allow us to:

1. question the 'morality without ethics' in the current political discourses on the right, centre and left by denaturalising the moral concepts such as 'good', 'evil' or 'justice' these discourses refer to, and by proposing instead a critical historical analysis of these concepts and values;
2. remain vigilant against moralism, which inevitably leads to a paralysing 'politics of conviction' (Brown 2001: 93–4) (cf. the war on terror against 'the axis of evil', charity wristbands sporting competing self-righteous slogans, 'ethical shopping', or even cultural studies' own moralism, which refuses to question its politics);
3. provide an ethical supplement to its political work by drawing on its own history – its content-free ethical injunction, manifesting itself in an openness to difference, to the marginalised, the non-canonical and the excluded;
4. offer a theoretical framework for the left, enabling it to conceptualise a responsible politics capable of accounting for its affective investments.

Critical of the institutional conditions of the university with its academic and corporate allegiances, and of its practical politics of inclusion and exclusion, cultural studies can also shift the boundary between the internal politics of the academic institution and the external politics of the 'wider world', on the transnational and local level. Its relatively 'marginal' position in both the traditional figurations of academic disciplinarity and in broader political movements can also be a position of strength – although I realise this proposition goes against the desire of many cultural studies practitioners to align themselves with wider political movements. But this 'marginal' position could allow for an intellectual critique and a responsible teaching that would not be immediately swallowed up by political activism, and that would keep a check on its moralist drives.

Taking a cue from Levinas as well as the more 'recognisable' cultural studies texts and thinkers mentioned above, a responsible ethical cultural studies would thus be able to help us envisage new conditions of possibility for a just being in the world, for its transformation, for rearranging its structures of power and producing new alliances and strategies of resistance – while also keeping the ethical promise open. Rather than focusing on a telos of a revolution led by a unified left, or indeed mourning the loss of this telos, cultural studies could work towards outlining a 'revolutionary politics of long duration' (McRobbie 2005: 24) interweaving longer socio-historical processes such as transformations of liberalism, Communism or democracy, seismic eruptions of different scales ('1968', '9/11') and hard-to-pin-down, more 'rhizomatic' developments (transnational flows of capital or desire, virtual communities). Like a collective, populist, twenty-first-century version of the Nietzschean philosopher, cultural studies scholars could thus guard society against the slave morality of 'quiet, virtuous resignation', a 'duplicity of impotence' that 'asks very little of life', as it already knows in advance what its conditions of possibility are and how far its moral horizon goes (Nietzsche 1956: 179).

Notes

1 http://news.bbc.co.uk/1/hi/uk_politics/1594264.stm, accessed on: 30 June 2005.
2 I would hesitantly add that this kind of moralisation in politics can also be observed in other neo-liberal democracies: we can mention here the 'moral panic' response to the assassination of the controversial politician Pim Fortuyn in 2002 and to the broader 'immigration and Islam' issue in the Netherlands, or the religiously motivated 2005 protests against the public recognition of homosexuality in Poland. However, we need to exercise caution in drawing parallels too quickly between all these different countries, and in looking at 9/11 as the sole origin of the moralisation of politics, which is why this chapter starts from interrogating the more easily traceable parallels between the US and the UK, and the way both countries explicitly rearticulated their international and national political agendas in the aftermath of the 9/11 attacks.
3 These ideas on zones of exception have been developed from Agamben (1998).
4 http://adbusters.org, accessed on: 30 June 2005.
5 By 'affective investments' I mean something different from just emotional influences. 'Affect' stands for me rather for the *capacity for transformation from one state to another*, involving 'an increase or decrease of the power of acting, for the body and the mind alike' (Deleuze 1988: 49). Affects thus involve both ideas and feelings – although my interpretation of affective investments falls in line more with psychoanalysis than with Deleuze's re-reading of Spinoza.
6 Philosophy is understood here as a discrete academic discipline, although I of course acknowledge that philosophical thought deeply permeates cultural studies.

7 This paragraph has been taken, in a revised form, from my book *The Ethics of Cultural Studies* (2005: 4).
8 There is no room for an analysis of Jacques Derrida's radicalisation of Levinas's concept of alterity and his rethinking of Levinasian ethics in terms of hospitality in this chapter, but I would like to refer the reader to Derrida's *Adieu: To Emmanuel Levinas* (1999) and his *Of Hospitality* (2000).
9 For a critique of cultural studies' inherent humanism, see Neil Badmington's chapter in this volume.

Bibliography

Agamben, Giorgio (1998), *Homo Sacer: Sovereign Power and Bare Life*, Stanford, CA: Stanford University Press.
Beckett, Andy (2005), 'Branded for Life' (review of Joseph Heath and Andrew Potter's *The Rebel Sell*), *Guardian*, review section, 4 June, p. 11.
Brown, Wendy (2001), *Politics Out of History*, Princeton, NJ, and Oxford: Princeton University Press.
Butler, Judith, Laclau, Ernesto and Žižek, Slavoj (2000), *Contingency, Universality, Hegemony: Contemporary Dialogues on the Left*, London and New York: Verso.
Carter, Erica (1984), 'Alice in Consumer Wonderland', in Angela McRobbie and Mica Nava (eds), *Gender and Generation*, London: Macmillan, pp. 185–214.
Deleuze, Gilles (1988), *Spinoza: Practical Philosophy*, San Francisco: City Lights Books.
Derrida, Jacques (1999), *Adieu: To Emmanuel Levinas*, Stanford, CA: Stanford University Press.
Derrida, Jacques (2000), *Of Hospitality: Anne Dufourmantelle Invites Jacques Derrida to Respond*, Stanford, CA: Stanford University Press.
During, Simon (1999), 'Introduction', in Simon During (ed.), *The Cultural Studies Reader*, 2nd edn, London and New York: Routledge, pp. 1–28.
Garnham, Nicholas (1997), 'Political Economy and the Practice of Cultural Studies', in Marjorie Ferguson and Peter Golding (eds), *Cultural Studies in Question*, London, Thousand Oaks and New Delhi: Sage, pp. 56–73.
Hall, Gary (2002), *Culture in Bits: The Monstrous Future of Theory*, London and New York: Continuum.
Hall, Stuart (1988a), 'New Ethnicities', in Kobena Mercer (ed.), *Black Film, British Cinema*, BFI/ICA Documents 7, London: ICA, pp. 27–31.
Hall, Stuart (1988b), *The Hard Road to Renewal*, London: Verso.
Hall, Stuart (1996a), 'Cultural Studies and its Theoretical Legacies', in David Morley and Kuan-Hsing Chen (eds), *Stuart Hall: Critical Dialogues in Cultural Studies*, London and New York: Routledge, pp. 262–75.
Hall, Stuart (1996b), 'The Meaning of New Times', in David Morley and Kuan-Hsing Chen (eds), *Stuart Hall: Critical Dialogues in Cultural Studies*, London and New York: Routledge, pp. 223–37.

Hall, Stuart, Critcher, Charles, Jefferson, Tony, Clarke, John and Roberts, Brian (1978), *Policing the Crisis: Mugging, the State, and Law and Order*, Basingstoke and London: Macmillan.
Hebdige, Dick (1979), *Subculture: The Meaning of Style*, London and New York: Routledge.
Laclau, Ernesto (1990), *New Reflections on the Revolution of Our Time*, London and New York: Verso.
Levinas, Emmanuel (1969), *Totality and Infinity: An Essay on Exteriority*, Pittsburgh: Duquesne University Press.
Levinas, Emmanuel (1998), *Otherwise than Being: Or Beyond Essence*, Pittsburgh: Duquesne University Press.
Littler, Jo (2005), 'Anti-Consumerism, Cultural Change and the Limits of Reflexivity', *Cultural Studies*, 19:2, March, pp. 227–52.
McRobbie, Angela (1991), *Feminism and Youth Culture: From 'Jackie' to 'Just Seventeen'*, London: Macmillan (reissued in 2000).
McRobbie, Angela (2005), *The Uses of Cultural Studies*, London, Thousand Oaks and New Delhi: Sage.
Moore, Kerry (2005), 'Policing the "Asylum Crisis": Anti-Detention Campaigns and Counter Discourse of Asylum in the UK', *Signs of the Times*, www.signsofthetimes.org.uk, 13 April.
Nietzsche, Friedrich (1956), *The Birth of Tragedy and The Genealogy of Morals*, New York: Doubleday.
Singer, Peter (2004), *The President of Good and Evil: Taking George W. Bush Seriously*, London: Granta Books.
Zylinska, Joanna (2005), *The Ethics of Cultural Studies*, London and New York: Continuum.

DO NOT ASK WHAT CULTURAL STUDIES CAN DO FOR YOU, BUT WHAT YOU CAN DO FOR CULTURAL STUDIES

CHAPTER 5

Cultural Studies and German Media Theory

Geoffrey Winthrop-Young

A chapter on 'German Media Theory' is an unusual choice for inclusion in a cultural studies book. What connections are there, if any? What makes *German* work on media more noteworthy than French, Japanese or American scholarship?[1] And why should we care? The Germans, after all, never cared much for cultural studies. The translation into German of key works by Raymond Williams and the CCCS met with little success; and subsequent publications like Mike Brake's *The Sociology of Youth Culture* or Dick Hebdige's *Subculture: The Meaning of Style* were treated as extended manuals for decoding juvenile subcultures. Cultural studies, in short, 'arrived late; its reception was highly selective, and it ended in a pedagogical discourse' (Horak 1999: 110). In most accounts the culprit behind this unresponsive welcome is the Frankfurt School. Its emphasis on the nefarious consciousness-shaping force of the culture industry could not but dismiss as an exercise in self-delusion any approach that valorised the critical agency of the subject to decode incoming media messages subversively. Hence many German theorists came to think as highly of British cultural studies as German automobilists think of British cars or German gourmets of British cuisine: that is, not very. No doubt this biased perception of cultural studies is as uninformed as the reverse stigmatisation of the Frankfurt School by cultural studies practitioners as reductionist and elitist. Only recently has the situation begun to change, though there is reason to believe that it is American rather than British cultural studies that is gaining ground, given that the more text-based American approach is more compatible with the philological bias of German scholarship (Mikos 2002).

So why should those with a vested interest in cultural studies care? Because in the words of Geert Lovink, possibly the most informed non-German observer, 'since the 1980s a vibrant, globally unique media theory production has evolved in the German-speaking areas' (Lovink 2004). But what does this alleged uniqueness consist of? Where did it come from? And again, why invite it across the channel or across the oceans? I will attempt to answer these questions in this chapter, albeit in a highly selective fashion. That said, I am *not* going to present a balanced, objective or comprehensive survey of 'German Media Theory.' Instead I will focus on just two theorists – Friedrich Kittler and Niklas Luhmann – and add minor references to a small number of others – among them, Peter Sloterdijk, Klaus Theweleit, Hartmut Winkler and Bernhard Siegert.[2] To be sure, some of these names will not meet with expert approval. It is highly questionable whether Sloterdijk or Theweleit can be labelled media theorists or whether Luhmann has contributed anything noteworthy to the study of media *technology*. And while Kittler may (still) be the most important German media theorist, he stands for an extreme position that few of his peers share. My approach, however, is based on the reverse assumption: I believe that German media theory (to echo Lovink's characterisations) is at its most vibrant where it is most extreme, and that these extremes are in fact very representative of the alleged uniqueness of German media-theoretical production. Furthermore, I am not going to provide objective accounts of Kittler and Luhmann. Instead, I will attempt to tease out some of their less conspicuous radical features. Here are – potentially exportable – ideas, thoughts, warnings, or signposts worth scrutinising.

Certain caveats are necessary. Despite what the title of this chapter may indicate there is no such thing as 'German Media *Theory*'. There is – to follow a lucid account by Austrian media scholar Stefan Weber – at best a motley crew of media-theoretical *paradigms* that pit incompatible basic approaches against each other, such as 'descriptive' versus 'prescriptive', 'realist' versus 'constructivist', 'instrumentalist' or 'anthropocentric' versus 'post'- or 'anti-humanist', and so on (Weber 2003). Another informed observer, Reiner Leschke, has argued that this fractured assemblage is due to the fact that at present in Germany media theories originating *outside* the domain of media (e.g. Critical Theory, cognitivism, systems theory, Foucauldian discourse analysis) are squaring off against media ontologies, that is, theories (those of Kittler and Vilém Flusser come to mind) that are based on the generalisation of *intrinsic* media operations (Leschke 2003). Regardless of how you describe this cacophony, the bottom line is that while in many countries media research tends to be organised around one or two hegemonic approaches, the German academic scene is marked by a conspicuous absence of such silverback alpha-theories. Intellectually, the German media-theoretical arena is up-to-date and then some, but socially it is stuck in the (very German) Middle

Ages; that is, it resembles a patchwork of jealously guarded fiefdoms whose in-fighting prevents the establishment of a central authority.

The absence of a theory enjoying a broadly acknowledged dominant status entails a lack of a common understanding of key terms. Just as there is no German Media *Theory* there is no German *Media* Theory in as far as there is no general agreement on what terms like 'medium' or 'media' refer to. For instance, despite their ideological differences, Birmingham-style cultural studies and Frankfurt-style critical theory share pretty straightforward views of what a mass medium is. But these conceptualisations are incompatible with, say, Niklas Luhmann's systems-theoretical definition of medium as a 'loose coupling' of elements as opposed to the 'rigid couplings' that go by the name of 'form', or Friedrich Kittler's esoteric account of media as data-processing techniques equipped with differing time-axis-manipulation capabilities that determine historically contingent discursive networks. As a result, theoretical connections or cross-fertilisations that could result in a generally more acceptable definition of media are both rare and difficult. Hartmut Winkler, one of the few practitioners involved in large-scale ecumenical ventures (Winkler 1997, 2002, 2004a), recently attempted a definition of 'medium' that would satisfy the most important positions espoused in Germany: tellingly, he needed no fewer than sixty-nine steps to do so (Winkler 2004b). Of course this cannot go on. The German education system is not known for its hospitality to intellectual unruliness. Increasingly German media theory is running into administrative and institutional pressure to get its house in order, clear up the mess, establish a binding paradigm, achieve an academically and didactically viable consensus on terms and definitions, and provide a mutually agreeable disciplinary ancestry – in short, to consolidate and canonise. But at this point in time such a demand amounts to building a house during an earthquake – an exercise that is as hazardous to perform as it is instructive to watch from a safe distance.

A first hypothesis: in Germany *media* managed to attract the intellectual energy that in Britain was invested in the equally fuzzy object *culture*. These academic foci have to be seen as deposits of differing historical experiences. German postcolonial scholarship – to cite the most obvious example – is but a fledgling shadow compared to its British counterpart. And how could it not be? The German colonial experience (including its aftermath) was geographically limited and of short duration; and its atrocities were conveniently forgotten.[3] Matters are different when it comes to questions of class. At the risk of oversimplifying matters I would argue that, due to the more pronounced British tradition of emphasising socio-cultural distinctions – more pronounced, that is, than in Germany – British cultural theory tends to focus on mechanisms of vertical differentiation. It is no coincidence that Pierre Bourdieu's work on social distinctions is more successful in Britain than in Germany; or that German cultural theory offers little that can compare to the pioneering British explorations of working-class culture. German scholarship is instead more prone to investigate questions of homogenisation. The latter is related to a succession of attempts to mold a nation, a people, a race, or a citizenry. These attempts range from the fusing together (by way of books or bombs) of a patchwork of regions into Germany, to the ideologically supercharged elimination of social inequality in the Third Reich – and the latter, if Götz Aly's widely discussed recent study of the connection between the Holocaust and relieving the German taxpayers' burden is to be believed, is the basis of the postwar welfare state, the last attempt to engineer a more egalitarian society (Aly 2005). Herein lies a key for the noticeable German focus on media and technology, for these attempts are inextricably linked to a highly visible deployment of media technology. It would require an extensive investigation to explain this in sufficient detail; here I will offer no more than a few abbreviated historical pointers.

First, compared to the development of 'normal' nations such as France or Britain – normal because their particular evolution has been internalised as the norm for the genesis of nation-states – Germany is said to be a 'delayed nation' (*die verspätete Nation*). This is usually attributed to the relative atrophy of trade and industry in combination with the strongly divisive political forces (both internal and external) shaping 'German' politics up until 1870/1. As a result, cultural production was seen for an extended period as the major cohesive factor in the face of political fragmentation. The very close relationship established right from the beginning of German literary scholarship between nurturing letters and nurturing the nation attests to the early awareness that Germany was a nation that, more than many others, had been written into being. Germany, to put it bluntly, is a kind of media product. (One often feels if it did not exist it would have been invented by theorists from Marshall McLuhan to Benedict Anderson to illustrate the complicity of print and nation.) This explains why so many of the current generation of German media scholars started out as scholars of literature. The noticeable decline in the status of literary studies is directly related to the rise of the importance of media studies. The large-scale escape into relevance from the growing insecurity of traditional humanities not only resulted in the marked philological bias of German media studies, it also ensured that the latter inherited some of the importance that in bygone days accrued to the study of literature. Where else, Winkler has asked, are media scholars so prone to overestimate their own capabilities, turning almost any question into a media problem, media themselves into a social a priori, and their own discipline into a presumptive master discipline (2004a: 189)? As already mentioned, many of the most important approaches imported from literary scholarship to the study of media were not originally developed for the study of literature. The ease with which literary texts were replaced by other media stems from the fact that in most cases there was no corresponding change of approach. This is why Lovink chose the 1980s as the point of emergence of the German scene, for it was during that particular decade that post-structuralist, systems-theoretical and constructivist theories (none of which was home-grown literary scholarship in the first place) migrated from literary studies to challenge the ruling media analyses shaped by the Frankfurt School and the German version of US-style communication studies.

Second, one of the most crucial developments for understanding modern German history is the rapid industrialisation following unification that, within one generation, transformed a primarily agrarian patchwork into an industrial superpower. This transition reached its climax in the technologised mass killings of World War I and was captured by Walter Benjamin's image of the generation 'that had gone to school in a horse-drawn streetcar' and now found itself in an open sky 'in a field of force of destructive torrents and explosions' (1969: 84). Among the many effects of this traumatic change was an intense intellectual and aesthetic engagement with technology, especially during the first half of the twentieth century. This included the broad spectrum of – frequently politically extreme – theories of technology or *Technikphilosophien* (featuring contributions by Oswald Spengler, Ernst Jünger, Benjamin and Martin Heidegger, among others), the rise of 'reactionary modernism' (Herf) as a distinctly German right-wing attempt to fuse quintessentially modern technology with pre-modern social philosophy, and the rich futurist imagery of Weimar culture. These concerns and obsessions are among the most important – though frequently forgotten or even actively suppressed – sources for the very high profile of technology-centred approaches in contemporary German media theory. As Siegfried Kracauer's famous book title has it, there may be a continuity *From Caligari to Hitler*; there certainly is one from Caligari to Kittler.

Third, it is important to realise the extent to which dictatorships and liberations in modern German history were experienced as media events. Albert Speer, the chief Nazi technocrat, once described the Third Reich as 'the first dictatorship of an industrial nation in the age of modern technology', in which newly developed communication devices made it possible to turn the state into a giant 'switchboard [which] could be controlled and dominated by someone's will' (1970: 522). As an analysis of the highly divisive power structure of the Third Reich this is misleading (not to mention self-exculpatory), but it does point towards the subjective experience of the regime's excessive cinematographic and radiophonic self-presentation.[4] Continuing this line of thought, Klaus Theweleit – who has not received the recognition he deserves as a media theorist – remarked that 1956/7 marked 'the most rapid' generational break ever in recent German history, because that was when American and British army radio stations started broadcasting the top ten rock 'n' roll tunes (2004: 56). Allied armies defeated Germany in 1945, but it took another ten years before rock' n'roll liberated Germans. If Theweleit's acclaimed *Male Fantasies* was an extended examination of the ways in which institutional and technological experiences drilled an entire generation into inhumanity, his succeeding works are – among many other things – an extended probing of the media experiences that shaped postwar Germany (cf. 1989: 347–87). Radio had a direct impact on young minds and bodies of the 1950s, an impact that served to exorcise the authoritarian or even Fascist voices that had tried to control these bodies previously. The media focus culminates in Sloterdijk's provocative portrayal of nations as stressed communities that 'belong' together because they listen and view the same media products and then get upset together (Sloterdijk 1998).

With this in mind a second, equally blunt hypothesis: a chain of (positively and negatively connoted) collective media experiences and socialisations over the last two centuries is the main reason for a common predisposition among German scholars to diagnose different kinds of media-based heteronomy – be it enslavement to the culture industry as sketched by the early Frankfurt School, Kittler's insistence that 'media determine our situation' (1999: xxxix), or Luhmann's equally apodictic assurance that 'whatever we know about our society, or indeed about the world in which we live, we know through the mass media' (2000: 1). And this is where matters get interesting. As Nicholas Gane pointed out, Kittler's work raises important questions regarding the relationship between technological mediation and social relations that need to be addressed in the context of a '*post-human* sociology' (2005: 40; emphasis in the original). The same could be said of Luhmann and certain other German theorists; and it also applies to what could be called 'posthuman cultural studies'.

Posthuman cultural studies? What does this imply? It is beyond the scope of this chapter to give an overview – an overview, no less, of something that is not yet *in* view because it is only currently emerging. The following points, however, strike me as pertinent when discussing the importance of certain branches of German media theory.

1. The prefix *post* does *not* imply that a new type of cultural studies must be developed to engage with a world that allegedly is no longer made by humans. It is not a matter of technologising theory in order to adequately deal with the new, media-based assemblage of cultural machineries and productions that have sidelined all wetware activities. This would once again invoke the old fallacy of supersession – first humans had the top billing in history, now they are being pushed aside by machines. Posthuman cultural studies does not take its cue from either euphoric or apocalyptic techno-theory but from approaches like the French *école des annals*, Manuel De Landa's *A Thousand Years of Non-Linear History* or even highly speculative mega-projects like Peter Sloterdijk's *Spheres* trilogy. The focus is on short-, middle- and long-term structuration processes that have taken place throughout history on various sub- and supra-human levels.
2. The focus on technology cannot be the only crucial foray into posthuman theory domains; it must be accompanied by a critical engagement with biological matters. Recent attempts to make animals an integral part of a new 'posthumanist theory' (Wolfe 2003) are as necessary as Kittler's media-technological grounding of cultural history (Kittler 2000), or Bernhard Siegert's archeology of the postal a priori (Siegert 1999). Ultimately, the goal is to provide the possibility for an analysis of history and of the present in terms of interacting 'grey' and 'green' ecologies – of the configurations that arise from the interaction of climate and computers, mammals and machines, media and microbes.

In this context the work of Luhmann takes on special importance, given that its basic blueprint is a vexing import into sociology of a biological model of differentiation (for more see Winthrop-Young 2003). So let us start with him. At first glance his presence in German media theory is a bit baffling: in contrast to the scope, originality and intellectual rigour of so many of his other studies, his only text that deals directly with mass media, *The Reality of the Mass Media*, is a disjointed, technologically superficial and not very original 'private aphorism collection' (Leschke 2003: 222). Ultimately, Luhmann's impact on German media scholarship has to do with the fact that his theory allows for an abstraction and generalisation of the concept of media beyond the technological, as well as for a sociological extension that precludes the naive treatment of media as mere means or transmitters which, if only 'liberated', will allow for truly humane, consensus-based communication. Scott Lash, perhaps the most prominent among the growing number of cultural theorists to have acknowledged Luhmann's importance, has singled him out alongside Gilles Deleuze as 'the paradigmatic thinker of the information age' because of his understanding 'that the social bond itself is no longer about exchange in the symbolic but has taken on proportions of the communication' (Lash 2002: 111). Keep in mind, however, that communication, as conceptualised by Luhmann, is something humans despite all their brains and conscious minds cannot do. 'Only communication can communicate' (Luhmann 1994: 371). The most radical aspect of this idea is not the tripartition of communication into information, utterance and understanding that constantly feed into each other, or the complex notion of structural coupling that ties this communication three-step to human minds. Nor is it the demotion of the liberal subject from its position as source and goal of communication. What is important is the prospect that the autopoeisis of communication allows it to be coupled to new machines instead of old minds:

> Already today computers are in use whose operations are not accessible to the mind or to communication ... Although manufactured and programmed machines, such computers work in ways that remain intransparent to consciousness and communication – but which by way of structural coupling nevertheless influence consciousness and communication. They are, strictly speaking, invisible machines. To ask whether computers are machines that operate in ways analogous to the mind or whether they can replace or even surpass it, is to pose the wrong question, if not to make light of the issue. Neither does it matter whether or not the internal operations of the computer can be conceived of as communications. Rather, one will have to drop all these analogies and instead ask what the consequences will be when computers can create a fully independent structural coupling between a reality they can construct and psychic or communicative systems. (Luhmann 1997: 117f.)

Luhmann did not pursue this line of thought, but his ideas were quickly seized upon by German media scholars influenced by Kittler. The result was one of the most bizarre productions ever performed on the German theory stage: the attempt to fuse the work of Kittler and Luhmann into a mighty hybrid alpha-theory able to occupy the vacancy left by the demise of Hegel's philosophy (cf. Maresch and Werber 1999; see also Winthrop-Young 2000). The inevitable knee-jerk reactions against such super-theories are gratuitous and miss out on the interesting components. Luhmann had briefly envisaged a scenario in which communication takes place (in) between machines and is thus completely severed from all human input. He hinted at a kind of silicon sociology that places inter-machine communications alongside their human counterpart. In addition, he insisted that the usual diagnoses – that 'invisible machines' are replacing and/or mimicking humans, for example – are insufficient. But he said all this with little insight into the technologies that enable his scenario. This is precisely where Kittler comes in. His work was to correct Luhmann's blind spot by supplying the informed focus on the materialities of communication. The project itself is quixotic, but it does provide a first delineation of a possible future posthuman cultural studies.

First, however, it is necessary to understand what Kittler is aiming at. In this context it is helpful to contrast his particular merging of poststructuralism and technology briefly with developments in the United States. Readers may recall that especially in the early 1990s certain sectors of US literary scholarship were aglow with the promise of computer-aided writing. George Landow's programmatically entitled *Hypertext: The Convergence of Contemporary Critical Theory and Technology* declared that 'hypertext creates an almost embarrassingly literal embodiment' of Derrida's emphasis on decentring and Barthes' conception of the readerly versus the writerly text (Landow 1992: 34), while Jay Bolter declared that the electronic writing space amounted to nothing less than 'a vindication of postmodern literary theory' (Bolter 1992: 24). 'Embodiment', 'literalization', 'dramatisation', 'instantiation', 'materialization' – such were the terms used to characterise the relationship between hypertext and French theory, most of which imply that the latter was in need of some kind of technological remediation. Much like an oversized airplane that arrives ahead of schedule in an underdeveloped region and is then forced to circle the clouds and wait for the ground crew to build an adequate runway, French theory appeared to be locked in a holding pattern with little chance of a touchdown in reality. But once the new technologies were in place they brought about nothing less than the promise/prospect of making theory itself superfluous, since 'what is unnatural in print becomes natural in the electronic medium and will soon no longer need saying at all, because it can be shown' (Bolter 1991: 143). In hindsight it is difficult not to make fun of this fortunate redemption of old-world theory through new-world technology. Lurking underneath this happy tale is an old intercontinental love story: robust and handy, yet somewhat unrefined American boy meets refined and sophisticated, yet somewhat awkward French girl. The dainty conquest is whisked off West, as it were, to earn her keep on the homestead, where she confers on her new abode a touch of class and cultured *je ne sais quoi*. Technology grounds theory, theory elevates technology.

While American theorists celebrated the new media-technological implementation of French theory, Kittler was out to uncover its media-technological basis. Rather than showing how electronic data processing was an instantiation of Parisian poststructuralism, Kittler argued, among other things, that Lacan's three registers of the imaginary, the symbolic, and the real grew out of the late nineteenth century's tripartition of data processing into film, phonography and mechanised (type)writing (1999: 15f.), and that Foucault's sudden epistemic breaks must be linked to media shifts (1999: 5). In essence Kittler replaced Foucault's 'historical a priori' with a 'technological-medial a priori' according to which 'social, cultural and epistemological structures presuppose technological conditions of mediation' (Spreen 1998: 7). Foucault's somewhat abstract notion of the episteme is concretised in the shape of discourse networks, defined as 'the network of technologies and institutions that allow a given culture to select, store and process relevant data' (Kittler 1990: 369). Culture itself turns into a vast data-processing machinery. To analyse the specificity of a given culture therefore requires a focus on those historically contingent technological and institutional features that regulate the input, throughput and output of data. And out of one of these techno-cultural configurations – to be precise: out of the restructured language and data-processing techniques of the 'discourse network 1800' – emerges the subject, that is, the 'imaginary and the consequent depth of the individual as a historical by-product' (Poster 2001: 85).

Once again, it is important to realise the radical implications. It is not the demotion of the subject to the status of a 'historical by-product', nor the reverse promotion of media to the status of historical subject. That's old theory news; Kittler certainly wasn't the first to broadcast it. What is remarkable is a Hegelian agenda that Kittler somewhat awkwardly hinted at in an interview:

> What I keep dreaming of and what people don't like to hear because they believe that technology and science are mere tools made for people in the street . . . is that machines, especially the contemporary intelligent machine age as conceived by [Alan] Turing in 1936, are not there for us humans – we are, as it were, built on too large a scale – but that nature, this glowing, cognizant part of nature, is feeding itself back into itself [*sondern daß sich da die Natur, dieser leuchtende erkennende Teil der Natur, mit sich selbst rückkoppelt*]. (Kittler 2002: 270)

Hegel's *Phenomenology of the Spirit* is subjected to a technologised despiritualisation. The processing facilities of the human mind are no more than a transitory stage in an ever finer, ever more accelerated and complex feedback cycle that – in Lacan's terms – aims at establishing direct connections between the symbolic without any recourse to the imaginary (Winthrop-Young 2005: 149–152). To combine this with Luhmann: Luhmann envisaged a scenario in which non-human communications exist independently and alongside communication systems that depend on human input or – to use terms that Luhmann only employed ironically – the agency of autonomous subjects. Focusing on the data-processing capabilities of the former, Kittler historicises this scenario by showing that human minds and bodies were only necessary intermediaries as long as the machine/nature interface was not in possession of more effective couplings. This, I would argue, is the framework for a truly posthuman cultural studies.

Two points must be added. First, it would be a mistake to believe that all this started with computers, the Internet or virtual technologies. The creation and subsequent exclusion of human subjects can already be plotted when analysing old media infrastructures that appear to be at the beck and call of said subjects. Bernhard Siegert, probably the most brilliant of the younger German media theorists writing in a Kittlerian vein, has shown this in connection with the post office (Siegert 1999). What Siegert has done is to ground Jacques Derrida's somewhat vague notion of the 'postal principle' (Derrida 1987; see also Chang 1996) in a succession of historically specifiable 'postal a prioris'. He shows how subjects are constituted by the postal delivery apparatus (rather than vice versa) and how, with the introduction of prepayment and the standardisation of all interfaces between the people and the postal network, the latter effectively became a closed circuit, for which the contingencies of sender and receiver are irrelevant as long as their position is predetermined in a postal grid. The post, in other words, emerges as a closed Luhmannian system (see Winthrop-Young 2002; Winkler 2004a: 94–109, 133–35).

Second, Siegert's insistence that Derrida's postal analysis must be linked to concrete innovations in the postal system is part of a noticeable unease among certain German media theorists. Increasingly, some of the critique levelled at hermeneutic and/or socio-economic approaches that are forgetful of their medial base are directed against Derrida . 'To be sure', Kittler conceded as far back as the late 1970s, 'nobody has as meticulously as Derrida deciphered philosophical discourse as a sort of text that claims not to be one but the silent voice of reason itself, but as long as deconstruction keeps referring occidental metaphysics to *one* other that by its name "arche-writing" (*Urschrift*) is already transcendental and categorical, it will remain mired in a philosophical space' (1979: 199). This early objection contains two important points that will return time and again whenever Kittler mentions Derrida. First, despite Derrida's obvious penchant for media-technological considerations (from Plato's wax tablets in 'Plato's Pharmacy' to the ultimately rather trivial ruminations on e-mail in *Archive Fever*), there is a strange disregard for concrete media shifts. *Of Grammatology* delineates a metaphysically charged privileging of voice over writing that connects Plato to Rousseau with little consideration of the intervening two thousand years, which saw a very deliberate promotion of writing over voice (Kittler 2003a: 500). Derrida, it appears, lacks a sufficiently technologically informed sense of history. Second, for all their formidable self-reflexivity Derrida's analyses do not adequately reflect upon their own medial constitution. According to Kittler, Derrida's notion of trace, for instance, requires a technological a priori in the shape of Edison's phonograph, which has the same stylus engrave and trace the groove: 'Which is why all concepts of trace up to and including Derrida's grammatological *ur*-trace, are based on Edison's simple ideas. The trace preceding all writing, the trace of pure difference still open between reading and writing, is simply a gramophone needle' (1999: 33).

This is not to say that all poststructuralist German media scholarship falls in line with Kittler. On the contrary, Kittler's insistence on the mediality of deconstruction has been countered with a reverse deconstruction of the notion of mediality (see, for example, Tholen 2002a, 2002b) that turns the table on Kittler's more Foucault-inspired approach by teasing out the conflicting significations contained within notions of medium and mediality. But going beyond such internal divisions, Kittler's work raises the possibility that there never really was such a thing as poststructuralism, or that at the very least it was less than it was made out to be since the term was made to include incompatible approaches (Kittler 2002: 31). In a recent essay on Thomas Pynchon, Kittler scoffed that critics are so prone to resort to the handy label 'postmodernism' because it allows them to avoid the far more important military-technological aspects of Pynchon's texts, in the face of which traditional scholarship cannot but 'miserably fail' (2003b: 123). Does the same apply to 'poststructuralism'? Despite its frequent engagement with technology it may turn out to be a verbose rearguard action aimed at avoiding the full implications of the analog–digital media shift. The Americans, then, were right to insist on the enactment of theory through technology; the Germans were right in insisting that it goes way beyond new forms of writing and that these new forms feed back into reflection. Kittler is fond of quoting Friedrich Nietzsche's assertion that 'our writing tools are working on our thought' (Nietzsche, quoted in Kittler 1999: 200). Nietzsche knew what he was talking about: he was the first philosopher to use (and reflect upon) a typewriter. But it is the self-reflexive twist that really counts: our writing tools are also working on our thoughts about our writing tools. That must be the baseline command of all media studies.

Ultimately, if not for anything else Kittler's and Luhmann's theories should be appreciated as a warning, an exaggerated signpost at the edge of theory. Much like dragons appearing at the margins of old maps, they represent a *non plus ultra*: you cannot, despite all elaborate theorising, proceed any further on your normal course, for at this point technology (always seen in a Heideggerian light as an essential frame exerting its power over the history of being or *Seinsgeschichte*) becomes a determining factor in cultural production, and communication removes itself from those who believe that they are its source and subject.

In conclusion, let us outdo this hyperbole with an even more outlandish exaggeration that may serve as the vanishing point for posthuman cultural studies. In 1991 Manuel De Landa published *War in the Age of Intelligent Machines*, a study of the evolution of military strategy and technology inspired in particular by Humberto Maturana's concept of autopoiesis (which became so important to Luhmann). Employing a formidable Brechtian defamiliarisation effect, De Landa writes as if he were a historiographically inclined artificial intelligence descended from intelligent weapons systems that has decided to write its own genealogy. Obviously such a 'robot historian' will look at humans in a very different light:

> The robot historian of course would hardly be bothered by the fact that it was a human who put the first motor together: for the roles of humans would be seen as little more than that of industrious insects pollinating an independent species of machine-flowers that simply did not possess its own reproductive organs during a segment of its evolution. Similarly, when this robot historian turned its attention to the evolution of armies in order to trace the history of its own weaponry, it would see humans as no more than pieces of a larger military-industrial machine: a war machine. (1991: 3)

Now imagine this robot historian suddenly developing humanist interests. What would it say about cultural evolution? How would it write a history of literature? The fact that humans were once indispensable nodes in the production of texts would be of little concern to it, for humans would once again be seen as nothing more than diligent insects necessary for intertextual fertilisation in those periods when machines were not able to write, process and transmit texts on their own, that is, without any recourse to an attached human consciousness. Authors, editors, publishers, critics, readers as parts of a large writing apparatus all become disposable once feedback mechanisms had evolved that surpassed limited human processing capabilities. If you apply this posthumanist vista to cultural production as a whole you have a glimpse of what Kittler's and Luhmann's theories are ultimately headed towards. Maybe the robot historian would spare a few complimentary words for its hominid German predecessors whose analyses of discourse networks, media structures and non-human autopoietic communication systems paved the way for its own work.

Notes

1 A note on *German*: with the exception of those passages that refer to the German university system or to specifically German historical experiences, the term is used as a shorthand replacement for the cumbersome 'German-speaking'; thus it includes Austria and the German parts of Switzerland. No proper engagement with 'German' media theory can afford to miss out on the work of Austrian media theorists such as Frank Hartmann (2000, 2003), although (or precisely because) some of them situate themselves apart from the more narrowly defined German tradition.
2 Even the most concise survey would have to include several contributions that I will not mention: Sybille Krämer's project on intermediality and performativity; Mike Sandbothe's infusion of pragmatism into media studies; Bernhard Dotzler's work on computer and paper machines; Wolfgang Hagen's work on media and electricity; or Michael Giesecke's extensive exploration of print culture. To date there is no such overview available in English, but glimpses can be found in Geisler (1999) and Werber (2003).
3 I have met several German academics who confessed that they first learned about the massacres of the Hereros by German troops from Thomas Pynchon's novels. Not until very recently has the topic been taught at (some) German schools.
4 With the role of the radio in the Third Reich in mind, it comes as no surprise that German media theorists have produced some of the most interesting work on the intersection of (radio) voice and power (e.g. Hagen 1991; Schmölders 2002; Gethmann and Stauff 2005).

Bibliography

Aly, Götz (2005), *Hitlers Volksstaat: Raub, Rassenkrieg und nationaler Sozialismus*, Frankfurt: Fischer.
Benjamin, Walter (1969), *Illuminations: Essays and Reflections*, New York: Schocken.
Bolter, Jay (1991), *Writing Space: The Computer, Hypertext and the History of Writing*, Hillsdale: Lawrence Erlbaum.
Bolter, Jay (1992), 'Literature in the Electronic Writing Space', in Myron C. Tuman (ed.), *Literacy Online: The Promise (and Peril) of Reading and Writing with Computers*, Pittsburgh: University of Pittsburgh Press, pp. 19–42.
Chang, Briankle (1996), *Deconstructing Communication: Representation, Subjects and Economies of Exchange*, Minneapolis: University of Minnesota Press.

De Landa, Manuel (1991), *War in the Age of Intelligent Machines*, New York: Zone Book.
Derrida, Jacques (1987), *The Post Card: From Socrates to Freud and Beyond*, Chicago and London: University of Chicago Press.
Gane, Nicholas (2005), 'Radical Post-Humanism: Friedrich Kittler and the Primacy of Technology', *Theory, Culture and Society*, 22:3, pp. 25–41.
Geisler, Michael (1999), 'From Building Blocks to Radical Construction: West German Media Theory since 1984', *New German Critique*, 78, pp. 75–107.
Gethmann, Daniel, and Stauff, Markus (eds) (2005), *Politiken der Medien*, Zurich and Berlin: Diaphanes.
Hagen, Wolfgang (1991), 'Der Radioruf: Zu Diskurs und Geschichte des Hörfunks', in Martin Stingelin and Wolfgang Scherer (eds), *HardWar/ SoftWar: Krieg und Medien 1914 bis 1945*, Munich: Fink, pp. 243–74
Hartmann, Frank (2000), *Medienphilosophie*, Vienna: WUV.
Hartmann, Frank (2003), *Mediologie*, Vienna: WUV.
Herf, Jeffrey (1984), *Reactionary Modernism: Technology, Culture, and Politics in Weimar and the Third Reich*, Cambridge: Cambridge University Press.
Horak, Roman (1999), 'Cultural Studies in Germany (and Austria), and Why There is No Such Thing', *European Journal of Cultural Studies*, 2:1, pp. 109–15.
Kittler, Friedrich (1979), 'Vergessen', in Ulrich Nassen (ed.), *Texthermeneutik: Aktualität, Geschichte, Kritik*, Paderborn: Schöningh, pp. 195–221.
Kittler, Friedrich (1990), *Discourse Networks 1800/1900*, Stanford, CA: Stanford University Press.
Kittler, Friedrich (1998), 'On the Take-off of Operators', in Timothy Lenoir (ed.), *Inscribing Science: Scientific Texts and the Materiality of Communication*, Stanford, CA: Stanford University Press, pp. 70–8.
Kittler, Friedrich (1999), *Gramophone, Film, Typewriter*, Stanford, CA: Stanford University Press.
Kittler, Friedrich (2000), *Eine Kulturgeschichte der Kulturwissenschaft*, Munich: Fink.
Kittler, Friedrich (2002), *Short Cuts*, Frankfurt: Zweitausendeins.
Kittler, Friedrich (2003a), 'Heidegger und die Medien- und Technikgeschichte. Oder: Heidegger vor uns', in Dieter Thomä (ed.), *Heidegger-Handbuch: Leben – Werk – Wirkung*, Stuttgart: Metzler, pp. 500–4.
Kittler, Friedrich (2003b), 'Pynchon und die Elektromystik', in Bernhard Siegert and Markus Krajewski (eds), *Thomas Pynchon: Archive – Geschichte – Verschwörung*, Weimar: VDG, pp. 123–36.
Landow, George (1992), *Hypertext: The Convergence of Contemporary Critical Theory and Technology*, Baltimore, MD: Johns Hopkins University Press.
Lash, Scott (2002), *Critique of Information*, London: Sage.
Leschke, Reiner (2003), *Einführung in die Medientheorie*, Munich: Fink.
Lovink, Geert (2004), 'Netzkompetente Philosophen', *Lettre International*, 64, p. 114.

Luhmann, Niklas (1994), 'How Can the Mind Participate in Communication?', in Hans Ulrich Gumbrecht and K. Ludwig Pfeiffer (eds), *Materialities of Communication*, Stanford, CA: Stanford University Press, pp. 371–87.
Luhmann, Niklas (1997), *Die Gesellschaft der Gesellschaft*, Frankfurt: Suhrkamp.
Luhmann, Niklas (2000), *The Reality of the Mass Media*, Stanford, CA: Stanford University Press.
Maresch, Rudolf and Werber, Niels (eds) (1999), *Kommunikation. Medien. Macht*, Frankfurt: Suhrkamp.
Mikos, Lothar (2002), 'Die Rezeption des Cultural Studies Approach im deutschsprachigen Raum', in Andreas Hepp and Rainer Winter (eds), *Kultur – Medien – Macht: Cultural Studies und Medienanalyse*, 2nd edn, Opladen: Westdeutscher Verlag, pp. 161–71.
Poster, Mark (2001), *What's the Matter with the Internet?*, Minneapolis and London: University of Minnesota Press.
Schmölders, Claudia (2002), 'Stimmen der Führer: Akustische Szenen 1918-1945', in Friedrich Kittler, Thomas Macho and Sigrid Weigel (eds), *Zwischen Rauschen und Offenbarung: Zur Medien- und Kulturgeschichte der Stimme*, Berlin: Akademie, pp. 195–226.
Siegert, Bernhard (1999), *Relays: Literature as an Epoch of the Postal System*, Stanford, CA: Stanford University Press.
Sloterdijk, Peter (1998), *Der starke Grund, zusammen zu sein: Erinnerungen an die Erfindung des Volkes*, Frankfurt: Suhrkamp.
Speer, Albert (1970), *Inside the Third Reich: Memoirs*, New York: Macmillan.
Spreen, Dierk (1998), *Tausch, Technik, Krieg: Die Geburt der Gesellschaft im technisch-medialen Apriori*, Hamburg: Argument.
Theweleit, Klaus (1989), *Buch der Könige 1: Orpheus Eurydike*, Frankfurt: Stroemfeld/Roter Stern.
Theweleit, Klaus (2004), *Tor zur Welt: Fußball als Realitätsmodell*, Cologne: Kiepenheuer and Witsch.
Tholen, Georg Christoph (2002a), *Die Zäsur der Medien: Kulturphilosophische Konturen*, Frankfurt: Suhrkamp.
Tholen, Georg Christoph (2002b), 'Media Metaphorology: Irritations in the Epistemic Field of Media Studies', *South Atlantic Quarterly*, 101:3, pp. 659–72.
Weber, Stefan (2003), 'Einführung: (Basis-)Theorien für die Medienwissenschaft', in Stefan Weber (ed.), *Theorien der Medien*, Konstanz: UVK, pp. 11–48.
Werber, Niels (2003), 'Media Theory after Benjamin – Neo-marxist?', in Hans Ulrich Gumbrecht and Michael Marrinan (eds), *Mapping Benjamin: The Work of Art in the Digital Age*, Stanford, CA: Stanford University Press, pp. 230–9.
Winkler, Hartmut (1997), *Docuverse: Zur Medientheorie der Computer*, Munich: Boer.
Winkler, Hartmut (2002), 'Discourses, Schemata, Technology, Monuments: Outline for a Theory of Cultural Continuity', *Configurations*, 10.1, pp. 91–109.
Winkler, Hartmut (2004a), *Diskursökonomie: Versuch über die innere Ökonomie der Medien*, Frankfurt: Suhrkamp.

Winkler, Hartmut (2004b), 'Mediendefinitionen', *Medienwissenschaft*, 1:4, pp. 9–27.

Winthrop-Young, Geoffrey (2000), 'Silicon Sociology, or, Two Kings on Hegel's Throne? Kittler, Luhmann and the Posthuman Merger of German Media Theory', *Yale Journal of Criticism*, 13:2, pp. 391–420.

Winthrop-Young, Geoffrey (2002), 'Going Postal to Deliver Subjects: Remarks on a German Postal a priori', *Angelaki*, 7:3, pp. 143–58.

Winthrop-Young, Geoffrey (2003), 'On a Species of Origin', *Configurations*, 11:3, pp. 305–349.

Winthrop-Young, Geoffrey (2005), *Friedrich Kittler zur Einführung*, Hamburg: Junius.

Wolfe, Cary (2003), *Animal Rites: American Culture, the Discourse of Species, and Posthumanist Theory*, Chicago: University of Chicago Press.

Part II: New Theorists

SPECIAL AFFECT

CHAPTER 6

Cultural Studies and Gilles Deleuze

Gregory J. Seigworth

One paradigm less

Underneath the large noisy events lie the small events of silence.
                                 Gilles Deleuze, *Difference and Repetition*

[O]ne has to seek a term for that which is not fully articulated or not fully comfortable in various silences, although it is usually not very silent. I just don't know what the term should be.
                                 Raymond Williams, *Politics and Letters*

More than twenty-five years ago cultural studies was new again for the first time. Although Stuart Hall's 1980 essay 'Cultural Studies: Two Paradigms' presented itself as an evenhanded assessment of the state of cultural studies, it was clear that 'structuralism' (the new paradigm in town) would be continuing along its path of ascendance as begun in the late 1960s and early 1970s. Meanwhile, 'culturalism' as the founding paradigm of cultural studies – exemplified, for Hall, in the work of Richard Hoggart, Raymond Williams and E. P. Thompson – was plainly receding.[1]

Sharing at best a fairly loose coherence, the so-called culturalists held to the notion that the realm of culture (as found in texts, in history, in lived experience) could not always be determinately fixed to the relations of production (society's economic base). Yes, people made history in conditions that were not of their own making, but history's motor – the capacity for agency, for change, for making history – could not be readily separated out from the 'whole way of life' (or, for Thompson, a 'whole way of struggle') that serves as history's ever-present fabric of relations. The structuralists grew itchy at what felt like a certain naivety in this formulation and began to chafe against such an overly woolly (seemingly woolly-headed) fabric. No longer able to abide the indissolubility of culture as a 'whole' expressive totality with no apparent emphasis granted to any particular thread (in either the first or last instance), the structuralists wanted to trace out the threads, to weave a more complex – that is, more specifically determinant (focusing mainly on the ideological effects of political economy) – set of determinations; and, thus, to form concepts that, in Hall's words, could 'cut into the complexity of the real, in order precisely to reveal and bring to light relationships and structures which cannot be visible to the naïve naked eye' (1980: 67). The 'culturalists', one might say, had spun a fabric that structuralists could now see straight through, revealing themselves as not quite emperors anymore.

Thus, by the late 1970s, the study of culture was rather far along in the process of aligning its own movements with the latest in continental theory: at that time, a heady amalgamation of structuralism, Marxism and psychoanalysis as forged largely by courtesy of Louis Althusser (although, soon enough, to be rendered slightly more supple through Antonio Gramsci's writings in general and his concept of 'hegemony' in particular). Hall's 1980 essay merely formalised what was already cultural studies' stepping into this new set of adventures, trying on a new set of clothes.[2]

What, then, of the potential for an even 'newer' set of adventures twenty-five years hence? In a more recent interview with the journal *Radical Philosophy*, Hall was asked if there might be a 'new notion of culture regulating the field today, in the way that these two paradigms did in the past? Or has the field become piecemeal, lost its theoretical core?' (Hall 1997: 25). Reflecting briefly on the initial paradigm shift from culture as 'a whole way of life' to culture as 'signifying practice', Hall concluded:

> If I were writing for students, those are still the two definitions I'd pick out, and I wouldn't say there is a third one. I suppose you might say that there was a postmodern one, a Deleuzian one, which says that signification is not meaning, it's a question of affect, but I don't see a break in the regulative idea of culture there as fundamental as the earlier one. (p. 25)

The current chapter will concur with Hall on this much: there is no need to imagine a new paradigm for cultural studies, or, if so, it should certainly not be called 'Deleuzian'.[3] Why not a third paradigm? Because if the work of Gilles Deleuze has a particularly productive entry point into the already existing theory-narrative of cultural studies, it would enter on the side of 'culturalism' (that is, as a return to and reinvigoration of many of the dawning premises of cultural studies), and only thereafter might it undertake renegotiation talks with many of the 'structuralising/signifying' tendencies still actively operating across the field. In sum, the argument here will focus on a cultural studies that has, after Deleuze, one paradigm less and not one more.

After a more than quarter-century-long detour through the dense and twisting theory-thickets of structural Freudo-Marxism and poststructuralising articulation theory (a detour that has been, by no means, fruitless), there is a sense – call it a pre-emergent structure of feeling – that many of those once presumably old-school, shopworn concerns of 'culturalism' have been steadily finding their way back onto the diverse agendas of a widely dispersed cultural studies. Of course, nowhere will one find these concerns presented as a single, united front, and far less should one expect to find any explicitly stated affiliation with the faintest residues of a 'culturalist' tradition. Still, what might be evidenced by this accidentally ad hoc twenty-first-century re-versioning of culturalism – besides, too, a certain collective exhaustion of structuralist (post- and otherwise) trajectories – can perhaps best be glimpsed in a revived emphasis upon such matters as: process, sensation and affect, movement and transition, rhythm, creativity, imagination, the connection of ethics and aesthetics, the virtual, expressive totality (the 'whole'), 'forces' of life (vitalism), the lived or experience, *bios* and non-human materiality, or what might be understood, quasi-collectively, as a renewed attention to 'empiricism'. Born long before cultural studies, this is an empiricism where 'experience' and 'experiment' are uttered (together, once again) in one and the same voice.

It is the latter – the concept of experience and a renewed sense of the empirical and empiricism – that will be a primary focus of this chapter. Not surprisingly, the quasi-collective features listed above also help to compose whatever might be seen as the present 'Deleuzian' boom in cultural studies. Deleuze declared himself, first and foremost, an 'empiricist' of the forgotten 'experiment-meets-experience' sort: where one 'is always experiencing, experimenting, not interpreting but experimenting, and what we experience, experiment with, is always actuality; what's coming into being, what's new, what's taking shape' (1995: 106). The goal is, as it had once been, to open up the concept of experience affectively to the (more-than-human) being of a sensate world, not allowing it to lodge only within the interpretative powers of a being's knowing sensibility. Much of what might fall under the name of 'Deleuzian cultural studies' today takes up this experimentally experiential ambition in one way or another and, thus, for all the right and wrong reasons, Deleuze has become very much of a theoretical darling for many graduate students and postgraduates in cultural studies and elsewhere.

While no longer holding such 'darling' status, Williams' culturalism (or, as he preferred, 'cultural materialism') adopted a remarkably similar ontological cast (despite never quite allowing itself to shake off fully, as

Deleuze would, certain remnants of humanism). Perhaps this is why imagining a secret, subterranean history of cultural studies where culturalism, circumventing its eclipse, meets up directly with Deleuze's empiricism – arriving sometime, say, in the mid-1970s and later taking structuralism on board as useful addendum, and not as a necessarily separate path or alternative paradigm – remains enticing in the possibilities still to be made.

Experience, for Williams, went beyond – perhaps, in a sense, also went below or continually slipped past – 'culture' as the regulative idea that has come to define the space of operations for cultural studies (yes, just imagine: cultural studies without culture?). Simply put, experience does not personally *belong* to a subject (the purported subject of experience), nor does it only arise in the mediating space of subject and object. How might experience be granted a certain relative autonomy, its own dynamic potential as active and changing, travelling farther afield than usually allowed in contemporary understanding? Williams dared to entertain such an idea: to unfix experience, to connect it with 'all that is present and moving, all that escapes or seems to escape from the fixed and explicit and the known, [from all that] is grasped and defined as the personal' (1977: 128). His concept of 'structures of feeling' was one other way to approach this whole matter of experience, and, not surprisingly, it was also consistently misunderstood.

Because experience was among the most harshly criticised of all the foundational blocks in the culturalist repertoire, bearing witness to some of Williams' tussles over it can prove tremendously enlightening. A particularly illustrative case in point can be found in the *New Left Review* interviews that make up Raymond Williams' career-retrospective volume *Politics and Letters* (1981). Over the course of the interviews Williams is taken to task, more than once, by his interlocutors, Perry Anderson, Anthony Barnett and Francis Mulhern, for utilising the concept of 'experience' in ways that they consider somewhat less than circumspect, and, indeed, even naive. This thoroughgoing interrogation of the status of 'experience' – as well as 'structures of feeling' – remains instructive for the nuanced parrying of point and counterpoint between Williams and his interviewers. But just as impressive throughout the more than four hundred pages of *Politics and Letters* is the distinct impression that Williams leaves; here is someone holding fast to the conviction that, like culture, cultural studies is itself 'a single indissoluble real process' and cannot too readily become a house divided.

The chief accusation levelled at the concept of experience was that it was never as free from ideological determination as Williams (and other culturalists) might have wished to believe. With cultural studies at its most fully immersed in the structural Marxist moment, there is even a point in the interviews where Williams is reminded that, for Louis Althusser, experience serves as 'simply a synonym for illusion' (Williams 1981: 168). In privileging the concept of experience, the culturalists were accused of conjuring up an unrealistic, theoretically insupportable voluntarism.[4] The human subject was – from the structuralist perspective – just too saturated, through and through, by ideological forces and other unavoidable socio-cultural/linguistic constructions.

Over the course of the interviews, perhaps the most illuminating moment comes as Williams replies to a question that attempts to link his concept of experience back to the pre-dawn of his own (and the culturalist) emergence. Williams is asked whether his reliance upon 'experience' and, by extension, his concept of 'structures of feeling', haven't merely recapitulated a certain 'Leavisian notion of "life"'. Unlike F. R. Leavis, Williams, in his own estimation, had not 'spiritualised' cultural production by longing for the organicism of a romanticised past; rather he had attempted to *materialise* it (though, certainly, this materialisation would encompass such relatively ephemeral life-processes as affect and emotion) in a way that was forward looking, orientated towards an emerging future. So, had this originary 'culturalist' paradigm, in the end, really travelled very far from its predecessors?

Until this moment in the interviews, Williams' immediate responses to even the most pointed questions about the place of experience in his work had been quite gracious, often conceding some amount of ground to his interlocutors (many of his answers begin with: 'Yes' or 'That seems fair' or 'I accept' or 'I concede'), but here his answer is quite emphatic in its disagreement. It is worth quoting at length:

> No. That should be very clear. For after all the basic argument of the first chapter of *The Long Revolution* is precisely that there is no natural seeing and therefore there cannot be a direct and unmediated contact with reality. On the other hand, in much linguistic theory and a certain kind of semiotics, we are in danger of reaching the opposite point in which the epistemological wholly absorbs the ontological: it is only in the ways of knowing that we exist at all. To formalist friends, of whom I have many, who affect to doubt the very possibility of an 'external' referent, it is necessary to recall an absolutely founding presumption of materialism: namely that the natural world exists whether anyone signifies it or not . . .
>
> . . . By contrast in the whole process of consciousness – here I would put a lot of stress on phenomena for which there is no easy knowing because there is too easy a name, the too easy name is 'the unconscious' – all sorts of occurrences cut across the established or offered relations between a signification and a reference. The formalist position that there is no signified without

a signifier amounts to saying that it is only in articulation that we live at all . . . (1981: 167)

Having here set out, rather succinctly, the limitations of the structuralist paradigm as he saw them, Williams then turns to directly address his own initiatives at reshaping the 'culturalist' enterprise and, in particular, the sustained attention given to the concept of experience.

While readily acknowledging the inherent (and inherited) difficulties with the term and what it encompasses, William refuses to let 'experience' be simply expunged from cultural analysis or to otherwise allow its ready subsumption under the too tidy lines and right angles of signifying articulations. 'Experience' by whatever name, including structure of feeling, is crucial to grasping what is in the process of change, in the very midst of flux and flow, moving along the cusp of semantic availability, present in 'all that escapes or seems to escape from the fixed and the explicit and the known' and, hence, in what has 'not yet come, often not even coming' (1977: 128 and 130). As Williams continues in his response to the *Politics and Letters* interviewers' question:

> . . . I have found that areas which I would call structures of feeling as often as not initially form as a certain kind of disturbance or unease, a particular type of tension, for which when you stand back or recall them you can sometimes find a referent. To put it another way, the peculiar location of a structure of feeling is the endless comparison that must occur in the process of consciousness between the articulated and the lived. The lived is only another word, if you like, for experience: but we have to find a word for that level. For all that is not fully articulated, all that comes through as disturbance, tension, blockage, emotional trouble seems to me precisely a source of major changes in the relation between the signifier and the signified, whether in literary language or conventions. We have to postulate at least the possibility of comparison in this process and if it is a comparison, then with what? If one immediately fills the gap with one of these great blockbuster words like experience, it can have very unfortunate effects over the rest of the argument. For it can suggest that this is always a superior instance, or make a god out of an unexamined subjectivity. But since I believe that the process of comparison occurs often in not particularly articulate ways, yet is a source of much of the change that is eventually evident in our articulation, one has to seek a term for that which is not fully articulated or not fully comfortable in various silences, although it is usually not very silent. I just don't know what the term should be. (1981: 167–8)

This insightful and far-reaching passage usefully highlights many core features in what was Raymond Williams' evolving project of 'cultural materialism' – with its balance of the ontological with the epistemological, its broader attention to various processes of consciousness (including the unconscious, non-conscious and so on), its elevation of the realm of affect and feeling (with 'tensions' and 'pressures' in lieu of determinations and linguistic significations), and its reinflection of 'experience' towards change/process, emergence, 'the lived'.

Williams' *Keywords* had first been published in the year prior to the *Politics and Letters* interviews and, somewhat curiously, contained no separate entry for the concept of 'experience' (an omission that his interviewers do not fail to point out), although it was added in the book's next edition. However, in the initial volume, a discussion of experience does appear, rather interestingly, under the headings for 'science' and 'empirical', where special note is made, in both of these entries, of what had once been the interchangeability of 'experience' and 'experiment' (as both share the common Latin root word *experiri*) until the latter third of the eighteenth century. In this splitting of experience and experiment, Williams noted that there followed an interrelated set of unfortunate consequences: (1) a distinction arises within 'empirical' between the practical and the theoretical (with experience cast as atheoretical or anti-theoretical); (2) a division in science occurs between an inner (subjective) knowledge and an external (objective) knowledge; and (3) there is a cultural/everyday delineation between 'experience past ("lessons") and experience present (full and active "awareness")' (1985: 127). Williams' work in cultural studies is known first and foremost for its appeal to 'wholeness', and so the mere fact that the contemporary understanding of 'experience' was now based upon a set of exclusions (of theory, of creativity, of the present and future) and upon a subjectively centred model of consciousness presented a serious problem desperately in need of resolution.

While the twists and turns and detours in the history of the concept of experience have been widely explored, most recently and comprehensively by Martin Jay's *Songs of Experience* (2005), key here to the project of a revived culturalism will be the insights of Gilles Deleuze, as well as Frankfurt School critical theorist Walter Benjamin. What do they share with each other and with Williams? Mainly, a desire to include the excluded of experience and to find a way out of the false problem of an interiorised subjectivity and an outside world. Not only do Deleuze and Benjamin coincide in their appeals for a reintegration of all of the exclusions of experience and overlap in their hostility at self-sufficient models of consciousness, they both point a finger at the work of one highly suspicious character in particular: Immanuel Kant. For Benjamin and Deleuze, it was, perhaps more than anything, Kant's rendering (or rending) of the concept of 'experience' that made him the focus of their enmity. Deleuze called his book on Kant's critical philosophy an affectionate study of 'an enemy' (1995: 6), while Benjamin proclaimed Kant one of his great adversaries, a 'despot' that he was determined to 'track down' (1994: 125).[5]

Looking back, like Williams, to transformations taking place in the latter part of the eighteenth century, Walter Benjamin levels the majority of his critique squarely at what he sees as Kant's (and the subsequent neo-Kantians') re-routing of experience through a 'hollow' epistemology: where experience is allowed only minimal significance by serving as the 'possibility' of knowledge (Benjamin 1996: 102). Benjamin was determined to produce what he considered a 'superior concept of experience' (Wolin 1989: 211): one that does not conflate 'experience' with 'knowledge of experience':

> Paradoxical though it sounds, experience does not occur as such in the knowledge of experience, simply because this is knowledge of experience and hence a context of knowledge. Experience, however, is the symbol of this context of knowledge and therefore belongs in a completely different order of things from knowledge itself. (Benjamin 1996: 95)

Benjamin adds that, although his choice of the word 'symbol' here might be 'unfortunate', he is using it 'simply to point to different conceptual realms' (1996: 95). The concept of experience had once possessed its own affectual, viscerally ontological sort of knowing, or what Benjamin called 'speculative knowledge'. After Kant, the concept of experience could no longer, of itself, provide its own kind of intuitive knowledge as the present/future-orientated *experiment* of experience (not at all unlike Williams' reference to 'experience present' as 'full and active "awareness"'). Experience for Kant was to serve only in the interest of a higher, adjudicating knowledge, as the faculty of intuition is submitted to the legislation of understanding.

Deleuze's own critique takes a similar approach, locating two intrinsic problems with Kant's version of experience. The first is that knowledge, contrary to Kant, bears absolutely no resemblance to the 'experience' that purportedly provides its ground. That is, experience and knowledge of experience do not work via some mode of resemblance or recognition. Deleuze draws attention to this implicit tracing operation: 'It is clear that . . . Kant traces the so-called transcendental structures from the empirical acts of a psychological consciousness: the transcendental synthesis of apprehension is directly induced from an empirical apprehension, and so on' (1994: 135). For both Benjamin and Deleuze, experience – categorically unbound and infinitely particulate – does not look like knowledge, nor does it arrive only in the harmoniously symmetrical synthesis of sensation and sensibility.[6]

As Deleuze would remark, those well-known Kantian 'conditions of possible experience' are always surrounded by and shot through with 'subjacent conditions of real experience' (1994: 232); these 'subjacent conditions' (peripherally beneath consciousness) still act but without rising to the status of knowledge. Because Kant also immediately derived the transcendental from the empirical, his philosophy perpetually turned the experiential into a field of 'possible experience from which nothing, the external as well as the internal, escapes' (Deleuze and Guattari 1994: 46). After all, as Williams said (in the lengthy quotation above): 'all sorts of occurrences cut across the established or offered relations between a signification and a reference'. As such, the conditions of experience are not subsumable or otherwise capable of ready assimilation with the dictates of conscious apprehension, nor do they fall under the too easy name of 'the unconscious', as Williams also noted. But these 'occurrences' or events do exert a force (or, better, a feeling or sensibility of force) – setting limits, maintaining pressures, presenting potentials – that will always exceed, in all directions, the possible experience of psychological consciousness or any all-enveloping epistemology.

The second major problem created by the Kantian concept of experience – before ever becoming transcendental – is that it leaves too much out of the experience equation that Benjamin and Deleuze argue, in their own ways, should be admitted. In fact, Benjamin deliberately sows the seeds of his own philosophy for the future in those very places that Kant ruled decidedly out of bounds. Benjamin complained that:

> Kant's epistemology does not open up the realm of metaphysics, because it contains within itself primitive elements of an unproductive metaphysics that excludes all others. In epistemology every metaphysical element is the germ of a disease that expresses itself in the separation of knowledge from the realm of experience in its full freedom and depth.... There is – and here lies the historical seed of the approaching philosophy – a most intimate connection between that experience, the deeper exploration of which could never lead to metaphysical truths, and that theory of knowledge, which was not yet able to determine sufficiently the logical place of metaphysical research. (1996: 102–3)

The Kantian understanding of experience acts to quarantine or eradicate all 'metaphysical germs' in a steady purification process that needs, in Benjamin's view, to be seriously contaminated. This is why fellow

Frankfurt School theorist Theodor Adorno would claim that Benjamin's insights appealed:

> to a type of experience that distinguished itself from the usual only by its indifference to the limitations and taboos to which a well-adjusted consciousness normally bows. Benjamin never once acknowledged the boundary taken for granted by all modern thought: the Kantian commandment not to trespass into unintelligible worlds . . . For Benjamin everything habitually excluded by the norms of experience ought to become part of experience to the extent that it adheres to its own concreteness instead of dissipating this, its immortal aspect, by subordinating it to the schema of the abstract universal. (1988: 4)

In Benjamin's work, the most seemingly ephemeral, most materially recalcitrant, other-than-human, non-sensuous and incorporeal aspects of experience were granted equal standing with the more 'knowing' world of human understanding and reason.

What Benjamin regards as the unfortunate conflation of 'experience' with the 'knowledge of experience', Deleuze refers to, with equal disdain, as the 'sensibility of Being' and, instead, proposes a concept of experience as the 'being of the sensible' (1994: 140). Here, again, experience is not strictly amenable to a mode of thought or any image of thought based upon resemblance, representation, or (re)cognition, but is more non-representational and affectual, belonging to neither subject nor object (neither inside nor outside). The conditions of experience are then reconceived as an immanent and open field of intensities, banal affectivities and sensations that can come to engage with faculties of knowing but without necessarily being replayed, realised, synthesised or somehow completely subsumed in the process.[7]

Benjamin, Deleuze and Williams, as a result of this winnowing down of experience following Kant, each came to develop his own alternative conceptualisation – respectively, 'non-sensuous similarity', 'virtual', 'structures of feeling' – to designate all that skirts along the edges or otherwise dwells in the far and near reaches of that 'blockbuster word' experience, in order to include all 'that which is not fully articulated or not fully comfortable in various silences, although it is usually not very silent'. Of course, this obstinacy over experience also did much to contribute to many of the criticisms often levelled at Benjamin, Deleuze and Williams, rendering each of them – in his own way – untimely, or, at least, habitually out of sync with his contemporaries.

Williams might have felt this untimeliness as much as – perhaps more than? – Benjamin and Deleuze; even his most forthright attempts to refine and clarify his positions did little to dispel continued critique of his views on experience. About a year after the release of *Politics and Letters*, Stuart Hall published a commentary review of the book that, while often self-effacing and gracious, remained flatly unconvinced by Williams's 'uninspected notion of "experience" which . . . produced the quite unsatisfactory concept of "structures of feeling" and which continues to have disabling theoretical effects' (1990: 62). Further, Hall reiterated that 'the "experiential" paradigm does continue to cause some theoretical fluctuations in Williams's work around such key problems as determination, social totality, and ideology' (p. 63). Such continuing fluctuations, of course, were believed to hasten the demise of the experiential or culturalist paradigm. But what if it is precisely the manner of this paradigm's 'theoretical fluctuations' that render it poised now, more than ever, for a return? Could an always untimely appeal be raised to reassert the conceptual and practical worthiness of a resurgent culturalist/experiential paradigm?

One initially instructive insight in this regard comes from Adorno, who found himself exasperated and perplexed more than once by the writings of his friend Walter Benjamin. Remarking on Benjamin's concept of experience, Adorno noted how it was far outside the mainstream of almost all modern philosophy and, thus, 'so at odds with these criteria [used by Benjamin's critics] that it never even occurred to him to defend himself against them as Bergson did' (1988: 4). Indeed, it was the work of early twentieth-century French philosopher Henri Bergson that served for Deleuze and Benjamin (although this would not be the case for Williams) as a crucial antidote to Kant.[8] Bergson was one of the most consistent and nuanced critics of Kant's metaphysics of experience and, as such, his thoroughgoing depictions of its conceptual limitations proved powerfully resonant for anyone looking for a way out of this box. In one especially vivid passage, Bergson wrote of how Kant's philosophy rests upon 'pouring the whole of possible experience into pre-existing molds' as if 'the great discoveries only illuminate point by point the line traced in advance, as, on a festival night, a string of bulbs flick on, one by one, to give the outline of a monument' (2002: 197). Benjamin and Deleuze readily signed on to such a portrait of Kant's experiential shortcomings.

However, this was not to be the case for Williams; he made barely any reference to Bergson's work.[9] This is not entirely a surprising state of affairs. Bergson's thought, once widely influential and highly regarded at the dawn of the twentieth century, had faded from view almost completely by the time of Williams' first writings.[10] In the face of prevailing post-World War II sensibilities, the philosophy of Henri Bergson had come to be regarded as too irrationalist, too mystical, too vitalist, too affirmatively optimistic and too unapologetically metaphysical. Such sentiments surely provided Williams with more than enough reason to give Bergson's writings the widest possible berth – even as he (Williams) continually directed his own work towards a remarkably similar set of concerns: to 'the creative mind', to an immersion in 'process' by putting historical data (and concepts) back 'into solution', to feeling/emotion and the affective, to the emergent and pre-emergent, to an open-ended materialism, and to the 'wholeness' of life.

Today's revived interest in Bergson can be largely credited to Deleuze; his works, such as *Bergsonism* and *Difference and Repetition*, have nearly single-handedly demonstrated how this untimely, process-orientated philosophy may have finally found its moment. Deleuze states that his 'return to Bergson' is meant not only as 'a renewed admiration for a great philosopher but a renewal or extension of his project today, in relation to the transformations of life and society, in parallel with the transformations of science' (1991: 115). In *Bergsonism*, three distinctive features – intuition, science and metaphysics, and multiplicities – are identified by Deleuze as having come into even sharper contemporary focus, and, hence, each offers insights that might continue 'along new paths which constantly appear in the world' (p. 115). Perhaps too these features might shed additional light on Williams' experiential/culturalist paradigm and reveal ways that culturalism can still speak to our contemporary moment. In short, could a revitalisation of culturalism find shared resonances with the recent revival of Deleuzian Bergsonism? At the outset, though, it is worth emphasising that any extended encounter between Williams' culturalism (or cultural materialism) and Deleuze's Bergsonism (or incorporeal materialism) must cut, even as it connects, both ways. That is, it cannot simply be a matter of mustering a defence of the former by or through the latter, but must also be one of acknowledging that each of these projects must be mutually transformed over the course of these momentary intersections (such as follows).

Intuition. Bergson links experience and experiment through the faculty of intuition that exceeds or overflows the intellect; this is his 'reversed Kantianism' as taken up by Benjamin and Deleuze in their own arguments, as outlined above (Mullarkey 1999: 115). Empirical before it is conceptual, intuition is experience put back into solution, where it 'follows the real in all its sinuosities' (Bergson 1998: 363). Bergson argues that intuition is 'nothing mysterious' but, instead, means starting always within the lived immediacy of mobility and continuity (2002: 199). Intuition takes place beyond the 'turn in experience', continuing as a single, immersive process: as memory (experience past, both conscious and embodied), in duration (the endured overfullness of experience present), while simultaneously remaining open to the future (experience as experiment). Or, as Deleuze says, 'beyond experience, toward the conditions of experience' (1991: 23).

Similarly, Williams – most especially in his *Marxism and Literature* – wanted to elaborate a 'practical consciousness [that] is saturated by and saturates all social activity . . . social and continuous (as distinct from the abstract encounters of "man" and "his world", or "consciousness" and "reality", or "language" and "material existence")' (1977: 37). He described this version of experience as reconstituting the 'lost middle term between the abstract entities, "subject" and "object"' (p. 37). Indeed, sounding a great deal like Bergson countering Kant, Williams states: 'Thus, mediation is a positive process in social reality, rather than a process added to it by way of projection, disguise, or interpretation' (pp. 98–9).

With intuition, experience is less a discrete place in the time past belonging to a subject, and more an immanent process of relation (beyond inside and outside, beyond subject and object). Williams' particular (unspoken, unspeakable) consideration of intuition finds its greatest conceptual purchase in his structures of feeling's grasp for the 'pre-emergent', or that which moves 'at the very edge of semantic availability' (p. 134): the 'kind of feeling and thinking which is indeed social and material, but . . . in an embryonic phase before it can become fully articulate and defined exchange' (p. 131). The 'practical consciousness' thus re-emphasises the role of the 'creative process' and, thereby, alters the perceived relationship between theory and practice. It means, wrote Williams, not only 'casting off an ideology or learning phrases about it, but confronting a hegemony in the fibres of the self and in the hard practical substance of effective and continuing relationships' (p. 212). It likewise means that one 'special function of theory' is creatively tied to 'exploring and defining the nature and variation of practice' – and looking to how 'excluded and subordinate' models and experiences might need to be readmitted and refitted in order to work towards 'the articulation and formation of latent, momentary, and newly possible consciousness' (p. 212).

Putting this method of theoretical intuition and concept-creation into practice places unique demands on writing. It strives to discover 'a new articulation and in effect a new formation, extending beyond its own modes' (p. 211) but without idealising or spiritualising the writing process: finding expression and opening a place for the not yet fully arrived. Fred Inglis captures this sense well when he observes that Williams 'commended to others to see that whatever is begotten, born and dies is always mobile, changeable, mortal, and that only by trying to grasp this changeful, ungraspable totality will we understand anything, and then only in passing' (1995: 245).

Science and metaphysics. Deleuze remarked that Bergson's intuition, as a method, leads 'to the open creative totality' extending beyond the human (1991: 111). Williams might have hastened to add that 'beyond' the human does not entail leaving 'the human' entirely behind or presenting one's project as 'anti-humanist' (and neither Bergson nor Deleuze nor Benjamin would disagree), yet there is ample reason to believe that the non-human, ahuman, more-than-human and so on also have a place in Williams' cultural materialism.[11] On the way towards 'the materialist recovery', Williams took the 'experiment' of experience quite literally: even, for example, telling his *Politics and Letters* interviewers that if he 'had one single ambition in literary studies it would be to rejoin them with experimental science' rather than 'a blending of concepts of literature with concepts from Lacan' (1981: 340). But perhaps more than any of his other writings, Williams' essay on Marxist philosopher Sebastiano Timparano reveals how he deliberately chose not to impose a priori limits on what should count in 'the materialist project':

> Too much social and cultural practice is necessarily directed beyond human history, to material that at once precedes and persists. To neglect or withdraw from these directions would be a major cultural defeat. For the enemies are various and powerful: from the spiritualisms that are flourishing within a disintegrating social order, through the contemporary mythologizing, often sophisticated, of so many of our least understood conditions and practices, to the now vaunting ambition of epistemology to become the universal science. (1980: 121)

In the face of an epistemological clampdown, Williams maintained that the problem was not with 'science' but with how concepts such as 'physical' or 'material' came to be defined. The way forward, said Williams, is to encourage 'the necessary social process through which the materialist enterprise defines and redefines its procedures, its findings and its concepts, and in the course of this moves beyond one after another "materialism"' (p. 122). Bergson's own interplay of metaphysics and science works, according to Deleuze, to produce a radically redrawn materialism that extends simultaneously into matter, bodies, and machines (technology) – as well as incorporealities, felt qualities and processes, finding in these, then, 'new lines, openings, traces, leaps, dynamisms' that might offer 'new linkings and re-linkings in thought' (1991: 116). By allowing metaphysical room for creative intuition, science – for cultural studies at least – escapes its ingrown tendency to reduce the world to the contents of our consciousness and, instead, points the way towards the more-than-conscious, towards multiplicities.

Multiplicities. Andrew Milner describes Williams' cultural materialism as engaging with 'a specifically "materialist" humanism, which acknowledged the differences in our present condition, precisely so as to distinguish eradicable inequity from desirable plurality and thereby to proceed, not to the abstractly universal, but to a concrete commonality' (2002: 166). This inherently political passage from desirable plurality to concrete commonality echoes Adorno's quotation (above) about Benjamin's trespassings through the Kantian prohibitions on experience, and also resonates with Deleuze's claim that he'd always felt he was 'an empiricist, that is, a pluralist' (Deleuze and Parnet 1987: vii). In these instances, this is not a rarefied move towards some higher level of abstraction, but rather the embrace of something quite vividly, even viscerally available: an affectively, experimentally empirical stance towards the world as a multiplicity in order 'to find the conditions under which something new is produced' (p. vii), and not a world where pre-existent concepts are always waiting to be conveniently superimposed.

As Deleuze continues:

> The essential thing, from the point of view of empiricism, is the noun multiplicity, which designates a set of lines or dimensions which are irreducible to one another . . . In a multiplicity what counts are not the terms or the elements, but what there is 'between', a set of relations which are not separable from each other. (pp. vii–viii)

A multiplicity takes into account the concrete variability of a thing's particularity or singularity, without lifting it out of the processes of its emergence or severing it from the context of relations that make it uniquely what it is. Deleuze's resituating of structuralism, in his essay 'How Does One Recognize Structuralism?', is based upon this very notion: 'To discern the structure of a domain is to determine an entire virtuality of coexistence which pre-exists the beings, objects, and works of this domain. Every structure is a multiplicity of virtual coexistence' (2004: 179). In unfolding this virtual co-existence of any single element *plus* its relations and its conditions of emergence, Deleuze is able to shift structuralism – as a method of analysis prone to stasis – subtly out of phase with itself, putting every structural moment into motion as a processual, mobile configuration.[12]

Or, as Raymond Williams might have completed this same thought: all such structural moments come to serve as 'indissoluble elements of a continuous social-material process'. Like Deleuze and Bergson, Williams favoured the thought-image of solution and precipitation as a means to describe the flows and fluxes between process and structure, between virtual co-existence and articulated determination, between the uninterruptedly continuous and the discontinuously discrete: in short, to describe the way any element or structure is inhabited by multiplicity. Williams often acknowledged, as ever-present (even if not always fully conscious), the process of comparison between thought and feeling, experience and experiment, the indivisible whole and its parts, the disarmingly simple and densely complex and, even more, how each could contain the other while also remaining itself. He hung his hopes (and their resources) for the future on this multiplicity, and in its realisation as our 'concrete commonality'.

Williams' final words in *Politics and Letters* state these hopes and their political impulses poignantly:

> I have been pulled all my life, for reasons we've discussed, between simplicity and complexity, and I can still feel the pull both ways. But every argument of experience and of history now makes my decision – and what I hope will be a general decision – clear. It is only in very complex ways that we can truly understand where we are. It is also only in very complex ways, and by moving confidently towards very complex societies, that we can defeat imperialism and capitalism and begin that construction of many socialisms which will liberate and draw upon our real and now threatened energies. (1981: 437)

There is still a long way to go (it is going to be, as Williams warned, a 'long revolution'), but maybe multiplicity, intuition and a metaphysically materialist science are among those simple and, finally, complex pathways that allow cultural studies to continue the necessary work of bringing such hopes ever closer to fruition.

Twenty-five years after splitting in two and then going 'piecemeal', there is arguably more than sufficient licence to wonder if a reinstated culturalist appeal to a vital and experiential empiricism returns now as an increasingly necessary critical endeavour. Deliberately echoing Williams, Francis Mulhern (one of the original *Politics and Letters* interviewers) writes, on the last page of his *Culture/Metaculture*, that the practice of cultural studies operates, today, in the space of an open-ended excess 'with no fixed composition or tendency. It is a heterogeneous mass of possibilities old and new and never mutually translatable, possibilities no longer or not yet and perhaps never to be chartered as bearing general authority, as proper norms of political judgment' (2000: 174). No longer. Not yet. Perhaps never. Then, too, it is never a matter of reaching back to a past that once was in order to restore some bit of its lustre, but of finding this lustre (minus its supposedly musty past-ness), always alongside, in this current heterogeneous mass of possibilities. Experience and experiment.

Williams remains our contemporary. If cultural studies were to find itself one paradigm less (via whatever route or new adventure it travels to get there – Deleuzian or not), it should not, in the end, be named either 'culturalist' or 'structuralist', nor should it be given some other designation. It should only have to be known, simply (and, finally, complexly), as 'cultural studies.'

Notes

1 It is important to remember that the tag 'culturalism' came from Richard Johnson and is not a name that Thompson, Hoggart and Williams ever chose to designate their own work. Nor was there ever any spoken or unspoken alliance between their projects. Given the various and subtle heterogeneities of the so-called 'culturalists', this chapter will limit itself to dealing almost exclusively with Williams' thought.
2 While it is not the aim of this chapter to enumerate all of the presumed pains and wrong turns that some argue followed in the wake of Stuart Hall's bifurcation of cultural studies into culturalists and structuralists (Hall 1980), interested readers might consult Milner (2002); Mulhern (2000); Pickering (1997).
3 After all, as Michel Foucault proclaimed (somewhat facetiously), the name Deleuzian should some day apply to the whole twentieth century (Foucault 1977: 165).
4 Martin Jay (2005: 199–215) efficiently summarises the fallout around 'the quarrel over experience in British Marxism': especially as regards Williams and Thompson. See also the 'Theory and Experience' chapter of Fred Inglis' *Raymond Williams* (1995: 240–65).
5 The key text is Benjamin's 'On the Program of the Coming Philosophy' (written in 1918 but unpublished in his lifetime). His critique of Kant's philosophical accounting of 'experience' is unremitting, even while it attempts to preserve certain other elements of the Kantian system (though Benjamin will, later, forego any pretence to perpetuate the system itself). In a 1918 letter to his friend Ernst Schoen, Benjamin is even less charitable to Kant:

> The greatest adversary of these thoughts is always Kant. I have become engrossed in his ethics – it is unbelievable how necessary it is to track down this despot, to track down his mercilessly philosophizing spirit which has philosophized certain insights that are among the reprehensible ones to be found in ethics in particular. Especially in his later writings, he drives and senselessly whips his hobbyhorse, the logos. (Benjamin 1994: 125)

6 See Daniel Smith's 'Deleuze's Theory of Sensation: Overcoming the Kantian Duality' (1996: 29–56).

7   See Brian Massumi's introduction to *Parables for the Virtual* for more on the 'field of emergence of experience' (2002: 15).
8   Lawrence Grossberg has also pointed a finger at Kant, arguing that cultural studies has 'gotten itself into something of a dead-end because . . . almost all of the available theories of culture can be traced back to and located within the terrain of a Kantian philosophical discourse' (1997: 19).
9   To the best of my knowledge, there is only a brief parenthetical mention of Bergson – with regard to 'idealist notions of the "life force"' (1989: 72) – in Williams' final collection of essays, *The Politics of Modernism*.
10 So popular was Bergson, at one time, that the first traffic jam in the United States has been attributed to his speaking appearance at Columbia University in 1913.
11 Félix Guattari argued that, while both Foucault and Deleuze 'emphasized the non-human part of subjectivity,' one should not misjudge and, then, 'suspect them of taking anti-humanist positions' (1995: 9). See Mulhern, who writes of Williams: 'His analysis of creativity was radically anti-essentialist, postulating experience as a historical formation of subjectivity, variable between and within societies, not a perceptual constant. And "the human", in his discourse, marked a social principle of inclusion, not a perennial moral nature' (2000: 90–1).
12 For a fascinating account of letters exchanged between Deleuze, Louis Althusser and Pierre Macherey (a student of Althusser's at the time) over the course of Deleuze's drafting of his 'Structuralism' essay, see Stolze (1998). See also Etienne Balibar (2003). For a more collective accounting of Althusser and structuralism, via Spinoza, see Fourtounis (2005).

Bibliography

Adorno, Theodore (1988), 'Benjamin the Letter Writer', in Gary Smith (ed.), *On Walter Benjamin*, Cambridge, MA: MIT Press, pp. 329–37.

Balibar, Etienne (2003), 'Structuralism: A Destitution of the Subject?', *differences: A Journal of Feminist Cultural Studies*, 14:1, pp. 1–21.

Benjamin, Walter (1994), *The Correspondence of Walter Benjamin, 1910–1940*, trans. Manfred Jacobson and Evelyn Jacobson, Chicago: University of Chicago Press.

Benjamin, Walter (1996), *Selected Writings: Volume 1, 1913–1926*, Marcus Bullock and Michael W. Jennings (eds), Cambridge, MA: Belknap Press.

Bergson, Henri [1907] (1998), *Creative Evolution*, trans. Arthur Mitchell, Mineola, NY: Dover.

Bergson, Henri [1903] (2002), 'Introduction to Metaphysics', in *The Creative Mind*, trans. Mabelle Andison, NY: Kensington pp. 159–200.

Deleuze, Gilles [1966] (1991), *Bergsonism*, trans. Hugh Tomlinson and Barbara Habberjam, New York: Zone Books.

Deleuze, Gilles [1968] (1994), *Difference and Repetition*, trans. Paul Patton, New York: Columbia University Press.

Deleuze, Gilles [1990] (1995), *Negotiations*, trans. M. Joughin, New York: Columbia University Press.

Deleuze, Gilles [1973] (2004), 'How Does One Recognize Structuralism?', in *Desert Islands and Other Texts, 1953–1974*, Los Angeles and New York: Semiotext(e), pp. 170–92.

Deleuze, Gilles and Félix Guattari [1991] (1994), *What is Philosophy?*, trans. Hugh Tomlinson and Graham Burchell, New York: Columbia University Press.

Deleuze, Gilles and Claire Parnet [1977] (1987), *Dialogues*, trans. Hugh Tomlinson and Barbara Habberjam, New York: Columbia University Press.

Foucault, Michel [1970] (1977), 'Theatrum Philosophicum', in *Language, Counter-Memory, Practice*, trans. Donald Bouchard and Sherry Simon, New York: Cornell University Press, pp. 165–96.

Fourtounis, Giorgos (2005), 'On Althusser's Immanentist Structuralism: Reading Montag Reading Althusser Reading Spinoza', *Rethinking Marxism*, 17:1, pp. 101–18.

Grossberg, Lawrence (1997), *Bringing It All Back Home: Essays on Cultural Studies*, Durham, NC: Duke University Press.

Guattari, Félix [1992] (1995), *Chaosmosis: An Ethico-Aesthetic Paradigm*, trans. P. Bains and J. Pefanis, Bloomington and Indianapolis, IN: Indiana University Press.

Hall, Stuart (1980), 'Cultural Studies: Two Paradigms', *Media, Culture, and Society*, 2:1, pp. 57–72.

Hall, Stuart [1980] (1990), 'Politics and Letters', in Terry Eagleton (ed.), *Raymond Williams: Critical Perspectives*, Cambridge: Polity, pp. 54–66.

Hall, Stuart (1997), 'Culture and Power', *Radical Philosophy*, 86, November–December, pp. 24–41.

Inglis, Fred (1995), *Raymond Williams*, London and New York: Routledge.

Jay, Martin (2005), *Songs of Experience: Modern American and European Variations on a Universal Theme*, Berkeley and Los Angeles: University of California Press.

Massumi, Brian (2002), *Parables for the Virtual: Movement, Affect, Sensation*, Durham, NC: Duke University Press.

Milner, Andrew (2002), *Re-Imagining Cultural Studies: The Promise of Cultural Materialism*, Thousand Oaks: Sage.

Mulhern, Francis (2000), *Culture/Metaculture*, London and New York: Routledge.

Mullarkey, John (1999), *Bergson and Philosophy*, Notre Dame, IN: University of Notre Dame Press.

Pickering, Michael (1997), *History, Experience, and Cultural Studies*, New York: St Martin's Press.

Smith, Daniel (1996), 'Deleuze's Theory of Sensation: Overcoming the Kantian Duality', in Paul Patton (ed.), *Deleuze: A Critical Reader*, Cambridge, MA: Blackwell, pp. 29–56.

Stolze, Ted (1998), 'Deleuze and Althusser: Flirting with Structuralism', *Rethinking Marxism*, 10:3, pp. 51–63.

Williams, Raymond (1961), *The Long Revolution*, New York: Columbia University Press.

Williams, Raymond (1977), *Marxism and Literature*, Oxford and New York: Oxford University Press.

Williams, Raymond (1980), *Problems in Materialism and Culture*, London: Verso.

Williams, Raymond (1981), *Politics and Letters: Interviews with the New Left Review*, New York: Verso.

Williams, Raymond (1983), *The Year 2000*, New York: Pantheon Books.

Williams, Raymond (1985), *Keywords: A Vocabulary of Culture and Society*, Oxford and New York: Oxford University Press.

Williams, Raymond (1989), *The Politics of Modernism: Against the New Conformists*, London and New York: Verso.

Wolin, Richard (1989), 'Experience and Materialism in Benjamin's Passagenwerk', in Gary Smith (ed.), *Benjamin: Philosophy, Aesthetics, History*, Chicago: University of Chicago Press, pp. 210–27.

CHAPTER 7

Cultural Studies and Giorgio Agamben

Brett Neilson

In an article published in *Le Monde* on 10 January 2004, Italian philosopher Giorgio Agamben declared his refusal to travel to the United States and publicly announced the cancellation of a course he was due to teach at New York University in March of the same year. The piece, entitled 'No to Biopolitical Tattooing' (2004b), links this decision to the then recently instated US law requiring visitors who carry a visa to leave their fingerprints when entering the country. Agamben's objection to this measure stems not simply from solidarity with criminals and political defendants, who are regularly subjected to such procedures. Rather, he contends, the practice signals a shift in the juridical-political status of citizens in the so-called democratic states. 'History', he writes, 'teaches us how practices first reserved for foreigners find themselves applied later to the rest of the citizenry.' And, by requiring the enrolment and filing away of the most private and incommunicable aspect of human subjectivity (the body's biological life), the US contributes to what Michel Foucault once called 'the progressive animalization of man which is established through the most sophisticated techniques' (Agamben 2004b).

While entreating other European intellectuals and teachers to take the same stance, Agamben recalls 'the sympathy that has connected me to my American colleagues and their students for many years'. It would not be unreasonable to suppose that a good many of these colleagues and students would, at least at some point in their careers, have either been part of or otherwise engaged with that diffuse set of intellectual practices known as cultural studies. After all, cultural studies underwent rapid expansion in the US from the time that Agamben began to accept visiting appointments there in 1994, particularly in literature programmes such as those in which Agamben taught (although as an interdisciplinary practice cultural studies also took hold in areas such as sociology, history, anthropology and communications). Still, even though it's not too difficult to identify a number of people in the field who draw on his work these days, such as the literary and cultural theorist Cesare Casarino or the critic of biotechnology Eugene Thacker, to track the precise intersections of Agamben's thought with cultural studies would be a complex task: both because cultural studies has in many institutional situations and circumstances become something of a catch-all term, used to describe a variety of conflicting approaches to the analysis of culture and power; and also, of course, because its global presence cannot be reduced merely to its uptake in the US academy.

By now a thoroughly international phenomenon with its strongest presence in the English-speaking world (or at least in countries where English is the dominant academic language), cultural studies has come a long way since it first entered the university through adult education programmes, small publishing enterprises and the like. It currently boasts considerable institutional power and, in many cases, in Australia especially, works at the policy interface with state powers that command measures such as that against which Agamben's *Le Monde* article protests. Nevertheless (or, indeed, perhaps precisely because of this), Agamben's work provides an enormous resource for those in cultural studies and beyond who are interested in rethinking the political dimensions of human life. Indeed, by arguing that *life itself*, and in particular the propensity to reduce complex human existences to bare organic matter, has been central to Western politics since the time of Aristotle, Agamben reconceives the very notion of the political. In so doing, he develops an understanding of the political that equates neither to a purely linguistic relation nor to grounded intervention in specific social or institutional contexts. And it is primarily for this reason, I would suggest, that his work is proving so important for a younger generation of cultural studies practitioners, a generation who have grown discontent with the tendency to classify research in the field either as being curiosity-driven and therefore political only at a gestural level; or as actively engaged with the solution of practical problems in an increasingly complex world.[1] By questioning the very possibility of political community and political action, Agamben suggests a different path for cultural studies: one that requires a thorough reassessment of the relations between theory and practice, agency and application, and means and ends.

A movement that is not there

In January 2005, Agamben participated in the first meeting of the Italian nomad university, an initiative organised by Antonio Negri and others to construct spaces for intellectual and political creativity beyond the formal academic system. The intervention he offered, entitled 'Rethinking the

Movement', was characteristically heterodox with respect to the ethos of action-orientated solidarity which was predominant among the social movement participants who formed the bulk of the audience. Reviewing the concept of movement elaborated by the German political theorist Carl Schmitt in his 1933 essay *State, Movement, People* (2001), Agamben (2005) offered the following motto as an 'implicit rule' for his thought: 'When the movement is there pretend it is not there and when it's not there pretend it is.' With this dictum he sought not only to question the viability of any political thought that claims autonomy from the state and/or people by associating itself with social movements, but also to relate this difficulty to complexities implicit in the notion of movement itself. As defined by Aristotle, movement or kinesis is an unfinished act, a relation between potential and act that is always incomplete or capable of not passing into fruition. Movement, in this sense, 'is always constitutively the relation with its lack, its absence of end or *ergon*, or *telos* and *opera*' – when it is there it is not there and vice versa. With respect to the political, Agamben explains: 'Movement is the indefiniteness and imperfection of every politics.' At stake is a kind of threshold that marks the indeterminacy of politics as such, a limit beyond which the political must be conceived in separation from actions or ends.

It is instructive to recall Agamben's motto with respect to debates concerning the politics of cultural studies. Consider Fredric Jameson's (1993) caricature of cultural studies as the attempt to outline a radical politics without a radical political movement. Jameson's point is a frequently made one about the institutionalisation of cultural studies in the university and its supposedly consequent separation from grassroots struggles. But if read in the light of Agamben's comments, Jameson's remark has quite a different implication. The absence of a political movement becomes the very condition that necessitates a rethinking of politics and, in this sense, can be understood as an enabling rather than a disabling condition. Agamben's reconceptualisation of the political in relation to potentiality rather than in relation to end-orientated activity presents a challenge to cultural studies, exposing the secret complicities that inhabit many of its internal debates concerning the political dimensions of cultural analysis. It reveals, for instance, the common assumptions that inhabit the thought of those, like Stuart Hall (1990), who understand cultural studies as a radical intellectual practice that prepares the way for an emerging historical movement, and those, like Tony Bennett, who advocate more modest and practical interventions in the realms of industry and government.

Although by now almost a decade old, Bennett's *Culture: A Reformer's Science* (1998) remains one of the most influential calls for an applied cultural studies that pragmatically engages with the wider social world. The book builds its case for such a version of cultural studies through an explicit contrast with the earlier Gramsci-influenced work of Hall. Bennett dismisses, as growing more improbable by the day, Hall's notion that cultural studies 'might furnish a stratum of intellectuals who will prepare the way for an emerging historical movement to which that stratum will then attach itself in a moment of organicity' (p. 32). Yet, as Gary Hall (2002) has pointed out, 'for all that he is critical of Hall's thinking in this respect', Bennett's proposal:

> that the relationship between cultural studies and the idea of the organic intellectual be reformulated in terms of the 'development of forms of work – of cultural analysis and pedagogy – that could contribute to the development of the political and policy agendas associated with the work of organic intellectuals . . .' (33) continues to operate very much within the terms of Hall's own juxtaposition of theory and politics. Witness [Bennett's] proposal for a 'pragmatics for cultural studies': a 'revisionary program' in which cultural studies is 'to be developed in close association with the policy concerns of government and industry as a means of developing a more prosaic concept of practice, one that will sustain actual and productive connections with the field of the practicable' (17). Rather than analysing the complexity of the relation between theory and political practice [as Agamben's thought impels us to do], Bennett, on his own admission, simply adopts what he regards as 'an appropriately more limited usage' of this relation. (Hall 2002: 147, n. 14)

Agamben's reconception of the political in terms of potentiality allows us to discern the shared tendency in both Hall and Bennett – thinkers whose positions are often understood as emblematic of a wider divide in cultural studies – to reduce the political to the field of the actionable.[2] To think the political outside the actual and actionable, however, is a seemingly impossible task since, at least in the Western tradition, politics is predicated on action. For Agamben, the notion of potentiality must include not only the potential to be but also the potential not to be. The architect who knows how to build a house has, at the same time, the potential not to build it. And, in this sense, potentiality welcomes non-being – it encompasses passivity as much as action. A politics of potentiality is thus a politics that does not canvas action or engagement as a means of bringing the real into alignment with the ideal. It is rather a politics of subtraction or withdrawal that, as Franchi (2004) suggests, bears affinity to that developed by Italian *operaista* thinkers like Mario Tronti and Antonio Negri in the 1960s and 1970s. The fundamental move of these Marxist intellectuals, whose work provided the theoretical backbone for a whole generation of protest movements in Italy, was to reverse the classical relationship between labour and capital. By arguing that capital is essentially a social power that requires productive labour, and which evolves through a series of attempts to control or co-opt workers, they introduced the notion that the withdrawal of labour and/or refusal to collaborate with capital in the organisation of labour (e.g. by making demands that could not possibly be met) would function to destroy the capitalist system. In so doing, they invented a new form of politics that consisted in the denial of action or, as Tronti (1966) famously called it, 'the strategy of refusal'.

It is a curiosity of intellectual history that just as these notions were displacing the stronghold of Gramscian thought on Italian Marxism in the 1960/70s, British cultural Marxists were adopting Gramsci's notion of hegemony as a theoretical tool for understanding the relations of culture and power in complex industrial societies. For Hall and other practitioners of the early 'Birmingham School' formation of cultural studies, the Gramscian concept of hegemony provided the principal means for explaining the role of culture in the practical and theoretical activities by which the ruling class not only justifies and maintains its dominance, but also wins the active consent of those over whom it rules. Implicit in this approach was an optimism about promoting the democratic and pluralistic aspects of civil society as a means of destabilising (or reabsorbing) the coercive powers of capital and the state – hence the emphasis upon the transformative possibilities of agency and popular engagement that, as we have seen in the case of Bennett, was only scaled back in more recent governmental and pragmatically applied versions of cultural studies. By contrast, the non-active politics that Agamben seems to share with *operaista* thinkers like Tronti and Negri presents a very different model of political life – one that separates itself from notions of agency and engagement to question the very constitution of the political in sociological notions of change.

To be sure, Agamben's relation to *operaista* thought is complex and uneven. Not only does it derive from a Heideggerian rather than a Marxist matrix, but it also expresses a deep scepticism about the possibility of ever fully escaping from the existing articulations of capitalist and state power (Neilson 2004). Despite his collaboration with prominent *operaista* thinkers such as Paolo Virno – with whom he worked on the journal *Luogo commune* in the early 1990s – Agamben's thought maintains a certain singularity that questions even the tendency for 'the strategy of refusal' or escape to exist merely as a form of reaction to dominant conditions. Key to understanding his attempt to develop a coherent notion of non-active politics is an interrogation of the way in which he consistently refers these questions back to the ontology of life. For Agamben, the *vita activa* or purposeful assumption of a political task is, in the final analysis, just a particular form of life that is primarily defined on the basis of the exclusion of bare life – that is, of non-rational (animal or vegetable) life. Indeed, Agamben believes such an act of exclusion to found the Western political tradition. This is why the question of political constitution is, for him, necessarily connected to the constitution of life. Indeed, it is in this nexus of politics and life (which, following Michel Foucault, he calls the biopolitical) that Agamben's work acquires its most powerful resonances – resonances that are heard across a wide field of contemporary philosophical debate, but which have a special relevance for attempts within cultural studies to rethink the question of governance in relation to constitutional and sovereign structures.

Life – an inaccessible object

If the subject of biopolitics assumed central importance in Agamben's work with the 1995 publication of *Homo Sacer* (1998), before that it still held a subterranean sway on his thought. In his first book in 1970, *The Man Without Content* (1999a), Agamben argues that critical judgement pertains not so much to art as to its absence: 'When we deny that a work of art is artistic, we mean that it has all the material elements of a work of art with the exception of something essential on which its life depends, just in the same way that we say that a corpse has all the elements of the living body, except that ungraspable *something* that makes of it a living being' (p. 42). Here, the issue of that ungraspable *something* that constitutes life appears as a wider philosophical question – one which Agamben inherited from Heidegger, with whom he studied at Le Thor in 1966–8. In his later years, Heidegger stressed the need for the philosopher to have faith in the limits of thought. For Agamben, this meant approaching the limits of thought as potential openings rather than irredeemable closures. By the time of the 1977 *Stanzas* (1993a), he had formulated this principle into a notion that would haunt his entire philosophical oeuvre. The quest of criticism, he wrote, consists 'not in discovering its object but in assuring the conditions of its inaccessibility' (p. xvi).

In books such as *Infancy and History* in 1979 (1993b), *Language and Death* in 1982 (1991) and *The Idea of Prose* in 1985 (1995), Agamben explores the implications of such a critical quest in relation to Benjamin's messianic conception of history, the links between Hegel and Heidegger on negativity, and Aristotle's writings on potentiality, among other literary and philosophical moments. By the time of *The Coming Community* in 1990

(1993c), his fascination with the inaccessible object acquires an explicitly political rationale. Here he contrasts the constituted political community of modern statehood with a 'community-to-come' organised around a principle of non-identity or what he calls the singularity of the 'whatever' – that is, an unnamable object that cannot be contained within the logic of generality and particularity. Moreover, he argues that future politics will 'no longer be a struggle for control of the State, but a struggle between the State and non-state (humanity), an insurmountable disjunction between whatever singularity and the State organization' (p. 84). From here, Agamben begins his extraordinary reflections on the paradoxes of sovereignty and the biopolitical condition of bare life.

The impetus for this biopolitical turn in Agamben's work comes from an engagement with the late writings of Michel Foucault. In '*Society Must be Defended*', from 1975–6 (2003), Foucault famously argues that, with the advent of the modern era in the seventeenth century, systems of political rule that refer to a unitary and transcendent sovereign power are gradually matched by a new formation that organises and differentiates subjectivities on a horizontal plane. This new system, which he calls biopower or governmentality, establishes *life itself* as a political object through more or less rationalised attempts to intervene upon the vital characteristics of human existence: morbidity, mortality, old age, reproduction, the general health of the population and so forth. In *Homo Sacer*, Agamben contests Foucault's historical and analytical distinction between sovereignty and biopower. He writes: 'the inclusion of bare life in the political realm constitutes the original – if concealed – nucleus of sovereign power. *It can even be said that the production of a biopolitical body is the original activity of sovereign power*' (p. 6). In this way, Agamben rejects Foucault's claim that modern politics represents a definitive break from classical sovereignty, tracing the concern with bare life or *life itself* back to the earliest political formulations of sovereignty in the West.

To develop his argument, Agamben draws on the influential work of German political theorist Carl Schmitt, who, in *Political Theology* (1985), claims that sovereignty consists not in the exercise of total control, but in the ability to declare an exception to the rule. For Schmitt, the defining characteristic of sovereign power is the ability to decide on the 'state of exception', or to declare an emergency in which normal legal and constitutional arrangements are suspended. Such a state of exception, Agamben explains, strips legal subjects of their constitutional rights, rendering them as merely living bodies or bare life. Furthermore, he follows Walter Benjamin's critique of Schmitt, in the eighth of the 'Theses on the Philosophy of History' (1969), to argue that modern politics is characterised by the extension and generalisation of the state of exception. In other words, he contends that the biopolitical regime of power operative in modernity is not, as Foucault claims, distinguished by the incorporation of life into politics, but by the fact that the 'state of exception comes more and more to the foreground as the fundamental political structure and ultimately begins to become the rule' (1998: 20). Agamben thus understands sovereign power to exist at once inside and outside the juridical-political order, establishing what he calls a 'zone of indistinction' where actions that do not have the value of law can acquire the force of law.

By far the most prominent example of this zone of indistinction in Agamben's work is the Nazi *Lager*, which occupies centre stage in *Remnants of Auschwitz* (1999a) – a text that explores the denuded condition of the concentration camp intern in relation to the problematics of witnessing and survival. However, it would be wrong to assume that the Holocaust is the only or ultimate instance of modern biopower for Agamben, since he is interested in how the state of exception haunts not only those regimes usually identified as totalitarian, but modern democratic polities, too. Thus, in *Homo Sacer*, he discusses the predicament of the Nazi camp intern alongside a host of more contemporary bodies that also inhabit the indistinct space between life and death, including the comatose patient, the subject of euthanasia and the detained migrant.

The link between this biopolitical thematic and Agamben's fascination with the inaccessible object of criticism becomes perhaps most evident in *The Open* of 2002 (2004c). This text explores the boundary between human and animal – a barrier that, for Agamben, is indistinct since the human always defines itself in relation to the animal. 'Everything happens', he writes, 'as if, in our culture, life were *what cannot be defined, yet, precisely for this reason, must be ceaselessly articulated and divided*' (p. 13). In this sense, life itself becomes an inaccessible object, and the attempt to define the human becomes caught in an 'anthropological machine' that, on the one hand, attempts to animalise the human and, on the other hand, to humanise the animal. Agamben understands these dual processes as essentially political since, as Aristotle recognised when he described 'man' as a political animal, the indistinction of human and animal coincides with the juridical threshold that constitutes Western sovereignty. The production of the human requires the creation of bare life – whether understood as merely living flesh, the animal, or some barbarous, less-than-human existence. Which is why the question of man's biological existence, today as much as in ancient times, cannot be separated from fundamental questions concerning political constitution and sovereign order.

Agamben's most sustained analysis of the contemporary operations of sovereign power, however, is *State of Exception* from 2003 (2005). Here he explores the constitutional mechanisms that, in all modern democracies, enable the declaration of the emergency. In particular, he remembers the military order delivered by George W. Bush on 13 November 2001 (subjecting non-citizens suspected of terrorist activities to indefinite detention and trial by military tribunals). The 'unlawful combatants' interned at Guantánamo Bay thus move to the centre of a meditation on the relation between sovereign power and legal order at a time of 'global civil war'. *Contra* Schmitt (1985), for whom the state of exception is established to protect and lead back to the constituted norm, Agamben contends that there is no essential connection between legal right and the violence that reduces humanity to bare life. In seeking to undo that which has been artificially and violently linked, he hopes to oppose the 'maximum planetary unfolding' of the state of exception. At stake here is not only the development of theoretical methods that enable a lucid analysis of the present articulation of exceptional powers, but also a personal refusal to accept as normal and humane practices of biopolitical control that seek to register and identify the very stuff of life. Chief among these refusals so far has been Agamben's resignation of his position at NYU and protest against the 'biopolitical tattooing' implicit in US security and border control regimes – a form of non-active politics that he has invited others to follow.

Another cultural studies – well, potentially

It would be wrong to presume that Berlusconi's Italy does not form part of the cabal of powers that have pursued the so-called 'war against terror'. But Agamben's refusal to enter the US raises a question about what form of political expression is appropriate for intellectuals within those 'Anglosphere' countries – the US, UK and Australia – that have most aggressively constituted the 'coalition of the willing'. Interestingly enough, these are the same countries where cultural studies has achieved its strongest institutional uptake. Although it would be disingenuous to suggest a correlation between the war-making activities of these states and the earlier ascendancy of cultural studies within their universities, it would also be naive to claim that this success can be abstracted from questions of governance. For, while the question of institutionalisation has been a persistent concern within cultural studies, the field has undeniably been shaped by the corporate transformations to the university, particularly the pressures for research to attract funding from 'external' sources, and the speeded-up, performance-assessed rhythm of work.[3] This has meant increased attention to practical questions and applied outcomes. In some cases, it has also prompted a return to a humanist ethos and more sociological modes of analysis, either because these are perceived as more amenable to funding bodies or because they are understood to offer minimal protections against the demands of utilitarianism.[4]

The question of how these changes affect the political dimension of cultural studies is complex. For a start, there are different versions of what it means to be political in cultural studies, including Gramscian notions of connection with organic intellectuality, demands for greater attention to political economy, feminist emphases on the personal and bodily aspects of political life, and calls for pragmatic engagement with government and community. To suggest that Agamben's attempts to rethink the political can assist in reorientating these debates is not simply to add another option to this list. Rather, it is to seek to understand the logic that drives this proliferation of alternatives. For by posing the question of the political in relation to potentiality, Agamben not only questions the possibility of political practice as such, but also exhibits the way in which potentiality cuts across various practices, establishing a zone of indistinction where they begin to interfere with one another. Moreover, he does this in a way that drives home the difficult and confrontational questions that cultural studies must face if it is to understand not merely how it is shaped by institutional and governmental processes, but also how it positions itself in relation to sovereign power at a time of seemingly interminable war.

To be sure, Agamben's thought has not been ignored in cultural studies. The notion of 'whatever' singularity developed in *The Coming Community* has informed a variety of studies, ranging from innovative approaches to the politics of textuality (Casarino 2002) to work on computer gaming and the global dispersion of information (Mackenzie 2002). Similarly, Agamben's reflections on the constitution of life have provided a theoretical direction for studies of the biotechnological developments in genetics and other life sciences (Cooper et al. 2005). Another area of influence has been ethical philosophy, with Agamben's discussion of the unassumable nature of responsibility in *Remnants of Auschwitz* prompting inventive work from theorists both in cultural studies (Zylinska 2002) and in adjacent fields (Mills and Jenkins 2004). Not surprisingly, Agamben's writing has also proved crucial for thinkers seeking to understand the political structure of the detention camp, whether in historical (Perera 2002) or current perspectives (Butler 2004; Whyte 2005; Santner 2005). But these interventions, partly because they exist at the borders of cultural studies or attempt to expand its jurisdiction in original ways, do not fully register the potential impact of Agamben's thought on the field. It has also to be recognised that there are thinkers within or closely associated with cultural studies who resist Agamben's efforts to bring the question of the sovereign exception to the centre of contemporary theoretical enquiry. And the influence of these figures, as much as that of Agamben himself, is likely to shape the future of the field.

In an article entitled 'Thoughts on the Concept of Biopower Today' (2003), Paul Rabinow and Nikolas Rose criticise Agamben for applying 'Schmitt's concept of "the state of exception" and Foucault's analysis of biopower to every instance where living beings enter the scope of regulation, control and government' (p. 6). The thrust of their argument is to pin Agamben's account of sovereignty and life to the totalitarian regime and thus to separate, via a literal acceptance of Foucault's sovereignty/ governmentality distinction, his understanding of sovereignty from the routine operations of biopower in contemporary society. 'It is important to analyse the role and powers of the state in this new governmental configuration', Rabinow and Rose write, 'but it is clear that they cannot be accounted for by reference to the figure of sovereignty either as historical model or conceptual diagram of power' (p. 9). At stake in their argument is an attempt to identify a horizontal plane of governance in which various state and non-state agencies interact in the regulation and control of life. Sovereign power becomes emptied of any unifying or transcendent force and the state's independence and authority over society is weakened to the point where it becomes merely an enabling or facilitating body. For Rabinow and Rose, Agamben's condensation of all power relations into a single modality of sovereign power ultimately implies an appeal to religious authority. Thus, in a move that suggests they understand modern secularism as an uncomplicated virtue, they contest his reference of the theory of sovereignty to the ancient Roman figure of *homo sacer* – the 'sacred man' who can be killed without being murdered.

Importantly, there are practitioners of cultural studies who question the way in which Foucault-inspired models of liberal governance view the state as 'something different from what it is in its own terms' – that is, a sovereign entity that exercises monopolistic political power within a finite territorial space (du Gay 2002: 12). But unlike Agamben, these thinkers tend to throw the accusation of theologisation back on to the theorists of liberal governance themselves, contending that the attempt to de-autonomise the state under the aegis of its status as a social construct works only if sovereignty 'is conceptualized as a once-and-for-all condition of hermetic self-sufficiency' (p. 13). Missing here is an attempt to understand the way in which sovereign power actually does operate in the exceptional manner described by Agamben, and no more so than in times of war.

Consider the slaying of Brazilian national Jean Charles de Menezes, shot eight times by British police in London's Stockwell underground station on 22 July 2005. Although subject to legal process, the killers of this man, who was incorrectly suspected of planning a suicide bombing, are highly unlikely to be prosecuted since, as police, they need only demonstrate their belief that the supposed threat merited a fatal intervention. The figure of *homo sacer* would not appear as remote from contemporary logics of rule as first appears. Episodes like this, not to mention the existence of spaces such as Guantánamo Bay, Abu Ghraib or internment camps such as Australia's Baxter, make it clear that the exertion of sovereign power over bare life is not a historical condition that can be safely consigned to the totalitarian past, but a logical and persistent condition that remains operative within contemporary democracies.

It is also important to note that the distinction between the sacred and the profane, or the religious and the political, has been an important feature of Western political theory, but its application to non-Western societies is clearly problematic. Agamben's understanding of sovereign power as closely related to the sacred, in the Western as much as in other traditions, allows a rethinking of the relation between politics and religion that is crucial at a time when global as well as domestic conflicts seem increasingly driven by faith-based initiatives. The questioning of the division between church and state by the US right, the intervention of Pope Benedict XVI in Italy's 2005 referendum on IVF (in vitro fertilisation), the French ban on the *hijab* in schools, the religious imperatives associated with many forms of terrorism, the description by George W. Bush of the 'war against terror' as a 'crusade' – these all are phenomena that cannot be analysed or opposed without an approach that can account for the relation of the sovereign to the sacred. And while the question of religion has not been altogether ignored in cultural studies (Mizruchi 2001), there has been little attention to the nexus of religious authority and the state highlighted by Agamben.

The lack of such an engagement can perhaps be explained by the tendency in cultural studies to deflect the question of politics from the state – a move that allows a series of questions to be asked, including ones concerning the role of consumption and consumerism as political forms, or the imbrications of science and technology in presumptions about political life.[5] But these questions, which often emphasise the operations of power at the micro-level, cannot in the present global environment be detached from the problem of sovereignty. Consider, for instance, the booming research into the cultural implications of genomic medicine – a field in which Rabinow and Rose are prominent authorities. There is a rich and complex debate in this area, which focuses on emerging paradigms for the management of the health of people and populations. The issues canvassed usually concern the relation between biotechnological research and capital investment, its effects upon public access to biomedical technologies, and the appearance of new forms of risk management that devolve responsibility for health from the state to individuals and market relations. It would be safe to say that almost all cultural researchers intervening in this area support and advocate the advancement of equitable public health measures. But what remains underinvestigated is the way in which, in the present 'war environment', biotechnological research is increasingly linked to sovereign notions of security and defence. In the US, for example, biodefence and biosurveillance measures are emerging as the predominant logic of public health. As Thacker (2005) explains, 'US biodefense policy has created an atmosphere in which it is impossible to distinguish national security from public health, war from medicine, terror from biological life. The inordinate amount of funding and emphasis given to biodefense nearly suggests that *public health can only be improved through the condition of permanent exception that is war.*'

Such observations need not be understood to imply that sovereign power is the only form of power. One persistent criticism of Agamben concerns the manner in which he develops the paradigm of biopolitical thought without focusing on the specific economic rationality of biopolitics (see Bröckling 2003). It is generally recognised that the current era of globalisation is one in which economics has triumphed over politics – a situation that has particular consequences for the tradition of political theology that Agamben inherits from Schmitt. Wendy Brown (2005), for instance, argues that the prevalence of theological imperatives in the rhetoric of contemporary political leaders stems from the fact that sovereign power has been eroded by economic forces. As the sovereign state loses control over its destiny, it can assert its power only by clinging to the theological supplement that has always animated its claims to autonomy. In this way, the triumph of the economy registers what Mario Tronti (1998: 196) calls the 'political atheism' of the present era. In a recent interview entitled 'From Political Theology to Economic Theology', Agamben (2004a) takes a somewhat different approach to this problem. The ascendancy of economic rationality, he suggests, cannot be explained within the frame of political economy, which has always assumed the dominance of politics over economics. Rather, there is a need to trace the forgotten history of what he calls economic theology, a mode of thought that has precedents in early Christian appropriations of the Aristotlean notion of *oikonomia* and which leaves traces on modern political economy – for example, Adam Smith's metaphor of the 'invisible hand'. While Schmitt deliberately suppressed all references to economic theology, Agamben believes it provides the key to understanding the contemporary dominance of economic pragmatism. But it is not a matter of altogether abandoning the ontological cast of the Schmittian tradition. Rather, it must be recognised that sovereignty and governmentality have always been intertwined: 'The dominance of ontology has hidden the presence of the economic-pragmatic element, which has been just as important and perhaps in the end more decisive. Today the situation is reversed. But both elements are necessary for the functioning of the system' (Agamben 2004a, my translation).

No less than the political order is the economic order a part of the state of exception. In this regard, Agamben offers new resources for thinking the pragmatic order of neo-liberal globalisation that, among other things, has reconfigured the university environment in which cultural studies largely exists. But he also offers strategies for breaking out of this exception. It must be stressed, however, that he does not seek to offer practical solutions. As always, Agamben's politics are articulated at the level of potentiality and, in particular, through the attempt to specify the potentiality of what, following Aristotle, he calls the 'happy life'. In the 1986 essay 'On Potentiality' (1999a), he writes that 'the greatness of human potentiality is measured by the abyss of human impotentiality' (p. 182). Furthermore, it is in this impotentiality (or in the potentiality not to be) that 'the two terms distinguished and kept united by the relation of [the sovereign] ban (bare life and form of life) abolish each other and enter into another dimension' (1998: 55). By rendering the opposition of these terms ineffective, Agamben believes, a potential politics opens a space in which life can survive, free from the sovereign decision, unhinging and emptying the 'traditions and beliefs, ideologies and religions, identities and communities' which have borne it (1993c: 83). This is what, for Agamben, enables a life directed towards happiness, or, as Negri (2003) describes it in his *Il Manifesto* review of *State of Exception*, 'a fully immanent redemption that never forgets the mortal condition'.

Despite his emphasis on the theological powers of sovereignty, then, Agamben imagines the 'happy life' as a purely immanent condition. This is why it would be disingenuous to present his work here as some kind of political foil to cultural studies, which has often tended to operate with a secular understanding of culture and everyday life. Agamben's thought concerns itself with the constitution of the political as such, with the indefiniteness and imperfection of every politics, with means without ends. In this sense, it remains an analytical tool that denies the reality of the object it analyses. The question Agamben presents to cultural studies is not one about the need to be more political in dangerous and compromised times. Rather it is about how to negotiate its very conception of the political under conditions where politics cannot simply be reduced to agency and engagement. For this reason, his work provides strategies for cutting across and identifying both the commonalities and fault-lines between the modes of political expression that proliferate in cultural studies. What remains to be seen is whether such a negotiation, if it ever did occur, would transform cultural studies from within or whether it would precipitate a mutation to practices that seek altogether another name.

Notes

1 For some reflections on the tendency to divide knowledge production within cultural studies between curiosity-driven and pragmatic interventions, see Ang (2004). Ang draws on the distinction from Gibbons et al. (1994) between Mode 1 knowledge production, which is driven by academic interests and codes of practice, and Mode 2 knowledge production, which seeks to address a specific problem recognised as relevant within a wider social context. Importantly, Ang wants to question the boundaries between these research modes. None the less, she recognises that cultural studies is increasingly practised in institutional and policy environments where such divisions are taken for granted and applied research options are favoured.
2 For an example of this tendency to take Hall and Bennett as emblematic of different strains within cultural studies, see Wickham (2005). Wickham takes Hall to represent what he sees as the dominant intellectual type in cultural studies, the ethical-must-be-moral type, who seeks ethically, through relation to a movement, to empower the disempowered. By contrast, Bennett, along with Ian Hunter, is taken to represent the civil-philosophy type, who makes more limited interventions in accordance with the political and juridical secularisation of civil governance.
3 For a somewhat dated but still useful series of debates surrounding the institutionalisation of cultural studies see Striphas (1998).
4 On the latter see Rutherford (2005), who argues that an anti- or post-human perspective in cultural studies provides no basis to oppose neo-liberal demands for practical research outcomes and the commercialisation of knowledge.
5 Clearly, this is a generalisation that cannot encompass all projects within cultural studies, including central and formative ones such as Hall et al. (1978) – a text that engaged with the powers of the state using theoretical ideas from Althusser. However, with the full impact of Gramscianism upon cultural studies, there was a general tendency to steer away from matters of state (Harris 1992). See also Lloyd and Thomas (1998: 8–16) for an account of the absence of a theory of state power in the influential works of Raymond Williams.

Bibliography

Agamben, Giorgio [1982] (1991), *Language and Death: The Place of Negativity*, Minneapolis: University of Minnesota Press.
Agamben, Giorgio [1977] (1993a), *Stanzas: Word and Phantasm in Western Culture*, Minneapolis: University of Minnesota Press.
Agamben, Giorgio [1979] (1993b), *Infancy and History: The Destruction of Experience*, London: Verso.
Agamben, Giorgio [1990] (1993c), *The Coming Community*, Minneapolis: University of Minnesota Press.
Agamben, Giorgio [1985] (1995), *The Idea of Prose*, Albany, NY: State University of New York Press.
Agamben, Giorgio [1995] (1998), *Homo Sacer: Sovereignty and Bare Life*, Stanford, CA: Stanford University Press.
Agamben, Giorgio [1970] (1999a), *The Man Without Content*, Stanford, CA: Stanford University Press.
Agamben, Giorgio [1986] (1999a), 'On Potentiality', in *Potentialities: Collected Essays on Philosophy*, Stanford, CA: Stanford University Press, pp. 177–84.
Agamben, Giorgio [1998] (1999a), *Remnants of Auschwitz: The Witness and the Archive*, London: Zone Books.
Agamben, Giorgio (2004a), 'Dalla teologia politica alla teologia economica', http://rivista.ssef.it/site.php?page=20040308184630627&edition=2005-05-01.
Agamben, Giorgio (2004b), 'No to Biopolitical Tattooing', www.truthout.org/cgi-bin/artman/exec/view.cgi/4/3249.
Agamben, Giorgio [2002] (2004c), *The Open: Man and Animal*, Stanford, CA: Stanford University Press.
Agamben, Giorgio (2005), 'Rethinking the Movement', www.generation-online.org/p/fpagamben3.htm.
Agamben, Giorgio [2003] (2005), *State of Exception*, Chicago: University of Chicago Press.
Ang, Ien (2004), 'Who Needs Cultural Research?', in Pepi Leistyna (ed.), *Cultural Studies: From Theory to Action*, New York: Blackwell, pp. 477–83.
Benjamin, Walter [1940] (1969), 'Theses on the Philosophy of History', in Harry Zohn (ed.), *Illuminations*, New York: Schocken Books, pp. 253–64.
Bennett, Tony (1998), *Culture: A Reformer's Science*, Sydney: Allen and Unwin.
Bröckling, Ulrich (2003), 'Menschenökonomie, Humankapital: Eine Kritik der biopolitischen Ökonomie', *Mittelweg*, 36:1, pp. 3–22.
Brown, Wendy (2005), '"Sovereign is He Who Decides": Global Capital as Absolute and Perpetual Power', keynote address, 'The Politics of Being', Annual Conference of the Australian Society for Continental Philosophy, University of New South Wales, 15–17 June.
Butler, Judith (2004), 'Indefinite Detention', in *Precarious Life: The Powers of Mourning and Violence*, New York: Verso, pp. 50–100.

Casarino, Cesare (2002), 'Philopoesis: A Theoretico-Methodological Manifesto', *boundary 2*, 29:1, pp. 65–96.
Cooper, Melissa, Goffey, Andrew and Munster, Anne (2005), 'Biopolitics, For Now', *Culture Machine*, 7, http://culturemachine.tees.ac.uk/frm_f1.htm.
Du Gay, Paul (2002), '"A Common Power to Keep Them in Awe": A Comment on Governance', *Cultural Values*, 6:1, 2, pp. 11–27.
Foucault, Michel [1975–6] (2003), '*Society Must be Defended*', London: Allen Lane.
Franchi, Stefano (2004), 'Passive Politics', *Contretemps*, 5, pp. 30–41, www.usyd.edu.au/contretemps/5december2004/franchi.pdf.
Gibbons, Michael, Limoges, Camille, Nowotny, Helga, Schwartzman, Simon, Scott, Peter and Trow, Martin (1994), *The New Production of Knowledge: The Dynamics of Science and Research in Contemporary Societies*, London: Sage.
Hall, Gary (2002), *Culture in Bits: The Monstrous Future of Theory*, London: Continuum.
Hall, Stuart (1990), 'The Emergence of Cultural Studies and the Crisis of the Humanities', *October*, 53, pp. 11–23.
Hall, Stuart, Critcher, Charles, Jefferson, Tony, Clarke, John and Roberts, Brian (1978), *Policing the Crisis: Mugging, the State and Law and Order*, Basingstoke: Macmillan.
Harris, David (1992), *From Class Struggle to the Politics of Pleasure: The Effects of Gramscianism on Cultural Studies*, London: Routledge.
Jameson, Fredric (1993), 'On "Cultural Studies"', *Social Text*, 34, pp. 17–54.
Lloyd, David and Thomas, Paul (1998), *Culture and the State*, New York: Routledge.
Mackenzie, Adrian (2002), *Transductions: Bodies and Machines at Speed*, London: Continuum.
Mills, Catherine and Jenkins, Fiona (eds) (2004), 'Unassumable Responsibility: New Perspectives on Freedom, Justice and Obligation', special issue of *borderlands e-journal*, 3:1, www.borderlandsjournal.adelaide.edu.au/issues/vol3no1.html.
Mizruchi, Susan L. (ed.) (2001), *Religion and Cultural Studies*, Princeton, NJ: Princeton University Press.
Negri, Antonio (2003), 'The Ripe Fruit of Redemption', www.generation-online.org/t/negriagamben.htm.
Neilson, Brett (2004), '*Potenza Nuda*? Sovereignty, Biopolitics, Capitalism', *Contretemps*, 5, pp. 63–78, www.usyd.edu.au/contretemps/5december2004/neilson.pdf.
Perera, Suvendrini (2002), 'What is a Camp?', *borderlands e-journal*, 1:1, www.borderlandsjournal.adelaide.edu.au/vol1no1_2002/perera_camp.html.
Rabinow, Paul and Rose, Nikolas (2003), 'Thoughts on the Concept of Biopower Today', www.molsci.org/files/Rose_Rabinow_Biopower_Today.pdf.
Rutherford, Jonathan (2005), 'Cultural Studies in the Corporate University', *Cultural Studies*, 19:3, pp. 297–317.
Santner, Eric L. (2005), 'Terri Schiavo and the State of Exception', www.press.uchicago.edu/Misc/Chicago/05april_santner.html.

Schmitt, Carl [1922] (1985), *Political Theology: Four Chapters on the Concept of Sovereignty*, Cambridge, MA: MIT Press.

Schmitt, Carl [1933] (2001), *State, Movement, People: The Triadic Structure of the Political Unity*, Washington, DC: Plutarch Press.

Striphas, Ted (ed.) (1998), 'Institutionalizing Cultural Studies', special issue of *Cultural Studies* 12:4.

Thacker, Eugene (2005), '*Nomos, Nosos,* and *Bios*', *Culture Machine*, 7, http://culturemachine.tees.ac.uk/articles/thacker.htm.

Tronti, Mario (1966), *Operai e capitale*, Turin: Einaudi.

Tronti, Mario (1998), 'Tesi su Benjamin', in *La politica al tramonto*, Turin: Einaudi.

Whyte, Jess (2005), 'The New Normal', *Signature*, 1, www.s7digital.com/signature/sig-stories.php?id=346.

Wickham, Gary (2005), 'Ethics, Morality and the Formation of Cultural Studies Intellectuals', *Cultural Studies Review*, 11:1, pp. 71–88.

Zylinska, Joanna (2002), ' "They're All Antisemitic There": Aporias of Responsibility and Forgiveness', *Culture Machine*, 4, http://culturemachine.tees.ac.uk/Cmach/Backissues/j004/Articles/Zylinska.htm.

KNOW YOUR ENEMY

CHAPTER 8

Cultural Studies and Alain Badiou

Julian Murphet

In this chapter we approach something that appears, at first glance, in the form of an implacable opposition. The title should, perhaps, read: 'Cultural Studies *or* Alain Badiou'. While cultural studies has been the most hospitable of disciplines, absorbing and assimilating no end of theoretical 'positions' in its muscular advance towards an adequate critical relationship with its world, there is the strong sense that, in the work of Alain Badiou at least, a limit has been reached. We will see below how hostile Badiou himself is to any *rapprochement* with a discipline he presumptively lumps together with the worst varieties of 'multiculturalism'; and we will further specify good reasons why cultural studies as it is presently constituted can have little immediate use for a philosophy, like Badiou's, predicated on truth, subjectivity, universals and 'pure art'. In the words of Badiou's most gifted English mediator, Peter Hallward: 'It is probably not much of an exaggeration to say that Badiou's work is today almost literally unreadable according to the prevailing codes – both political and philosophical – of the Anglo-American academy' (2003: xxiii). And if there is little chance that these two critical protocols might learn to read each other in a common project, then perhaps the force of this irreconcilability amounts to an injunction to decide, *to decide in favour of decision*, rather than cling to the dream of conciliation. Yet the question remains: is *this* antagonism the 'right' one for us to be deciding? And furthermore, is it *really* the antagonism it appears to be?[1] At the conclusion of this chapter we will ask these questions more insistently, and probe the possibility of a conjuncture between two such seemingly mutually exclusive critical positions.

Let us briefly summarise a few principles and premises that might be said to confer at least the semblance of unity on the proliferation of practices going ahead in the name of cultural studies (though each of these tenets is arguable, even within 'the discipline'):

1. *Truth* is a discursive construct always implicated in the operations of power and fundamentally unavailable for effective critical reclamation.
2. Any truck with the *universal* must be resisted. Only concrete particularities and their combinations can responsibly be treated.
3. *Difference* is good, 'sameness' is bad.
4. *Multiculturalism* is 'a core value of the discipline' (During 2005: 160).
5. Culturally, the impure is simply *what is*, and is, as such, good. Any attempt to 'purify' the impure (à la Mallarmé and Ezra Pound, who both offered to 'purify the dialect of the tribe' with their forbidding works) is a totalitarian gesture.
6. Cultural studies 'tends to regard all cultural practices and objects as value-equivalent' (During 2005: 7).

Every one of these tenets is categorically opposed by the philosophy of Alain Badiou, who affirms a philosophy of *truth*, in the name of *universalism*, the *immortal subject*, an ethics of the *Same*, and the *value* of the *purity of art*. Clearly, this requires some explanation.

Badiou, who came to intellectual maturity under the auspices of Louis Althusser, proceeds from a basic conviction: that mathematics, particularly post-Cantorian set-theory, resolves one of philosophy's most enduring problems – namely, the question of Being. 'Ontology is nothing other than mathematics as such' (Badiou 2004: 45). Mathematics *thinks* pure being, and does so perfectly adequately, in terms of its immanent multiplicity, its infinite extension from within. Passionately hostile to all philosophies of the 'One', Badiou embraces the 'inconsistent multiple' of mathematical infinity as the ultimate horizon of all thought and practice.

Truth is the name of philosophical responsibility before the universality of mathematical logic. One of Badiou's more exasperated asides berates cultural relativism as a 'barbaric' retreat from this universality:

> The extreme forms of this relativism . . . claim to relegate mathematics itself to an 'Occidental' setup, to which any number of obscuranitst or symbolically trivial apparatuses could be rendered equivalent, provided one is able to name the subset of humanity that supports this apparatus. (Badiou 2003: 6)

Badiou insists on mathematics as a universal condition of thought, against any attempt to relativise it. But *truth* itself is not mathematical – far from it. Mathematical ontology is descriptive; it enables us to think being, but in a more or less tautological way. Set-theory elucidates the infinitely multiple constitution of any given situation, and insists on the gap between this raw multiplicity and the 'count-for-one' that represents it as a 'state' (for instance, a political state consists of *these* elements: politicians, trades unions, capitalists, media institutions, and so forth; and *not others* that are none the less 'inside' it: illegal immigrants, homeless and mentally ill persons), but it does not explain how it is that anything could *happen* within a situation to change it. Set-theory and the 'difference' it underscores as constitutive and therefore banal cannot explain *events*; and for Badiou the realm of truth proper is reserved only for events.

To grasp what he means by an event, consider the 'state' of painterly practices in France around 1906–7. We could account for all the many schools and impulses within this field, and produce an exhaustive description of its parts. An element named 'Picasso' (26 years old, Spaniard) would be enumerated within this manifold ('wistful, etiolated nudes, circus folk, and beggars he had been painting up to 1905' (Hughes 1980: 20)); but there would simply be no way of inferring from this the event of *Les Demoiselles d'Avignon* in 1907, a painting which horrified even Picasso's closest comrade Georges Braque 'by its ugliness and intensity'. And yet, galvanised by that event and in solidarity with its immense implications, Braque would join Picasso and for the next several years enact something called Cubism. All of twentieth-century art took place within the aftermath of this event, which was not reducible to its situation, and finally transformed it completely.

When Badiou says that events are irreducible to their situations, he means that although they can be seen to emerge from a situation (they are not miracles), they cannot be said to belong to it either. Their 'evental site' is near the *void* of any given situation, its interiorisation of the infinite, the gap between its official elements and its infinite distribution of parts, the counted and the uncounted – an 'ugly' mole in an amorous situation, for example, or the homeless in a political state. In the moment of their taking place, events cause their situations to bend and buckle. One glance at the beloved's mole can suddenly transform the lover's mind into a roiling chaos; an effective protest by the homeless might have sufficient power to force the entire political system into crisis. For Badiou, these events are the passages of *truths*. Truths have nothing to do with situations, sets, states of affairs ('knowledge' deals with these); they have to do only with the events that shatter situations. Truths are thus local and particular in origin, but they collapse all the existing hierarchical elements of their situations into a 'generic multiple', and thus attain the universal.

> What happens . . . is precisely this: a fragment of multiplicity wrested from all inclusion. In a flash, this fragment (a certain modulation in a symphony by Haydn, a particular command in the Paris Commune, a specific anxiety

preceding a declaration of love, a unique intuition by Gauss or Galois) affirms its unfoundedness, its pure *advent*, which is intransitive to the place in which 'it' comes. (Badiou 2004: 101)

Truths are what Badiou calls 'universal singularities'. They emerge singularly, completely by chance, out of determinate states of affairs, and cannot be predicted or categorised in advance. Because their status is so murky and undecidable (is *Les Demoiselles* really an event, or just ugly nonsense? have our demands to end the death penalty really been met, or is this a temporary cynical capitulation?), they are always in danger of disappearing for ever, reabsorbed by the status quo. But their implications, once declared, are universal: this painting isn't just a local resolution to specific procedural problems in representation, it fundamentally redirects *the course of art itself*; if we have succeeded in forcing this demand to end the death penalty here and now, then the death penalty is *universally evil*; and so on.

In order to become true, events must be named and sworn to by human agents, who, torn from their regular roles, now become what Badiou calls *subjects of a truth*. In their declarations of fidelity to events that most people have not even discerned, these subjects (the *only* genuine subjects) take leave of things as they are, of routines and opinions. Kitty Shcherbátsky in *Anna Karenina* experiences this break as profoundly as any: 'On that day when . . . she had silently gone up and given herself to him – in her soul on that day and hour there was accomplished a total break with her entire former life, and there began a completely different, new life, totally unknown to her' (Tolstoy 2003: 453). Subjects tread a dangerous path: a selfless dedication to the universal implications of something which only 'happened' because they have decided to declare it. In remaining faithful to the event, subjects become *immortal*: 'to be the immortal that he is', writes Badiou, is the highest task of 'man' (2001: 14; *sic*). For Badiou, 'subjectivity' and 'immortality' have nothing to do with the routine identity of a 'self' – they are inhuman processes of depersonalisation in the name of *singular universals*, or truths: scientific, political, amorous or artistic.

Take Badiou's privileged example, St Paul. Although Saul (a Jew and Roman citizen) was for many years an ardent persecutor of Christians, he was struck one day on the road to Damascus by the realisation that he himself was a Christian. From that moment forward, he was no longer Saul, persecutor of Christians, but Paul, apostle of a Christ he had never met, declaring the truth of an event he never witnessed (the resurrection), a position that made life extremely hazardous for him as a human being, but which guaranteed his immortality as a subject. For Badiou, Paul is the very type of the subject of a truth, the courageous 'new figure of the militant'. Paul's Christian 'I am' is the subjective 'I am' as such: a perilous project of faith and consistency in the face of violent social opposition, sustained by conviction, hope and love, and by the co-workers whom his faith conscripted around him. And this subjectivation can happen to *anyone* and implies *everyone*. In Paul's astonishing words, which resound in the present with such perdurable force, 'there is no such thing as Jew or Greek, slave or free man, man or woman, . . . for you are all one person in Jesus Christ'. The event of the resurrection (whether it happened or not; the point lies in Paul's conviction that it did) laid bare the generic truth of its situation. All 'cultural identities' were as nothing when seen in the light of this truth: *human beings are equal in the love of Christ*. The lesson was clear: 'Adapt yourself no longer to the pattern of this present world, but let your minds be remade and your whole nature thus transformed' (Romans 12.2).

Badiou's presentation of truth, as a passionate subjective attachment to an accidental occurrence whose ramifications threaten the entire order of things, is to say the least eccentric. Hitherto, philosophy has approached truth either as transcendental, as positivistic, as consensual, or as a rhetorical vestment of power, but never in such a perverse blend of absolutism and voluntarism as this. In essence, what it amounts to is an admission of politics into the highest philosophical values – truth can only be understood politically, and fundamentally there is no truth without the political praxis that brings it into being. Politics saturates all four of Badiou's 'truth precincts' (love, art, science and politics proper), because the subjective conscription to a cause of any sort involves irreversible decisions, struggles for power and the formation of sects and cells (even if the membership is limited to one). If we are now to shift gears and begin to spell out some of the relations between Badiou's militant philosophical Platonism and the ground-level practices of cultural studies, this question of politics seems a good place to start. After all, in a certain tradition of cultural studies, politics is construed as foundationally as in Badiou's project. The difference, of course, lies in the place of *truth* and the meaning of *culture* within either paradigm.

How are the concepts of politics and culture related to each other in cultural studies? Nick Couldry's book *Inside Culture* has argued that cultural studies is undergirded by a commitment to a 'broad notion of citizenship' and the quest for a 'common culture', which he defines as 'the attempt to build a common *space* where cultural differences can be mutually negotiated, explored, reflected upon – a space of speaking and listening between "concrete others"' (2000: 142). More recently, Simon During has tried to group the panoply of cultural studies trajectories under three modalities: 'It takes into account the perspective of the marginalized and oppressed; it nurtures cultural celebration and affirmation, and encourages fandom; and it aims to frame its analyses and critiques in relation to everyday life' (2005: 214). These two examples suggest powerful underlying frames of reference, drawn from cultural studies' interdisciplinary origins in anthropology, ethnography, literary studies, sociology and political theory. The bedrock assumption is not hard to miss: 'concrete' and 'marginalized others' are to be 'affirmed' in their everyday cultural values, even if the structures governing everyday life have to be 'critiqued'. This – what can only be described as a kind of radical liberalism – has obvious affinities with the mainstream project of multiculturalism, which During has declared to be 'a core value of the discipline' (2005: 160). It is indeed, despite the complex theoretical contributions to the discipline of intellectuals such as Gayatri Spivak, Judith Butler and Donna Haraway, difficult to dissociate ground-level cultural studies from an ongoing belief that 'other' cultures, as much as 'our own', constitute the primary frames in which the majority of people enact their political lives.

The pre-eminence in cultural studies of categories such as the everyday, the ordinary (Williams 1997) and the popular points to the discipline's celebration of the political valency and wealth of existing human cultural practices: their diversity and tenacity, their traditions, both inherited and invented, their active and passive moments. At present, of course, this field is riven by clear political inequalities; and in Henry Giroux's words, 'culture as a terrain of struggle shapes our sense of political agency and mediates the relation between materially based protests and structures of power and the contexts of daily struggles' (2000: 139). However, the 'common culture' putatively lying within reach of these 'struggles', a global citizenship which much cultural studies would like to see consolidated by a web of mutual respect and 'listening', is perhaps a specious fetish, constructed by Western liberals and a few of their Third World cohorts to palliate the existential and historical burden of guilt. Such at least is the thrust of Badiou's critique of what he calls 'culturalism', a tendency of which institutional 'cultural studies' is symptomatic:

> The objective (or historical) foundation of contemporary ethics is culturalism, in truth a tourist's fascination for the diversity of morals, customs and beliefs. . . .
> Against these trifling descriptions (of a reality that is both obvious and inconsistent in itself), genuine thought should affirm the following principle: since differences are what there is, and since every truth is the coming-to-be of that which is not yet, so differences are then precisely what truths depose, or render insignificant. . . .

Only a truth is, as such, *indifferent to differences*. This is something we have always known, even if sophists of every age have always attempted to obscure its certainty: a truth is *the same for all*. . . .

It is only through a genuine perversion, for which we will pay a terrible historical price, that we have sought to elaborate an 'ethics' on the basis of cultural relativism. (2001: 27–9)

No one is arguing that cultural studies is reducible to 'cultural relativism' – the study of difference in and between cultures does not reduce to relativism. Badiou's critique here is absolute, however: *cultural differences are simply the way things are*. They are thus politically meaningless and philosophically devoid of interest. There can be no 'critique', in the strong Kantian sense of the word, of those differences whose oft-proclaimed 'ordinariness' suggests as much. The 'obvious and inconsistent' terrain of culture is precisely what truths 'depose' and render insignificant; cultural studies must therefore, logically, be untrue.

Badiou's 'return to truth' strikes right to the core of cultural studies as it is most often practised, since the discipline's claims for political relevance are so often pinned to the democratic vista of a realised 'space' of cultural 'negotiation' and 'recognition'. Couldry sees the political promise of cultural studies as a progressive pedagogical enlightenment: 'This means as many people as possible getting critical skills, demystifying the processes of representation through examining how meanings are produced, and becoming aware of the underlying politics of representation. . . . opening up our experiences of living inside contemporary mediated, commodified cultures to reflection and dialogue' (2000: 42). This sounds admirable as far as it goes, but alas it goes nowhere. Reflexive immanence is arguably the very name of the system we inhabit: its modus operandi, nowhere hidden, is reflected back at us before we have a chance to refract it inwardly. Dialogue itself is a vacuous category, outside of a context defined by antagonistic aims. In the absence of any 'truth procedure' (in Badiou's sense), 'people' are simply unable to transform the open secret of 'critical' knowledge into anything more than *cynical reason*. The awareness that what is being done to me (my culture) is a fraud, and my acceptance of that as inevitable, has even become pleasurable, and is meant to be so. Ours are cultures that ceaselessly 'study' themselves, and publicly proclaim their relativity and absence of truth. What is a discipline devoted to the critical study of such 'obviousness' supposed to do? For all its oppositional rhetoric, how *critical* is cultural studies?

Simon During has written that, 'from within cultural studies, the discipline's rise is consistently narrated in terms of its struggle against elitism, Eurocentrism and cultural conservatism; yet from the outside it often looks like a beneficiary of the new market-orientated political economy and economistic models of university governance' (During 2005: 11). Cultural studies has, here and there, even become a way of intervening in the management of culture. This position, espoused by Tony Bennett, has the critical advantage of clarifying the 'programmatic, institutional and governmental calculations in which cultural practices are inscribed' (1992: 28), and urges a realpolitik view of culture, whose ultimate goal is 'a politics which might take the form of an administrative program, and . . . a type of cultural studies that will aim to produce knowledges that can assist the development of such programmes' (p. 29). As Adorno put it long ago, 'Whoever speaks of culture speaks of administration as well . . . the single word "culture" betrays from the outset the administrative view, the task of which, looking down from on high, is to assemble, distribute, evaluate and organize' (1991: 93). Cultural studies and cultural administration are difficult to keep apart in practice. Graduates of the discipline often end up at one level or other of the culture industries. In the words of Lauren Berlant, cultural studies has tended at key moments to become a mode of 'affirmative culture', an uncritical affirmation of what is, rather than a labour of intellectual negation (2004). Or, to cite Michael Bérubé, 'For most people, "cultural studies" is not about evaluating and historicizing complex cultural forms, . . . it is all about celebrating the transgressive possibilities afforded by Madonna's video for "Vogue" ' (2005: 8).

How, then, does cultural studies avoid becoming more than merely descriptive, telling, as Meaghan Morris once put it, 'the same old story' in playfully revised forms (Morris 1999: 409)? What, ultimately, are we to make of its claims to political relevance, framed in terms of 'resistance' and 'opposition', when so much of the critical focus to this point has been 'on cultural consumption' (Garnham 1999: 495) and the nurturing of 'dialogue' and 'respect'? Perhaps one answer lies in aesthetics. The great advantage of Badiou's philosophical project is that it remains completely uninterested in the ironies of cultural competency and critique. Culture, for Badiou, is categorically without truth and therefore is of no concern to philosophy. Art, on the other hand, is intimately related to truth. And the nature of that truth rests entirely with what Badiou terms art's 'subtraction' from culture – just as all truth consists in the 'subtraction' of a subject from a 'self', of an event from a situation. Culture, in all its complexity and difference, is just the 'situation', the 'state of affairs' in which a work of art sometimes takes place. In the words of Peter Hallward:

> Against any notion of art as cultural therapy, as particularist, as identitarian or communitarian, as 'imperial' or representative, Badiou affirms the

production of contemporary works of art, universally addressed, as so many exceptional attempts 'to formalize the formless' or 'to purify the impure'. The sole task of . . . art is the effort to render visible all that which, from the perspective of the establishment, is invisible or nonexistent. (2003: 195)

Badiou's remarkable readings of Beckett, Mallarmé and Pessoa proceed from a belief that works of art bring truths into the world by *purifying* their merely 'cultural' environs. What Badiou calls 'inaesthetics' is the faithful act of declaring these movements of purification; observing how it is, for instance, that a poem moves out of 'discourse' to become a truth. 'A truth begins with a poem of the void, continues through the choice of continuing, and comes to an end only in the exhaustion of its own infinity' (2005: 56). The artwork does precisely what 'culture' can never do; it is an *event*, an act in which, to paraphrase Mallarmé, *something will have taken place other than the place*. 'Culture' is the situation in which *nothing can take place but the place*: a continual reaffirmation of the way things are. Again, we can see how apolitical the affirmation of culture per se is in this context; only works of art can have any correspondence with political choice, although they have no direct relation to political truths as such.

A recent initiative in cultural studies has seen a movement towards a renewed articulation with aesthetics, from which, as Michael Bérubé reminds us, a certain line of cultural studies has never really been estranged. And yet, when Bérubé asks, rhetorically:

> Can politically motivated criticism have anything interesting to say about the *form* of cultural forms? What is the role of aesthetic evaluation in such criticism? How should we understand the emergence of the aesthetic as a realm of experience, and its relation to the institutions of modernity? Can an understanding of the aesthetic augment an understanding of social movements, or is one necessarily a distraction from the other? (2005: 9)

we are a long way from any kind of engagement with what Badiou thinks of as the radical purification of artworks. Truths cannot be accounted for via any discourse working with such terms as 'social movements', 'relations to social institutions' or 'aesthetic evaluation', since these terms are already predisposed towards a conception of art that stresses 'the functional and situational character of judgment, and . . . the place of aesthetic judgement in the system of social differentiation' (Bérubé 2005: 8). I suggest that *Les Demoiselles d'Avignon* can be approached *either* in terms of its functional role in constituting a new regime of value ('modernism' and the industry of discourse associated with that); *or* in terms of its truth as such, its purification of a painterly regime of sense and the subjective fidelities it calls into being; but *not* both at once.

What we are then confronted with is the apparent form of a *decision*. On the one hand is a theoretical enterprise proceeding from a neo-Gramscian notion of hegemony and a virtual fusion of the realms of politics and culture. On the other hand is a rigorous, Platonic conception of truth as a process of radical subtraction from the 'state of affairs', and a model of subjectivity defined purely by the fidelity it declares to those truths. Culture is either the field of the possible, replete with political openings; or it is what forestalls the 'impossible', situation-specific truth that alone announces the authentic, singular political intervention. How to choose? Or better: *why* choose?

Badiou himself insists on the necessity of 'taking sides', disavowing pluralisms and interrupting the consensual codes of a prevailing mediocrity. His thought rigorously divides the camps, between a 'serious' philosophical commitment to truths, and a consensus of opinions about the Other that unconsciously mimics the logic of capital itself. And that is its undoubted attraction. In these terms, however, a decision becomes both vitally important and curiously impossible. Daniel Bensaïd has aptly written:

> The absolute incompatibility between truth and opinion, between philosopher and sophist, between event and history, leads to a practical impasse. The refusal to work within the equivocal contradiction and tension which bind them together ultimately leads to a pure voluntarism, which oscillates between a broadly leftist form of politics and its philosophical circumvention. (2004: 101)

Badiou's militant advocacy of the singularity of truths, the radically subjective nature of fidelity, and the non-relational field of the multiple, all render his political thought strangely 'voluntarist' in the sense that Bensaïd charges. What results is 'a worrying refusal of relations and alliances, of configurations and contradictions' (Bensaïd 2004: 105). This is, of course, inversely the very strength of cultural studies, the domain of contemporary thought in which conjunctural, relational and hybrid practices have been most elaborately codified and critiqued. The blind spots of Badiou's political thought (contradictions, relations, coalitions and so on) are ironically illuminated to the richest extent in the intellectual camp of the 'multiculturalist' enemy he most despises. While, from one perspective, this has led cultural studies perilously close to an accommodation with existing relations of power, and an unwitting celebration of 'controlled protests, captive resistances, reactions subordinated to the tutelary fetishes they pretend to defy' (Bensäid 2004: 100), nevertheless the outstanding record of works by writers as diverse as Dick Hebdige, Nancy Fraser and Rey Chow is ample testament to the fact that cultural contradictions and contestations are alive with political implications that make no blip on the austere radar of Badiou's universalism.

Meanwhile, cultural studies' primary deficiency is in providing a satisfactory theory of the event. Cultural studies has been remarkably tight-lipped about the various reasons why so many people have made history by rejecting their cultures in favour of something that happens to render them null and void: the rapture of listening to a prophet who liquidates everything one has previously stood for; the staggering implications of a drought, a depression or an alien encounter. The discipline should learn again the extraordinary political passions implicit in St Paul's epistle to the Romans, the great and serious joy many millions of people have experienced over the centuries in *abandoning* their existing cultural coordinates, for truths that dance all over them like sheet-lightning. If it can recognise the profound significance of truths' shattering passage athwart the matrices of everyday life, and the revolutionary responsibilities of fidelity to such events, then it will have managed to come face to face with the deep paradox of its own constitution as a discipline, as an analytic of the ordinary which refuses to decide on the purport of its own capacities for critique.

The powerful opposition here between *truth* and *culture* is not an accidental one, and one can no more decide for or against either Badiou or cultural studies than one can imagine some magical synthesis of the two. The aporia teaches us something vital about how critical intelligence is itself ultimately determined and deformed by the pressures of material existence. For ultimately, this powerful conceptual antinomy represents a stalled capacity of our own imaginations before the totality of social relations today. On the one hand, there is a profound satisfaction with the sheer diversity and radiant particularity of the human adventure in its present articulation, a celebration of the fact that, despite everything, we have managed to achieve extraordinary acts of resistance and continue to be resilient, inventive and cunning beyond the wildest dreams of our forebears. On the other hand, however, there is the uncanny and sickening sense that all of this is being administered to us as a bribe for the most stultifying and oppressive pall of orthodoxy yet suffered by humankind, a foreclosure of possibilities so extreme and nightmarish that it makes the idea of letting 'our minds be remade and our whole nature thus transformed' attractive as never before. It is just that no event has yet transpired to enlist us in the cause of its radical refashioning of existence. Prior to that event, however, there is one way we can begin to nourish our beleaguered imaginations.

Slavoj Žižek has suggested that, despite their manifest opposition on so many scores, cultural studies and Badiou's thought coincide on at least one point: '[Badiou's post-Althusserianism] shares with its great opponent, Anglo-Saxon Cultural Studies and their focus on the struggles for recognition, *the degradation of the sphere of the economy*' (Žižek 2004: 75). It is also the case that both camps emerged from the very same 'sphere' they currently 'degrade'. Cultural studies 'as an enterprise came out of a set of assumptions about political economy. It continues to carry that paradigm within itself as its grounding assumption and its source of legitimation as a "radical" enterprise' (Garnham 1999: 493). So, too, Badiou's project is steeped in the rhetoric of its Maoist and Communist past, which it can no more dispense with than cultural studies can supersede the Marxism that haunts it like the spectre of a future it too often refuses to acknowledge. It is time for the repressed origins of these antithetical currents in contemporary thought to return to the surface. Certain cultural studies intellectuals are already hard at work forcing the discipline into this inevitable re-encounter with its past. A renewed critique of political economy may seem an unglamorous undertaking, but it should once again ignite utopian passions and prepare the way for what Badiou prophesies but cannot imagine. 'From what source', he asks, 'will man draw the strength to be the immortal that he is?' (Badiou 2001: 14). Arguably, we will draw the strength of our 'immortality' neither from Badiou's adventitious 'truths', nor from cultural studies' fascination with the 'patterns of the present world', but from critical knowledge of 'the equivocal contradiction and tension which bind them together' (Bensäid 2004: 101). And the name of that tensile web is *capital*. Truths and cultures are the warp and woof of our existence, and between them make the future a habitable place; but so long as they languish in the coils of an economic system that divides the spoils in favour of their mutual enemy, they will remain as opposed in fact as they are in the unreconciled theoretical domains sketched here.

Note

1 Recent work on Badiou by one of the contributors to this volume would suggest that it perhaps isn't. See Zylinska (2002); Goffey and Lowe (2003).

Bibliography

Adorno, Theodor (1991), 'Culture and Administration', in Jay M. Bernstein (ed.), *The Culture Industry: Selected Essays in Mass Culture*, London: Routledge, pp. 93–113.

Badiou, Alain (2001), *Ethics: An Essay on the Understanding of Evil*, trans. Peter Hallward, London and New York: Verso.
Badiou, Alain (2003), *Saint Paul: The Foundation of Universalism*, trans. Ray Brassier, Stanford, CA: Stanford University Press.
Badiou, Alain (2004), *Theoretical Writings*, ed. and trans. Ray Brassier and Alberto Toscano, London and New York: Continuum.
Badiou, Alain (2005), *Handbook of Inaesthetics*, trans. Alberto Toscano, Stanford, CA: Stanford University Press.
Bennett, Tony (1992), 'Putting Policy into Cultural Studies', in Lawrence Grossberg, Cary Nelson and Paula Treickler (eds), *Cultural Studies*, London: Routledge, pp. 23–37.
Bensaïd, Daniel (2004), 'Alain Badiou and the Miracle of the Event', in Peter Hallward (ed.), *Think Again: Alain Badiou and the Future of Philosophy*, London: Continuum, pp. 94–105.
Berlant, Lauren (2004), 'Critical Inquiry, Affirmative Culture', *Critical Inquiry*, 30:2, pp. 445–51.
Bérubé, Michael (2005), 'Introduction: Engaging the Aesthetic', in Michael Bérubé (ed.), *The Aesthetics of Cultural Studies*, Oxford: Blackwell, pp. 1–27.
Couldry, Nick (2000), *Inside Culture*, London: Sage.
During, Simon (2005), *Cultural Studies: A Critical Introduction*, London and New York: Routledge.
Garnham, Nicholas (1999), 'Political Economy and Cultural Studies', in Simon During (ed.), *The Cultural Studies Reader*, London and New York: Routledge, pp. 492–503.
Giroux, Henry A. (2000), 'Public Pedagogy as Cultural Politics', in Paul Gilroy, Lawrence Grossberg and Angela McRobbie (eds), *Without Guarantees: In Honour of Stuart Hall*, London and New York: Verso, pp. 134–47.
Goffey, Andrew and Lowe, Shannon (2003), 'The Caesura of Consensus', *Journal for Research in Cultural Values*, 7:1, pp. 97–104.
Hallward, Peter (2003), *Badiou: A Subject to Truth*, London and Minneapolis: University of Minnesota Press.
Hughes, Robert (1980), *The Shock of the New: Art and the Century of Change*, London: BBC.
Morley, David (2000), 'Cultural Studies and Common Sense: Unresolved Questions', in Paul Gilroy, Lawrence Grossberg and Angela McRobbie (eds), *Without Guarantees: In Honour of Stuart Hall*, London and New York: Verso, pp. 245–53.
Morris, Meaghan (1999), 'Things to do with Shopping Centres', in Simon During (ed.), *The Cultural Studies Reader*, London and New York: Routledge, pp. 391–409.
Tolstoy, Leo (2003), *Anna Karenina*, trans. Richard Pevear and Larissa Volokhonsky, London: Penguin.
Williams, Raymond [1958] (1997), 'Culture is Ordinary', in Ann Gray and Jim McGuigan (eds), *Studies in Culture: An Introductory Reader*, London: Arnold, pp. 5–14.

Žižek, Slavoj (2004), 'The Lesson of Ranciere', in Jacques Ranciere, *The Politics of Aesthetics*, trans. G. Rockhill, New York: Continuum, pp. 69–79.
Zylinska, Joanna (2002), ' "*Arous[ing] the Intensity of Existence*": The Ethics of seizure and Interruption', unpublished paper presented at the international conference 'Ethics and Politics: The Work of Alain Badiou', Centre for Critical and Cultural Theory, Cardiff University, 25–6 May.

ARE YOU NOW OR HAVE YOU EVER BEEN A POSTSTRUCTURALIST?

CHAPTER 9

Cultural Studies and Slavoj Žižek

Paul Bowman

The *Guide* is definitive. Reality is frequently inaccurate.
Douglas Adams, *The Restaurant at the End of the Universe*

Friends or *faux amis*?

In recent years the Slovenian philosopher and political and cultural critic, Slavoj Žižek, has had an increasing amount to say about cultural studies – a field in which his work has had a marked impact since the explosive arrival of his first book in English, *The Sublime Object of Ideology* (Žižek 1989). As Michael Walsh observes, even though Žižek was unpublished in English as recently as 1988, he has since published 'an average of more than one monograph a year, not to speak of a [growing] number of edited collections', works which have proved so influential that today 'a speaker giving a presentation at a scholarly conference may now find that s/he is giving the second or third Žižekian talk in a row. For full-blown appearance on the intellectual scene, then, Žižek has few rivals' (Walsh 2002: 390). There are perhaps two glaring reasons for Žižek's phenomenally successful arrival. The first is suggested by Catherine Belsey, who observes that 'when Žižek slips easily and wittily between Kantian philosophy and demotic jokes, Hegel and Hitchcock, the effect is exhilarating' (Belsey 2003: 27). So, Žižek is *fun* (at least for an academic readership used to very dry scholarship), a lively and enthralling read, combining philosophy with popular culture in novel and interesting ways. The second reason is provided by Terry Eagleton, whose now-famous description of Žižek as 'the most formidably brilliant exponent of psychoanalysis, indeed of cultural theory in general, to have emerged from Europe in some decades' now graces the back covers of many of Žižek's publications.

Žižek's theoretically lucid and radically politicised cultural criticism, with its use of examples taken from film, popular culture and everyday life, would thus seem tailor-made for cultural studies. Given this, the fact that most of what Žižek has actually written about cultural studies is often scathingly critical may seem surprising. Tony Myers notes the irony: Žižek's work is increasingly 'a staple on cultural studies programmes' at the same time as it is becoming more and more clearly marked by a growing 'disavowal of cultural studies' (Myers 2003: 124). However, what I want to suggest in this chapter is that Žižek's disavowal of cultural studies is *deliberate* and *strategic* (whilst the knee-jerk adoption or rejection of his work within cultural studies is not always so well considered); that Žižek's strategic and apparently belligerent relation to cultural studies actually offers something of a 'royal road' for approaching and understanding his work; and that making sense of this peculiar relation in fact provides us with a number of important insights into his entire orientation. So this chapter will first examine Žižek's polemics against cultural studies, and assess the grounds and value of this often downplayed aspect of his work for cultural studies. It will do so with the aim of questioning – as Žižek regularly does – the place, role, responsibilities and significance of cultural studies in the contemporary world. After detailing why cultural studies should maintain a critical but affiliative relation to Žižekian theory, the chapter will then conclude by arguing that, from a Žižekian point of view, Žižek actually ought in future to reorientate his strategic relation to cultural studies; and that cultural studies should in turn regard Žižek's critiques as serious theoretical challenges to be engaged with, no matter how problematic they may also appear.

Of *naïfs* and relative fools

Tellingly, Žižek actually contends that cultural studies exists and operates right at the heart – indeed, on the 'radical' side – of a dispute that divides and structures the entire contemporary academic world. That is, he takes cultural studies to be the exemplary case of a strand of scholarship that he characterises (variously) as postmodernist, deconstructionist, relativist, historicist or postcolonialist, which he then opposes to an entity that he calls the 'standard' or 'naïve cognitivist approach' of most other contemporary scholarship (Žižek 2001a: 223). Many may baulk at such a schema and at what may well be taken as a reductive or unjustly simplifying representation of, we must remember, *the entire academic world*. But this is typical Žižek: his work is saturated with (and organised by) sweeping statements, stark oppositions and binary schemas – binaries that ultimately become tripartite, once Žižek's own position is added to the mix. Here, for instance, Žižek is ultimately using those strands of scholarship he sees as being embodied by cultural studies on the one hand, and by the 'cognitivist popularizers of the "hard" sciences' (Žižek 2001a: 210) on the other, merely to argue for his own position, which 'transcends' – or at least trumps – them both. So, quite distinct from scholars like Jacques Derrida, of whose cultural studies 'acolytes' Žižek is most critical, and whose main strategy involves 'microscopic' readings of specific texts (often in order to comment upon wider issues, problems, institutions or phenomena (Derrida 1998: 40)), Žižek's approach is chiefly one of quickly conjuring up such wider issues (through allusion and assertion), so that he can diagnose them in terms of his own preferred categories (Laclau 2004: 327). This is quite problematic, and we will return to this aspect of Žižek's approach in due course. At this stage, it is sufficient to note that when Žižek bandies around terms like 'cultural studies', he is not interested in trying to demonstrate, justify or prove any of his points or assertions. He simply wishes to set the scene quickly for his own philosophising on issues he treats as if already self-evident, widely known and in general circulation.

Žižek's primary claim in relation to cultural studies is that his work has nothing in common with it. This is because he views himself as an 'authentic philosopher' (Žižek 2001b: 125). He views cultural studies as 'ersatz philosophy' (Žižek 2001a: 224). In fact, it is always clear that Žižek himself values and identifies with Philosophy overall. But this leads him to project his own values onto other objects (here, cultural studies is represented as wanting to be philosophy), and to interpret them entirely in his own terms. So, cultural studies is simply 'ersatz philosophy', while the rest of the university is allegedly dogged by the shackling anti-philosophical animus of a 'naive cognitivist approach' (Žižek 2001a: 223). As he puts it, characteristically polemically, his position vis-à-vis these alternatives is neither that of 'today's twin brothers of deconstructionist sophistry and New Age obscurantism' (Žižek 1998: 1,007), nor the 'capitulation itself' of most other social and political thinking, such as that of the 'Third Way' ideologues like Anthony Giddens or Ulrich Beck, whom he regards as the lapdogs of neoliberalist ideology (Žižek 2002: 308, 2001b: 32–3). This pejorative view makes more sense when it is understood that by 'capitulation' Žižek means 'the acceptance of capitalism as "the only game in town", the renunciation of any real attempt to overcome the existing capitalist liberal regime' (Žižek 2000: 95). This 'resignation' to capitalism is something he sees and decries everywhere: in the positions of all 'standard' social and political thinkers, in all political and cultural movements that are not explicitly anti-capitalist (and even, it seems, most that are), as well as, in a different way, in what he calls 'naive cognitivism', or 'the standard functioning of academic knowledge – "professional", rational, empirical, problem-solving' scholarship (Žižek 2001a: 226). For even scholarship that is allegedly neutral, objective and supposedly non-political *is* political precisely because it is that of the status quo (which is a political formation).

Against simple 'capitulation', cultural studies, deconstruction and postmodernism are 'sophistry' because (like New Age mysticism) they do not properly engage with the 'truth', or with 'material reality' (Žižek 2001a: 1–2). The only saving grace that deconstructionism and postmodernism (but never New Ageism) can sometimes have, in his eyes, is that they do not *completely* capitulate to the status quo of today's 'capitalism'. In fact, as we will see, Žižek does think that there is something fundamentally intellectually and politically radical and potentially transformative about cultural studies. This is because integral to the differences he sees between cultural studies and cognitivism is the 'deconstructionist' and otherwise *theoretical* character of cultural studies as opposed to the philosophical naivety of 'standard' scholarship – the ingenuous operating assumption that humans can simply, immediately and directly access the truth of reality in unbiased, unmediated and untheoretical ways. Thus, argues Žižek, there is 'a dimension that simply eludes its grasp'; a dimension 'properly visible only from the standpoint of Cultural Studies' (Žižek 2001a: 223). This dimension is the insight that *all* knowledge, even 'objective' knowledge, is constitutively and inescapably 'part of the social relations of power' (2001a: 225). Despite this insight, however, despite the grain of truth that it holds as its starting point (that we are barred access to the truth, because we are limited, partisan, and flung into a world made up of different discourses and ideologies), the problem with cultural studies is that it does not engage with material reality *properly*. Instead, it contents itself with the 'cognitive suspension' of refusing to ask direct ontological questions about reality in favour of discussing 'different discursive formations evaluated not with regard to their inherent truth-value, but with regard to their socio-political status and impact' (2001a: 219). This, for Žižek, is a cop-out. Thus, he complains, the cultural studies-style scholarship of incessantly 'historicising' and 'contextualising' in terms of politics and power actually *avoids* the hard questions of truth and reality – questions which, to its credit, cognitivism takes on, albeit naively.

The inauthentic relative

Žižek, then, sees mushy, wishy-washy relativists to the left of him and diligent knaves to the right. We might well critique him on the basis of this simplifying schema – as Ernesto Laclau does when he says that Žižek's style often reminds him of the parable of a 'village priest . . . who in his sermons imagined a stupid Manichean to be able to more easily refute Manicheanism' (Laclau 2004: 327). And this tendency in Žižek is certainly problematic. Yet there is a sense in which to criticise Žižek without taking on board *why* he proceeds in this manner is to miss something important. For his target is the anti-theoretical, anti-philosophical, intellectually 'naïve' character of much scholarship, on the one hand, and the overtheoretical but misguided intellectual 'sophistry' of cultural studies in its 'postmodernist, deconstructionist, historicising' forms, on the other. (Žižek is entirely uninterested in any version of cultural studies other than its 'high theory' incarnations, consigning all empirical work to the status (quo) of 'the standard functioning of knowledge'.) In other words, cognitivism is a non-starter while cultural studies stumbles at the first hurdle because of an unfortunate tendency to *relativism*:

> Why is [cultural studies-style] radical historicising false, despite the obvious moment of truth it contains? Because *today's (late capitalist global market) social reality itself is dominated by what Marx referred to as the power of 'real abstraction'*: the circulation of Capital is the force of radical 'deterritorialization' (to use Deleuze's term) which, in its very functioning, actively ignores specific conditions and cannot be 'rooted' in them. It is no longer, as in the standard ideology, the universality that occludes the twist of its partiality, of its privileging a particular content; rather, it is the very attempt to locate particular roots that ideologically occludes the social reality of the reign of 'real abstraction'. (Žižek 2001a: 1–2)

Thus, the postmodern claim of relativism *would* be true were it not for the objective and universal truth of capitalism, which behaves predictably (it commodifies, it exploits, subjecting all to the logic of the market) and obscures its simple actions by blinding us all with a chimerical sense of the all-consuming complexity, disconnectedness or *unmasterableness* of it all. Žižek claims to be able to cut through this misunderstanding by way of his 'authentic' tripartite paradigm, consisting of a combination of the insights of Hegel, Marx and Lacan. Hegel provides a universally applicable (meta-transcendental) way of understanding the logic of historical development (not to mention a proto-Lacanian account of the fundamental human condition in the master-and-slave dialectic (Hegel 1977), a dialectic which renders human identity as always inextricably bound up in complex identifications with significant others, and which Žižek maps onto Freud's Oedipus Complex and into Lacanian theory). Žižek marries this to the ('crude') Marxian claim that the truth of today's material reality is governed by the logic of capitalism. Meanwhile, the problems of the limited, biased contextuality of all viewpoints Žižek 'resolves' through appeal to a series of

Lacanian psychoanalytic insights, wherein, for example, because any viewer's 'gaze is inscribed into the "objective" features' of material reality (2001a: 150), what is required in order to step out of the deadlock between naivety and relativism is for cognitivist science (and everyone else, for that matter) to retheorise objectivity in line with the lessons of Lacanian psychoanalysis. Accordingly, science and other forms of scholarship both need to be psychoanalysed and need to psychoanalyse, and indeed to be contextualised and historicised. But *not* 'relativised'. This is because, for Žižek, there *is* an objective truth and a determinant reality that governs human society: it is the 'material reality', 'objective conditions' and 'logic' of capitalism into which we psychoanalysable subjects find ourselves thrown. Thus, as can be seen from the passage quoted above, relativism may be *relatively* true, but the objective reality of the universality of capitalism has circled around to undercut relativism, by simultaneously *using* relativism's apparent truth (mushy relativism becoming the ideology of capitalism) and *thereby* invalidating it (for in reality, there is no relativism: capitalism is 'universal').[1]

These are the key coordinates of Žižek's claim of 'authenticity'. His Hegel offers a transcendental philosophy of the logical (dialectical) processes of history. This is completed by Marxist knowledge of the 'logic' of capitalism, plus Lacanian psychoanalytic insights into the human condition. In fact, the person that Žižek thinks best managed to '*act*' most successfully against the systemic stranglehold of capitalism was Lenin, and Žižek's ultimate ambition is that of 'repeating Lenin' (Žižek 2001c, 2002). In other words, as Žižek sees it, 'for an authentic philosopher, *everything has always-already happened*; what is difficult to grasp is how this notion not only does *not* prevent engaged activity, but effectively *sustains* it' (2001b: 125). Žižek sees his theoretical responsibilities to be those of 'holding the place' (2000), of repeating the 'truth' of his insights into capitalism, ideology and subjectivity: namely, that although ideology 'goes all the way down' (Walsh 2002: 393), and the 'fundamental level of ideology . . . is not that of an illusion masking the real state of things but that of an (unconscious) fantasy structuring our social reality itself' (Žižek 1989: 33), this is set against the real backdrop of capitalism. Žižek's approach is to insist upon these truths until such a time as . . . as . . . well . . . until such a time as *someone* will 'act' decisively. To put it another way, in Žižek's political theory there is the universal 'system', on the one hand, and on the other the individual (exemplified by Lenin) who has the potential to 'act' in a revolutionary manner, to change this system.

Now this position harbours more than a few difficulties and limitations, and has some highly problematic consequences. One is its apparent superciliousness. As Michael Walsh explains, 'there's no arguing with a thoroughgoing Hegelian; theirs is a position that always-already anticipates (or sometimes just "implies") anything of value that is subsequently voiced' (Walsh 2002: 391). Another is with this very *combination* of a meta-transcendentalist position claiming to know the universal truth of history (Hegel), with a putatively materialist economico-political position claiming to know the truth of contemporary reality (Marxism), and a psychoanalytical position claiming access to the fundamental truth of the human condition (Lacan). In Žižek, they are all presented as if *simply* overlaying, consolidating and unproblematically reinforcing each other, such that Žižek can 'dialectic' his way out of any corner and make pronouncements and diagnoses on apparently *any* subject. This leads to the serious problem of the formulaic repetition that one often finds in Žižek, and the wreaking of a kind of 'violence' on all other forensic, argumentative and methodological considerations. In Žižek, that is, one rarely finds detailed textual analysis (what's the point when you already know what you will find?), no real genealogical, archival or historiographical examination (there is no need when a Marxian and/or psychoanalytic explanatory matrix is already to hand), nor indeed any contextual analysis, whether of his own position or of whatever is under discussion. This is because, from a position always confident that it *already* knows and speaks the truth, there is no need to contextualise one's own 'position' (it *is* the correct one).

Žižek's, one might say, is consequently a very peculiar 'philosophy' or 'theory' – one that does not really *think* (or *read* or *study*) as such. Indeed, Žižek views with suspicion any intellectual position, work or methodological considerations other than those he discerns in Hegel, Marx and Lacan – unless he can represent it as somehow being Hegelian/Marxian/Lacanian. In particular, Žižek is suspicious of cultural studies, because in its historicising, contextualising, relativising, 'positioning', 'politically correct' impulses, it seems both to corrupt his 'authentic' position and to repackage it in an ideologically acceptable form. Indeed, he claims that in contemporary cultural studies, erstwhile radical

> notions of 'European' critical theory are imperceptibly translated into the benign universe of Cultural Studies chic. At a certain point, this chic becomes indistinguishable from the famous Citibank commercial in which East Asian, European, Black and American children playing is accompanied by the voice-over: 'People once divided by a continent . . . are now united by an economy' – at this concluding highpoint, of course, the children are replaced by the Citibank logo. (Žižek 2002: 171)

In other words, for Žižek, despite all appearances, *it's always the economy, stupid!* And, to Žižek as to Marx and Engels, capitalism is a vampire.

So, when it comes to cultural studies, Žižek's critique is based on the claim that any move towards retheorising or rethinking either politics, or the obligations of an engaged intellectual (Hall 2002), necessarily entails a 'silent suspension of class analysis' (Žižek 2000: 96), and hence a regressive move away from 'authentic' (Marxist, class-based) political engagement. As he theorises it, the

> post-modern Leftist narrative of the passage [of cultural studies-type scholarship] from 'essentialist' Marxism, [which viewed] the proletariat as the unique Historical Subject, [and entailed] the privileging of economic class struggle, and so on, to the postmodern [argument about the] irreducible plurality of struggles . . . leave[s] out the resignation at its heart – the acceptance of capitalism as 'the only game in town', the renunciation of any real attempt to overcome the existing capitalist liberal regime. (Žižek 2000: 95)

Not only does Žižek view all of the 'posts-' associated with cultural studies to be politically 'resigned and cynical', then, he ultimately contends that *if* cultural studies is at the radical, challenging, cutting edge of anything at all, that thing is quite simply the advancement of the ideology of contemporary capitalism. In other words, although cultural studies may perhaps tout as radical its preoccupations with such subjects as democracy, emancipation, egalitarianism, identity-formation, multiculturalism, postmodernism, feminism, queer studies, anti-racism, postcolonialism, marginality, hybridity and so on, in actual fact these are simply struggles at the cutting edge of the 'politically correct' ideology of capitalist expansion. For Žižek, cultural studies is thus a trail-blazer of neo-liberal ideology, which pushes 'political correctness' in order to ensure everyone is invested chiefly in their own 'individuality' and 'difference'. This is unfortunate because it precludes effective political struggle, solidarity and agency. For, of course, individuality and difference are construed by Žižek as chiefly manifesting in different, pseudo-individual forms of consumption and leisure activities.

This, for Žižek, is an exemplary travesty, and a corruption of what cultural studies could and therefore should be. Rather than working towards 'true' emancipation (anti-capitalist revolution), cultural studies merely furthers 'politically correct', tolerant, consumer, multiculturalist relativism. It may *seem* 'radical' but, he counters, 'in the generalized perversion of late capitalism, transgression itself is solicited' (2001b: 20); 'transgression itself is appropriated – even encouraged – by the dominant institutions, the predominant doxa as a rule presents itself as a subversive transgression' (2001a: 141); or, 'to put it in Hegel's terms, the "truth" of [any] transgressive revolt against the Establishment is the emergence of a new establishment in which transgression is part of the game' (2001b: 31). Needless to say, to Žižek's mind, this rings true even for such supposedly radical, emancipatory or otherwise transformative intellectual efforts as the 'progressive' cultural studies impulse towards inter-, post- and anti-disciplinarity that developed 'to overthrow the Eurocentrist curriculum' (Žižek 2001a: 215; Hall 1992). To him, it is merely another facet of the 'deconstructive' or 'deterritorialising' logic of capital.

Of course, Žižek was not the first and will surely not be the last to regard the international proliferation of cultural studies within and at the limits of capitalism with some suspicion (Rutherford 2005; Readings 1996; Lyotard 1984).[2] Stuart Hall, for instance, once confessed to being 'completely dumbfounded' by the 'rapid professionalization and institutionalization' of cultural studies in the USA (Hall 1992: 285), and he too suggested that this 'professionalization and institutionalization' could 'formalize out of existence the critical questions of power, history, and politics' (286). Žižek regularly returns to the 'professionalization' of cultural studies, even remarking anecdotally and with a certain incredulity that he has heard of American cultural studies professors who play the stock market (2002: 171–2). This is why he suggests that perhaps 'the field of Cultural Studies, far from actually threatening today's global relations of domination, fit their framework perfectly' (2001a: 225–6). What cultural studies needs to do, he asserts, is to take a dose of its own medicine, take stock of itself, and remember its roots:

> Academically recognised 'radical thought' in the liberal West does not operate in a void, but is part of the social relations of power. Apropos of Cultural Studies, one has again to ask the old Benjaminian question: not how do they explicitly *relate to* power, but how are they themselves *situated within* the predominant power relations? Do not Cultural Studies also function as a discourse which pretends to be critically self-reflexive, revealing predominant power relations, while in reality it obfuscates its own mode of participating in them? So it would be productive to apply to Cultural Studies themselves the Foucauldian notion of productive 'bio-power' as opposed to 'repressive'/prohibitory legal power: what if the field of Cultural Studies, far from actually threatening today's global relations of domination, fit their framework perfectly, just as sexuality and the 'repressive' discourse that regulates it are fully complementary? What if the criticism of patriarchal/identitarian ideology betrays an ambiguous fascination with it, rather than an actual will to undermine it? Crucial here is the shift from English to American Cultural Studies: even if we find in both the same themes, notions, and so on, the socio-ideological functioning is completely different: we shift from an engagement with real working-class culture to academic radical chic.

Despite such critical remarks, however, the very fact of *resistance* against Cultural Studies proves that they remain a foreign body unable to fit fully into existing academia. (2001a: 225–6)

Now, despite the appearances caused by the crescendo of *ad hominem* insinuations here, this is not simply an entirely untenable argument about sincerity versus pretence, nor an easy anti-Americanism argument. It is certainly problematically phrased, particularly in the claim that cultural studies no longer engages properly 'with real working-class culture' (whatever this might ever be taken to mean – and it might be taken to mean lots of different things), having become instead mere 'academic radical chic' in 'the shift from English to American Cultural Studies'. As a Lawrence Grossberg essay title puts it, 'Where Is the "America" in American Cultural Studies?' (Grossberg 1997). For key to cultural studies is the questioning of such distinctions as this one, between 'English' and 'American' cultural studies. Of course, as we have seen, this is a tendency that Žižek thinks exacts a cost on 'an engagement with real working-class culture'. Either way, it should perhaps be assumed that Žižek is simply using the distinction as shorthand, in much the same way that Stuart Hall uses this same schematic in order to discuss the palpably different institutional contexts of cultural studies' reception, development, 'professionalization and institutionalization' (Hall 1992: 285). For, Žižek wants basically to challenge cultural studies to apply some of its own stock insights *to itself*. This is not a new idea, of course. (Indeed, the fluency and fluidity with which Žižek poses the question could itself be taken as a sign of cultural questions having been formalised 'out of existence', or of the main thing that Stuart Hall cautions against in this essay, namely easy 'theoretical fluency', which indicates institutional comfort and political complacency. In Hall's terms, then, Žižek *himself* could be taken as an exemplary case of the institutionally comfortable theoretical formalist.) Similarly, the 'bastard child of capitalist ideology argument' is not a new argument against cultural studies: thinkers like Bourdieu and Readings (Bourdieu 1998; Readings 1996), for instance, have variously argued that cultural studies is unable to comprehend or 'grasp its own condition of possibility' precisely because 'the concepts at its disposal . . . are forged out of a structural mis-recognition of their corporate and ultimately US corporate derivation' (Mowitt 2003: 178). In other words: cultural studies fetishises 'resistance', but the theme of 'resistance' is equally *de rigueur* in the marketing and advertising of brands of jeans, meaning that resistance really is useless.

Specifically, Žižek's argument is actually to do with the vicissitudes of time, place and (yes) capitalism: 'even if we find in both the same themes, notions, and so on, the socio-ideological functioning is completely different'. So the crux of his argument is that when cultural studies first began, its engagement with working-class culture was an involvement with an active and potentially transformative form of politics (working-class, socialist). But subsequently, as socialist class politics were increasingly discredited by mainstream culture, politics and ideology; cultural studies began to prefer 'difference', 'individuality', 'consumption', 'identity politics', and so on. So the extent to which the growth of cultural studies in Western universities is marked by an increasing 'celebration' of such things signifies to Žižek that cultural studies is coming more and more into line with mainstream ideological discourse – whilst still claiming to be somehow radical.

Conclusion: 'When the hurly-burly's done'

So *is* cultural studies really a hapless dupe, or an ignorant, unknowing, unaware pawn of 'capitalism'? Is 'deconstructionism' really a political and theoretical mistake? Is the move from 'essentialist' studies of 'class' to the broadening of the theoretical, ethical and political agenda to embrace questions of ethnicity, gender, sexuality, place and so on really a costly mistake, to the benefit only of 'capitalism'? As Derrida once stated of deconstruction vis-à-vis questions of politics:

> All that a deconstructive point of view tries to show, is that since convention, institutions and consensus are stabilisations (sometimes stabilisations of great duration, sometimes micro-stabilisations), this means that they are stabilisations of something essentially unstable and chaotic. Thus, it becomes necessary to stabilise precisely because stability is not natural; it is because there is instability that stabilisation becomes necessary; it is because there is chaos that there is a need for stability. Now, this chaos and instability, which is fundamental, founding and irreducible, is at once naturally the worst against which we struggle with laws, rules, conventions, politics and provisional hegemony, but at the same time it is a chance, a chance to change, to destabilise. If there were continual stability, there would be no need for politics, and it is to the extent that stability is not natural, essential or substantial, that politics exists and ethics is possible. Chaos is at once a risk and a chance, and it is here that the possible and the impossible cross each other. (Derrida 1996: 84)

Far from relativism, such deconstruction is an impetus to responsible politicisation – a claim of the political character of all institutions, interpretations and establishments. This Žižek would not dispute. But, on the basis of the political character of interpretation (reading/rewriting), Derridean deconstruction asserts the importance of 'microscopic' readings/rewritings of texts (Derrida 1998: 40). Žižek has no patience for this; evidently worrying that there is a mutually exclusive *choice*, an *either-or*: *either* deconstruction (and endless questions about interpretation and textuality) *or* Marxism and politics; *either* theorising *or* action; *either* scholarship *or* politics; *either* theory *or* practice. Now, neither Derridean deconstruction (Derrida 1992; Protevi 2001) nor cultural studies (Hall 1992), nor indeed 'deconstructive cultural studies' (Mowitt 1992, 2002; Hall 2002) – nor even *Žižekian theory itself* – could be satisfied with such a simple opposition between theory and practice, theory and politics. As Žižek notes with approval, cultural studies is aware of its ensnarement within the social relations of power and the political consequentiality of the biases of such key social institutions as the university and its disciplines. However, his strategic polemic in defence of 'pure' revolutionary politics leads him to refuse to theorise politics any further than supposedly free, individual, totalising, voluntarist 'revolutionary acts'.

This has the consequence that Žižek's theory of political change is somewhat limited. According to Simon Critchley, his rigid 'theoretical grid' leads him 'to a complete ultra-leftist cul-de-sac' (Critchley 2003: 65–6). Moreover, as scholarship, this 'type of analysis sacrifices the texture of any particular production for a preemptory political evaluation' (Mowitt 1992: 17). This synthesises into problematic and limiting dogmatism and refusals. His core assertion is that all everyone needs to do is to begin 'finally, again conceiving of capitalism neither as a solution nor as one of the problems, but as *the* problem itself' (2002: 308). Thus, laments Laclau, Žižek 'transforms "the economy" into a self-defined homogeneous instance operating as the ground of society – . . . that is, he reduces it to a Hegelian explanatory model' (Laclau 2005: 237). This has the peculiar double consequence of causing Žižek to refuse apparently *all* political efforts and, paradoxically, all *study of* capitalism. Thus, he even claims that activities 'like *Médecins sans frontières*, Greenpeace, feminist and anti-racist campaigns' provide a 'perfect example of interpassivity: of doing things not in order to achieve something, but to prevent something from really happening, really changing. All this frenetic humanitarian, Politically Correct, etc., activity fits the formula of "Let's go on changing something all the time so that, globally, things will remain the same!"' (2002: 170). As Laclau observes: Žižek refuses 'to accept the aims of all contestatory movements in the name of pure anti-capitalist struggle, [so] one is left wondering: who for him are the agents of a historical transformation? Martians, perhaps?' (Laclau 2004: 327). Simon Critchley goes further: 'What he is unable to think, in my view, is *politics*. That's because he's thinking politics on the basis of the wrong categories, namely psychoanalytic categories. I remain doubtful as to whether Lacanian psychoanalytic categories are going to be able to bring you any understanding of politics, certainly in the way Žižek uses them' (Critchley 2003: 65–6).

In a study of cultural studies, Gary Hall observes that, often, 'the last thing that is raised in all this talk about the importance of politics for cultural studies *is* the question of politics . . . Politics is the one thing it is vital to understand, as it is that by which everything else is judged. But politics is at the same time the one thing that *cannot* be understood; for the one thing that cannot be judged by the transcendentally raised criteria of politics is politics itself' (Hall 2002: 6). In Žižek, the things that it is vital to understand are not only 'politics' but also 'capitalism'. Yet it seems that these are the very things upon which Žižek can shed no strategic light. 'Capitalism' is simply the 'empty signifier' of pure negativity that organises Žižek's entire orientation. It is the tautological start and end-point of his whole thinking. This is a problem, both theoretically and politically; one that Žižek and Žižekian scholars, theorists and activists (whatever a Žižekian activist might be) must address. Cultural studies could be of assistance here – although without pretending to know the answers already. For cultural studies and Slavoj Žižek share an incomplete project, which hinges on the theory and practice of how to make effective ethical and political interventions. Reciprocally, if cultural studies is indeed 'a politically committed questioning of culture/power relations which at the same time theoretically interrogates its own relation to politics and to power' (Hall 2002: 10), then Žižek's demand that it address the political and ideological ramifications of its orientations should constitute the rest of the grounds of an ongoing dialogue between cultural studies and Slavoj Žižek. Of course, Žižek's polemical tone should be addressed. However, cultural studies need never take offence. For Žižek's own approach suggests an unequivocal interpretation of his apparent dismay at and disapproval of cultural studies: in its 'inverted and true form', Žižek's critique is a complement, demonstrating his conviction of the importance of cultural studies. The gauntlet he throws down for cultural studies is merely this 'difficult question: how are we to remain faithful to the Old in the new conditions? *Only* in this way can we generate something effectively New' (Žižek 2001b: 32–3).

Notes

1 In this, Žižek is reminiscent of Michael Hardt and Antonio Negri, who argue that today 'power itself' chants with the postmodernists, postcolonialists, and

all other supposed radicals 'Long live difference! Down with essentialist binaries!' (Hardt and Negri 2000: 139). They argue that 'Power has evacuated the bastion [that most "radicals"] are attacking and has circled round to their rear to join them in the assault in the name of difference' (2000: 138).

2 In a recent issue of the journal *Cultural Studies* (itself only one more instalment in the long-running engagement of cultural studies with the question of the field's position with regard to economics, politics and other 'social relations of power'), Jonathan Rutherford begins his reflection on 'Cultural Studies in the Corporate University' by recalling the memorable edict from his superiors that, even as an academic, his 'priority should be costs' (Rutherford 2005: 297). This prompts the following observations, in a narrative that will be representative of many others working within cultural studies:

> When I got my first permanent, full-time lecturing post ten years ago, my ideal of an academic was modelled on Gramsci's organic intellectual: 'The mode of being of the new intellectual can no longer consist in eloquence . . . but in active participation in practical life, as constructor, organiser, "permanent persuader" and not just a simple orator' (Gramsci 1988). Cultural Studies was about the world beyond the university. I saw the institution itself as a benign presence, the neutral, depoliticised element in the equation. This rather naive view failed to survive the market-based reforms of the subsequent decade. I found myself increasingly preoccupied with the university itself, and my relationship with it. The site of political change was no longer 'out there', but right here in the practice of being an academic and a university employee. I can't recall what it was I lectured about when I first began, but it undoubtedly reflected my own recent struggles in the library, studying postcolonialist texts by Gayatri Spivak or Homi Bhabha. There is an irony in the resurgence of neo-colonialism because Media and Cultural Studies' modules that might incorporate these ideas are sold to institutions in China, India and East Asia. Our universities pursue business in countries with governments who have scant regard for academic freedom and where academics are locked up for writing the wrong kinds of history. This is not the realisation of the dream of international exchange and dialogue. The university is a global business and Media and Cultural Studies finds itself a commodity at the heart of it. (Rutherford 2005: 298)

Bibliography

Belsey, Catherine (2003), 'From Cultural Studies to Cultural Criticism?', in Paul Bowman (ed.), *Interrogating Cultural Studies: Theory, Politics and Practice*, London: Pluto Press, pp. 19–29.

Bourdieu, Pierre (1998), *Acts of Resistance: Against the New Myths of Our Time*, Cambridge: Polity.

Butler, Judith, Laclau, Ernesto and Žižek, Slavoj (eds) (2000), *Contingency, Hegemony, Universality: Contemporary Dialogues on the Left*, London: Verso.

Critchley, Simon (2003), 'Why I Love Cultural Studies', in Paul Bowman (ed.),

Interrogating Cultural Studies: Theory, Politics and Practice, London: Pluto Press, pp. 59–75.

Derrida, Jacques (1992), 'Mochlos, or, The Conflict of The Faculties', in Richard Rand (ed.), *Logomachia: The Conflict of The Faculties*, Lincoln, NE, and London: University of Nebraska Press, pp. 1–34.

Derrida, Jacques (1996), 'Remarks on Deconstruction and Pragmatism', in Chantal Mouffe (ed.), *Deconstruction and Pragmatism*, London: Routledge, pp. 77–88.

Derrida, Jacques (1998), *Resistances of Psychoanalysis*, Stanford, CA: Stanford University Press.

Gramsci, Antonio (1988), *A Gramsci Reader*, London: Lawrence and Wishart.

Grossberg, Lawrence (1997), *Bringing It All Back Home: Essays on Cultural Studies*, Durham, NC, and London: Duke University Press.

Hall, Gary (2002), *Culture in Bits: The Monstrous Future of Theory*, London: Continuum.

Hall, Stuart (1992), 'Cultural Studies and its Theoretical Legacies', in Lawrence Grossberg, Cary Nelson and Paula Treichler (eds), *Cultural Studies*, London: Routledge, pp. 277–94.

Hardt, Michael and Negri, Antonio (2000), *Empire*, London: Harvard University Press.

Hegel, G. W. F. (1977), *Phenomenology of Spirit*, Oxford: Oxford University Press.

Laclau, Ernesto (2004), 'Glimpsing the Future', in Simon Critchley and Oliver Marchant (eds), *Laclau: A Critical Reader*, London: Routledge, pp. 279–328.

Laclau, Ernesto (2005), *On Populist Reason*, London: Verso.

Lyotard, Jean-François (1984), *The Postmodern Condition: A Report on Knowledge*, Manchester: Manchester University Press.

Mowitt, John (1992), *Text: The Genealogy of an Antidisciplinary Object*, Durham, NC: Duke University Press.

Mowitt, John (2002), *Percussion: Drumming, Beating, Striking*, Durham, NC, and London: Duke University Press.

Mowitt, John (2003), 'Cultural Studies, in Theory', in Paul Bowman (ed.), *Interrogating Cultural Studies: Theory, Politics and Practice*, London: Pluto Press, pp. 175–188.

Myers, Tony (2003), *Slavoj Žižek*, London: Routledge.

Protevi, John (2001), *Political Physics: Deleuze, Derrida and the Body Politic*, London: Athlone.

Readings, Bill (1996), *The University in Ruins*, London: Harvard University Press.

Rutherford, Jonathan (2005), 'Cultural Studies in the Corporate University', *Cultural Studies*, 3, pp. 297–317.

Walsh, Michael (2002), 'Slavoj Žižek (1949–)', in Julian Wolfreys (ed.), *The Edinburgh Encyclopaedia of Modern Criticism and Theory*, Edinburgh: Edinburgh University Press, pp. 390–8.

Žižek, Slavoj (1989), *The Sublime Object of Ideology*, London: Verso.

Žižek, Slavoj (1998), 'A Leftist Plea for "Eurocentrism"', *Critical Enquiry*, 2, pp. 988–1009.
Žižek, Slavoj (2001a), *Did Somebody Say Totalitarianism?: Five Interventions in The (Mis)use of a Notion*, London: Verso.
Žižek, Slavoj (2001b), *On Belief*, London: Routledge.
Žižek, Slavoj (2001c), *Repeating Lenin*, Zagreb: Arkzin.
Žižek, Slavoj (ed.) (2002), *Revolution at the Gates: Selected Writings of Lenin from February to October 1917*, London: Verso.

Part III: New Transformations

CULTURAL STUDIES™

CHAPTER 10

Cultural Studies and Anti-Capitalism

Jeremy Gilbert

Let me make one thing very clear before I start. I am not at any point going to argue that something called 'cultural studies', or those who practise it, *ought to* ally itself with something called 'anti-capitalism'. I am going to consider some reasons why they might want to do so, and what some of the logical consequences might be if they did. This is not the same thing as arguing that they should. I might even hope that they will, and declare myself personally committed to such a position. Yet again, I say, this is not the same thing as making an argument that cultural studies necessarily *should* be anti-capitalist. I do not believe that an argument for or against such a position could logically be sustained, because I do not think that there are any absolute and objective grounds upon which it could be argued that cultural studies *should* do anything. That doesn't stop me hoping that it might. With those provisos out of the way, I will offer some considerations as to why those of us working within cultural studies might want to ally ourselves in some sense with 'anti-capitalist' politics. There are several such reasons, relating in part to the long history of cultural criticism in English, in part to the specific history of cultural studies, in part to the political and institutional position in which people working in the field (as students or teachers) find themselves today, in part to the implicit and explicit political orientation of most of the philosophical positions informing much cultural studies.

If cultural studies has a founding text then it is almost certainly Raymond Williams' *Culture and Society* (1982), first published in 1958.[1] One of the key themes of this work is the extent to which the intellectual tradition it identifies and into which it critically inserts itself is one consistently motivated by a critical attitude to the social effects of capitalist modernisation. Although Williams did not use an explicitly Marxist vocabulary until later in his career, it's clear that from the very beginning he was interested in the fact that what links figures such as Burke and Cobbett, Eliot and Cauldwell is partly their shared scepticism towards capitalism as a social form and its various aesthetic manifestations. At the same time, what marks the emergence of cultural studies as a specific discipline, distinct from this longer tradition of cultural criticism, is as much as anything the turn by Williams and then Hall to an explicitly Marxist orientation (cf. Mulhern 2000: 83–92, 124–31). As such, we might well say that a generally sceptical attitude towards capitalism is constitutive of the whole tradition of cultural criticism from which cultural studies emerges, while observing that it is precisely the replacement of that vague, often conservative and reactionary, anti-capitalism with the more complex and politically focused attitude made available by the Marxian critique of capital that constitutes the emergence of cultural studies as a specific discipline with a characteristic methodology.

We should be careful here, however. It would be too simple to see this as a shift from a vague anti-capitalism to an explicit one. Indeed, it is important to understand that, in precise terms, the anti-capitalism of, say, T. S. Eliot is much less ambiguous than that informed by any attentive reading of Marx. Eliot simply disliked capitalism in general, and thought, like many Anglophone writers of his generation (J. R. R. Tolkien having proved the most lastingly influential, perhaps), that capitalist modernity in its entirety had been a mistake which we ought to do our best to reverse (Eliot 1982). Marx, by contrast, was an enthusiast for capitalism's transformatory power, seeing it as the only social system dynamic enough to raise the productive forces to a level which could make socialism possible (Marx and Engels 2002). And, indeed, a powerful populist current runs through cultural studies, which has been both self-articulate and read at various times in terms of a democratic Marxism, a feminist anti-authoritarianism and a liberal celebration of late capitalism. Despite their political differences, this thread links Williams' account of the 'Long Revolution' (Williams 1961) – which saw modernity fundamentally, but not inevitably, as a process of social, political and cultural democratisation, some time before Lefort wrote of 'the modern democratic revolution' (Lefort 1994: 172) – to the often unfairly reviled 'cultural populism' (McGuigan 1992) of the 1980s and beyond. This line of thought has always been concerned with identifying those features of contemporary capitalist culture which can be understood as progressive, according to the norms of a generally unspecified liberal and egalitarian politics. None the less, it is hard to avoid the sense that the eventual adoption of an explicitly Marxian orientation by key writers in cultural studies is indissociable from their initial explicitly anti-capitalist stance. Why exactly should this be so?

I would suggest the reason is as follows. The adoption of Marxism by writers such as Hall and Williams was the concretisation of a position already present in the 'pre-Marxist' or non-Marxist writing of Williams and Richard Hoggart (the other key figure in founding the discipline), which is what really marked it out from the earlier 'culture and society' tradition of cultural criticism. This is a position which specifically orientated itself to the culture and goals of the British labour movement. In particular, it was the long struggle of that movement to establish more egalitarian social conditions than those enabled by an unregulated liberal capitalism to which these writers allied cultural studies at its formative moment. This commitment has remained largely intact within the mainstream of the discipline until very recently, and the overriding importance of this affiliation in determining the political identity of cultural studies surely cannot be overestimated. Cultural studies' 'politics', then, was never primarily a function of the abstract theoretical positions taken up by its key practitioners, but rather a question of the relationship between these positions and those informing wider political struggles. This is precisely the point which commentators such as Francis Mulhern and Terry Eagleton have patently failed to grasp. Routinely condemning cultural studies for its overvaluation of the field of 'culture' and consequent occlusion of the field of 'politics', such writers seem to project their own disengagement from any political project outside the academy onto the objects of their critique (Mulhern 2000; Eagleton 2000).

The fact is that 'cultural studies' – or at least its mainstream, as represented by Hall and Williams – has never claimed that either it or some more widely conceived field of 'culture' could ever substitute for 'politics' or become the sole sphere of meaningful political activity. The sheer weight of commentary offered by Williams and Hall on mainstream parliamentary 'politics' throughout their careers makes a nonsense of this notion (see Williams 1989; Hall 1988). Rather, their project has always been to develop critical positions primarily for those whose social function was to study and teach in universities the humanities which could correlate meaningfully with the core philosophical assumptions of certain radical political movements. This is a much more modest project than that which the likes of Mulhern, Eagleton and Tony Bennett (Bennett 1998) routinely accuse cultural studies of engaging in, but it is one which conversely depends on a much larger and more complex understanding of politics and its relationship to other spheres of activity than that which such commentators seem able to deploy. It is *not* the same thing as substituting intellectual or cultural work for political activism, nor is it even necessarily to argue that intellectual and cultural work are species of activism. It is rather a matter of developing critical positions within the humanities which *correlate* to those of certain social and political movements, for the simple reason that if one is a partisan of those movements then it is preferable for such perspectives to prevail, even in the modest space of the seminar room, than it is for opposing ones to do so.

I should make clear that this is not a formulation ever offered explicitly by Williams, Hall or any other key writer in the field to my knowledge. It may even be one with which they would disagree. What I am offering is not a direct transcription of their reflexive accounts of their practice, but a logical account of what cultural studies has actually been and done which is as uncontroversial and objective as possible. From a contemporary vantage point, it seems clear that cultural studies began life with an explicit commitment to the project of the British labour movement, that it adopted a specifically Marxist position at precisely the moment when an increase in militancy amongst students and workers put Marxism into more general circulation on the Anglophone left, and that it was then persistently modified in the 1970s by an extending series of commitments to the politics of the student revolts, second-wave feminism, anti-racism, anti-imperialism and gay liberation, as those various movements gathered strength and prominence. It also seems fairly uncontroversial to argue that the relative strength and weakness of those movements and their various internal disputes has consequently been the primary source of political and theoretical debate and fragmentation within cultural studies. Logically, this account implies that it makes little sense to consider the changing politico-theoretical make-up of cultural studies simply in terms of some internal narrative of shifting positions and theoretical breaks. Instead, we have to appreciate that the political identity of intellectual work within a discipline like cultural studies will always come to some extent from *outside* the boundaries of that discipline. In the case of cultural studies as such, it is very clear that the positions adopted by its key practitioners have been informed by a sympathy with those strands of the British labour movement which were most committed to a democratic socialism, and that they have changed along with the transformations that those strands have undergone (Williams 1989; Hall 1988). The radical democratic tendencies in the British labour movement and the mainstream of cultural studies should not be confused with each other, but it is the commitment of the latter to the political project of the former which has informed cultural studies' political and philosophical positions for much of its history.

The question which this formulation might raise is that of why the cultural studies practitioner, or even the potential cultural studies practitioner, should choose to adopt a position which is allied to any given political movement at all. My response to this is fairly straightforward: properly considered, this is simply not a question that can be answered from 'within' cultural studies, for it is not one whose answer could ever be limited or specific to cultural studies. The issue of why one adopts a given ethical or political position at all is one of the fundamental themes of philosophy, and it is one that some of the finest minds have considered to be definitively unanswerable (Derrida 1999). Nevertheless, several types of response are usually offered to this question, which tend to answer it by positing such a fundamental ethico-political decision as necessarily consistent with either pure self-interest or some identifiable set of logical principles, and I will shortly consider some versions of these in relation to the current position of cultural studies.

First, however, it is necessary to consider where the story of cultural studies and its relationship to political movements has got to recently. In doing so, it is indispensable to consider the ongoing political crisis of the left since the early 1970s. This is to some extent a global phenomenon. Despite the messianic triumphalism of millenarian commentators such as Michael Hardt and Antonio Negri (Hardt and Negri 2000, 2004), it is hard to disagree that the past three decades have been bad for the labour movement and organisations committed to its traditional political goals, pretty much all over the world. At least in Britain and the US, trade unions have shrunk significantly in size and influence, and anything recognisable as traditional social democratic approaches to policy and politics have more or less disappeared from the agendas of even those political parties that are directly funded by trade unions. This is a situation which poses major problems for anyone – inside or outside cultural studies – who remains committed to a politics whose egalitarian aims are incompatible with the demonstrable social effects of unregulated economic liberalisation within a wholly capitalist economic framework (Crouch 2004; Harris 2005), as most cultural studies practitioners to date have been. This situation might, at its most drastic, be thought to render wholly invalid an intellectual current which has staked its claims to political relevance on the viability of such politics. This is illustrated in the fate of Western European Communism, which, having been relatively significant and well organised throughout the postwar period, disappeared almost overnight following the collapse of the Soviet Union, predicated as it always had been on the possibility that political democratisation in the Soviet bloc might not lead to the complete collapse of actually existing socialism (Sassoon 1997: 730–7). Is this what should happen to the tradition of socialist cultural studies which has dominated the discipline since its inception? Should it accept that socialism and social democracy have been utterly defeated and give it up? Maybe. Should it suspend the idea of commitment to concrete political movements or ideals and instead interrogate its most fundamental *ethical* assumptions, to consider what their intellectual, social, cultural and political implications would be in this new context? It should, as it happens, and I refer the reader to the relevant chapter by Joanna Zylinska in this volume. But would such a move necessarily prevent us from returning, eventually, to some concrete political commitments? By no means. Would such commitments have to entail an abandonment of the New Left tradition and all of its legacies? Perhaps. Perhaps not.

One reason for thinking not is that this tradition was never uncritical in its support for the British labour movement. More than this, it was precisely the intellectual current to which Raymond Williams and Stuart Hall (amongst others) were central which offered the first diagnoses of the immanent crisis of that movement and which accurately forecast the shape of the political problems it was likely to face in the 1980s and 1990s. From the late 1950s, and most notably in the later 1970s and 1980s, the 'New Left' and its legatees, in the form of writers such as Hall and Eric Hobsbawm, warned that the changing social, economic and cultural make-up of the UK would render the traditional politics of 'labourism' – which had always been undemocratic, anti-intellectual and bureaucratic – untenable, appealing only to a shrinking minority of 'traditional' propertyless, white, male manual workers (Hall 1988). This current was committed to that broader movement to formulate a democratic, internationalist, feminist socialism which was not irredeemably hostile to emergent trends in youth culture, or 'lifestyle' politics and so forth, and which manifested itself in forms such as the policies of Ken Livingstone's Greater London Council and the project to modernise and democratise the Labour party in the 1980s. This was a politics which therefore correlated closely with the consistent but rarely specified politics informing the vast majority of work in cultural studies: egalitarian, libertarian, democratic, anti-elitist and concerned primarily with issues of class, 'race', gender and sexuality. Until as late as the early 1990s leading figures in both the British Labour party and the Democratic party in the US gave voice to perspectives which were unmistakably informed by a very similar agenda (for example, Robert Reich, Bill Clinton's first secretary of labour, and Robin Cook, the first foreign secretary to be appointed by Tony Blair). As such, practitioners in the mainstream of cultural studies, committed to a politics which was broadly that of the New Left and its descendents, could reasonably be said to be deploying critical perspectives which correlated to those informing major political movements with realistic agendas for social change and reasonable chances of success in implementing them. But of course, that was before Blair and Clinton.

There is little doubt that the writings of commentators such as Hall had a direct influence on the thinking of key figures in the formation of New Labour: not least on Tony Blair himself (Finlayson 2003: 116–24). There is also now no question that the political conclusions drawn by Blair et al. were radically at odds with those of figures such as Hall, despite the fact that they shared a range of observations as to the historical conditions which made possible the triumph of the New Right over the postwar social-democratic consensus. This relatively simple situation produced a good deal of confusion in many quarters for a long time. The fact that New Labour was, like the New Democrats in the US, not a legacy of the New Left but a product of its final defeat took a long time to sink in. While many hoped that New Labour's short-term accommodation to neo-liberal common sense would give way in time to a more progressive programme of economic and political democratisation, this has not been what has happened at all. Consequently, the political isolation of figures such as Hall has mirrored a larger situation whereby the 'academic left' has found itself detached from any actually existing political movement. The direct conclusion drawn by Angela McRobbie is that 'left-academic endeavours, like cultural studies, must rely more on the academic environment and the university for their continued existence . . . Voices like that of Hall now have to function as "productive singularities", and there is a certain loneliness in such distinctiveness' (McRobbie 2005: 38).

This may be true. Indeed, one can add here the observation that the massive expansion of the university sector and the emergence of the 'knowledge economy' is creating a situation in which universities are much more deeply embedded in the fabric of our social life, and hence much more important sites of political activity, than they once were. Relying on the academic environment of the university may therefore not amount to the retreat from public engagement it might once have done. None the less, I want to raise some questions concerning the assertion that Hall's voice is necessarily distinctive and lonely. It certainly is, if one's view of politics is confined to the field of national parliamentary politics. In that arena, the views espoused by a figure like Hall today lack any significant correlate. However, there is a wider world out there, in which 'the left' has not ceased to exist and has not made such a full accommodation with neo-liberalism that it now lacks any meaningful political identity. It is precisely in the vacuum created by the collapse of Communism and social democracy and in opposition to the full hegemony of neo-liberalism that contemporary 'anti-capitalism' has emerged as a distinctive political formation in recent years. Even more significantly, this 'movement of movements' defines its difference from the traditional lefts of Communism, labourism and social democracy in precisely the same terms that the New Left once did, and in many cases there is a direct lineage linking the libertarian, anti-soviet Marxism of the 1950s, the radical upsurge of the 1960s and the 'new social movements' of the 1970s to the 'anti-capitalist' politics of today. As such, there remains a strong correlation between the positions taken by Hall and emergent international movement for social change, even if Hall's direct discernible influence on the 'anti-capitalist' movement has been negligible.

There isn't space here to elaborate at length on the history and details of the 'anti-capitalist movement'. It is of the nature of this definitively postmodern radicalism that its sources are multiple, its histories discontinuous and its agendas multifarious. One thing that is certain is that 'anti-capitalism' (see Tormey 2004 for an expert explanation of this term) or the 'movement of movements' (Mertes 2004) is at the very least a partially imaginary construct, a concept whose function is not to name something that already exists but performatively to will into existence a coherent entity. It would be easy to say that behind this label lay nothing but an international diffusion of sporadic resistances to neo-liberal hegemony. This may well be true, but it also changes nothing, because the same could be said of almost all political movements, at least at key junctures in their history. The notion of the working class as an organised political force, of the 'class struggle' as a coherent challenge to the power of capital, even the idea of the 'labour movement' where one might have seen simply a random assortment of trade unions and reformist political parties, are and were all to some extent imaginary. So any attempt to relate the history of the 'anti-capitalist movement' is going to be inevitably partial and controversial. What follows should therefore be treated as a provisional sketch rather than a definitive history.

During the 1990s, the various strands of the movement emerged into the spaces vacated by the organised left following its global political defeat at the hands of neo-liberal capitalism. Led by the New Right governments of Thatcher and Reagan but supported also by nominally socialist governments such as Mitterand's in France and Hawke's in Australia, the project to dismantle much of the apparatus of the welfare state in the West and to destroy Eastern European socialism met with little effective resistance in any quarter. It is in the hope of offering resistance to the otherwise unchallenged hegemony of liberal capitalism and its socially and environmentally destructive consequences that the new movement has arisen. From the 'refounded' militant wing of the disbanded Italian Communist party (Rifondazione Comunista) to the 'direct action' radical ecology movements of the UK and North America (McKay 1998), most of its key elements in the Northern hemisphere draw one way or another on the organisational forms and libertarian, radically democratic rhetoric of the 'new social movements' (in particular deep ecology, the peace movement and second-wave feminism). In the South, this movement has also drawn on indigenous traditions of non-hierarchical organisation and a long history of democratic and socialist militancy in parts of Latin America and India. It had two particularly spectacular manifestations in the 1990s.

First, 1994 saw the beginning of the Zapatista uprising in Mexico. From that date up until the present time, this group of indigenous rebels led by the former Marxist intellectual 'subcommondante Marcos', whose characteristic rhetoric combines a penchant for poetry with an obvious familiarity with and sympathy for postmodernist, radical democratic and postcolonial critiques of classical revolutionary politics (Marcos 2001), has gathered worldwide support for their non-violent campaign of opposition to the Mexican government and the North American Free Trade Agreement through their use of the worldwide web (Tormey 2004: 129–36). Second, the cycle of semi-violent protests against the World Trade Organisation (WTO) and its policies which began in the late 1990s culminated in a perceived victory when the 1999 meeting of the WTO at Seattle was effectively prevented from concluding its business by a well coordinated campaign of disruption by large numbers of activists (Tormey 2004: 38–69). These are only two examples of the 'movement' in action, however. Others include the anti-sweatshop campaigns on US campuses documented in Naomi Klein's international bestseller *No Logo* (Klein 2000), the radical farmers' movement led by French militant José Bové (Bové and Dufour 2001), and large sections of the organised opposition to the US-led invasion of Iraq.

The decisive turning point, however, has almost certainly been the establishment and success of the World Social Forum (WSF), because of its attempt to create and make permanent a new kind of democratic institution rather than simply to engage in short-term tactical disruption of commercial or political activity by governing institutions. Initially conceived as a counter-conference to the World Economic Forum, held in the Brazilian city of Porto Alegre, the first WSF was attended by some 20,000 activists and NGO workers from around the world. By 2005, the now-annual gathering was attracting 150,000 and had spawned countless regional equivalents around the world, from the European social forums in Florence, Paris and London to the city-based social forums in places as distant as Genoa and Boston (Cassen 2004; Wainwright 2003: 42–69). Essentially an interconnected set of rolling and recurrent conferences, the WSF process has far to go before it impinges directly on, say, electoral politics, especially in the North (although some credit the success of the Forum with helping the left-wing Worker's Party to win state power in Brazil in 2002). None the less, the sheer existence of this unprecedented exercise in international deliberative democracy stands as a major achievement, and evidence that the movement against neo-liberalism must be seen now as something more than merely a disparate collection of impotent protests. While some may complain that this 'anti-capitalism' lacks any positive programme, others might argue that the coalition bound together by the politics of 'one no, many yeses' (Kingsnorth 2003) is precisely that required by philosophical positions such as radical democracy, a socialist deconstruction or the philosophy of difference, which would reject the hegemony of neo-liberalism without imposing a single model of the future. This anti-capitalism is therefore not a revolutionary utopianism, but just the kind of open-ended, pluralistic refusal to endorse the hegemony of contemporary capitalism that the New Left always argued for. Seen in this context, Hall's is very far from being a lonely voice: never have so many been raised in condemnation of neo-liberalism and in calls for a truly democratic alternative which could realise the legacy of the radical movements of the late twentieth century.

The 'left-academic', then, should she or he wish to, certainly has the choice today to be something less lonely than a 'productive singularity' (a pedantic excavation of this terminology might lead to the conclusion that no singularity is ever actually lonely, and that if it was it could not be productive, because every singularity is also a node in an infinite network of relations which constitutes the field of its potential productivity – see Nancy 2000 – but we'll leave that to one side for now). These academics can, if they want to, adopt a position which correlates with that of a vibrant, international and forward-looking political movement. Given that this movement happens to have inherited most of the attitudes and much of the history of those political traditions which have informed the mainstream of cultural studies to date, this shouldn't be a terribly traumatic transition, and it's one for which contemporary cultural studies is equipped with plenty of resources. So what would the consequences of such a move be? They would not necessarily – let us be clear – involve any kind of direct political activism, but they would involve the orientation of teachers, researchers and students to a range of perspectives which are typical of the 'movement of movements'. In many ways, this would involve no change at all from cultural studies' established practices, because the politics of class, race and gender are all important themes within the movement. Nonetheless, it would involve engagement with a range of themes which have had relatively little explicit prominence within cultural studies in recent years, and it is worth considering what some of these might be.

While it is notoriously difficult to extrapolate a coherent programme from the multifarious strands and demands of the 'anti-capitalist' movement, certain issues have emerged as central to its aims, rhetoric and philosophy. Most obviously, an emphasis on the defence of 'the common' or even 'the commons' has become a central means by which to resist the normative hegemony of neo-liberalism and its philosophical assumptions (Klein 2004). This terminology draws a deliberate historical parallel with the history of the enclosures in the UK: that process by which lands which had been held and farmed 'in common' by peasant communities for centuries were enclosed and appropriated by local gentry, creating the necessary conditions for the capitalisation of agriculture in the eighteenth and early nineteenth centuries and expropriating a population which was thereby forcibly transformed into the world's first true industrial proletariat. It sees the privatisation and marketisation of essential services – water, health care, housing, education – typical of recent government policies the world over as an equivalent process, and one which can only be resisted in the name of an ideal of human collectivity and mutuality at odds with the neo-liberal ideology of competitive individualism and relentless privatisation.

This politics has a clear resonance with some of the very earliest work in cultural studies: Williams' interest in the formation of communities and the possibility of a 'common culture' (Williams 1982: 332) was constitutive of his entire project. Thinking through the conditions of possibility of common life and interrogating the hegemonic normativity of certain kinds of individualism are tasks which cultural studies has been undertaking since the moment of its inception, but they are also tasks which this political situation lends a new urgency (for those who want to carry them out at all) and which cultural studies has become somewhat unaccustomed to. The critiques of racism, patriarchy and homophobia which came into cultural studies from the social movements of the 1970s, which at the time could be mobilised directly against active elements of hegemonic ideologies, are still often wielded as if nothing much had changed in the past thirty years. Today, in the era of cosmopolitan capitalism, when the right-wing administration of President George Bush can promote a black woman (Condoleezza Rice) to one of the highest offices of state, and a large part of gay culture consists of a highly public and depoliticised sector of the leisure industry, there is little friction between the hegemonic ideology of competitive, consumerist individualism and a liberal feminism or anti-racism divorced from its socialist antecedents. As I have remarked elsewhere (Gilbert 2003), students today often receive the critique of identity-essentialism as nothing more than a restatement of individualist liberal humanism: 'these cultural differences are not essential, therefore they are superficial to our real individualities'. The only way out of this impasse is to renew the critique of individualism once associated with Marxism and class politics, which today finds a new correlate in the politics of the common in a way which refuses the class essentialism of that earlier moment. This is not merely a matter of returning to the roots of cultural studies, however. The attempt to rethink the politics of collectivity is one of the key themes of recent work in those strands of contemporary philosophy – poststructuralism and post-Marxism – which have been most central to cultural theory in recent years. One could cite here Giorgio Agamben or Jean-Luc Nancy, both prominent philosophers concerned to elaborate a contemporary thematics of community (Agamben 1993; Nancy 1991, 2000). The most famous example, however, must be Hardt and Negri's account of 'the Multitude', the collectivity that is not a meta-subject, which is an explicit contribution to this philosophical discussion and to the global anti-capitalist movement with which they ally themselves (Hardt and Negri 2004).

This is a useful example because it can illustrate the kind of relatively subtle modification to existing practice which would be required of a cultural studies which was explicitly committed to thinking in solidarity with the anti-capitalist movement. Hardt and Negri draw attention to the symbiotic conflict between the endless creativity of the multitude and what they call 'Empire': the complex network of power, mediated by various state, inter-state and corporate institutions, which governs contemporary capitalism. A good example of this relationship is that between the vast network of fans, musicians, producers, DJs, programmers and so on who constitute today's global music culture and the complex network of institutions – record labels, shops, royalties agencies, legal institutions, industry bodies – attempting to control its production and distribution for profit: the music industry, in other words. Jason Toynbee, in two recent works, has commented on the lengths to which the industry must go in order to transform the products of music culture, which almost always emerge from a process of 'social authorship', into commercial commodities identifiable as the private property of named individuals or corporations (Toynbee 2000, 2002). The continuity between Toynbee's analysis, Hardt and Negri's conceptual framework, and the political orientation of the anti-capitalist movement is striking, even though Toynbee himself deploys a largely conventional Marxist analytical framework. All are predicated on an appreciation of creativity as inherently social in character and of collectivity as inherently productive. In exposing the arbitrary working of individualist culture, Toynbee deploys a critical perspective which correlates with the anti-individualist politics of the common, and in the process illuminates an important aspect of contemporary power relationships from a perspective potentially allied to the anti-capitalist movement. As such he offers an exemplary exercise in anti-capitalist cultural studies, and one wholly in tune with current anti-capitalist politics.

Not all of the major concerns of the anti-capitalist movement fit so easily into established frames of reference for cultural studies. One of the main strands of this movement is radical ecology, as represented by a range of organisations from mainstream NGOs such as Friends of the Earth through the various European Green parties to the militant 'green anarchism' of Earth First. The implications of green politics are deep and wide-ranging for any established political position. In particular, it raises major questions concerning the viability of any social model based on ever-intensifying levels of material consumption. The mainstream of cultural studies has been characterised since the 1960s by a populist rejection of any puritan condemnation of popular culture, and since the 1980s by an emphasis on consumption as a potentially creative act which cannot be condemned or analytically marginalised without skewing our entire understanding of human social life (and particularly, in the advanced consumer economies, the role of women). In the context of ecological crisis, any naive celebration of consumer culture looks increasingly anachronistic, but this is not to say that the insights of the consumer populist tendency ought to be abandoned. Rather, cultural studies is faced here with an urgent set of questions: how far are contemporary cultural forms inherently bound up with an unsustainable system of production/consumption? What would be the cultural implications of a shift towards sustainability, and what cultural conditions would make such a shift politically possible? This is not the place to begin trying to answer those questions, but it is worth observing that, once again, intellectual resources with which to engage them already exist within the traditions of British cultural studies and post-structuralism: both Raymond Williams and Félix Guattari wrote books on ecological themes (Guattari 2000; Williams 1975), and the emergent fields of bio-ethics and ecocriticism may provide invaluable tools in developing them for the twenty-first century.

Further examples could fill several volumes, and many of the chapters in this book could be read as elaborations on these speculative suggestions. This all leaves open some significant questions, however: what have been the attitudes of cultural studies writers and 'anti-capitalists' to each other to date? What would be the implications for the movement of an 'anti-capitalist cultural studies'? In response to the first question, it has to be said that the two groups have largely ignored each other. The most striking exception is probably the New York-based academic Andrew Ross, who having begun his career as a writer clearly within the tradition of cultural studies, has, in his engagement with the concerns of political tendencies such as the anti-sweatshop movement, turned increasingly to a kind of straightforward political journalism as his characteristic mode of writing (to be clear – this is not a criticism) (e.g. Ross 2004). More typical is the attitude exhibited by McRobbie in the remarks cited above, and the relative lack of interest in the emergent anti-capitalist movement displayed by Hall and his colleagues during the 1990s (Bird and Jordan 1999). As I have suggested elsewhere (Gilbert 2004), the Gramscian New Left's parochial focus on the British experience has tended, and is still tending, to define the parameters of its political vision, and within those parameters the anti-capitalist movement does not matter at all.

On the other side, anti-capitalist literature and practice rarely if ever demonstrate any awareness of cultural studies' existence. A partial exception is Naomi Klein, who counterposes the anti-sweatshop movement to the campus-bound narcissism of identity politics (Klein 2000), while also directly and indirectly drawing on work in the cultural studies tradition in making its arguments about the commodification of the image in the emergence of brand culture. But Klein's tendency to reinvent the Situationist/Frankfurt-School wheel is also depressing to anyone with an undergraduate knowledge of cultural theory. More widely, the movement in fact displays many of the features of the Anglophone left which helped to provoke cultural studies into existence in the first place. A complete failure even to begin to understand what might be at stake in winning popular support and a self-righteous contempt for the totality of popular culture are the main features of any discussion of cultural issues within the anti-capitalist literature. More striking, however, is the simple absence of such discussion at all. A glance at any Indymedia site reveals the extent to which the general engagement with 'cultural' issues – from the 'arts' to 'lifestyle' questions – is at best marginal and more commonly non-existent. A puritanical abstention from ordinary cultural life – apart from the obligatory attendance at samba drumming classes and occasional punk gigs – is a notorious feature of 'activist' life.

It was just this kind of 'cultural illiteracy' from which many in cultural studies once sought to save the Anglophone left, and this could be a task which a new strand in the discipline might set itself: to give to the emergent movement a vocabulary and a space in which wider reflection on life beyond the protest and the action can take place. However, a related contribution might be made which is both subtler and arguably more important. The mainstream, 'New Left', Gramscian cultural studies tradition has always maintained that politics is a 'war of position', a long-term process of trench warfare in which winning over large numbers of relatively 'passive' supporters is as important for success as cultivating highly committed cadres of activists. It's this which, in countries like the UK, 'anti-capitalism' has so far proved extremely bad at doing. And it's this which can't happen unless anti-capitalism begins to emerge, not only as a discontinuous set of oppositional political currents, but as a family of attitudes on a range of interconnected issues. From this point of view, as I have already suggested, simply by existing, by informing the ordinary academic work of lectures, seminars, journal articles and research projects, an anti-capitalist cultural studies could make a contribution. This need not be a matter of practitioners focusing all their attention on explicit questions of hard politics, or on addressing the elusive, imaginary, 'wider audience' which seems always out of the reach of academics, but of researchers, teachers and students carrying out their work from a position of quiet but explicit sympathy with the forces struggling against neo-liberalism, in the terms outlined above.

The question that remains for this chapter is why, having said all this, should anybody want to bother? Why trouble ourselves with an 'anti-capitalist' cultural studies when we could instead practise a cultural studies whose commitment to libertarian individualism, avant-garde digital aesthetics and casual multiculturalism, justified in terms of a crude misreading of Deleuze or Derrida which would make them apologists for any kind of destruction, would render it enormously attractive to corporate funders and government agencies? Why indeed? Many are already heading down that path, and many more undoubtedly will. I can't offer much in the way of inducement, I'm afraid. There are a few things to reflect on, however.

If, as McRobbie implies, the university is to be a safe haven not just for the 'left-academic' but for any kind of independent intellectual work, then it will have to be defended. Anyone who thinks that the university as a space not entirely governed by the logic of corporate power and the commodification of all knowledge can be saved without some wider defence of the public sector is living in a dream world. Anyone who thinks that existing political elites in the North will protect it because it is the decent thing to do is ignoring the last thirty years of political history. Almost without exception, governments of all political persuasions throughout the world have been intent on dismantling as much of the public sector as possible, for more than a generation now. Layer after layer has been peeled away, and today in the UK even secondary schools are increasingly in the hands of private corporations with an explicit remit to deliver education tailored to the needs of the entrepreneurial economy (Whitfield 2001). Those who think that universities are going to remain safe places for long are in for a shock. If even the 'productive singularities' of the academic left are to retain a home in the twenty-first century, then it will have to be fought for one way or another. This is exactly the fight that the anti-capitalist movement is engaged in today. Of course, as I have insisted, even an explicitly anti-capitalist cultural studies will not amount to a very major contribution to this fight. Only levels of political militancy which the professional classes are not historically inclined to display, except at real moments of crisis, are likely to have any chance of defending such privileges as academic autonomy and liberal education for students. If you want a reason, as a researcher, teacher or student, to orientate your cultural studies in an anti-capitalist direction, then that reason will only be that you want to orientate your politics in that direction too. You may or may not wish to do that, and in the end I doubt that I could write anything to persuade you either way. But if you want to be free to practise cultural studies at all, then you may soon have no choice.

Note

1 Of course, Richard Hoggart's *The Uses of Literacy* was published a year earlier, but its long-term impact on the overall shape of the discipline was considerably less.

Bibliography

Agamben, Giorgio (1993), *The Coming Community*, trans. Michael Hardt, Minneapolis: University of Minnesota Press.

Bennett, Tony (1998), *Culture: A Reformer's Science*, London: Sage.

Bird, Tessa and Jordan, Tim (1999), 'Sounding Out New Social Movements and the Left: Interview with Stuart Hall, Doreen Massey and Michael Rustin', in Tim Jordan and Adam Lent (eds), *Storming the Millennium: The New Politics of Change*, London: Lawrence and Wishart, pp. 195–215.

Bové, Jose and Dufour, François (2001), *The World is Not For Sale: Farmers Against Junk Food*, trans. Anna de Casparis, London, Verso.

Cassen, Bernard (2004), 'Inventing *ATTAC*', in Tom Mertes (ed.), *A Movement of Movements*, London: Verso, pp. 152–74.

Crouch, Colin (2004), *Post-Democracy*, Cambridge: Polity.

Derrida, Jacques [1991] (1999), *Donner la Mort*, Paris: Galilée.

Eagleton, Terry (2000), *The Idea of Culture*, Oxford: Blackwell.

Eliot, Thomas Sterns [1939] (1982), *The Idea of a Christian Society*, London: Faber and Faber.

Finlayson, Alan (2003), *Making Sense of New Labour*, London: Lawrence and Wishart.

Gilbert, Jeremy (2003), 'Friends and Enemies: Which Side is Cultural Studies On?', in Paul Bowman (ed.), *Interrogating Cultural Studies*, London: Pluto, pp. 145–6.

Gilbert, Jeremy (2004) 'The Second Wave: The Specificity of New Labour Neo-Liberalism', *Soundings*, 26:1, pp. 25–45.
Guattari, Félix (2000), *The Three Ecologies*, trans. Ian Pindar and Paul Sutton, London: Continuum.
Hall, Stuart (1988), *The Hard Road to Renewal: Thatcherism and the Crisis of the Left*, London: Verso.
Hardt, Michael and Negri, Antonio (2000), *Empire*, Cambridge, MA: Harvard University Press.
Hardt, Michael and Negri, Antonio (2004), *Multitude: War and Democracy in the Age of Empire*, New York: Penguin.
Harris, John (2005), *So Now Who Do We Vote For?*, London: Faber and Faber.
Kingsnorth, Paul (2003), *One No, Many Yeses: A Journey to the Heart of the Global Resistance Movement*, London: Free Press.
Klein, Naomi (2000), *No Logo*, London: Flamingo.
Klein, Naomi (2004), 'Reclaiming the Commons', in Tom Mertes (ed.), *A Movement of Movements*, London: Verso, pp. 219–29.
Lefort, Claude [1981] (1994), *L'Invention Démocratique*, Paris: Fayard.
Marcos, Subcommandante Insurgente (2001), *Our Word Is Our Weapon: Selected Writings of Subcommandante Insurgente Marcos*, New York: Seven Stories Press.
Marx, Karl and Engels, Friedrich [1848] (2002), *The Communist Manifesto*, London: Penguin.
McGuigan, Jim (1992), *Cultural Populism*, London: Routledge.
McKay, George (ed.) (1998), *DiY Culture: Party and Protest in Nineties' Britain*, London: Verso.
McRobbie, Angela (2005), *The Uses of Cultural Studies*, London: Sage.
Mertes, Tom (2004), *A Movement of Movements*, London: Verso.
Mulhern, Francis (2000), *Culture/Metaculture*, London: Routledge.
Nancy, Jean-Luc (1991), *The Inoperative Community*, trans. Peter Connor, Lisa Garbus, Michael Holland and Simon Sawhney, Minneapolis: University of Minnesota Press.
Nancy, Jean-Luc (2000), *Being Singular Plural*, trans. Robert D. Richardson and Anne E. O'Byrne, Stanford, CA: Stanford University Press.
Ross, Andrew (2004), *No Collar: The Humane Workplace and its Hidden Costs*, Philadelphia: Temple University Press.
Sassoon, Donald (1997), *One Hundred Years of Socialism*, London: Fontana.
Tormey, Simon (2004), *Anti-Capitalism: A Beginner's Guide*, Oxford: Oneworld.
Toynbee, Jason (2000), *Making Popular Music*, London: Arnold.
Toynbee, Jason (2002), 'Beyond Romance and Repression: Social Authorship in a Capitalist Age', www.opendemocracy.net/media-copyrightlaw/article_44.jsp.
Wainwright, Hilary (2003), *Reclaim the State: Experiments in Popular Democracy*, London, Verso.
Whitfield, Dexter (2001), *Public Services or Corporate Welfare*, London: Pluto Press.

Williams, Raymond (1961), *The Long Revolution*, London: Chatto and Windus.
Williams, Raymond (1975), *The Country and the City in the Modern Novel*, Oxford: Oxford University Press.
Williams, Raymond [1958] (1982), *Culture and Society*, London: Hogarth Press.
Williams, Raymond (1989), *Resources of Hope*, London: Verso.

THE UNITED STATES OF CULTURAL STUDIES

CHAPTER 11

Cultural Studies and the Transnational

Imre Szeman

The 'transnational' follows perhaps only the 'global' as *the* central buzzword of the contemporary era, a concept-metaphor that is meant to describe the general conditions of the contemporary era as such. Replacing the older concept of the 'international' as the name for the play of ideas, identities and communities beyond the nation, the transnational opens up new conceptual and theoretical spaces for imagining solidarities, social formations and cultural practices which (at least potentially) might exceed what many feel to be the parochialisms and paternalisms of the nation and the politics of the nation-state era. One could argue that compared to the related and today more commonly employed concept of 'globalisation' – which has now come to be fixed, in the academic and public imagination alike, as having to do almost solely with the global spread of the institutions and ideologies of neo-liberal economics – the political valence of the transnational is still undecided in a way that makes it useful for forms of cultural analysis that aim to interrupt established forms of power and their legitimation through and by culture, especially as such power is theorised as circulating beyond the nation as well as within it.

The use of the word 'transnational' originates as a description of corporations that not only have a presence in different countries (which would make them 'multinationals'), but whose commercial and financial activities have allowed them effectively to transcend national boundaries and the legal and legislative controls once exerted on them by nation-states. This is the sense of the 'transnational' invoked by the former CEO of General Electric, Jack Welch, who once described the ideal location for his company to be a giant barge that could be lugged around the world as needed to take advantage of shifts in the economic climate.[1] But this is only one sense of the 'transnational.' As Bruce Robbins has pointed out in reference to the related concept of 'cosmopolitanism', 'Capital may be cosmopolitan, but that does not make cosmopolitanism into an apology for capitalism' (1998: 8).

The same could be said for the transnational. It is a concept that is theoretically productive, not only because it captures the present mode of a capitalism that very effectively mobilises bodies, money and energies across national boundaries, but also because it holds open the promise of a new politics beyond the dead-end of the (so-called) representative democracies of contemporary liberal states. In this later sense, the 'transnational' acts as an incitement for new kinds of theoretical manoeuvres that might help to produce human communities and solidarities no longer in thrall to global capitalism and which cut across the always artificial boundaries of national belonging, while nevertheless maintaining the lived reality of cultural 'disjuncture and difference' (Appadurai 1996).

As a concept that names both the conditions of contemporary economic, social, political and cultural life, as well as the new situation that a left-cultural politics would want to bring into existence, it could be claimed that much recent theoretical work has been written with the problems and possibilities of the transnational in mind. While eschewing the declaration of universalising theoretical schemas, contemporary theory has come to see the conceptualisation of extra- or post-national forms of belonging (political, social and cultural) as one of its major problematics. Examples of the range of recent work on the transnational include the vast literature on globalisation and its discontents (from Arjun Appadurai's *Modernity at Large* (1996) to Saskia Sassen's writings on global cities (2001)), the revolution introduced by new communication technologies and new media (from Manuel Castells (1996) to Lev Manovich (2001)), the re-visioning of universalisms and cosmopolitanisms (as in Jacques Derrida's *On Cosmopolitanism and Forgiveness* (2001), Judith Butler et al.'s *Contingency, Hegemony, Universality* (2000) and Pierre Bourdieu's essays in *Acts of Resistance* (1998), albeit in different ways), the return of the discourse of ethics (e.g. in the work of Alain Badiou – see Murphet's chapter in this volume), the implications of the transnational for ideas of disciplinarity and the university (e.g. Gayatri Chakravorty Spivak's *Death of a Discipline* (2003) and Bill Readings' *The University in Ruins* (1996)), and all of the fascinating theoretical work related to the analysis of the global character of contemporary capitalism and its implications for politics today (e.g. Giorgio Agamben's *Homo Sacer* (1998) and *State of Exception* (2005), and Michael Hardt and Antonio Negri's *Empire* (2000) and *Multitude* (2004) – see the chapters by Neilson and Hall in this volume).

These texts are heterogeneous enough to make it evident that work on the transnational does not constitute a clearly defined 'school' or distinctive theoretical approach (like Marxism, deconstruction or psychoanalysis). Indeed, its presence in the themes and problematics of such a wide range of different analyses might make it seem that, like the concept of 'postmodernism' before it, the transnational is largely a periodising concept whose specific contents are worked out in highly variable and distinct ways in the writings of different theorists. Yet while the problematic named by the transnational may be broader and more general than many other concepts that have emerged in recent years, it can nevertheless today be seen to play an essential role in the activities of both cultural studies *and* what is in this book being called theory, albeit in different ways. At the same time, the general problematic named by the transnational has also generated important reflections on the grounds and origins of both practices. As theory and cultural studies have gone global, and have found themselves circulating outside their spaces of 'origin,' both have of necessity had to examine their potential cultural biases and inflections in their efforts to open themselves to and, indeed, encounter ideas and concepts from 'elsewhere' in all of their destabilizing and productive Otherness. Of course, theory and cultural studies both regard themselves as self-critical practices attentive to their own analytic and conceptual limits. Nevertheless, within this, theory contains a certain potential to push cultural studies beyond the latter's own understanding of the implications and challenges of the transnational, at least to the extent that cultural studies has tended to focus primarily on the epistemological issues and quandaries that the transnational raises for a politics of culture carried out with the entire globe in mind. What it has consequently often failed to consider adequately in doing so is the broader deformations and transformations of the category of *culture* itself, which have both accompanied and helped to produce the massive changes in contemporary economics, society and politics that are identified with the transnational. For the transnational forces us to consider seriously that the very object of cultural studies – culture – has been radically changed in ways that require the activity of the field to shift from what has remained its basic orientation: the study of cultural objects and practices of everyday life in relation to power. I begin here by first describing the relationship of cultural studies to the transnational (which holds lessons and insights for the global spread of theory, too), before examining the engagement of some contemporary theorists with the transnational (including Jameson, Hardt and Negri, and Yúdice) and showing how such work can help us to generate new ideas about the transnational and cultural studies alike.

The transnational functions within cultural studies on at least three distinct levels. The evocation of the transnational signifies perhaps first and foremost the spread of cultural studies beyond the national sites and spaces with which it has been typically identified – beyond that familiar trajectory that begins with Birmingham, before splintering off to the United States, Australia and Canada. In this first instance, cultural studies becomes transnational when it has exceeded the spaces of its Anglo-American origins, still finding itself in the UK, but now also in Finland, Taiwan, Turkey and Brazil, thereby becoming as globalised as the popular cultural forms with whose analysis it is still often identified. For a field that has always viewed its transformation into a 'discipline' warily, the emergence of cultural studies as a globalised academic practice has been one of the signal developments of the past several decades. One of the chief markers of this development has been the creation of the (International) Association of Cultural Studies (ACS), which has held its bi-annual meetings at Tampere, Finland (1996, 1998 and 2002), Birmingham, UK (2000), and Urbana-Champaign, USA (2004), with the 2006 meeting scheduled for Istanbul, Turkey. There are now cultural studies associations in Austria, Australia/New Zealand, Canada, Japan, Taiwan, Switzerland, the UK and the USA; centres, networks and programmes in many more nations, including China, Croatia, Denmark, Finland, Germany, India, Israel, Jamaica, the Netherlands, South Korea, Sweden, Turkey and Venezuela; with conferences and colloquia held in still other locations, such as Portugal and Greece.[2] In addition, the past decade has seen the birth of a number of new journals whose explicit aim is to enable movement across 'state/national/sub-regional divisions, scholarship and activism, modalities/forms of knowledge, and rigid identity politics of any form' ('Editorial Statement' 2000: 5), including *Inter-Asia Cultural Studies*, *Public Culture* (published by the Society for Transnational Cultural Studies) and the *International Journal of Cultural Studies*. Even if we were to measure the presence of cultural studies around the world only through these most visible institutional signs, it is apparent that cultural studies as a professional practice is now truly transnational (or, at a minimum, multinational) in a way that it was not only a decade ago.

A second connection between the transnational and cultural studies, one that operates at a different level from the first, relates to the sites of cultural analysis themselves. No longer focused primarily on national contexts or local situations related (in the last instance) to the national, cultural studies has come increasingly to explore genuinely transnational scenes and scapes – for instance, the new media cultures generated by Turkish television broadcast to European audiences, the practice of filmmaking in the West by diasporic directors from the Third World, the audiences for Bollywood films in Central Africa and Lebanon, the social implications of the global commodity trade in sugar and coffee, and even the use made by East Asian consumers of McDonald's, that prototypically 'American' cultural-consumer space (Aksoy and Robbins 2000; Naficy 2003; Mottaheddeh 2004; Hitchcock 2003; Watson 1997). This second iteration of the transnational in cultural studies draws attention to the limits of cultural analyses that fail to read the politics of cultural production and consumption without due attention to the now globalised 'flows' of power, people and discourse – flows that have reorganised significantly the long-imagined cultural fidelity of the local to the national, or of individuals to their physical communities. It is not simply that some examples of cultural studies can still focus on the details of location while others now mine the cultural spaces between nations. It is rather that an awareness of the transnational forces recognition of the fact that the local is always already organised by global forces, institutions and structures that play an essential role in the dynamics of specific situations and circumstances. If in the first instance pairing cultural studies with the transnational is meant to suggest that the former is an academic practice that is now (almost) everywhere, this second level forces a reconsideration of the typical analytical focus of cultural studies away from the national and the local. What has accompanied this shift of analytic focus to the transnational is a renewed attention to the political economy of culture and the material conditions of possibility of social and cultural forms in the context of 'global circuits constituted by the long-term historical trajectories of geo-political and neo-colonial structures' (Chen 1998: 4). Much work in cultural studies that focuses on the circumstances and contexts of globalisation approaches the transnational at this level.

The third function of the concept of the 'transnational' in cultural studies takes this analytic and epistemological challenge one step further. Even assuming that the narrative of the rise of cultural studies in Birmingham (and for many, its fall in the US) is correct,[3] the 'transfer' of cultural studies to other intellectual, social, political, national and indeed transnational contexts raises serious and difficult questions about the politics of this intellectual inheritance. As mentioned above, theory and cultural studies are both characterised by a heightened self-reflexivity concerning the historical and social conditions for the emergence of specific approaches, problematics, themes and topics. It thus comes as no surprise that those who would seek to make cultural studies 'work' in other situations would also be conscious of the problems of 'travelling theory' – that unequal sharing of theoretical resources around the globe that uncannily mirrors dominant economic flows. The production and export of 'Theory' (and theory) in the West (and primarily in English and French) for consumption in 'secondary' markets in Latin America, Asia, Eastern Europe and Africa situates it as part of the larger sphere of contemporary cultural production (films, television and so forth) through which critics have argued that Western (capitalist, cultural) hegemony has been relentlessly affirmed. Likewise, the subaltern origins of cultural studies in Antonio Gramsci's Italian South, in adult education classes in post-World War II Britain, or indeed in relation to other disciplines, does not guarantee that it retains this status in its shift from North to South. It is telling, for instance, that the official formation of the ACS at the 2002 meeting was greeted with criticism by some participants for the still small role played by scholars and students outside of North America, Australia and Western Europe. And for all the diverse national sites at which cultural studies finds itself institutionally represented today, one cannot avoid considering the significant absences as well, such as Africa, where (with the notable exception of South Africa) institutional formations of cultural studies exist at present only in a minor form, if at all. It has today become essential to consider the politics of the internationalisation of theoretical discourse in general, whether in so-called 'high theory', literary studies, postcolonial studies (where an especially rich dialogue around these issues has taken place) or cultural studies.

Though these three levels at which the transnational operates in and on cultural studies are distinct, they are nevertheless related in an intimate and inseparable way. The fact that there are practitioners of 'cultural studies' in Taiwan and Turkey (and not just scholars, but associations, journals, university programmes and so on) brings the other two methodological levels into play immediately, and with them, a whole host of difficult and important questions. Just what kind of cultural studies is this, and what affinities or family resemblances does it have to cultural studies in the UK, for example – itself a disparate, changing and difficult-to-categorise formation that exists both in and outside of universities?[4] Does cultural studies in Taiwan and Turkey need to have such affinities still to be 'cultural studies'? And is the research that takes place at these new locations 'transnational' or does it focus on local and national issues? There is often an assumption that, say, Asian cultural studies is transnational, or contributing to the transnationalisation of cultural studies, without taking into account the content of that work – which can at times be anything but transnational in its scope. Last, but not least, certainly as far as this book is concerned, what roles can and does theory play in all this as something distinct from cultural studies? For instance, I earlier suggested that what is in this volume being called and understood as theory (the work of Agamben, Butler, Derrida, Laclau, Spivak, Žižek and so on) can help move cultural studies beyond the limits of the latter's own understanding of the implications and challenges of the transnational. But are there other forms of theory in other parts of the world that are different from 'Western theory' in significant ways, too? Or does this question, which is meant to attend to difference, represent in fact yet again a desire for an exotic theoretical 'other'? Is theory primarily a 'Western' mode of discourse? Is the very idea which underpins this book, that of thinking about cultural studies in relation to theory, only really appropriate in relation to Western formations of cultural studies? Might it not be somewhat contradictory, if not indeed impossible, to do so in other places? Though some of these questions have been addressed (numerous times) in other fields in the context of other recent intellectual debates – for instance, in discussions of cosmopolitanism in postcolonial studies – the presence of institutions of cultural studies around the world and the increasing attention to the analysis of transnational contexts make them more pressing for cultural studies than ever. It is the challenge of these questions that I want to bring to bear on the already available body of writing concerned with analysing the implications of the transnational for cultural studies.

Clearly, there is a link between the newly transnational contexts and forces within which cultural studies now takes place and is disseminated, and the political promise of the transnational discussed at the outset – that is, between the existing politics of knowledge and power on a global scale, and the possibility of creating genuinely new forms of knowing that might challenge and interrupt dominant forms of power. Consequently, an interrogation of the potential cultural parochialisms and conceptual blind spots of cultural studies constitutes, for me, one of the most important and compelling 'theoretical' projects in the field today, and is in fact a necessary precondition for any serious study of that other transnationalism to which so much attention is currently being paid: that of global institutions and forces, extra-national identities and global culture, transnational communications systems, new global social movements and the like.

What is at stake for cultural studies with respect to the transnational in this regard can be seen in Akbar Abbas's and John Nguyet Erni's introduction to their recent anthology *Internationalizing Cultural Studies* (2005). The title of the book draws attention to the central task they have set for themselves in compiling the collection. Rather than reflecting a cultural studies that is already 'internationalised' (an adjective of a completed process), Abbas and Erni want to intervene in the uneven flow of knowledge in contemporary cultural studies, 'internationalizing' it by bringing together work from outside the dominant streams of Anglo-American cultural studies. They write:

> A certain parochialism continues to operate in Cultural Studies as a whole, whose objects of and languages for analysis have had the effect of closing

off real contact with scholarship outside its (Western) radar screen. In the current moment of what we call the 'postcolonial predicament' of Cultural Studies, in which a broad hegemony of Western modernity is increasingly being questioned among Cultural Studies scholars from around the world, we must consider any form of internationalization as an effort – and a critical context – for facilitating the visibility, transportability, and translation of works produced outside North America, Europe and Australia. (2005: 2)

The process of internationalising cultural studies in the way Abbas and Erni propose demands more than simply adding representative works from outside of the West to a pre-existing sense of what constitutes cultural studies: received ideas of cultural studies need to be challenged, examined, rethought – and changed. To achieve a genuine pluralisation of cultural studies, Abbas and Erni argue that 'we must allow the notion of "elsewhere" to retain its critical and interrogative edge' (2005: 2). The essays collected in their book are thus intended already to be other than work necessarily or explicitly part of an identifiable history of cultural studies written with Birmingham at its centre. Rather, these works are to be seen as connected to the writing of other genealogies of cultural studies, whose origins lie in the work of such diverse figures as José Martí and Frantz Fanon, the Brazilian literary critics António Candido and Roberto Schwarz (Cevasco 2000), the social and literary criticism of Wole Soyinka and Chinua Achebe in Nigeria, or, in China, the work of both the early twentieth-century writer Lu Xun and Fredric Jameson's influential lectures on postmodernism at Beijing University in 1985 (Hutters 2003). Cultural studies as imagined by Abbas and Erni is distinguished from other practices that have engaged with 'elsewhere' (pre-eminently the discipline of anthropology) by its insistence on an otherness that does not constitute in the main an 'epistemological problem', blocking the acquisition of knowledge, but one that is 'capable of looking back and talking back' (2005: 3). Instead of generating universal knowledge that is impeded by the Other, cultural studies is thus seen as moving us 'towards a [general] politics of knowledge and culture, which we believe is the major trajectory in Cultural Studies' (2005: 4). As it is transnationalised, cultural studies is seen as a critical practice that is able to challenge its own origins in Western modernity in such a way as to effectively make use of the dislocating energies of knowledges from 'elsewhere'.

But it is here that we can begin to see some of the ways in which the encounter of cultural studies with the transnational does not push far enough. For instance, as positive as Abbas and Erni's view of transnationalised cultural studies might be, one cannot pass over some of the epistemological (and political) problems that arise out of such a project. To follow up on one of the questions posed earlier: in what sense is the cultural studies described here still identifiably 'cultural studies'? Jon Stratton and Ien Ang (1996) have pointed out that if the encounter between cultural studies produced at different sites and within distinct intellectual traditions is to be 'as open-ended and open-minded as cultural studies itself wants to be, the "internationalization" of cultural studies cannot mean the formation of a global, universally generalisable set of theories and objects of study. At the same time, a *rendez-vous* [of intellectual traditions] would be useless if it were merely a juxtaposition of already fixed positions of difference' (1996: 363). Abbas and Erni, and indeed, many of the other critics who have explored the promises and problems of the transnationalisation of both theory and cultural studies (Ang and Stratton 1996a, 1996b; Chen 1996a, 1996b, 2000; Denning 2001; During 1997; Hitchcock 2003; Lee 2003; Mato 2001, 2003; Morris 2004) are right to insist on the need to pluralise cultural studies. In many respects, the vision of a cultural studies defined neither by fixed juxtapositions of pre-existing differences, nor by agreement on a generalised set of theories and objects, can be seen as a rearticulation on a greater geographic scale of the anti-disciplinary and conceptual looseness that has characterised cultural studies all along. Nevertheless, even in such a conceptually open discipline, the process of opening up and pluralising the range of work that is considered to in fact be 'cultural studies' threatens to expand the category so widely that it risks losing all meaning and significance. After all, analysis of 'the politics of knowledge and culture' – the minimal connective tissue suggested by Abbas and Erni to hold together different kinds of work – has become a signal feature of critical work in *and* outside of universities across the world, whether or not it is done explicitly under the banner of cultural studies. The work of essayists, critical journalists, non-fiction writers, cultural producers, anti-globalisation activists and the like has focused just as intently on the political uses and abuses of knowledge and culture as has cultural studies, which has come increasingly to signify only the academic version of such practices. We might then want to ask whether such a broad category – a 'politics of knowledge and culture' – is sufficient to enable work from different regions to find enough of significance in common to constitute the broader intellectual and political project that has been associated with cultural studies. Does the concept of the transnational create the conditions for an internationalised academic practice called 'cultural studies', or does it in fact radically pluralise what we understand as cultural studies in ways that go beyond what Abbas and Erni and other critics imagine?

If the project of a transnational cultural studies is understood to be one whose constitution is always in the process of being produced, never to be definitively arrived at, always alive to the promise of difference, then the latter seems to be the result: a vastly expanded sense of cultural studies that goes well beyond the academy. The transnational challenges cultural studies to take seriously the idea that the practices associated with academic work in cultural studies are to be found in other social and cultural spaces, especially if the forms that theory takes 'elsewhere' are considered; it also requires that we go beyond the enumeration of those institutional sites and spaces in different national contexts that constitute the most obvious level at which cultural studies has gone transnational. Stratton and Ang insist that contemporary cultural studies be assessed as 'a geographically dispersed plurality of intellectual trajectories and movements, largely in the post-1960s period in Western, English-speaking countries, which, under precise historical conditions which need to be further explored, converged into the aforementioned international *rendez-vous*' (1996: 375). It should come as no surprise that these diverse trajectories and material circumstances have produced different forms and spaces in which the questions of the power of knowledge and culture have been taken up, and that as cultural studies moves outside of the English-speaking world a far broader plurality of 'intellectual' practices and movements would come into focus. This is in fact one of the key points made by Venezuelan theorist Daniel Mato, who argues that cultural studies in the West relies on too narrow an understanding of both 'the intellectual' and the range of practices comprising cultural studies to capture or explain accurately what constitutes 'cultural studies' in Latin America. To take just one concrete example: there is no Brazilian academic association of cultural studies on a par with the Cultural Studies Association of Australasia, nor a journal devoted to work in the field. At the same time, *Mais!*, the Sunday arts and culture supplement to the São Paulo daily newspaper *Folha de São Paulo*, features work by a range of cultural producers (critics, poets, politicians, activists and so on) that directly addresses the politics of knowledge and culture that Abbas and Erni identify as the 'major trajectory in Cultural Studies' (2005: 4). Popular music in Brazil has made explicit interventions into the links between culture, knowledge and power (Brown 2003; Veloso 2003), and from the World Social Forum movement to the Landless Peasant Movement (Movimento sem Terra) there are ongoing challenges to accepted definitions of knowledge throughout all sectors of civil society.

Such a radical expansion of the practices of cultural studies, which would include op-ed columns, demonstrations, political pamphleteering and so on, does not, however, seem to be what Abbas and Erni (or indeed, most of those who have discussed the transnationalisation of cultural studies) have in mind. They describe their aim of 'internationalising' cultural studies to be the production of a 'critical project that can satisfy two interrelated necessities: (a) the need to rediscover neglected voices and (b) the need to challenge the constructed singular origin of Cultural Studies' (2005: 5). Their primary goal would appear to be the reconstitution of cultural studies as a field, retaining the critical energies of cultural studies while being attentive to the way in which all fields exclude ideas and concepts as much as it brings them together. But they express another goal for a transnationalised cultural studies as well: to 'cultivate the ground for comparisons over *structured* differences (rather than random differences) under the conditions of globalization' (2005: 5). If the transnational prompts a re-evaluation of what 'counts' as cultural studies, it also insists on the need to undertake comparative work that would, among other things, help us to understand the important contiguities and interrelations of 'the broad and dispersed project of cultural decolonization around the world' (2005: 9). Such comparative work can point to differences across regions as well as to more general, global logics, and can be productive without having to insist on the 'formation of a global, universally generalisable set of theories and objects' (Stratton and Ang 1996: 363). Indeed, thinkers with very different attitudes about the degree of danger posed by Western-centred theory and theoretical discourses have insisted on the intellectual productivity of placing even very different spaces into comparative analysis. While highly attentive to 'local' theories and theorists in her own situation, Maria Elisa Cevasco, a Brazilian literary and cultural critic who has written extensively on the work of Raymond Williams, describes the introduction of a postgraduate programme in cultural studies at the University of São Paulo as an opportunity to 'counteract the seemingly endless proliferation of particularisms and random difference that marked much contemporary cultural theory, and show that different projects were determined by the same world order, which helps explain their structural similarities' (2000: 436). Mato meanwhile examines the geo-historical points of connection between cultural studies in Asia and Latin America, noting that what is shared in cultural studies as practised in these regions, but lacking in the US, is attention to 'labour movements and trade unions, human rights, imperialism, the Cold War, decolonization, neo-liberal reforms, militarization, state violence, political repression, democratization, etc.' (2001: 489). In the work of Cevasco, Mato and other thinkers, comparative work produces not only insights into local circumstances, but new understandings of the shape and character of the practices of cultural studies in which they themselves are engaged. Points of connection across regions and vital points of difference and particularity are brought into focus in a way that bears out the productivity of thinking of 'internationalising' or 'transnationalising' cultural studies as an ongoing process, without this necessarily transforming cultural studies into a catch-all category that might confirm in a negative way Angela McRobbie's famous characterisation of cultural studies as a practice whose 'authors are making it up as they go along' (1992: 722).

The overall impact of the transnational on cultural studies is thus to pull it as an academic practice towards a consideration of the globe (institutionally, epistemologically and analytically) and to push it in a direction that it has always wanted to go – out of the academy and into the world. But in both this push and pull lurk still greater challenges for the practice of cultural studies that cannot, it seems, emerge out of cultural studies' own attempts to address the transnational. It is here that theory provides ways of thinking about the transnational that could and should produce further shifts in how we understand the practice of cultural studies beyond those discussed so far. For the most part, even in work as careful as Abbas and Erni's, cultural studies seems to take the transnational at its most obvious: as the name for what is understood to be a primarily geographic phenomenon, whose most significant implications are themselves geographic – the global spread of culture and cultural studies – and, at one remove, epistemological. In response to the transnational, the old insistence of cultural studies on preserving and enabling plurality and difference against those hegemonic forces that push in the opposite direction is simply writ large over the globe. That this is accompanied by appropriate epistemological anxieties about the possible hegemonic aspirations of cultural studies itself does little to problematise or question the fact that what remains at the core of even a transnationalised cultural studies is a largely unaltered or unquestioned idea of what constitutes 'culture' and the politics and theoretical approaches adequate to it. Confronting the transnational does not seem to require that cultural studies confront, too, how it conceives of culture in the wake of the transnational, even as it sets out to make sense of a world it understands to be characterised by enormous change. The transnational is taken as a description of a new condition for culture related to the sudden dissolution of its old boundaries and its increased global motility. Yet the culture that is suddenly mobile and deterritorialised retains its older, 'affirmative' form: as a concept which Herbert Marcuse argues 'plays off the spiritual world against the material world by holding up culture as the realm of authentic values and self-contained ends in opposition to the world of social utility and means. Through the use of this concept, culture is distinguished from the civilization and sociologically and valuationally removed from the social process' (1988: 94–5). The transnational insists on the end of thinking about culture primarily in relation to geographic space – the end of the link, for instance, of culture to nation that originates in Romanticism in the work of thinkers such as Johann Gottfried Herder or Hippolyte Taine. Shouldn't we expect then, too, that it would have an impact on the very way we understand 'culture', and thus on how we practise cultural studies, above and beyond worries about the politics of travelling theory explored thus far?

If cultural studies has focused primarily on the geographic implications of the transnational, in contemporary theory the transnational has come to name the structured, interconnected, and global social transformation that has accompanied the final decisive spread of capitalism to every corner of the globe (the proletarianisation of every hitherto unproletarianised population, the real and not just formal subsumption of labour into capital, and so on); the dissolution of national boundaries and cultures, so fundamental to a geographic understanding of the transnational, plays a role here, too, but more as symptom than as ultimate cause. In the work of theory, especially in forms of contemporary post-Marxism, the transnational names not just a change in the scope of culture, but a fundamental shift in the operations of culture, power and the relations between them. To some extent, an investigation of this shift has been an ongoing concern since World War II, from work on the implications of mass culture on society and politics in Max Horkheimer and Theodor Adorno's 1947 *Dialectic of Enlightenment* (1988) to Jean Baudrillard's investigations of the politics of the simulacrum and the question of the postmodern more generally. What the transnational insists on is the need to explain such shifts and transformations in relation to dispersed but integrated networks of power that take in the entire globe, and not just in 'developed' countries where we might expect to find Guy Debord's 'society of the spectacle' most advanced. It is in prompting a rethinking of culture as the name for specific techniques or elements of such a global system of power that theory can push cultural studies past the limits it reaches and sets with respect to the transnational. These limits are signalled symptomatically above by the dissolution of cultural studies into cultural criticism in general, on the one hand, and by the relatively innocuous insistence on the productivity of comparative work, on the other. The challenge posed by the transnational for cultural studies goes beyond this; and it is what I see as theory's greater willingness to address the kind of structural and systematic questions that are capable of offering a view of the changed grounds of culture that makes a rigorous engagement with it so important for contemporary cultural studies.

Marcuse's description of the 'affirmative' character of culture, which arises out of the tendency for criticism to focus on specific cultural objects or practices as opposed to general 'cultural' processes or structures, was meant to draw attention to the limits of traditional forms of humanistic and evaluative criticism. One of the aims of cultural studies has been to reveal the hidden politics of older forms of cultural criticism precisely by focusing on process and structure, in part through an expansion of the range of what 'counts' as culture from 'high' culture to the everyday life of the popular and the mass. In the process, however, there has emerged a tendency in cultural studies to imbue the practices and objects it studies with a more or less traditional 'cultural' character through its very insistence on the distinctiveness of these practices and objects from the world of 'social utility and means'. Process and structure are in turn gainsaid, nowhere more so perhaps than in the surprising inability of cultural studies to see the category of culture as historical through and through, and thus open to change and significant reorientation.

David Lloyd and Paul Thomas argue that contemporary understandings of 'culture' emerge as part of the modern state's development of institutions geared to the development of manageable citizen-subjects in the wake of the expansion of formal democratic rights. In its modern usage, culture patches over 'the division of intellectual and manual labor [that] was increasingly formative of specialized or partial individuals' (1998: 2) through an insistence on 'the harmonious cultivation of all the capacities of the human subject' (1998: 2). If the nation has not entirely disappeared with the transnational, its institutions and the functions of culture articulated in and through it have radically changed: today, it is not manageable national subjects that are required, but self-managed transnational ones with changed social roles and functions – a shift that goes well beyond the obvious articulations about the globalisation of American mass culture that are often taken to signal an engagement with the consequences of the transnational on culture. Theoretical approaches to the transnational have focused on just this radical transformation of culture at a moment of extensified and intensified globalisation. For instance, beginning with his own work on the postmodern, Fredric Jameson has insisted on the need for theory to grapple with what he describes as the 'prodigious expansion of culture throughout the social real, to the point at which everything in our social life . . . can be said to have become "cultural" in some original and yet untheorized sense' (1991: 48). The modernist idea of culture which located its power in its transcendence of the social – an idea that continues to fuel the politics of cultural studies as much as it does the identity of various avant-gardes – no longer holds in a situation in which 'aesthetic experience is now everywhere and saturates social and daily life in general' (Jameson 1998: 100). In *The Expediency of Culture*, George Yúdice focuses similarly on the myriad ways that transnationalism has created a situation in which culture today has become a resource for 'socio-political and economic amelioration' (2003: 9). 'No longer experienced, valued, or understood as transcendent' (Yúdice 2003: 12), culture is appealed to as an engine of capitalist development through 'creative cities' initiatives, the production of 'authentic' difference for touristic purposes and so on, in ways that challenge 'many of our most basic assumptions about what constitutes human society' (Rifkin, cited in Yúdice 2003: 12).

The expansion and transformation of culture to fill the entire space of the social necessitates new forms of cultural studies that no longer rely on essentially modernist or affirmative understandings of the relationship of culture to the social and to power, but which engage with this new situation in which, somehow, everything is cultural, though not in the way we have long imagined culture. The precise forms such a cultural studies might take remain to be seen, though an intimation of the shape of such future cultural studies can be seen in theoretical works that take up the challenge of the transnational directly, such as Hardt and Negri's *Empire* (2000). One need not agree with the overall conclusions or even many of the specific arguments made by Hardt and Negri to see the productivity of their use of Michel Foucault's notion of biopolitics, and Gilles Deleuze's description of a 'society of control', in conjunction with an analysis of the transnational character of the production and reproduction of social life. At one point, Hardt and Negri controversially argue that 'postmodern' and 'postcolonial' theories end up 'in a dead-end because they fail to recognize adequately the contemporary object of critique, that is, they mistake today's real enemy . . . a new paradigm of power . . . [that has] come to replace the modern paradigm and rule through differential hierarchies of the hybrid and fragmentary subjectivities that these theorists celebrate' (2000: 138). The same could equally be said even of a cultural studies that has taken up the transnational: however attentive it might be to the multiple modalities of culture today, it nevertheless misses the new operations of culture in relation to a new paradigm of power. What cultural studies now has to understand – well beyond the vocabulary of coercion and consent – are the complexities of the biopolitics of 'culture' as these are differentially arrayed across the globe. Though Hardt and Negri are interested in understanding as precisely as possible the mechanisms through which power operates today, they in fact say very little about culture per se. But this is not because 'culture' no longer has a role to play. The 'prodigious expansion of culture' that Jameson and Yúdice identify as part of the transnational is indeed a key part of Hardt and Negri's discussion of the generalisation and intensification of forms of power 'throughout the brains and bodies of citizens' (2000: 23) that characterise a society of control. The problem posed by the transnational is how to understand culture as one of the signal ways in which forms of control are internalised and legitimated, without falling back on ideological models of cultural forms and practice; in turn, it forces us to consider these cultural practices not in the form of some impossible autonomy from the social, but as examples of the 'creative and intelligent manipulation' (2000: 293) of symbolic tasks that make-up one aspect of the forms of immaterial labour that Hardt and Negri argue constitute an increasingly important part of contemporary capitalist production.

Lawrence Grossberg has described cultural studies as the practice that investigates 'how specific [cultural] practices are placed – and their productivity determined – between the social structures of power and the lived realities of everyday life' (1997: 238). To date, the exploration of the transnational within cultural studies has tended to consider how its own activity is impacted on by the demands of thinking beyond the nation. This is not unimportant. However, what also need to be taken into account are the fundamental changes announced by the transnational to precisely those social structures of power and lived everyday reality in which cultural practices are placed. The kind of investigation that has thus far characterised much of the discussion on the globalisation of culture (i.e. investigations into the breaking of culture's boundaries) is in fact remarkably banal: culture was mixed, impure and hybrid long before the invention of national culture or the advent of the transnational era. Cultural studies is correct in its intuition that there is something new about culture and power in relation to the transnational, even if it only gets the story half-right. Can we not envision a cultural studies that takes the new conceptual possibilities of the transnational as an invitation to see culture in an entirely new way, that is, as an incitement to understand the continuing function of 'culture' within forms of control that are immanent to the global social body? This is the crucial contribution theory can make to the transnational adventures of cultural studies in this new century, even as cultural studies can provide theory with a model articulation of the dilemmas and difficulties of the politics of knowledge in the global era.

Notes

1 Though the term 'transnational' has been used freely to describe all manner of business practice, Michael Mann cautions that transnationalism proper exists

mostly in forms of finance capital: 'The national bases of production and trade seem undiminished. Ninety per cent of global production remains for the domestic market . . . Furthermore, almost all the so-called "multinational corporations" are still owned overwhelmingly by nationals in the home-base country, and their headquarters and research and development activities are still concentrated there' (Mann, in Robbins 1998: 16–17, n. 32).

2   The Association for Cultural Studies maintains an up-to-date list of cultural studies associations and programmes around the world. See www.cultstud.org/links.htm.

3   See John Frow and Meaghan Morris's introduction to *Australian Cultural Studies: A Reader* (1993) for an alternative genealogy of cultural studies in Australia, or Will Straw's account of the links between cultural studies and communications theory in Canada in his contribution to *Relocating Cultural Studies: New Directions in Theory and Research* (1993), for two representative challenges to the Birmingham origin tale.

4   For an assessment of cultural studies in the UK today, see Webster (2004).

Bibliography

Abbas, Akbar and Erni, John Nguyet (2005), 'General Introduction', in Akbar Abbas and John Nguyet Erni (eds), *Internationalizing Cultural Studies: An Anthology*, Oxford: Blackwell, pp. 1–12.

Agamben, Giorgio (1998), *Homo Sacer*, trans. Daniel Heller-Roazen, Stanford, CA: Stanford University Press.

Agamben, Giorgio (2005), *State of Exception*, trans. Kevin Attell, Chicago: University of Chicago Press.

Aksoy, Asu and Robbins, Kevin (2000), 'Thinking across Spaces: Transnational Television from Turkey', *European Journal of Cultural Studies*, 3:3, pp. 343–65.

Ang, Ien and Stratton, Jon (1996a), 'Asianing Australia: Notes toward a Critical Transnationalism in Cultural Studies,' *Cultural Studies*, 10:1, pp. 16–36.

Ang, Ien and Stratton, Jon (1996b), 'A Cultural Studies without Guarantees: Response to Kuan-Hsing Chen,' *Cultural Studies*, 10:1, pp. 71–7.

Appadurai, Arjun (1996), *Modernity at Large*, Minneapolis: University of Minnesota Press.

Bourdieu, Pierre (1998), *Acts of Resistance*, trans. Richard Nice, New York: New Press.

Brown, Nicholas (2003), 'Bossaposbossa, or, Postmodernism as Semiperipheral Symptom', *CR: The New Centennial Review*, 3:2, pp. 117–59.

Butler, Judith, Laclau, Ernesto and Žižek, Slavoj (2000), *Contingency, Hegemony, Universality*, New York: Verso.

Castells, Manuel (1996), *The Rise of Network Society*, Oxford: Blackwell.

Cevasco, Maria Elisa (2000), 'Whatever Happened to Cultural Studies: Notes from the Periphery', *Textual Studies*, 14:3, pp. 433–8.

Chen, Kuan-Hsing (1996a), 'Cultural Studies and the Politics of Internationalization: An Interview with Stuart Hall', in David Morley and Kuan-Hsing Chen (eds), *Stuart Hall: Critical Dialogues in Cultural Studies*, New York: Routledge, pp. 392–408.

Chen, Kuan-Hsing (1996b), 'Not Yet the Postcolonial Era: The (Super) Nation-State and Trans*nationalism* of Cultural Studies: Response to Ang and Stratton', *Cultural Studies*, 10:1, pp. 37–70.

Chen, Kuan-Hsing (1998), 'Introduction: The Decolonization Question', in Kuan-Hsing Chen (ed.), *Trajectories: Inter-Asia Cultural Studies*, New York: Routledge, pp. 1–53.

Chen, Kuan-Hsing (2000), 'The Imperialist Eye: The Cultural Imaginary of a Subempire and a Nation-State', *Positions: East Asia Cultural Critique*, 8:1, pp. 9–76.

Denning, Michael (2001), 'Globalization in Cultural Studies: Process and Epoch', *European Journal of Cultural Studies*, 4:3, pp. 351–64.

Derrida, Jacques (2001), *On Cosmopolitanism and Forgiveness*, trans. Mark Dooley and Michael Hughes, New York: Routledge.

During, Simon (1997), 'Popular Culture on a Global Scale: A Challenge for Cultural Studies?', *Critical Inquiry*, 23, pp. 808–33.

'Editorial Statement' (2000), *Inter-Asia Cultural Studies*, 1:1, pp. 5–6.

Frow, John and Morris, Meaghan (eds) (1993), *Australian Cultural Studies: A Reader*, Sydney: Allen and Unwin.

Grossberg, Lawrence (1997), *Bringing it All Back Home*, Durham, NC: Duke University Press.

Hardt, Michael and Negri, Antonio (2000), *Empire*, Cambridge, MA: Harvard University Press.

Hardt, Michael and Negri, Antonio (2004), *Multitude*, New York: Penguin.

Hitchcock, Peter (2003), *Imaginary States: Studies in Cultural Transnationalism*, Chicago: University of Illinois Press.

Horkheimer, Max and Adorno, Theodor [1947] (1988), *Dialectic of Enlightenment*, trans. John Cumming, New York: Continuum.

Hutters, Thedore (2003), 'Introduction', in Wang Hui, *China's New Order*, Cambridge, MA: Harvard University Press, pp. 1–39.

Jameson, Fredric (1991), *Postmodernism, or the Cultural Logic of Late Capitalism*, Durham, NC: Duke University Press.

Jameson, Fredric (1998), *The Cultural Turn*, New York: Verso.

Lee, Richard E. (2003), *Life and Times of Cultural Studies*, Durham, NC: Duke University Press.

Lloyd, David and Thomas, Paul (1998), *Culture and the State*, New York: Routledge.

Manovich, Lev (2001), *The Language of New Media*, Cambridge, MA, and London: MIT Press.

Marcuse, Herbert (1988), *Negations: Essays in Critical Theory*, trans. Jeremy Shapiro, London: Free Association Books.

Mato, Daniel (2001), 'Not Exotic, But Too Familiar', *Inter-Asia Cultural Studies*, 2:3, pp. 487–90.

Mato, Daniel (2003), 'Intellectual Practices in Culture and Power: Transnational Dialogues', *Cultural Studies*, 17:6, pp. 747–50.

McRobbie, Angela (1992), 'Post-Marxism and Cultural Studies: A Postscript', in Lawrence Grossberg, Cary Nelson and Paula Treichler (eds), *Cultural Studies*, New York: Routledge, pp. 719–30.

Morris, Meaghan (2004), 'Transnational Imagination in Action Cinema: Hong Kong and the Making of a Global Popular Culture', *Inter-Asia Cultural Studies*, 5:2, pp. 181–99.

Mottaheddeh, Negar (2004), 'Hollywood Remakes, Bollywood Samples and the Global Film Market', presented at 'Globalization and Indigenous Cultures' conference, Zhengzhou University, China, 7 June.

Naficy, Hamid (2003), *An Accented Cinema: Exilic and Diasporic Filmmaking*, Princeton, NJ: Princeton University Press.

Readings, Bill (1996), *The University in Ruins*, Cambridge, MA: Harvard University Press.

Robbins, Bruce (1998), 'Introduction Part I: Actually Existing Cosmopolitanism', in Pheng Cheah and Bruce Robbins (eds), *Cosmopolitics: Thinking and Feeling Beyond the Nation*, Minneapolis: University of Minnesota Press, pp. 1–19.

Sassen, Saskia (2001), *The Global City*, Princeton, NJ: Princeton University Press.

Spivak, Gayatri Chakravorty (2003), *Death of a Discipline*, New York: Columbia University Press.

Stratton, John and Ang, Ien (1996), 'On the Impossibility of Global Cultural Studies: "British" Cultural Studies in an "International" Frame', in David Morley and Kuan-Hsing Chen (eds), *Stuart Hall: Critical Dialogues in Cultural Studies*, New York: Routledge, pp. 361–91.

Straw, Will (1993), 'Shifting Boundaries, Lines of Descent: Cultural Studies and Institutional Realignments in Canada', in Valda Blundell and Ian Taylor (eds), *Relocating Cultural Studies: New Directions in Theory and Research*, London: Routledge, pp. 86–102.

Veloso, Caetano (2003), *Tropical Truth: A Story of Music and Revolution in Brazil*, New York: Da Capo Press.

Yúdice, George (2003), *The Expediency of Culture*, Durham, NC: Duke University Press.

Watson, James L. (ed.) (1997), *Golden Arches East: McDonald's in East Asia*, Palo Alto, CA: Stanford University Press.

Webster, Frank (2004), 'Cultural Studies and Sociology At, and After, the Closure of the Birmingham School 1', *Cultural Studies*, 18:6, November, pp. 847–62.

www.newculturalstudies.net

CHAPTER 12

Cultural Studies and New Media

Caroline Bassett

On being less forgetful

Digital codes currently direct themselves against letters, to overtake them . . . a new form of thinking based on digital codes directs itself against procedural 'progressive' ideologies, to replace them with structural, systems-based, cybernetic moments of thought . . . a sudden almost incomprehensible leap from one level to another. (Flusser, *Die Schrift: Hat Schreiben Zukunft?*, cited in Strohl 2002: xxxiii)

Although 'New media theory' does open the way for the decline or end of mass communication, it has not really introduced any fundamentally new issues of communication theory. (McQuail 2002: 19)

A flashback

Two summers ago, in Washington, DC, I encountered what was popularly supposed to be the city's first flashmob. A sudden flock of cell phone users descended on Books A Million in Dupont Circle and read magazines together. Old media became the content of a new media action. As DC militarised and the concrete barriers around the administrative centre of America at war multiplied, this 'happening', faintly redolent of situationism but utterly lacking its political heart, made the pages of the *Washington Post*, which subtitled its story '"Flashmobs" Gather Just Because'. Perhaps Terry Eagleton had a point when he said that sometimes some culture is not the most important thing (Eagleton 2002: 51).

Despite its apparent emptiness, or because of it, this event poses some interesting questions for the theorisation of new media, one of which is how media actions can be understood not only in relation to the historical and geo-political contexts within which they take place, but also in relation to questions of technology and medium. The flashmob event might be understood within critical horizons that locate technology in a dominant relation to culture (or vice versa), or within less dichotomous frameworks, for instance those that place technology and culture on an immanent plane.

Flashmobs, of course, are part of a larger new media ecology predicated on media technologies/media systems arising through processes of digital convergence. Convergence began in the 1980s, with the rise of popular personal computing and the rapid expansion of global computer networks, and continues today. It describes a process through which previously discrete media forms, media industries and media contents are drawn together, so that many old media forms are re-mediated, and many new forms are produced, although distinctions between new, old and recombinant media are rarely absolute. The mobile phone, a highly converged object within a highly converged system, is thus typical in that it contains old media forms alongside new ones and recombines them in new ways. The extent and reach of convergence, and in particular the degree to which digitalisation has redrawn or dissolved distinctions between media systems and other forms of material culture, are fiercely debated within the academy (by political economists, sociologists and media theorists in particular), and beyond it (by those who play the markets, by those who are players in the media industry, and by those who legislate, for instance). Fuelling the arguments is a series of different assessments of the scope and power of these new media forms/new media systems and of the degree to which they impose new modes of significance or instantiate new cultural logics.

The place of cultural studies within all this is interesting. Its interdisciplinary constitution, its history of engagement with the new, the unsanctified and the marginal, and its commitment, at least in some versions, to the study of questions of power mean it ought to be a useful or even a 'natural' site for the analysis of the converging, boundary-breaking, heterogeneous forms that constitute the new media landscape. This has not been the case. Instead, a different formation has emerged. Most strikingly, within writing that explores techno-culture (defined here as 'techno-cultural theory'), an increasingly influential body of work that finds its roots in medium theory and media philosophy has rejected cultural studies more or less entirely. This work finds inspiration in the German tradition of medium theory exemplified by Kittler and by Luhmanite systems theory (see, for instance, Hayles 2002, as well as Winthrop-Young in this volume) and has also relied heavily on the monist philosophy of Deleuze and Guattari (see Rossiter 2003; Rodowick 2001). A number of these theorists, while acknowledging work on cybernetics and information theory by intradisciplinary pioneers such as Kittler (1997) and Flusser (2002), also tend to draw directly on first- and second-wave cybernetics and information theory, reconsidering the work of Shannon and Wiener (see Terranova 2004, and below). The aim has been to build new models for the study of new media, based not only on cybernetics' modelling of complex feedback loops, and on information theory as a system for message transmission and control, but also on the logics of probability on which these sciences draw.

This development has been balanced by the burgeoning of fine-grained empirical work on new media and new media use emanating from a 'sociological turn' within media studies (Mansell 2004: 96), evidence of which can frequently be found in journals such as *New Media & Society*. This work stands in stark contrast to the often highly speculative critical-theoretical accounts described above, but is different again from the 'mainstream' cultural studies accounts that do exist, not least because the latter are marked by their tight focus on the discursive construction both of techno-cultures and of technological artefacts/systems 'themselves' (see Penley and Ross 1991 for an early example; or Sterne 2003 for an excellent later one).

Finally, the *focus* of study within techno-cultural writing is also changing. Many scholars who were active in the field of new media in the 1990s are now fixing their gaze on new 'new horizons' (biotechnology, nanotechnology, genomics) and moving away from the 'media sector' as it is narrowly defined – I recognise that this last term begs a question.

The splits and divisions now developing within the field of techno-cultural writing need to be understood in relation to the popular and critical techno-cultural hysteria that accompanied the explosive growth of networked technologies in the 1990s. This period was marked by a series of accounts of techno-culture which were highly celebratory and which often, despite their theoretical abstraction, simply tail-ended corporate boosterism, *processing* the industry's tales of the networking revolution that would render us all free rather than critiquing their fundamental assumptions – one of which might be what constitutes freedom in the first place. (As Barbrook and Cameron (1995) pointed out, this 'Californian' ideology only found its mirror image in the 'European dystopianism' that was also in vogue at the time.) Taking the techno-cultural narratives offered by the marketing wings of the new media corporations for real was bound to fail. The software industry has been famous for vapourware of all kinds; accurate prediction was never really the point, which was rather to gain support for a particular version of the future – to be guaranteed by one or other software standard. It is because they are essentially all the same that corporate visions of new media worlds were and are revealed to be ideologically loaded. As Kittler put it, in one of his lighter moments, cyberspace ideology is the 'foam packaging' of the products of the software industry 'turned to the outside' (Kittler, cited in Johnston 1997: 3).

I am interested here in why techno-cultural theory so often cleaved to the info-corporate line, and in whether it is likely to do so again, perhaps when faced with *new* new media technologies. Do the theoretical approaches currently being undertaken look likely to avoid such a reversion in the future? These are the questions addressed in this chapter, which is also an appeal for a form of cultural studies that is less forgetful, less susceptible to the scouring power of the new. This form of cultural studies needs to relate to, but not collapse into, other recent approaches to the study of new media, including some of those adumbrated above. One of my questions, indeed, is whether the turn to media philosophy and medium theory could mark a rewriting/rewiring of cultural studies, rather than registering as a hostile response to it.

The chapter comes in two parts. The first half looks at early encounters between cultural studies and computer science, exploring technology and forgetfulness. The second half considers Jameson's account of cyberpunk and dirty realism, in the context of Terranova's conception of informational culture, reading both in relation to speculative software, here understood as a critical art practice, as a form of tactical media, and possibly as a way of 'doing' cultural studies.

Under the sign of language

> Traditionally, mass communications research has conceptualized the process of communication in terms of a circuit or loop. (Hall 1992a: 128)

Contemporary medium theory is marked by a series of returns to the early cybernetics and information theory of Shannon and Wiener, which was developed alongside computers themselves, in the nascent Cold War contexts of the 1940s and on. These returns come as hard science attempts to wrest ownership of 'theory' from cultural studies and from the humanities, demanding that science is understood in its 'own' terms (see Žižek 2002: 19); that its own response to the 'systematic, totalizing claims of philosophy' (Weber 2000) produces a valid and complete understanding of a totality that encompasses the social and the physical world, perhaps.

There are some parallels here. Cybernetics in particular was formulated as a '*general* concept' model, one 'capable of modelling command and control systems '*in man and machine*' (Wiener 1961; Johnson 1997: 7; my italics), and the potential for this new 'computer science' to cross over from the hard sciences to the social and human sciences was recognised – and championed – early on. Studies of formally organised cross-over events such as the Macy conferences have begun to document this activity (see Gere 2002: 52) but only brush the surface of a process of diffusion that was largely informal and no less pervasive for that. Indeed, in the decades following its inception, the direct and indirect influence of cybernetics and information theory within the humanities was profound. Briefly, this influence is evident in structuralism/poststructuralism (e.g. Barthes 1982), psychoanalysis (e.g. Lacan 1988), apparatus and screen theory (e.g. Metz 1974) and mass communications theory (Carey 2002). In the post-Cold War years, however, cybernetics was consigned to relative obscurity, certainly falling out of favour as a model equally capable of describing the social world and the human psyche and of defining the dynamics of (information) machines. Information theory too became understood as operating in a more restricted field.

Cultural studies itself was not developed in ignorance of first-wave cybernetics/information theory or of systems theory. In fact it might be said to be an indirect response to the extension of various scientific and functionalist models of analysis in the humanities, and was certainly, at least in its Birmingham years, a very *direct* response to dissatisfaction with the dominance of mass culture/mass communication theories (the latter being itself directly influenced by information theory). Stuart Hall points out that any search for the origins of cultural studies is largely an illusory process (Hall 1992b: 16), but 'Encoding/Decoding' *is* an extremely important and influential text within a particular era and tradition of cultural studies and in it Hall broke with cybernetics and information theory's models and principles, rejecting the more or less absolute division between communication and meaning posited by these theories, and with it the view that interference in the system amounted to 'noise' and should be set aside (Hall 1992c: 118).

In the place of cybernetics' and information theory's transmission models and feedback loops Hall set a circuit of culture. This encompasses production and reception, but prioritises the semiotic moment, ensuring that 'the symbolic form of the message has a privileged position in the communicative exchange' (Hall 2002: 303). Cultural studies thus works 'under the sign of language'. Indeed, there is nothing in this model that is *outside* of language since, as D'Acci notes, despite the inclusion of moments of production and reception, the circulant in the encoding/decoding model is semiotic/discursive (D'Acci 2004: 425). This linguistic model produces particular lacunae, one of which concerns media technology. As Joshua Meyrowitz, a long-standing medium theorist, comments: 'most studies of the impact of media ignore the study of the media themselves . . . [since] the medium itself is viewed as a neutral delivery system'

(Meyrowitz 2002: 101). While the turn to language in cultural studies certainly enabled some encounters to be staged (arguably it allowed the encounter between Marxism and psychoanalysis begun in *Screen* theory to be continued on new grounds), it ruled out others. In particular, this turn meant that technology was either rendered into discourse or set aside (set *outside*), irrelevant to questions of signification or significance.

This is inevitably schematic, but now, having pointed to a break, I want to flag the degree to which Hall's encoding/decoding model *retains* traces of these earlier histories, in the sense that it clearly remains a *communicational* model. As such, it tends to reduce the complexity and breadth of culture to communication (or even transmission), thus ignoring its more expansive and/or ritual aspect. This is a point Lawrence Grossberg has made from within cultural studies (Grossberg 1997; see also D'Acci 2004: 430), drawing on James Carey's early exploration of ritual aspects of culture and communication to do so (see, for instance, Carey 2002: 43). In sum, Hall's model for cultural studies, apparently resolutely linguistic, is haunted by the technological, which comes in the form of an informing structural model or, to put it another way, *in the form of an abstraction*. What's more, if models employed by communication studies, themselves influenced by cybernetics/information theory, still influence cultural studies in particular ways, *biasing* the latter towards communication, this certainly isn't often acknowledged in relation to new media – and although Steve Jones' consideration of the 1990s rhetoric of the information superhighway takes up some of these points in suggestive ways (Jones 2001: 57), what is not acknowledged is the technological redoubling involved here.

Theorisations of contemporary forms of networked new media have been conditioned by this early and often forgotten encounter between information technology (in its first-wave cybernetic moment) and cultural theory. The widespread adoption of strong theories of social construction within media studies' explorations of media technology and everyday life might be understood within this trajectory (marking a move to remain within the media studies/cultural studies tradition whilst grappling with the technological); however, it also begins to suggest why many contemporary techno-cultural scholars have tended to move away from the (attenuated) communications model Hall et al. offer (where what is attenuated is precisely the materiality of media technology; the medium), instead either returning to forms of medium theory *avowedly* influenced by cybernetic models and by information theory, or turning to empirical social science, but in both cases rejecting cultural studies.

The first cybernetics/information theory moment is thus key to thinking through some of the distinctions between contemporary cultural studies models and medium theory/medium philosophy's treatments of new media. Consideration of the dynamics of innovation and diffusion of media technologies – of the question of the new – can add to this account in useful ways. This is provided in the next section in relation to amnesia.

Technology and forgetfulness

> [A] technical invention as such has comparatively little significance. It is only when it is selected for investment towards production, and when it is consciously developed for particular social uses – that is, when it moves from being a technical invention to what can properly be called available technology – that the general significance begins. (Williams 1989: 120)

The continuous process of innovation influences popular and critical understandings of media technologies and the cultures in which they arise. New media technologies tend to be understood (given to us) as determinant and it is only later, *when they are no longer new, when the next new media technology has come along*, that they are reassessed and explored in terms of their social shaping. This process operates in the critical sphere as well as the popular and produces a form of oscillatory amnesia, an incapacity to hold technology and culture in view simultaneously. As Stallabrass notes, such amnesia often extends from the object under consideration to become a general condition (Stallabrass 1999: 108–10), so that within these amnesiac circuits each significant new media technology in turn appears to hold the promise of revealing information's nature, *as if for the very first time*. This 'nature' is later forgotten as the moment of innovation is exhausted. That is, a previously new media technology (if it survives) becomes an accepted part of everyday life, and is largely forgotten *as a technology* (in this case as an information technology). Put yet another way, the popular invisibility that comes with consumption is paralleled by *dematerialisation* in the theoretical register. Raymond Williams' claim that technologies gain their significance and meaning as they are used and deployed as 'available technology' (Williams 1989: 120) suggests how this might operate. Examples can also be found in the cases of electricity (Marvin 1988), television (Silverstone and Hirsch 1992) and cinema (in much reception theory). In all of these cases the passage of the media technology in question into everyday use has been marked in large part by its dissolution as an object. Slotted into a worldview characterised by a strong sense of social construction, the material specificity of these technologies is forgotten and technological objects become cultural placeholders or fetishes, as Latour notes (2000). In sum, not only the status of particular new media technologies, but the status of technology per se, thus *oscillates* within these circuits.

Reviewing the recent history of techno-cultural theory in relation to these circuits is interesting. The early technophobia described above occurred at a moment of innovation, a moment in which specific new technologies (notably the Internet) appeared to be extraordinarily powerful *as technologies*, and in which the relationship between technology and culture was reassessed and the power of the former to rewrite the latter affirmed. Today we have reached a different point in the circuit, and the cyber-theoretical works of the early cyberspace years – futurological, speculative, snake-oily, revolutionary, celebratory – have been largely taken over by the micro-sociological, by the media-philosophical, or by medium theory of a more considered kind, as I've noted above. In addition, the trend towards the reterritorialisation of new media into old disciplines (particularly noticeable in film studies) suggests that others agree with Denis McQuail's robust claim that not much fundamental has changed in the media/communications scene and that therefore no new models are needed. Finally, some of the early attempts to produce a political response to the expected transformations of information appear to be exhausted. Donna Haraway, patron saint of all forms of boundary-breaking within cyberculture, has abandoned her cyborg in favour of another other(ed) species, this time canine rather than robotic (Haraway 2003). Man's best friend has become a cyborg surrogate for cultural studies' most famous cyberfeminist. Truly, we live in slightly odd times.

The kinds of amnesiac circuits outlined here are not to be read mechanically, and certainly operate simultaneously, in overlapping ways, and at various scales. They do, I believe, produce particular recursions and lacunae and have resulted in a history of thinking about innovation that is marked by abrupt shifts and turns, ruptures, breaks and (absolutely) new starts.

These circuits offer a new perspective on the haunted history of cultural studies, described above. As I read it, a certain form of cultural studies, marked both by its first encounter with cybernetics and systems theory in general, and by its retreat from that encounter, has switched into an absolutely cultural mode, operating either within semiotic/discursive channels typical of cultural studies or within fairly strong versions of social construction (to this extent poststructural and phenomenological or everyday-life theorisations mesh). This form of cultural studies has therefore been rendered problematic as a discipline able to handle new forms of science and/or new forms of technology. In other words, in relation to technology, cultural studies has been more *oscillatory* than it has been genuinely *interdisciplinary*.

Sadie Plant has argued that cultural studies exhibits a form of interdisciplinarity that confirms rather than breaks boundaries. As a consequence it sets out to legitimate what is already known rather than exploring 'how and to what extent it is possible to think differently' (Plant 1996: 216). This argument is revealed here to operate with some force. Plant's response is to reject cultural studies entirely, in favour of new forms of connectionism, based on a second-wave cybernetics (Plant 1996: 213). My sense is that, despite these problems, cultural studies remains a site for productive forms of thinking. Which raises the question: would it be possible to break the amnesiac circuit? Would it be possible to read and use the past differently, to deploy it in order to reconnect with some of the impulses that produced cultural studies as a critical discourse in the first place, whilst not losing the impulse to insist on the materiality of the object that continues to power medium theory?

Taking this up, the second half of the chapter seeks forms of cultural theory and practice that have been less forgetful in their attempts to think through connections between information and cultural form. It begins with Tiziana Terranova's bid to combine new left cultural studies and medium theory through a return to, and updating of, cybernetics and information theory.

'Informational culture?'

> Network culture is inseparable from a kind of network physics and a network politics. (Terranova 2004: 3)

Tiziana Terranova claims that 'cultural processes are increasingly grasped and conceived in terms of their informational dynamics' and that, as a consequence, there is 'no meaning outside of an informational milieu' (Terranova 2004: 7–9). Her project is at once a commentary on these developments and part of them, since the concept of 'informational culture' as she develops it is not understood purely as a form of cybernetics. Rather, it rethinks the *connections* between new and old forms of cybernetics and the contemporary cultural horizons that are developing as a result of the rise of informational dynamics. Terranova's premise (like Plant's in fact) is that while old forms of information science are problematic models for culture, newer systems based on second-order cybernetics, Artificial Life (AL) and chaotic systems, all of which allow for generation or emergence, are much more hopeful prospects. As she puts it:

> We are no longer mostly dealing with information that is transmitted from a source to a receiver, but increasingly also with an informational

dynamics – that is with the relation of noise to signal, including fluctuations and micro-variations, entropic emergencies and negentropic emergences, positive feedback and chaotic processes. (Terranova 2004: 7)

Terranova herself defines the *terms* of the connections she explores through the (Deleuzian) concept of the correlative. Different models of computer science are explored not as they are instantiated in culture, but as they correlate. This marks a break with the ways in which earlier generations understood cybernetics to be operational. However, the claims to general applicability at the heart of the cybernetics project, which are the basis for the proposed epistemological break information produces, remain and continue to produce particular consequences for reading the relation between theory and real-world effects, so that, as Saul Ostrow puts it, digital media systems 'dissolve our ability to differentiate, on the level of the natural and the artificial, between such [digital media effects] and those of the theoretical import of information theory and cybernetics' (Ostrow 1997: xii). The argument that new forms of information theory avoid the reductive modernism (see Plant 1996) of early cybernetics, enabling less totalising ways of thinking about informational culture that might also avoid the paradeictic privileging of science 'itself', cannot therefore be entirely justified. 'Informational culture' switches between science and culture (correlatively), but also makes arguments based on the assertion that these are the same, or indeed, that they always already operate on the same plane.

The wriggle room here is that Terranova's account does not operate through a simple delete-and-insert process (i.e. the deletion of one cybernetically determined worldview and the insertion of the next). Instead, a more-or-less simultaneous consideration of different *generations* of information science exposes distinctions between contemporary cultural (now informational) forms. Thus, while the medium theory of Kittler tends to erase medial difference even while expanding the terrain of media into a general information-scape (Kittler 1997: 31), Terranova's approach exposes the new forms such differences might take. In particular, distinctions made between communication and information, or discourse and dialogue, are here put into play and considered not in terms of representation, but in terms of medium specificity. The paradox of re-mediation is that these 'medium-specific' qualities may migrate onto older or newer platforms: being informational they become general, although they flourish in some environments and not others (Innis's sense of media bias might pertain here) (Innis 1991). Informed by this paradoxical specificity, Terranova develops an account of an informational regime in which the active, conscious practices of activists or tactical media operators are distinguished from a new form of mass audience, while both are integral to a new media ecology (Terranova 2004: 136). This '*other* mass', the 'television public held hostage by powerful media monopolies in a topsy-turvy world of propaganda and simulation' (Terranova 2004: 135), is as integral to the informational landscape as the net activists, and in that sense is (also) made by new media.

Of course, throughout its history cultural studies has looked at the supposedly inert mass and found within it active movements of various kinds. The difference is that the mass described here arises *after* the end of an era in which *encoding/decoding*-style theorisations of reception might pertain, *after* the epistemic break information produced (which is to say within 'informational culture'). In this sense it arises *after* cultural studies, at least of the kind that cleaves to Hall. This mass is read as a terminal 'for the receptive power of images' existing where 'meaning no longer takes hold' and where 'all mediations have collapsed', 'where images are not encoded but absorbed' (Terranova 2004: 138–40). The prospects for new forms of network politics arise when this terminal mass changes state. For Terranova this is when it becomes *virtual*.

Dirty realism

A precursor to Terranova's concept of 'informational culture' can be found in Fredric Jameson's exploration of 'dirty realism', a term he uses to interrogate the informing process of information on (global) culture in 'The Constraints of Postmodernism' (in Jameson 1994). In Jameson's hands, dirty realism, a figure for the cultural logic of informed capital, implies 'the ultimate rejoining and re-identification of the organic with the mechanical that Deleuze and Haraway . . . theorize and celebrate; but within a category – that of *totality* – alien to either of them' (Jameson 1994: 138). This totality is described partly through an exploration of a Rem Koolhaas cube, a design for the Library of France. Within this vast cube are various organs – stairs, rooms, pipes – bounded by but also floating freely within their container, which certainly cannot be grasped from the inside. Jameson argues that an archetypal form of dirty realism is also to be found in the cyberpunk-inspired environment of Ridley Scott's film *Blade Runner*, both in the forms of everyday life that the vertiginous blocks of the city (which produce a different version of an enclosure that cannot be grasped) and the crowded streets enable, and in the erasure of a certain viewing distance.

If cyberpunk 'realism' (resolving impossible geographies) is here held up in opposition to forms of naturalism, what is 'dirty' is 'the collective as such . . . the traces of mass, anonymous living and using' (Jameson 1994: 158) that are found in and illuminate *Blade Runner*'s dark (*noir*) streets. For Jameson, *Blade Runner* is a prefiguration of the end of traditional forms of community, an ushering in of 'a form of society beyond the end of the civil society' that will produce new forms of action and interaction (Jameson 1994: 160). These include new possibilities for 'corporate comebacks' as capital finds *its* uses for street uses of technology. Jameson's account of these new forms of collective life forcibly brings to mind Hardt and Negri's (later) account of the biopolitical multitude in *Empire*, and this latter is a work Terranova explicitly draws on. Whereas Terranova's multitude operates in an immanent plane *beyond* the degree-zero of the political, however, some form of historical horizon remains in Jameson's account of connections made on the street, even if this horizon is beyond reach. Having said that, Terranova's sense of the vitality of the multitude that springs to life after meaning clearly resonates with Jameson's account of the libidinal connotations of dirty realism, and above all with that vitality (the life that burns brightly and too fast) found in *Blade Runner*'s androids themselves. In both cases there is a utopian gesture, a hope for new kinds of cultural politics that might be founded on forms of human interaction with the machine – although of course Jameson's utopian moment, in contrast to Terranova's, is configured in fiction, and also in the text.

Tactical media: 'How low can you go?'[1]

With the exception of the telephone we dialogue with each other in the same way as those who lived during the Roman age. At the same time discourses raining down on us avail themselves of the most recent scientific advances. However, if there is hope in preventing the totalitarian danger of massification through programming discourses, it lies in the possibility of opening up the technological media to dialogue. (Flusser, cited in Strohl 2002: xix)

Operating in a very different sphere from Jameson's cultural semiotics but sharing his sense of the importance of what the street can do, and resonating also with Terranova's concern to explore the phase change that switches the mass to the multitude, are new forms of medium activism. These trade in software itself. They seek to get low (for real), rather than getting dirty within the text or remaining purely within the grounds of theory, and use media technology to provoke various kinds of disturbance.

One approach to tactical media is found in speculative software. This is defined by Matt Fuller as a form of art production and a form of cultural critique that 'plays with the form not the content [of new media] or rather refuses the distinction while staying on the right side of it' (Fuller 2003: 14). Tactical media/speculative software thus begins with a focus on the medium itself. It certainly involves playing tricks in code (Rtmark's notorious web redirects, or the recent Google hacks linking 'Bush' and 'Blair' with various search terms, might be understood as speculative software), and also exposes tricks in the code of others. Clearly these tactical interventions do not confine themselves to the medium. They rather refuse – and therefore expose – naturalised distinctions between form and content. These distinctions include those that are conventionally drawn between higher- or lower-level layers in complex software architectures, governed by various protocols, which are assumed to be more or less 'transparent' or 'neutral'. Playing with this, one of Fuller's works, for instance, explores the ways in which Microsoft Word shapes user productions through its menu-driven interface 'options'.

In refusing form/content distinctions at all levels, speculative software breaks with traditional hacker values, which are predicated on a modernist kind of cybernetics and which therefore also valorise form over content. The desire to 'get close to the metal', a paradoxical way of expressing that wish to find 'the truth in code', is recognised as characteristic of a particular era of hacking (see Taylor 1999). It amounts in the end to a *romance* of information and is a form of media sublime (Rossiter 2003). Kittler's modernist approach to information shares this characteristic since for Kittler, too, the only honest way to approach information technology and the only possibility for democracy in information society is through the granting of full or unmediated access to the machine-level code. The interface is *intrinsically* dishonest, denying access to the system, the latter being understood only *as* code. In refusing this romance of code, speculative software is thus also rejecting an essentially structural view of information technology in favour of an exploration of the *processual* characteristics and possibilities of a medium that is only understandable in use, and in terms that include the user. This exploration, both critical and political, interventionist and speculative, is a form of cultural politics. As Fuller puts it, speculative software is 'built to critically expose the mainstream model of the user – whilst at the same time creating *social* utopias in computer code' (Fuller 2003: 3, my italics).

Speculative software and tactical media thus try to harness the force of new media to oppositional ends. In doing so, they both create and draw on medium theory. However, while tactical media might find a new god in software, it most certainly refuses the injunction of all good cybernetic gods, which is to keep the *noise* down.[2] Its point indeed is to practice a form of pollution; precisely to open the system. Despite tactical media's supposed hostility to cultural studies, then, and despite its firm commitment to the medium, its refusal to dissolve technology into discourse, as Terranova once put it (2000), we are not so far from Stuart Hall here as it might at first appear.

Which raises the question: does tactical media offer a form of cultural politics that is amenable to cultural studies? And what might Terranova's and Jameson's accounts have to offer in this respect? It is important to be mindful of the very real differences in their respective approaches, whilst also considering the connections. One link between tactical media's bid to reconfigure and reimagine 'using', Terranova's vision of the mass turned multitude, and Jameson's reading of *Blade Runner* is the shared concern to find a cultural politics within this new milieu, and to do so by rethinking the relationship between communication and culture. What I mean by this is that all of these accounts explore the possibilities for rethinking new media politics around forms of *communion* that might oppose or undermine what Deleuze aptly called communicational stupidity, and all to some extent do so by considering forms of communication *in process*.

There are of course *distinction*s to be made between tactical media as medium action, dirty realism as a cultural semiotics, and Terranova's systems-influenced account of informational culture. These are very evident in the form that the particular turn (or return) to the medium takes in each case, as I have shown. Jameson embarks on an exercise in cognitive mapping in a coming information milieu, described textually. Terranova does this by way of a return to cybernetic theory that is largely if not entirely immanent to the cultural forms she explores. Tactical media sets out to remap the possibilities for use and does so partly through an insistence on cultural politics as (also) practice.

Flash forward

I close the chapter with three doubts. My first is that tactical media, at least in its less theoretically engaged forms, is all too easily subsumed within cultural studies' discourses of resistance, so that despite the hostility of some of its practitioners, it comes to be viewed as (just) another form of subcultural activity. As such, it might lose its medium specificity, since this derives less from the potential of an information system in the abstract than from a sense of what the possibilities are for politics within a new sphere of engagement or interaction between humans and machines, when this interaction begins with the medium.

My second doubt is that this neglects what is most interesting about tactical media, which is its insistence on breaking the barrier between critical theory and critical practice. Many, like the unfortunate electronic Zapatistas, have had their moment in a cultural studies sun that, at its worst, does more to warm those who *study* forms of resistance than it does to contribute to a movement. This works the other way around too, since, in so far as contemporary medium theory and medium practice lionise the 'processual as political', it is in danger of repeating, albeit in the register of medium specificity rather than in relation to media 'content', both cultural studies' old fondness for the romance of resistance and its incapacity to register the limits of this resistance. This is to disparage neither theory nor tacticalism/hactivism. It is to question certain presumed connections between theory and (creative) practice, and more broadly to question the connections drawn between (system) theory and the world it models.

My third doubt concerns the degree to which a focus on tactical media obscures a strength of cultural studies, which is its capacity to consider forms of practice that do not register as explicitly political, and that do not require the kinds of active skills or expert knowledge that the free software movement valorises and that tactical media employs, but which none the less do not conform.

A return to forms of cultural studies sensitive to questions of material creativity, material creative practice, and the material use of material technologies within broader historical and economic contexts might avoid these obstacles. This amounts to a demand for the (re)incorporation of the political economy of the new media into cultural studies, here taking the notion of political economy at its broadest, and reading cultural studies in its most interdisciplinary and least *oscillatory* moment: which is to say in its least forgetful moment. To abjure oscillation is not to abandon the hope of political transformation, or of critique.

Terranova's insistence that the 'other' mass, a *many* rather than the expert few, can change state insists on the inherently political possibilities contained in all cultural forms and cultural practices. A flashmob that refused the injunction 'only connect' and in doing so refused the injunction to *disperse* might be significant in all kinds of new ways.

Acknowledgement

This chapter stems from a research abroad period funded by the Leverhulme Trust and I would like to acknowledge their support. Thanks also to Clare Birchall and Gary Hall for their comments and suggestions.

Notes

1 Slogan for 'The Next Five Minutes', Tactical Media conference, Amsterdam, 1999.
2 The demand of the gods of Gilgamesh.

Bibliography

Barbrook, Richard and Cameron, Andy (1995), 'The Californian Ideology', *Mute*, 3, Autumn, pp. iv-v.
Barthes, Roland (1982), *Image, Music, Text*, London: Flamingo.
Carey, James (2002), 'A Cultural Approach to Communication', in Denis McQuail (ed.), *McQuail's Reader in Mass Communication*, London: Sage, pp. 36–45.
D'Acci, Julie (2004), 'Cultural Studies, Television Studies and the Crisis in the Humanities', in Lynn Spigal and Jan Olsson (eds), *Television After TV*, London: Routledge, pp. 418–46.
Eagleton, Terry (2002), *The Idea of Culture*, Oxford: Blackwell.
Eagleton, Terry (2003), *After Theory*, Harmondsworth: Penguin.
Flusser, Vilém (2002), *Vilém Flusser, Writings*, London: University of Minnesota Press.
Fuller, Matthew (2003), *Behind the Blip: Essays on the Culture of Software*, London: Autonomedia.
Gere, Charlie (2002), *Digital Culture*, London: Reaktion Books.
Grossberg, Lawrence (1997), *Bringing it all Back Home: Essays on Cultural Studies*, Durham, NC, and London: Duke University Press.
Hall, Stuart [1973] (1992a), 'Encoding/Decoding', *Culture, Media and Language*, London: Routledge, pp. 128–138.
Hall, Stuart (1992b), 'Cultural Studies and the Centre: Some Problematics and Problems', *Culture, Media and Language*, London: Routledge, pp. 15–47.
Hall, Stuart [1973] (1992c), 'Introduction to Media Studies at the Centre', in *Culture, Media and Language*, London: Routledge pp. 117–21.
Hall, Stuart [1973] (2002), 'The Television Discourse; Encoding and Decoding', in Denis McQuail (ed.), *McQuail's Reader in Mass Communication*, London: Sage, pp. 302–9.
Haraway, Donna (2003), *The Companion Species Manifesto*, Chicago: Prickly Paradigm Press.
Hardt, Michael and Negri, Antonio (2000), *Empire*, London: Harvard University Press.
Hayles, Katherine (2002), *Writing Machines*, London: MIT Press.
Innis, Harold [1951] (1991), *The Bias of Communication*, Toronto: University Of Toronto Press.
Jameson, Fredric (1994), *The Seeds of Time*, New York: Columbia University Press.
Johnston, John (1997), 'Introduction: Friedrich Kittler: Media Theory after

Post-Structuralism', in Friedrich Kittler, *Essays: Literature, Media, Information Systems*, ed. John Johnston, London: G&B Arts, pp. 2–26.

Jones, Steve (2001), 'Understanding Micropolis and Compunity', in Charles Ess and Fay Sudweeks (eds), *Culture, Technology, Communication*, New York: State University of New York Press, pp. 53–66.

Kittler, Friedrich (1997), *Essays: Literature, Media, Information Systems*, ed. John Johnston, London: G&B Arts.

Lacan, Jacques (1988), *The Seminars of Jaques Lacan. Vol. 1: The Ego in Freud's Theory and in the Technique of Psychoanalysis*, Cambridge: Cambridge University Press.

Latour, Bruno (2000), 'When Things Strike Back', *British Journal of Sociology*, millennium special issue, 51:1, pp. 107–24.

Lessig, Lawrence (2004), *Free Culture*, New York: Penguin, www.free-culture.cc/freeculture.pdf.

Libre Society (2004), *Libre Culture Manifesto*, www.libresociety.org/library/libre.pl/Libre_Manifesto.

Mansell, Robin (2004), 'Political Economy, Power and New Media', *New Media and Society*, 6:1, pp. 96–105.

Marvin, Carolyn (1998), *When Old Technologies Were New*, New York: Oxford University Press.

Mattelart, Armand and Mattelart, Michelle (1995), *Theories of Communication*, London: Sage.

McQuail, Denis (2002), 'Introduction', in Denis McQuail (ed.), *McQuail's Reader in Mass Communication*, London: Sage, pp. 1–20.

Metz, Christian (1974), *Film Language: A Semiotics of Cinema*, New York: Oxford University Press.

Meyrowitz, Joshua (2002), 'Media and Behaviour – A Missing Link', in Denis McQuail (ed.), *McQuail's Reader in Mass Communication*, London: Sage, pp. 99–109.

Ostrow, Saul (1997), 'Preface', in Friedrich Kittler, *Essays: Literature, Media, Information Systems*, ed. John Johnston, London: G&B Arts, pp. vii–viii.

Penley, Constance and Ross, Andrew (1991), *Technoculture*, Minneapolis: University of Minnesota Press.

Plant, Sadie (1996), 'The Virtual Complexity of Culture', in George Robertson, Melinda Mash, Lisa Tickner, John Bird, Barry Curtis and Tim Putnam (eds), *Futurenatural: Nature, Science, Culture*, London: Routledge, pp. 203–17.

Rodowick, David (2001), *Reading the Figural Or, Philosophy after the New Media*, Durham, NC: Duke University Press

Rossiter, Ned (2003), 'Processual Media Theory', *Symploke*, 11:1–2, pp. 104–31.

Silverstone, Roger and Hirsch, Eric (1992), *Consuming Technologies: Media and Information in Domestic Spaces*, London: Routledge.

Sterne, Jonathan (2003), 'Bourdieu, Technique and Technology', *Cultural Studies*, 17:3–4, May–July, pp. 367–89.

Stallabrass, Julian (1999), 'The Ideal City and the Virtual Hive', in John Downey and Jim McGuigan (eds), *Technocities*, London: Sage, pp. 108–20.

Strohl, Andreas (2002), 'Introduction', in *Vilém Flusser, Writings*, Minneapolis: University of Minnesota Press.

Taylor, Paul A. (1999), *Hackers: Crime in the Digital Sublime*, London: Routledge.

Terranova, Tiziana (2000), 'Infallible Universal Happiness', in Angela Dimitrakaki, Pam Skelton and Mare Tralla (eds), *Private Views, Spaces and Gender: Contemporary Art from Britain and Estonia*, London: WAL, pp. 110–20.

Terranova, Tiziana (2004), *Network Culture: Politics for the Information Age*, London: Pluto Press.

Weber, Samuel (2000), 'The Future of the Humanities: Experimenting', *Culture Machine*, 2, www.culturemachine.tees.ac.uk.

Wiener, Norbert (1961), *Cybernetics, or Control and Communication in the Animal and the Machine*, Cambridge, MA: MIT Press.

Williams, Raymond (1989), *The Politics of Modernism: Against the New Conformists*, London: Verso.

Žižek, Slavoj (2002), 'Cultural Studies versus the "Third Culture"', *South Atlantic Quarterly*, 101:1, Winter, pp. 19–32.

Part IV: New Adventures in Cultural Studies

SPACE WARS

CHAPTER 13

Cultural Studies and Rem Koolhaas' Project on the City

J. Macgregor Wise

You approach these books cautiously; their sheer size alone takes you aback; but you are none the less attracted, curious. One book cover is red plastic, the other black. They look heavy. The red one, naturally, is on China. Opening it you find photographs of billboards – first of Deng Xiaoping and then of housing projects, future office towers. Pictures (buildings, landscapes, people), diagrams (blueprints, time lines, maps, charts of construction footage) and texts (histories, diaries, analyses) follow. In over 700 pages the images clearly dominate. One flips here, and back, pauses (Donald Duck in a landscape design, golf courses, bridges under construction, Mao swimming the Yangtze), and flips again. The black volume, on shopping, is even bigger (800 pages this time). Page after page of historical and contemporary shopping spaces – the Crystal Palace flips by as does the Mall of America and mall scenes in Las Vegas, Kyoto, Basel, all looking remarkably similar. A time line of shopping spills over the pages, layer upon layer of graphics; information excess. And then pictures of museums, downtowns, escalators, Disneyland, churches. Charts, diagrams, texts. You flip, you surf, you feel at sea. You glance at the clock, astonished at the time that has passed, at the gravitational pull of these pages. These books create a space, or set of spaces, through which one moves – or rather these are territories which express something (or other).

These are the volumes of the Harvard Design School's Project on the City: Volume 1 is the *Great Leap Forward* (Chung et al. 2001a), about the staggering urban growth of the Pearl River Delta (PRD) in China, and Volume 2 is the *Guide to Shopping* (Chung et al. 2001b). What's interesting about these books is not simply what they are about but what they *do*; however, what they do has very much to do with what they are about, for they are about a crisis of urban space and the inability of many to even understand this crisis. The Project on the City derives its central concerns from its director, the iconoclastic, internationally renowned architect

Rem Koolhaas, and his frustrations with architecture as a discipline. Architecture, he feels, cannot make sense of, much less theorise, the radical growth and transformation of the city globally. In the online course description for the Project on the City, Koolhaas writes:

> As cities modernize beyond professional control, no longer is the architect/ urbanist/landscape architect able to sufficiently describe, let alone influence, large areas of the urban realm as even in the recent past. This double condition of runaway development and disciplinary paralysis warrants the urgent need to study the evolving agents, relationships and consequences of contemporary urbanization.[1]

The Project on the City is a sprawling attempt to describe, document and theorise these changes and at the same time to rethink architecture itself. In doing so, it opens up new territories for architecture and design, territories that cultural studies would do well to map and explore. However, my concern in this chapter is with more than simply describing new territories for cultural studies; it is to set up a perhaps instructive parallel between Koolhaas' project and cultural studies' position in the early twenty-first century.[2] This volume is, after all, about a certain frustration with cultural studies' ability (or lack of it) to come to terms with, much less theorise, recent radical changes in culture. In an era marked by globalisation, neo-liberalism, neo-conservatism, terrorism, pandemics and societies of control, not to mention sprawling urban transformation, old models of cultural studies and cultural critique seem to have little purchase. I would argue that this is a challenge *for* cultural studies rather than a challenge *to* cultural studies – cultural studies as an ongoing project is vitally important today; it just needs to find its sea-legs.

Contemporary cultural studies tends to find itself entrapped in the habits and structures of academic argument, safe within the covers of journals and academic press books. It has become too comfortable and complacent in this milieu, too theoretically fluent.[3] There is an old debate about whether or not cultural studies should write for more 'popular' audiences. I think those arguments should reconsider the terms of the debate – it is not a question of audience or rigour (rigour should be expected no matter what). Cultural studies needs to explore other forms – essay, visuality and so on – not because they are more 'popular' but because these forms have the potential for different effectivities. They *do* different things. It is these effectivities that cultural studies needs to explore. Perhaps the example of Koolhaas and his project not only presents new experiences instructive to cultural studies but raises important questions as well. How, in the end, do we think not only architecture differently but cultural studies as well?

The Project on the City

The Project on the City is actually an innovative cross-disciplinary graduate course/thesis research course at Harvard University's School of Design. The Project, headed by Koolhaas, draws students from across the Design School who collaboratively and independently research common topics suggested by Koolhaas. So far the Project has had five phases. The first was the work on the Pearl River Delta, which resulted in the *Great Leap Forward* volume; the second was on shopping, which resulted in the *Shopping* volume; the third, fourth and fifth are continuing projects which have not yet been published (except as extracts in *Content* (Koolhaas 2004) or *Mutations* (Koolhaas et al. 2001)): the deurbanisation of Lagos, Nigeria and the Roman city as operating system for modernity, and work on Communism and its architecture. Each of these projects focuses on coming to grips with a different process affecting the city: theorising hyperdevelopment (in the context of Communist China); theorising everyday life as an expression of shopping; theorising mutability, chaos and deterritorialisation as the future of the city (as Koolhaas is fond of putting it: 'Lagos is not catching up with us. Rather, we may be catching up with Lagos' (Koolhaas et al. 2001: 653)); and theorising the Roman city to discover the abstract machine governing urbanisation and globalisation.

It is not just the project itself but the texts produced which are of interest here. These texts are a sumptuous tangle of concepts, images and lines of flight.

> [T]exts could, more in keeping with the thinking of Gilles Deleuze, be read and used more productively as little bombs that, when they do not explode in one's face (as bombs are inclined to do), scatter thoughts and images into different linkages or new alignments without necessarily destroying them. Ideally, they produce unexpected intensities, peculiar sites of indifference, new connections with other objects, and thus generate affective and conceptual transformations that problematize, challenge, and move beyond existing intellectual and pragmatic frameworks. (Grosz 2001: 58)

The space/territory/assemblage created by these texts is arguably a new way of conceptualising the crisis of urban space, or creating links, drawing lines – mapping the visual, demographic and affective contours of the urban through an overwhelming excess. These books are not about detailed points (though they have more than their share of these) but about ways of moving from point to point – by link, by resonance, by chance.

Volume I: The *Great Leap Forward*

Based on fieldwork conducted in 1996, the *Great Leap Forward*[4] concerns the ultra-rapid development of the Pearl River Delta (PRD, which stretches from Hong Kong to Guangzhou to Macau), the Special Economic Zone or test-bed of socialist-capitalist experimentation. The Project seeks both to describe and to theorise this development. The book traces Mao's anti-urban policies through Deng's refocus on the urban through an ideology the authors refer to as *Infrared* – 'a covert strategy of compromise and double standard' (Chung et al. 2001a: 67) to realise the utopian dream of Communism by other means, hidden, underground. What it reveals is the idea of *The City of Exacerbated Differences (COED)*, a city with 'the greatest possible difference between its parts . . . [i]n a climate of permanent strategic panic' (2001a: 29). The *COED* is at the heart of the hyperdevelopment in the PRD.

The PRD has experienced staggering growth over the last twenty years. It consists of five major cities with a total population of over twelve million people, expected to increase to thirty-six million people by 2020. The rapid growth is exemplified by the fact that Shenzhen had 450 high rise towers in 1993 and less than ten years later had over 900. The focus in the Project on the City volume is on four of the cities in the region (Shenzhen, Dongguan, Zhuhai and Guangzhou), taking each city to exemplify a theme of their analysis. Shenzhen is an attempt by the People's Republic of China (PRC) to construct a mirror image of Hong Kong just across the border from Hong Kong itself. The authors use the example of Shenzhen to elaborate the concepts of *Red* (Communist ideology, especially as applied to the urban) and *Infrared* (the strategy of maintaining a Communist ideology and goals while ostensibly compromising with global capitalist economic developments). Shenzhen is also the opening example used to describe architecture as a practice in the PRC, especially under conditions of hyperdevelopment. For example, China has one tenth of the number of architects of the United States, but they do five times the work of those in the United States; if one divides the total construction volume in China by the number of architects, on average each Chinese architect produces a thirty-storey building every year; and buildings are designed ten times faster in China than in the US (this is termed *Shenzhen Speed* (2001a: 161)). The second city is Dongguan, a city that is not really a city, working in the shadow of Shenzhen, which competes with that city but stealthily. Dongguan is used to discuss money, economics, and pleasure in the PRD. The third city is Zhuhai, a garden city consisting of tourist resorts and golf courses (the city is 30 per cent green space). And the fourth city is

CULTURAL STUDIES AND REM KOOLHAAS' PROJECT   245

Guangzhou (formerly Canton), historically China's link to the outside world, which spurs the discussion of politics, policy, sovereignty and diplomacy.

The goal of the *Great Leap Forward* volume is to theorise this unprecedented urban development, inventing appropriate concepts to understand the situation.[5] These include not only the concepts of *Red*, *Infrared*, and *Shenzhen Speed* listed above, but also a myriad of others: *Concession* as a tactic, *Floating* as a condition of the migrant workers (which involves up to two thirds of the population of the region), the idea of *Zones* rather than cities, and many more. These concepts provide the primary links or ways of moving through the PRD volume. Concepts beget concepts; concepts return in other contexts to draw attention to underlying principles. One is given a new vocabulary to discuss new developments in a socio-economic context quite removed for the most part from that which generated our current critical and architectural vocabulary. The other way the space of this volume is navigated is through the images, most printed without margins so that they overspill into one another. Many are blurred, in movement, perhaps snapped by the Project team themselves. One is often unsure what one is looking at, or what one should be seeing, which gives movement through the book a certain restlessness, punctuated by blocks of text and the pinpoints of concepts (printed in red).

The volume is in many ways as overwhelming as the regional developments themselves. And though it may capture the culture of architecture in the PRD, it is relatively abstracted from the everyday lives and culture of those living there (except for brief slices of floating lives).[6] A quite notable omission (apart from a very short two-page discussion in a volume of over 700 pages) concerns the return of Hong Kong and Macau to China in 1997, despite the fact that such a transition was occurring the year after the fieldwork and has the potential to transform the region radically.[7]

Volume II: The *Guide to Shopping*

The *Guide to Shopping* volume has received more attention than that on the PRD. In some ways, in terms of presentation and design, it is the more creative endeavour, forgoing geographical or even long-thematic organisation in favour of forty-two more or less short chapters arranged in alphabetical order by title. The volume encompasses essays on the histories of air conditioning, the escalator and the mall, ruminations on the Crystal Palace, on branding, on the urbanism of Victor Gruen (the inventor of the shopping mall), on consumer marketing, on the Japanese Depato and so on. Colourful charts set out retail area in square meters per person per country

(US = 2.9 square metres, of which 2.2 is mall-space; the UK is 0.9, Singapore is 0.6), total retail area measured as a factor of Manhattan (world = 33 times Manhattan's land area, US = 12.7 Manhattans, etc.), as a factor of Mall of Americas, and so on. The volume is a host of fun facts: if retailers were countries Wal-Mart would have the twenty-fourth largest GDP, ahead of Hong Kong and Poland.

The *Guide to Shopping* sets itself in the context of the decline of the mall and even the projected decline of the big box 'category killer' stores, and the dot-com online retail shakeout of 2000–1. The contention of the book is that shopping has become the essential experience of everyday life – all aspects of social and cultural life are reduced to shopping. For example, the authors argue that shopping used to take place within the city, and now the city takes place within shopping. Urban redevelopment redesigns urban spaces as malls; churches draw on mall design to draw followers to the new mega-churches; and airports have become very profitable retail spaces (the average American mall has retail sales of $250 per square foot, while Heathrow has retail sales of $2,500 per square foot), and so on.

Movement through the *Shopping* volume is similar to that through the PRD volume – skipping across glossier images this time, chapters interconnected through detailed cross-references in the text – but also crucially different. Given the shortness of the chapters and their apparent random order, the book itself becomes a kind of mall: the reader browses, tries something on, and moves on.

Despite its core theoretical contention, for the most part the *Guide to Shopping* is atheoretical in that it uses little theoretical language and contains few attempts to theorise these contemporary and historical conditions, seeming content to describe. Indeed, the histories presented, while interesting, are fairly linear and more than a bit technologically determinist (the air conditioner, the elevator, the escalator . . .), while other entries are more journalistic and decidedly non-critical, such as that on Disney. But there is a theoretical frame which is worthy of note. It consists of two essays by Sze Tsung Leong (one at the beginning and one at the end of the book)[8] and one by Rem Koolhaas ('Junkspace', which literally sits at the heart of the book, overspilling its margins). Leong's first essay, '. . . And Then There Was Shopping', serves as an introduction, putting the first eighty pages of images, charts and statistics in the context of the argument that all human existence is becoming one with shopping.[9] This situation is the result of 'the unfettered growth and acceptance of the market economy as the dominant global standard' (Chung et al. 2001b: 129). Shopping becomes the most common form of collective social behaviour, provides a common cultural experience, and provides the template for the restructuring of social institutions: school, health care, religion, even the construction and refitting of urban centres. Leong concludes: 'In the end, there will be little else for us to do but shop' (2001b: 135). The essay is not groundbreaking in its argument, but notable for its totalised vision: the utter submission of everything to shopping as fait accompli. Leong's closing essay, 'Ulterior Spaces', argues that 'the shape of the contemporary city is no longer cohered by physical, visible characteristics such as form, iconography, or density, but arrived at by default, as the residue of ulterior motives' (2001b: 767). Those ulterior motives are the motives of control. Control space is a mobile, flexible, fluctuating map of information.[10] It is the space of smart cards, radio frequency identity (RFID) chips, demographic profiling and surveillance. Its by-products are residual spaces, obsolescent spaces from abandoned box stores to the boredom of endless rows of products.

Though not focused on control/residual space as a couplet, Koolhaas theorises contemporary space as Junkspace, a transient impermanence which is the residue of modernisation. Junkspace is at the heart of shopping. Junkspace is not about architecture, not about buildings (architects, he argues, never grasp space, only objects and structure, and Junkspace itself 'cannot be remembered' (2001b: 408)), but an endlessly connective space that is larger and infinitely less permanent than monuments of old. It is not, Koolhaas points out, a space of flows; it is much too anarchic to cohere into flows. It is space which is branded, derelict, renovated, controlled, open, formless but endlessly proliferating, transient, freeing yet suffocating, dazzling with stylistic surfaces which soon sag, leak, tear. Junkspace encompasses buildings, streets, highways, airports – constantly new, beginning to rot, always politely under construction. It is space that is obfusticating, nurturing, entertaining, sedating. Obviously the Junkspace essay itself is contagious, bringing the world into its habits of thought, rhythms, phrasing, images. It is not a way of critiquing architecture, but a way of thinking architecture differently.

Thinking architecture differently

With increasing critical attention paid to theories of space, especially spaces of modernity, postmodernity, the urban, the cosmopolitan or the global, not least in the disciplines of cultural studies and human geography, the field of architecture takes on increasing relevance and importance. Theorists and practitioners of built space, architects are in a prime location to understand and respond to these conditions. As Koolhaas puts it, there is a 'rediscovery of architectural thinking' (2002/3: 3). However, he also points out that architecture is often theorised and idealised by those outside the profession.

One of those looking at architecture from the outside is feminist scholar Elizabeth Grosz, who, inspired by the philosophy of Gilles Deleuze, asks 'how to *think* architecture differently?' (2001: 59). To think of a Deleuzian architecture entails asking the questions: 'can architecture be thought, in connection with other series, as assemblage? What would this entail?. . . Can architecture work (its or an) *outside*? What is it to open up architecture to thought, to force, to life, to the outside? . . . Can architecture survive such assaults on its autonomy?' (2001: 71).

From *inside* architecture, Koolhaas seems well positioned to think architecture differently, the Project on the City to think the city differently. Koolhaas is famously frustrated with architecture; he is an architect who seems to write as much as he builds (Foster 2001). He feels architecture has become passive before capitalism (one waits for a commission before one begins even to think, or plan, or analyse, or design). It also has become too slow. Koolhaas came to the realisation that architecture simply wasn't up to the task of responding to the changing nature of global everyday life.[11] Any major architectural project spends up to five years in development, which is unworkable in the rapidly transforming economics and culture of contemporary urban space. But not only is the profession itself too slow, its current self-definition won't allow it to comment on or participate in these processes in the ways others think that they should.

> I think it a pity that the core values of our profession resist our participation in the discovery of another kind of architecture, because ironically, if everything is architecture and architectural, we could extend our domain astronomically – we could think of everything, and we could participate in everything. We are marooned in the definition of a profession that is more reactionary and more conservative than the rest of the world is willing to grant us. (Koolhaas 2002/3: 3)

In 1995 Koolhaas, with graphic artist Bruce Mau, published *S, M, L, XL*, a sprawling 'architectural novel' which overviewed the work of his architectural firm, the Office of Metropolitan Architecture (OMA), and revolutionised architectural publishing. In many ways it previewed the style and approach of the Project on the City volumes. The style and function of these texts could best be described as verging on Deleuzian. Recall Elizabeth Grosz's earlier words on texts as 'little bombs' that rearticulate relationships and rework affective maps. It seems Koolhaas' idiom to cast 'little bombs' into the field of architecture in terms of either buildings or writings. In response to the frustrations summarised above, and perhaps to position himself better to address these other challenges to architecture, Koolhaas founded the Architecture Media Organization (AMO – the mirror image of OMA) to free architecture or architectural thinking from actually having either to wait for a commission or to build anything. 'Maybe, architecture doesn't have to be stupid after all', he writes. 'Liberated from the obligation to construct, it can become a way of thinking about anything – a discipline that represents relationships, proportions, connections, effects, the diagram of everything' (2004: 20). AMO became the virtual version of OMA, or the version of OMA focused on the virtual, on media, communication and information, the very things so profoundly altering the ground on which architecture worked.[12] Koolhaas and AMO were hired as consultants to Conde Nast especially to work on *WIRED* magazine and *Lucky* (a fashion magazine) – a collaboration which produced a special issue of *WIRED* in 2003 edited by Koolhaas et al. AMO also designed a colourful bar-code flag for the European Union.

The article 'Junkspace' and an earlier essay 'The Generic City' (in Koolhaas and Mau 1995) represent Koolhaas's attempts to think architecture differently, to invent new ways of thinking and writing – not the importation of theoretical concepts or frameworks, but generated from the moments themselves. Ackbar Abbas, commenting on 'The Generic City', writes: 'it discussed questions like repetition and seriality – a whole new discourse on the city which might allow us to rethink the ways we produce it. Naming what is going on and by doing so, intervening in the process of creating a new urban space' (in Lovink 1997). This desire to find new ways of thinking, describing and theorising the city and space is obvious in the 'Junkspace' article. As Fredric Jameson writes of 'Junkspace' in an essay on the Project on the City volumes, 'it is the new language of space which is speaking through these self-replicating, self-perpetuating sentences, space itself become the dominant code or hegemonic language of the new moment of History – the last? – whose very raw material condemns it in its deterioration to extinction' (2003). The Project itself represents a new way of presenting, describing and theorising architecture.

But do Koolhaas and the Project think architecture and the city differently enough? To be sure, Koolhaas thinking architecture and its outside is quite different from what Grosz has in mind when she asks, 'can architecture work (its or an) outside?' Grosz is much more radical, concerned with spaces and peoples much more othered. For instance, she describes as an example of the limits of architecture what Alphonso Lingis called the community of those who have nothing in common – the outcast, the rejected, the pure excess. How can architecture build for them? Koolhaas looks at Lagos' mammoth city dump in the Project on the City and sees it as a 'form of spatial organisation. Pure accumulation, it is formless, has an uncertain perimeter and location' (2003: 137). This shapeless, perpetually transforming space is seen as a triumph of human potential – people live on the dump (it's on fire, by the way) and scavenge. 'Freedom from order' is the lesson of the Lagos dump for Koolhaas. But this ignores the lived reality of the dump; its obscenity. There is a blind spot here: why are people (the outcasts living with the cast-offs) living on the dump? And there are broader blind spots in the Project as well – for example, the sweatshops which make possible both shopping and the PRD development are effectively ignored.[13]

Cultural studies and the Project on the City

For the remainder of this chapter I would like to ask two questions. First, how can we see the Project *as* cultural studies? And second, how can we pose the same questions from Grosz to cultural studies? How, in other words, can we think cultural studies differently? Can it be thought as an assemblage? Can it address its outside?

Fredric Jameson has declared that the Project volumes 'escape other disciplinary categories (such as sociology or economics) but might be said to be closest to cultural studies' (2003), and *Artforum* claims that Koolhaas is '[p]ackaging architecture, statistical analysis, and cultural studies into one cool Brand' (Lieberman 2002: 99). However, it is unclear what cultural studies means in these contexts, except as some sort of academic remainder bin. What *is* clear from the above quotations is that these volumes *should* be cultural studies, or at least this is work that cultural studies should be doing. So, as a way of exploring the first of my questions, concerning the congruencies and disparities between cultural studies and the Project on the City, I wish to start by considering what Lawrence Grossberg (1997) has described as one of the defining features of cultural studies, its *radical contextuality*. Grossberg defines the term as follows: 'An event or practice (even a text) does not exist apart from the forces of the context that constitute it as what it is. Obviously, context is not merely background but the very conditions of possibility of something' (1997: 255). The theoretical work of cultural studies is also radically contextual ('theory is always a response to specific questions and specific contexts' (Grossberg 1997: 262)) and in this the *Great Leap Forward* volume is closest to cultural studies in its generation of concepts from the milieu of the PRD. The Project itself works here by creating unique responses to the problem of mapping particular dimensions of contemporary urban space. However, though the arrangement and presentation of the *Shopping* volume is a specific response to that dimension of everyday space, otherwise the volume seems, well, a shopping expedition.

Part of cultural studies' radical contextuality is its emphasis on politics (which is also understood contextually, for cultural studies is not a project with a rigid political agenda). Cultural studies is not simply a description or analysis but an intervention into social and cultural conditions. Elizabeth Grosz writes:

> Think of politics as the question of how to live. And if politics is defined in terms of how to live, then clearly architecture is of central relevance to political issues, as is philosophy, as are the visual arts, and so forth. None of them are outside of the terrain of the political. . . . If the goal is not to create a wedge or rift between something like architecture and something like politics but rather to show what modes of exclusion architecture is necessarily committed to – not compliant with but complicit . . . then it seems to me that we are all complicit. (Grosz in Davidson 1995: 233–4)

Her comment was made in the context of a discussion of politics and architecture. Koolhaas undoubtedly would not deny the political dimensions of architecture, but argues that by the nature of the work architecture can never consist purely of critique.[14] In response to Grosz's statement above, he argues:

> My problem with this reigning discourse of architecture and architectural criticism is its inability to recognize that in the deepest motivation of architecture there is something that cannot be critical. In other words, to deal with the sometimes insane difficulty of an architectural project, to deal with the incredible accumulation of economic, cultural, political, and logistical issues, requires an engagement for which we use a conventional word – complicity – but for which I am honest enough to substitute the word engagement or adhesion. (Koolhaas in Davidson 1995: 234).

But there is a difference between engagement and the blithe ignoring of critique (just as there is a difference between critique and politics). Both Project on the City volumes clearly avoid other critical work done on their topics (especially *Shopping*). Koolhaas prefers the messy balance of complicity and critique – the in-between place of a pragmatic discipline building for those with capital and power articulated to a discourse that lays bare the functioning of Junkspace and control space. He is therefore fond of politically ambiguous projects, such as constructing the new headquarters for Chinese State Television (CCTV) in Beijing (see Koolhaas 2004; Zalewski 2005), and pays no mind to the contradictions and ironies of overseeing more expressly political books like *Content* (2004) (which includes, for example, Michael Hardt taking on President George W. Bush and Koolhaas quite subtly taking apart Martha Stewart) while designing Prada stores. One could state that Koolhaas' critique is an immanent one – not standing above or outside globalisation, capitalism, or Junkspace, but messily within it – surfing the contradictions of modernity.[15] His is an attempt to make architecture be what others think it is – to move outside the spaces and projects of high architecture but to remain a high architect.

So when Grosz speaks of 'a radically antifunctional architecture, an architecture that is anti-authoritarian and anti-bureaucratic. An architecture that refuses to function in and be a part of, as Deleuze names them, "societies of control"' (2001: 155), Koolhaas cannot agree. While the Project on the City certainly recognises, for example, the control society or Junkspace, it certainly does not work outside it. There is a crucial difference between working immanently while remaining complacent and working immanently while drawing a line of flight out. Whereas in the face of the societies of control Deleuze writes of resistance, for the Project on the City control space simply closes in over our heads. Critique becomes aesthetic and not political, unless one counts the 'politics of acquiescence' (Leach 2000: 83).[16] For example, Koolhaas' Prada stores incorporate as stylistic features RFID tags and other techniques of control space described in the *Shopping* volume. Despite his own critique of the reactionary work of contemporary architecture, perhaps Koolhaas remains acquiescent, accepting the notion that the culture-ideology of consumerism or shopping or control space has indeed permeated everything. Junkspace just goes on and on and on . . . The Project volumes are an aesthetic response to the crisis of the urban, but far from a political response.[17] Whereas '[c]ultural studies is about understanding the possibilities for remaking contexts through cultural alliances and apparatuses, the very structures of which (and the relations between them) are the product of relations and struggles over power' (Grossberg 1997: 260), the possibilities for remaking Junkspace, control space, the *COED*, are frustratingly vague – though the act of identification and description is crucially important in understanding the politics of these conditions.

But perhaps it is simply too much to ask a working architect to undermine architecture's basic conservative principles and open it to radical alterity, the Other, excess or chaos. 'The only legitimate relationship that architects can have with the subject of chaos is to take their rightful place in the army of those devoted to resist it, and fail', Koolhaas wrote in *S, M, L, XL* (1995: 969). Perhaps we would be better off raising the other form of Deleuzo-Guattarian politics: the politics of the minor. Grosz, for example, wants to raise questions 'in order to unsettle or make architecture itself, if not stutter, then tremble' (2001: 61). Koolhaas indeed likes to make architecture stutter. The Project on the City is, in many respects, architecture stuttering, trembling, trying out new resonances, new rhythms. It is encouraging, perhaps, that as Koolhaas (2002/3) himself proudly points out (though he admits he isn't quite sure what it means), in marked contrast with other classes of Harvard architects seeking high-powered corporate positions, half of those involved in the Project on the City drop out of the profession altogether.

Finally, there is one more dimension of cultural studies' radical contextuality I wish to consider here: its own self-reflective practice. For example, another blind spot not addressed by either the Project on the City or Koolhaas is the socio-economic position from which they mount their investigations, and the privileges of that position (Koolhaas does, after all, design Prada stores and not K-Marts). One cannot ignore the elite status of Harvard itself. This is putting it far too simply, but the tours by and access for Koolhaas and his students in the PRD or Lagos necessarily colour their observations (not to mention how one approaches shopping). By necessity, these projects can be only partial and fragmentary – in part because of the breadth of their subject matter and also because of the disciplinary limitations of the authors – these are design and architecture students, after all, and not historians of Chinese politics, trained ethnographers, or people deeply schooled in marketing or cultural analysis. We get interesting probes (to borrow a term from Marshall McLuhan) but ultimately superficial takes on the histories and processes described. The problem is not the identity or institutional location of these individuals but the lack of reflection 'on one's own relation to the various trajectories and dimensions, places and spaces, of the context one is exploring and mapping: theoretical, political, cultural, and institutional' (Grossberg 1997: 268) – a self-reflection critical to cultural studies practice. That these volumes are shaped by institutional location and disciplinary limitation is understandable and acceptable. What's at issue here is that their very massive, sprawling presentation, discourse and institutional imprimatur (it is, for example, the Harvard Design School *Guide to Shopping*), offer these projects as masterworks, comprehensive and totalising. The volumes do create their own spaces and maps in which and through which we wander for hours, overwhelmed by the seeming totality of the data, numbers and discourse (shopping is everything). Yet these spaces are ultimately self-enclosed worlds, their assemblages bend back self-referentially, never moving beyond these 1,500 pages. The spaces of these books remain trapped within their plastic covers, never opening up to their outside.

Thinking cultural studies differently

Despite their limitations, Koolhaas and his project can provide a generative starting point for rethinking cultural studies, and not just insights into contemporary urban conditions and new ways of theorising and new languages of space. Koolhaas has a knack for tackling issues also of concern to critical theory, from redirecting our focus on the cutting edges of globalisation to the abstract machine of shopping in everyday life. The creativity of these texts as responses to contemporary conditions is an important model for cultural studies to consider (a model with inherent dangers, of course).

This returns us to Grosz's questions – posed to architecture but now to cultural studies. Can we think cultural studies differently? Can we think of its practice as the production not of texts but of spaces or assemblages? Can it provide 'little bombs' to make the Junkspace of contemporary cultural studies, and contemporary culture, stutter or tremble? Imagine a cultural studies that performs its critique, its detour through theory; that acts through the creation of affective spaces, assemblages of images, ideas, sounds, textures. Such texts are not unknown to cultural studies, but tend towards the exception rather than the rule, and none has ever been mounted on the scale of the Project on the City. Perhaps they should be. Cultural studies is at its best when it functions as an assemblage. Recall the collective work, writing and projects of the Birmingham Centre for Contemporary Cultural Studies, tackling subcultures, mugging and the rise of Thatcherism. This was a cultural studies of the moment. It does no good to repeat it because that moment has passed. What we need is a cultural studies that is engaged and immanent in the contemporary moment; a cultural studies that is once again radically contextual in terms of its methods, concepts and writings; and a cultural studies project as sprawling, diverse, focused, multi-perspectival and affectively charged as Koolhaas' project. Koolhaas describes architecture as being devoted to the resistance against chaos. This is not the path for cultural studies (or for architecture, for that matter). While its project is to articulate, to create assemblages, organisations against chaos, it also when appropriate must disarticulate, to open up to chaos to release the forces of creativity and force.[18] It is only through engaging in these processes of deterritorialisation and reterritorialisation, of articulation and disarticulation, that cultural studies can (to respond to Grosz's other question) open up to an outside, to stutter and tremble.

Cultural studies has become too complacent in its acceptance of critique as the appropriate means of engaging the conjuncture. And Koolhaas is right in that we can't build based on critique alone. To build is to take risks, to make commitments, to establish new and lasting structures. We need a cultural studies that builds, that engages the politics of building and the politics of the minor, the multitude. That is a new adventure indeed.

Acknowledgement

I wish to thank those at the Conjunctures meeting in Montreal in 2005 for their helpful comments on a preliminary draft of this chapter, and also to thank Clare Birchall and Gary Hall for their feedback and support through the revision process.

Notes

1 www.gsd.harvard.edu/people/faculty/koolhaas/courses.html, accessed on: 26 January 2005.
2 'Cultural studies' is used as a term of convenience to raise these issues with contemporary North American and European cultural studies more generally. However, I wish to acknowledge that such sweeping terms are problematic; there is no one cultural studies and never has been.
3 Over a decade ago, Stuart Hall critiqued the 'astonishing theoretical fluency of cultural studies' (1992: 280), a critique which still holds true today. For more on cultural studies' 'theoretical fluency', comfort and complacency, see the introduction by Gary Hall and Clare Birchall and the chapter by Paul Bowman, in this volume.
4 It is unclear exactly what relationship the title is supposed to imply between contemporary urban developments and Mao's historical Great Leap Forward (a deurbanising movement). Considering that an estimated twenty million or more people died of starvation as the result of the Great Leap Forward, the title is either insensitive and inappropriate or devastatingly critical.
5 These terms are all copyrighted and accompanied by the copyright symbol (e.g. *Infrared©*).
6 Compare, for example, Eric Ma's much more limited 'methodological experiment with visual ethnography' in Dongguan as an attempt to engage the lifeworlds of the workers in that city's factories (Ma and Tse 2005).
7 Perhaps the prospect of addressing Hong Kong was too controversial if the team wanted greater access on the PRC side of the border (and Hong Kong is built on a very different economic and architectural model from the rest of the PRD).
8 '. . .And Then There Was Shopping' is actually the second essay in the book after a history of air conditioning, but close enough to the front matter to stand as an introduction. Leong's other theoretical essay, 'Ulterior Spaces', closes the volume. The alphabetic organisation of the book gives the

impression of randomness, if not an encyclopedia-like quality, but such organisation can be easily manipulated by altering essay titles. For example, portions of 'Ulterior Spaces' appeared in the *Mutations* volume under the better title 'Control Space' but the new title allows it to close the book.

9 Unfortunately, the concept of shopping itself is taken as a universal term and not unpacked or theorised. For example, the book takes for granted the seeming uniformity of shopping itself, locating its origins in 7,000 BCE when the city of Çatalhöyük was founded for the trade in commodities, as if shopping is the same in all places and at all times; that is, as if buying vegetables for the day's meals is the same as cruising through one of Koolhaas' Prada stores.

10 The essay shares much with Gilles Deleuze's society-of-control essays (both in Deleuze 1995). But unlike Deleuze's call to look for resistance 'at the level of our every move' (1995: 176), Leong simply gives up: 'In the end, there will be little else for us to do but shop' (2001b: 135).

11 A crisis point for Koolhaas and his architectural firm was a commission from Seagram/Universal to build a new corporate office in Los Angeles to celebrate what was then a huge merger. It was a commission 'to represent a commercial intention' (Koolhaas 2004: 44) – the merging of liquor, film, music and Internet companies. However, within six months 20 per cent of the company had disappeared. 'The company was mutating as fast as a virus' (2004: 44). What was first thought to be a follow-up to Mies van de Rohe's Seagram building was, half a century later, an unworkable mess.

12 Emphasising this focus on the virtual, cyberpunk guru Bruce Sterling even overviews AMO for the festschrift volume *Considering Rem Koolhaas and the Office for Metropolitan Architecture* (Patteeuw 2003).

13 Joan Ockman writes in *Architecture* about the Project on the City volumes: 'Of course, what might have been more revolutionary to expose in over 1500 pages on shopping and Chinese modernization is the sweatshop economy that has underwritten both – images conspicuously missing from the fashionably fuzzy photos' (2002: n.p.).

14 'It is impossible to make a creative statement that is based purely on criticism' (Koolhaas in Davidson 1995: 234). However, in saying this he conflates politics with critique, ultimately sidestepping the question of politics – a characteristic Koolhaasian move.

15 'Such mediation was also the mission of several avant-gardes after the war, Situationism prominent among them: to ride the dialectic of modernisation in a way that might keep these projects alive for the future. Koolhaas surfs this dialectic better than anyone else around, but his very skill has made for some ambiguous moves' (Foster 2001).

16 Leach here is critiquing Paul Virilio's work along similar lines. He argues that Virilio's critique of the transformations of architecture in the face of communication and information technology is essentially aesthetic. 'In the aesthetics of disappearance, it would seem, it is not the aesthetic which disappears, but

the political. Yet in reality the political never fully disappears. For what lurks beneath the veneer of the aesthetic is a more insidious form of reactionary politics: the politics of acquiescence' (Leach 2000: 83). In her critique of the Project volumes, Joan Ockman references Peter Sloterdijk's notion of 'enlightened false consciousness': 'the intellectual stance of understanding the disparities of power and pain in the world but acting as if there is nothing to do about them' (2002).

17 'One can't help but recoil at the prospect of an aestheticized album about the pathological dysfunction of that impoverished Nigerian city, among the most hellish places on earth' (Ockman 2002).

18 I have in mind here the conclusion to Deleuze and Guattari's (1994) *What is Philosophy?* on chaos and the umbrellas raised against it.

Bibliography

Chung, Judy, Chihua, Inaba, Jeffrey, Koolhaas, Rem and Leong, Sze Tsung (eds) (2001a), Harvard Design School *Project on the City: Great Leap Forward*, Cologne: Taschen.

Chung, Judy, Chihua, Inaba, Jeffrey, Koolhaas, Rem and Leong, Sze Tsung (eds) (2001b), Harvard Design School *Guide to Shopping*, Cologne: Taschen.

Davidson, Cynthia C. (ed.) (1995), *Anyplace*, Cambridge, MA: MIT Press.

Deleuze, Gilles (1995), *Negotiations 1972–1990*, trans. Martin Joughin, New York: Columbia University Press.

Deleuze, Gilles and Guattari, Félix (1994), *What is Philosophy?*, trans. Hugh Tomlinson and Graham Burchell, New York: Columbia University Press.

Foster, Hal (2001), 'Bigness', *London Review of Books*, 23:23, www.lrb.co.uk/v23/n23/print/fost01_.html. Accessed on: 26 January 2005.

Grossberg, Lawrence (1997), 'Cultural Studies: What's in a Name? (One More Time)', in *Bringing it All Back Home: Essays on Cultural Studies*, Durham, NC: Duke University Press, pp. 245–71.

Grosz, Elizabeth (2001), *Architecture from the Outside: Essays on Virtual and Real Space*, Cambridge, MA: MIT Press.

Hall, Stuart (1992), 'Cultural Studies and its Theoretical Legacies', in Lawrence Grossberg, Cary Nelson and Paula Treichler (eds), *Cultural Studies*, New York: Routledge, pp. 277–86.

Jameson, Fredric (2003), 'Future City', *New Left Review*, 21, www.newleftreview.net/NLR25503.shtml. Accessed on: 17 September 2005.

Koolhaas, Rem (2002/3), 'Introducing the Harvard Design School Project on the City', *Harvard Design Magazine*, 17, pp. 2–3.

Koolhaas, Rem (2003), 'Wasteland', *WIRED*, p. 137.

Koolhaas, Rem (ed.) (2004), *Content*, Cologne: Taschen.

Koolhaas, Rem and Mau, Bruce (1995), *S, M, L, XL*, New York: Monacelli Press.

Koolhaas, Rem, Boeri, Stefano, Kwinter, Sanford, Tazi, Nadia and Obrist, Hans Ulrich (2001), *Mutations*, Barcelona: Actar.

Leach, Neil (2000), 'Virilio and Architecture', in John Armitage (ed.), *Paul Virilio: From Modernism to Hypermodernism and Beyond*, Thousand Oaks: Sage, pp. 71–84.

Lieberman, Rhonda (2002), 'One and Two: A Project for *Artforum*', *Artforum*, February, pp. 98–9.

Lovink, Geert (1997), 'Hong Kong and the Culture of Disappearance: An Interview with Ackbar Abbas', posted to nettime-l. www.nettime.org/Lists-Archives/nettime-l-9707/msg00085.html/. Accessed on: 1 February 2005.

Ma, Eric and Tse, Ducky (2005), 'Working and Spending in South China: A Methodological Experiment with Visual Ethnography', *South-Asia Cultural Studies*, 6:1, pp. 113–25.

Ockman, Joan (2002), 'The Yes Man', *Architecture*, 91:3, pp. 76–9. Accessed via: ArtFullText 1/00–6/05 ERL WebSPIRS.

Patteeuw, Veronique (ed.) (2003), *Considering Rem Koolhaas and the Office of Metropolitan Architecture: What is OMA*, Rotterdam: NAi.

Zalewski, Daniel (2005), 'Intelligent Design: Can Rem Koolhaas Kill the Skyscraper?', *New Yorker*, 14 March, pp. 110–25.

HUMANIMALFUNCTION

CHAPTER 14

Cultural Studies and the Posthumanities

Neil Badmington

Greetings from Cardiff University's Humanities Building. Wish you were here. From my window, I can see a supermarket, a library, the railway line that runs north to the valleys, and, on the other side of the tracks, the skeleton of the unfinished Optometry Building. Apart from the occasional asbestos outbreak, the Humanities Building is a fairly uneventful place. Departments only really communicate with each other in standardised memos these days, as there is no shared common room. The only occasion on which I can remember a group of people from different parts of the Humanities Building talking to each other at length, in fact, was during a march through the city to protest against the invasion of Iraq. For an hour or two on a cold winter's day in 2003, there was a hum of humanities in Cardiff. It happened far from our building, though, and we went our silent, separate ways as soon as we stepped back through the automatic doors.

I give myself three wishes, one for each of the trains that I have just been watching thunder past my window. I wish for the destruction of this cold, grey building. I wish for the dissolution of the departments that lie within its walls. I wish, finally, that from the rubble would rise the Posthumanities Buildings. This chapter will no doubt be like a profession of a lack of faith. I do not believe in the humanities.

Cultural studies and the humanities

There is a sense in which cultural studies emerged out of a dissatisfaction with the shape of the humanities. The early work of Raymond Williams, for instance, stood up for the stories that the humanities had traditionally written out of the world. When figures such as Matthew Arnold or F. R. Leavis handled their subject matter in terms of value judgements, they contributed, Williams argued, to an understanding of culture that made the humanities a form of ignorance:

The concept of a cultivated minority, set over against a 'decreated' mass, tends, in its assertion, to a damaging arrogance and scepticism. The concept of a wholly organic and satisfying past, to be set against a disintegrating and dissatisfying present, tends in its neglect of history to a denial of real social experience. (Williams 1963: 255)

Culture, Williams countered, is simply a way of life. It is absolutely 'ordinary, in every society and in every mind' (Williams 1989a: 4).

Written from deep within the humanities in the late 1950s, *Culture and Society* could not, of course, find support for its propositions in any existing academic discipline.[1] A new space was needed. When cultural studies formally emerged some years later, its approach to culture, as is well known, owed much to Williams. As Paul Willis once put it, the new discipline took its subject matter to be 'not artifice and manners, the preserve of Sunday best, rainy afternoons and concert halls . . . [but] the very material of our daily lives, the bricks and mortar of our most commonplace understandings' (Willis 1979: 185–6). 'Clearly', he continued:

> this is a special use of the concept of culture. In part it can be thought of as an anthropological use of the term, where not only the special, *heightened*, and separate forms of experience, but *all* experiences, and especially as they lie around central life struggles and activities, are taken as the proper focus of a cultural analysis. (186; emphases in original)

The ground had shifted. It was now possible to pay attention to ways of life that had previously been pushed beyond the pale of the university. Williams' call for a rewriting of syllabuses 'to a point of full human relevance and control' (1989a: 15) had apparently been answered.

This is a familiar story, and others have mapped the shift in far more detail than I can offer here (Turner 1990; Davies 1995; Hartley 2003, for instance). I have no desire to tell the tale anew. I want, rather, merely to acknowledge before I go any further the dramatic difference that cultural studies has made to the humanities. Things are clearly better now than they were half a century ago. Culture has lost some of its limits, been thrown open to possibilities that once lay silent, and I do not wish for one moment to roll back the wheel of history. I think, though, that a problem remains. While cultural studies has transformed the humanities, it has not, in my opinion, questioned one of the most troubling aspects of the humanities. A limit has yet to be addressed. A 'damaging arrogance' – to recall Williams – remains in play. There is work to be done, a step still to be taken. This will have been the business of the posthumanities.

Cultural studies and the posthumanities

The problem to which I am alluding is phrased with power and precision in the opening pages of *Animal Rites*, where Cary Wolfe argues that cultural studies is commonly founded upon the repression of 'the question of nonhuman subjectivity' (Wolfe 2003: 1). Because the discipline tends to take 'it for granted that the subject is always already human', it remains 'locked within an unexamined framework of *speciesism*' (1; emphasis in original). Although it has sought to break down a series of oppressive barriers, cultural studies has systematically reaffirmed the hierarchical border between the human and the inhuman. Wolfe immediately adds another startling blow:

> That my assertion might seem rather rash or even quaintly lunatic fringe to most scholars and critics in the humanities and social sciences only confirms my contention: most of us remain humanists to the core, even as we claim for our work an epistemological break with humanism itself. (1)

Why, precisely, does humanism remain at work? Why does 'Man' man cultural studies? The answer, I think, lies in the very idea of the humanities.

This brief intervention is not the place to unfurl the coiled tale of the humanities. Instead, I simply wish to recall something that both Jacques Derrida (2002b: 207) and Samuel Weber (2001: 236) have pointed out: the humanities both presuppose the figure of the human *and* confirm what is proper to 'Man'. This was brought home to me with particular force when I recently revisited 'The Idea of the Humanities', where R. S. Crane proposes that the concept of *humanitas*, which he unearths in the writings of Cicero and Quintilian, established 'the nature and basic terms of the discussion of the humanities that has gone on from the Renaissance to our day' (1967: 158):

> When the Romans first spoke of *humanitas*, they used the word to mark off those activities of man by which he is most completely distinguished from the animals, and they identified these with the activities by which man brings to perfection the twin faculties of speech and reason. In this broad sense, then, 'humanity' may be said to consist in the possibilities or powers which men realize, in varying degrees of excellence or completeness, when they develop languages, produce works of literature and art of all kinds, or build philosophical, scientific, or historical constructions; the objects of humanistic study would therefore be precisely these things. (1967: 167)

These lines occur towards the end of Crane's survey, and he soon follows them by returning to the question with which, more than 160 pages earlier, he began:

What, then, are the humanities? It will not do merely to say that they are human achievements in language, art, philosophy, and science, though they are these. We must also take into account the methods and arts by which such achievements may be constituted as humanistic subject matters distinct from the subject matters of scientific enquiry. (Both subject matters, however, may include the same objects, in the sense of languages or literary works having the same names or dates.) And here, I think, one major distinction will be clear if we consider what is left over after language or literature has been analysed and explained by the factual methods of science. What is left over is precisely the question of the nature and value of the language or literature *as a human achievement*, and as an object, therefore, not merely of curiosity concerning its circumstances or genesis or natural laws, but of understanding and appreciation for what it is. (167–8; emphasis added)

The humanities, that is to say, contribute to the wider discourse of humanism, which insists that the figure of 'Man' is absolutely, naturally, ontologically different from – and superior to – all other beings. They are, in fact, the natural habitat of the humanist.[2] What truly interests Crane – and many of the more recent defenders of the humanities, such as Edward W. Said (2004) and Geoffrey Galt Harpham (2005) – is language *as a human achievement*, as a phenomenon that is essentially human.

This belief in the distinction of the human has, of course, been called into question by posthumanism. As I have pointed out elsewhere (Badmington 2004: 87), while the term '*post-Human*' – with its hyphen, capital letter, and italicisation – can be traced back to 1888, it is only in more recent times that posthumanism, as a critical force, has found its feet and its followers. This breakthrough is largely an effect of Haraway's 'Cyborg Manifesto' (1991), the first version of which appeared in 1985, where the monadic subject of humanism finds itself replaced by a nomadic confusion of the organic and the inorganic, the natural and the cultural. Technology, Haraway argues, can no longer be separated from everyday life; its influence is so powerful, its integration so seamless, that it no longer makes sense to think of ourselves as human beings. 'By the late twentieth century', she concludes, 'our time, a mythic time, we are all chimeras, theorized and fabricated hybrids of machine and organism; in short, we are cyborgs' (Haraway 1991: 150).

Taking this trembling of tradition as its starting point, posthumanism has, to put matters in somewhat general terms, interrogated the myth of humanism by activating the moments of pollution and the slow slide of certainties that have habitually been drowned beneath the white noise of uniqueness. The figure of 'Man' has, accordingly, been cut down to size, opened to intimate invasions from what once lay only on the side of the inhuman. Not content to have unleashed the cyborg, for example, Haraway has let OncoMouse out of its cage (1992), and, more recently, traced how companion species hound humanism to its death bed (2003). Drawing upon Haraway, N. Katherine Hayles (1999) has written an influential chronicle concerning how the human has been refigured in recent decades as disembodied information, and Elaine L. Graham (2002) has mapped the difference that phenomena such as 'Frankenstein foods', the Human Genome Project and technologically assisted reproduction make to what she repeatedly calls the 'ontological hygiene' of humanism. Cary Wolfe, meanwhile, has charted how work in animal studies has weakened the familiar boundary between humans and animals by showing that many of the traits habitually deemed uniquely human – self-awareness, boredom, altruism, tool-making and tool-using, love, friendship and even (non-verbal) language – are actually shared by animals (Wolfe 2003: 40).

There is, though, a curious irony in the fact that much posthumanist scholarship has been produced within the humanities, within the space that marks and makes 'Man'. It is time, I think, to iron out this irony. My point is not to denounce anyone for 'working for the enemy'; I, too, as my introduction deliberately made clear, find myself within the walls. I want, rather, now that posthumanism has made its presence felt, to question the relevance of the idea of the humanities to the analysis of culture.

It seems to me that a genuinely *critical* posthumanism – I borrow the addition of the crucial adjective from Jill Didur (2003: 112) – should resist the seductions of the humanities. If 'the human' is no longer a credible category, how can the humanities remain something in which to have faith? Such faith might not always be formally professed, of course, but, as Cary Wolfe has acutely observed (2003: 2), the discourse of species regularly operates *at the level of the unconscious*. If the study of culture fails to question the idea of the humanities, therefore, I think that it fails to address its speciesism. And if such a thing is allowed to happen, injustice looms large. Wolfe expands upon this latter point with particular clarity:

> It is understandable, of course, that traditionally marginalized peoples would be skeptical about calls by academic intellectuals to surrender the humanist model of subjectivity, with all its privileges, at just the historical moment when they are poised to 'graduate' into it. But . . . as long as this humanist and speciesist *structure* of subjectivization remains intact, and as long as it is institutionally taken for granted that it is all right to systematically exploit and kill nonhuman animals simply because of their species, then the humanist discourse of species will always be available for use by some humans against other humans as well. (7–8; emphasis in original)

It is precisely this 'humanist and speciesist *structure* of subjectivization' that I see as entangled with the idea of the humanities. 'We' learn – quietly, calmly, sometimes secretly – to naturalise 'ourselves' as ontologically distinct and eternally superior in the humanities. In the reckoning with what Crane calls 'human achievement', the human achieves dominion over its others.

Not all incarnations of cultural studies formally dwell within the humanities, of course. But it seems to me that the human has also underwritten cultural studies – wherever it has been practised – at the very level of culture itself. While the discipline has successfully wrestled culture away from the Cambridge teashop, to recall an image from Raymond Williams (1989a: 5), its redefinition has tended to go no further than the borders of the human. Culture, in short, remains *human* culture; it is what *we* produce, reproduce, challenge. Clifford Geertz's famous definition is, in this respect, absolutely decisive:

> The concept of culture I espouse . . . is essentially a semiotic one. Believing, with Max Weber, that man is an animal suspended in webs of significance he himself has spun, I take culture to be those webs, and the analysis of it to be therefore not an experimental one in search of law but an interpretive one in search of meaning. (Geertz 1973: 5)

Culture consists of meanings, and these have been woven by 'Man'. While 'he' is described by Geertz as an 'animal', 'he' is an animal that is *capable of culture*, and this essential difference is constitutive. And while it is true that Geertz's account is not wholly humanist – the webs of significance are, after all, transpersonal networks that exceed the grasp of the self-fashioning individual – it remains faithful to 'Man' at the level of the signifier and, more generally, in what Erica Fudge terms 'the exclusive connection between humans and culture' (2002: 135).

At the heart of this particular problem lies anthropology itself, which automatically authorises *anthropos*. And cultural studies, as I see it, has tended to do the same. What Paul Willis called – in the quotation to which I turned above – the discipline's 'anthropological use' of the signifier 'culture' certainly brought about a significant methodological shift, but this shift, *precisely because it was anthropological*, did little to disturb the reign of the human. Geertz's 'webs of significance', in other words, lead back to the *humanitas* of which R. S. Crane writes. What cultural studies inherits from anthropology is *anthropos*. And in its eagerness to expand the syllabus to what Williams called a level of 'full human relevance and control', cultural studies, for all its real victories, has spread a fundamental injustice every step of the way. Only the human is relevant. Even when it has moved outside the humanities, the discipline has seeded the divisive discourse of species with every sounding of culture. Even when the latter has been reimagined as inhuman 'webs of significance', behind and before those webs stands the figure of 'Man', as author, actor, agent. Popular music, fashion and teen subcultures, for instance, are now recognised as instances of culture, but they are at once manifestations of ways of life, of struggles and practices, of identities, that are ultimately and unmistakably human.

What is to be done? What might cultural studies do to address this injustice? In a critique of Geoffrey Galt Harpham's defence of the humanities (Harpham 2005), Jonathan Culler takes an initial step towards an answer to these questions. 'Perhaps', he writes, 'a helpful approach to the crisis of the humanities would be to try to invent a new name, so that our disciplines would not be characterized by a name that carries with it a potentially misleading ideology' (Culler 2005: 42). As Culler does not offer the 'new name' towards which he is reaching, I want to propose a possibility: the posthumanities.

In my writings on posthumanism, I have always been cautious about my use of the 'post', and that caution needs to be remembered here. As I have argued at length (Badmington 2004: 109–22), I do not take the 'post' of posthumanism to mark a clean and clear break. In my account, posthumanism is never that which simply follows – chronologically, apocalyptically – humanism. Taking my inspiration from Jean-François Lyotard's work on the postmodern, I have instead preferred to read the 'post' as the sign of a 'working-through' (in the Freudian sense of *Durcharbeitung*), a paced and patient reckoning with what is at stake. With this in mind, I see the 'post' of 'posthumanities' not as the announcement of the end of the humanities, but as the mark of a critical and gradual engagement with the relationship between the humanities and the figure of 'Man'.

I am not proposing an increase in interdisciplinarity. While interdisciplinary work is regularly rolled out as an object of desire in contemporary higher education, I think that J. Hillis Miller is right to argue that the very idea of interdisciplinarity confirms the purity of the disciplines that precede the communion (Miller 1998: 62). It is, I think, time to inter the 'inter'. The posthumanities, rather, would come into being with the overdue recognition that culture does not begin and end with what 'we' – as a 'we' – call 'human'. In the posthumanities, Geertz's webs of significance would be traced across the traditional ontological abyss between the human and its others. The uniqueness to which R. S. Crane appealed would no longer be of interest, would no longer guide reading, thinking, writing. If cultural studies is concerned with meaning, wherever it flourishes, then it cannot cling to an idea – the humanities – that confines complex signification to the human, for the belief that 'Man' is the only real creator of subtle signs is now profoundly suspect.

The implications of this latter point have, of course, been addressed at length by various critics whose names are associated with the specific fields of posthumanism and animal studies (Wolfe 2003; Fudge 2002, for instance). It seems to me, though, that the wider analysis of culture – even if it occurs outside the humanities – must rethink its most fundamental presuppositions in the light of such research. As long as culture remains the exclusive property of *anthropos* or *humanitas*, cultural studies wounds the world.

Does my imagining of the posthumanities chime with Jacques Derrida's profession of 'faith in the Humanities of tomorrow', in 'the new Humanities' (Derrida 2002b)? Not quite. I cannot, for once, be fully faithful. There is, I should like to add without hesitation, much that I find compelling in 'The University Without Condition'. Perhaps now, more than ever, it is crucial to demand at every turn that the university 'be the place in which nothing is beyond question' (Derrida 2002b: 205), in which experimentation be allowed to occur in peace. Modern Western universities – and even humanities departments – are, after all, increasingly run by people who unleash an idiot wind every time they move their mouths.

However, it strikes me as somewhat curious that Derrida, who devoted so many of his final pages to querying the humanism of Western understandings of 'the animal' (Derrida 2002a, 2003; Derrida and Roudinesco 2004: 62–76, for instance), should be unwilling to equate a working-through of the humanities with a loss of faith in the humanities. The 'new Humanities' will, he insists, 'have to study their history, the history of the concepts that, by constructing them, instituted the disciplines and were co-extensive with them' (Derrida 2002b: 230). And this deconstructive work, which must occur *within* the humanities:

> would treat the history of man, the idea, the figure, and notion of 'what is proper to man'. [The new Humanities] will do this on the basis of a non-finite series of *oppositions* by which man is determined, in particular the traditional opposition of the life form called 'human' and of the life form called 'animal'. I will dare to claim, without being able to demonstrate it here, that none of these traditional concepts of 'what is proper to man' and thus of what is *opposed* to it can resist a consistent scientific and deconstructive analysis. (Derrida 2002b: 231; emphases in original)

I am in complete sympathy with these propositions, and I recognise the impossibility of making an apocalyptic break from the humanities. I am uneasy, however, about 'the new Humanities', and not merely because the phrase reminds me of the 'neohumanism' for which Robert Scholes called in 'The Humanities in a Posthumanist World', his symptomatic presidential address to the MLA in 2004 (Scholes 2005: 732). Regardless of the lengths to which Derrida goes in order to explain the term, its second signifier does not, in my opinion, do justice to the essay's rigorous deconstruction of the humanism harboured in the third word.

It is on precisely these grounds that I prefer 'the posthumanities' to 'the new Humanities'. 'Post' can, of course, commonly signal the same kind of razed modernity as the term 'new', but, as I have already stated, I am using the prefix in a specifically Lyotardian manner. In that crucial sense, the posthumanities correspond with 'the new Humanities', for, in 'The University Without Condition', Derrida returns to the concerns of earlier texts such as 'Cogito and the History of Madness' (1978) and 'The Ends of Man' (1982), where he challenged the belief that it is possible to make a clean and clear break from humanist discourse: the working-through takes place within. If, therefore, 'The University Without Condition' is calling for a rewriting of humanism from within the walls of humanism itself, its project matches my description of posthumanism as 'the acknowledgment and activation of the trace of the inhuman *within* the human' (Badmington 2004: 157; emphasis added). 'The new Humanities' could, that is to say, be renamed 'the posthumanities' without loss of ground, but with the loss of the troubles of the 'new'.

I have a further reason for preferring 'the posthumanities'. Typographically, Derrida's phrase grants its final term two notable privileges. First, the capital 'H' heads in the direction of hierarchy. It might even be seen, following Cixous, as 'the stylized outline of a ladder' (1993: 4), the way to a higher ground. (I am mindful, moreover, of the fact that 'ladder' and 'school' are served by the same signifier – '*ysgol*' – in the Welsh language that surrounds me as I write, and that '*ysgol*' duly graduates into '*prifysgol*', the word for 'university'.) I have no desire for the humanities to ascend to a position of greater capital. Second, the 'new' preserves a literal space between itself and its successor. The 'Humanities' is allowed a comfort zone, room to breathe, the protection of distance. In 'the posthumanities', by way of contrast, the questioning is inscribed more intimately on the page, for the space has been reduced to its bare minimum (and the capital has, of course, been cut down to size). The beheaded 'humanities' is now coupled to its 'post'; the one follows the other, follows the other wherever it goes.

I do not expect my faith in the posthumanities to be popular. And, in one very immediate sense, I can understand the reluctance of anyone who works in the humanities to go along with my call for their 'post-ing'. Lives and jobs are at stake, and a lapse of faith in the humanities is surely something that the circling bureaucrats would relish. Wouldn't abandoning the humanities in the name of the posthumanities finally allow the old enemies – the idiots – to win? Isn't my faith in the posthumanities deeply and dangerously *irresponsible*?

Not necessarily. I would like to end with two pre-emptive observations:

1. 'Giving up' the humanities in the name of the posthumanities would not require the giving up of anything more than the humanities' fidelity to the human. The same texts, for instance, could continue to figure, but their *contexts* would change in their meeting and mixing with what was once beyond the pale. This is not about burning books or bridges; it is, rather, a question of working without the measure of 'Man', without culture being 'ours' alone.

Appropriately enough, perhaps, discussions about posthumanism have taken me outside the humanities in recent years, and I think that the posthumanities might learn from, among other things, the work of certain geographers whose approach strikes me as thrillingly alien to the idea of the humanities. I first became aware of their research at the annual conference of the Royal Geographical Society/Institute of British Geographers in 2003. I have a vivid memory of, several weeks before the gathering, writing in a state of blind panic to Noel Castree, who had invited me to address a session entitled 'Post-human/Post-natural Geographies' that he and Catherine Nash had organised. 'But I didn't even take "O" Level Geography. How on earth will I fit in?', I fretted. Noel calmly suggested that I read Sarah Whatmore's *Hybrid Geographies* (2002) to put my mind at ease.

As usual, he was right. What immediately impressed me about the book is its commitment to what baffles an idea of culture that is coterminous with 'the human'. Whatmore is, as she puts it elsewhere, 'an advocate of geographies attentive to, and sustaining of, more-than-human worlds' (2004: 1361), and *Hybrid Geographies*, in this spirit, celebrates the moments at which humanism's narratives are revealed to be partial, feeble, mythical. To view Duchess – an elephant housed at Paignton Zoo – in purely taxonomical terms, for instance, is to miss part of the animal's tale. Her time in captivity has spun a web of significance that makes a radical difference:

> Zoo animals like Duchess and the 30,000 or so in the herds of Chobe National Park may be kindred under the taxon *Loxodonta africana*, but in many other senses they are worlds apart. For all the scrutiny, veterinary

invention and population management, the elephants of Chobe still lead nomadic, socially rich and ecologically complex lives ... Duchess has become habituated to a more impoverished repertoire of sociability, movement and life skills that will always set her apart. (Whatmore 2002: 56)

Duchess, in short, is different in *culture* from the elephants of Chobe. Meanings move without the human; culture does not begin and end with 'us'.

Whatmore does not seem anxious about her disavowal of humanism, and I detect – as, I must stress, an outsider – a similar jubilation elsewhere in the field of geography, in Nigel Clark's infectious reading of everyday viruses (2004), Steve Hinchliffe's notion of 'entangled humans' (1999), and Nigel Thrift's work on automobility (2004), for instance. My dream for the posthumanities is that the insights and energies of critics working – like Whatmore, Clark, Hinchliffe and Thrift – beyond the humanities come to interface with those of figures who have already begun to foster posthumanism *within* the humanities. The rewriting of humanism from within will be easier and quicker with a little help from without.

2. Irresponsibility – the fact of failing to *respond* – is something at which the humanities have traditionally excelled, precisely because they have never known how to respond to what is not human with anything other than institutional ignorance. Cultural studies grew in reaction to injustice, to hierarchies and entrenched outlooks. If it is now to remain faithful to its initial promise, it must move towards the posthumanities. As long as the humanities guarantee the many privileges of 'Man', a structure of silence holds sway. The 'damaging arrogance' of which Williams wrote survives in the discourse of species. Faith in the humanities is faith in injustice. A cultural studies that cares about the politics and ethics of its work and its world should begin to imagine its role in the building of the posthumanities.

Acknowledgement

A version of this chapter was delivered at the nineteenth annual conference of the SLSA, Chicago, November 2005. I am grateful to all those who commented, particularly Stefan Herbrechter and Ivan Callus. I also owe thanks to Nigel Clark for the transmission of viruses.

Notes

1 Williams would later suggest, though, that the activities of the various British adult education programmes in the 1930s and 1940s could, in hindsight, be seen as de facto cultural studies (Williams 1989b: 154).

2 It is not mere coincidence that many critics use the term 'humanist' simply to describe one who works within the humanities. See, for instance, Crane (1967: 4); Said (2004: 2); Harpham (2005: 21); Scholes (2005: 726).

Bibliography

Badmington, Neil (2004), *Alien Chic: Posthumanism and the Other Within*, London and New York: Routledge.
Cixous, Hélène (1993), *Three Steps on the Ladder of Writing*, trans. Sarah Cornell and Susan Sellers, New York: Columbia University Press.
Clark, Nigel (2004), 'Infectious Generosity: Vulnerable Bodies and Virulent Becomings', paper given at the 'Life Science' conference, Queen Mary, University of London, 5 November.
Crane, Richard S. (1967), 'The Idea of the Humanities', in *The Idea of the Humanities and Other Essays Critical and Historical*, Chicago and London: University of Chicago Press, 2 vols, vol. 1.
Culler, Jonathan (2005), 'In Need of a Name? A Response to Geoffrey Harpham', *New Literary History*, 36:1, pp. 37–42.
Davies, Ioan (1995), *Cultural Studies and Beyond: Fragments of Empire*, London and New York: Routledge.
Derrida, Jacques (1978), 'Cogito and the History of Madness', in *Writing and Difference*, trans. Alan Bass, London: Routledge and Kegan Paul, pp. 31–63.
Derrida, Jacques (1982), 'The Ends of Man', in *Margins of Philosophy*, trans. Alan Bass, Hemel Hempstead: Harvester Wheatsheaf, pp. 109–36.
Derrida, Jacques (2002a), 'The Animal that Therefore I Am (More to Follow)', trans. David Wills, *Critical Inquiry*, 28:2, pp. 369–418.
Derrida, Jacques (2002b), 'The University Without Condition', in *Without Alibi*, ed. and trans. Peggy Kamuf, Stanford, CA: Stanford University Press, pp. 202–37.
Derrida, Jacques (2003), 'And Say the Animal Responded?', in Cary Wolfe (ed.), *Zoontologies: The Question of the Animal*, Minneapolis and London: University of Minnesota Press, pp. 121–46.
Derrida, Jacques and Elisabeth Roudinesco (2004), *For What Tomorrow . . . A Dialogue*, trans. Jeff Fort, Stanford, CA: Stanford University Press.
Didur, Jill (2003), 'Re-Embodying Technoscientific Fantasies: Posthumanism, Genetically Modified Foods, and the Colonization of Life', *Cultural Critique*, 53, pp. 98–115.
Fudge, Erica (2002), *Animal*, London: Reaktion.
Geertz, Clifford (1973), *The Interpretation of Cultures*, New York: Basic Books.
Graham, Elaine L. (2002), *Representations of the Post/Human: Monsters, Aliens and Others in Popular Culture*, Manchester: Manchester University Press.
Haraway, Donna J. (1991), 'A Cyborg Manifesto: Science, Technology, and Socialist-Feminism in the Late Twentieth Century', in *Simians, Cyborgs, and Women: The Reinvention of Nature*, London: Free Association Books, pp. 149–8.

Haraway, Donna J. (1992), 'When Man™ is on the Menu', in Jonathan Crary and Sanford Kwinter (eds), *Incorporations*, New York: Zone, pp. 38–43.
Haraway, Donna J. (2003), *The Companion Species Manifesto: Dogs, People, and Significant Otherness*, Chicago: Prickly Paradigm Press.
Harpham, Geoffrey Galt (2005), 'Beneath and Beyond the "Crisis in the Humanities"', *New Literary History*, 36:1, pp. 21–36.
Hartley, John (2003), *A Short History of Cultural Studies*, London: Sage.
Hayles, N. Katherine (1999), *How We Became Posthuman: Virtual Bodies in Cybernetics, Literature and Informatics*, Chicago and London: University of Chicago Press.
Hinchliffe, Steve (2000), 'Entangled Humans: Specifying Powers and their Spatialities', in Joanne Sharp, Paul Routledge, Chris Philo and Ronan Paddison (eds), *Entanglements of Power: Geographies of Domination/Resistance*, London: Routledge, pp. 219–37.
Miller, J. Hillis (1998), 'Literary and Cultural Studies in the Transnational University', in John Carlos Rowe (ed.), *'Culture' and the Problem of the Disciplines*, New York: Columbia University Press, pp. 45–67.
Said, Edward W. (2004), *Humanism and Democratic Criticism*, Basingstoke: Palgrave Macmillan.
Scholes, Robert (2005), 'The Humanities in a Posthumanist World', *PMLA*, 120:3, pp. 724–33.
Thrift, Nigel (2004), *'Driving* in the City', *Theory, Culture & Society* 21:4/5, pp. 41–59.
Turner, Graeme (1990), *British Cultural Studies: An Introduction*, Boston: Unwin Hyman.
Weber, Samuel (2001), *Institution and Interpretation*, expanded edn, Stanford, CA: Stanford University Press.
Whatmore, Sarah (2002), *Hybrid Geographies: Natures, Cultures, Spaces*, London and Thousand Oaks: Sage.
Whatmore, Sarah (2004), 'Humanism's Excess: Some Thoughts on the "Posthuman/ist" Agenda', *Environment and Planning A* 36.8: 1360–3.
Williams, Raymond (1963), *Culture and Society 1780–1950*, Harmondsworth: Penguin.
Williams, Raymond (1989a), 'Culture is Ordinary', in *Resources of Hope: Culture, Democracy, Socialism*, London and New York: Verso, pp. 3–18.
Williams, Raymond (1989b), 'The Future of Cultural Studies', in *The Politics of Modernism: Against the New Conformists*, London and New York: Verso, pp. 151–62.
Willis, Paul (1979), 'Shop Floor Culture, Masculinity and the Wage Form', in John Clarke, Chas Critcher and Richard Johnson (eds), *Working-Class Culture: Studies in History and Theory*, London: Hutchinson, pp. 185–98.
Wolfe, Cary (2003), *Animal Rites: American Culture, the Discourse of Species, and Posthumanist Theory*, Chicago and London: University of Chicago Press.

EXTREME EVERYTHING

CHAPTER 15

Cultural Studies and the Extreme

Dave Boothroyd

> By definition, the extreme limit of the 'possible' is that point where, despite the unintelligible position which it has for him, man, having stripped himself of enticement and fear, advances so far that one cannot conceive of the possibility of going farther. (Bataille 1988: 39)
>
> The object of research cannot be distinguished *from the subject at its boiling point*. (Bataille 1995: 10)

First image: X-ray vision

In Roger Corman's 1963 sci-fi movie *The Man with X-Ray Eyes*, the protagonist, Dr Xavier (Ray Milland), experiments with a drug he hopes will enhance his vision such that he can improve his work as a surgeon. At first its effects are promising and he finds he can diagnose the internal conditions of his patients simply by looking at their bodies – as well as cheat at cards and slyly admire the physiques of the unsuspecting people around him. Before long, however, his newly won superhuman capacity turns into something increasingly unbearable. With repeated use of the drug his vision achieves ever more extreme penetration into the physical environment around him, with the consequence that it becomes increasingly difficult for him to see the world as humans ordinarily do. The once-familiar modern, high-rise cityscape, for instance, becomes a surreal light show which he describes as 'a city that is newborn, hanging as metal skeletons, signs without support'. Driven by the urge to see ever further and deeper, he takes yet more of the drug, which this time renders his vision almost supernatural: 'I'm closing in on the gods', he tells a colleague who attempts, to no avail, to warn him of his dangerous hubris. Slipping into an irreversible state of increasing visual dissolution, he plunges into the sheer materiality of the world and begins to 'see through the centre of the universe'. Unable to discern anything at all by virtue of seeing everything at once, he becomes, finally and paradoxically, both blind and all seeing – an 'impossible', terrifying condition. Unable to be part of society, he is for a while exploited by a freakshow owner and finally he ends up wandering, lost in the desert. There he encounters an evangelical preacher who enjoins him: 'If thine eye offend thee, pluck it out!' And he does so.

There is an obvious Oedipal-Promethean axis to this tragic tale that any detailed reading of the film would have to explore – but that is not to be my theme here. I begin with this vignette of *The Man with X-Ray Eyes* because the image of 'extreme vision' it provides can also be read as an allegory of the television culture in which we all live. I use the term 'television' here not simply in the senses of either the ubiquitous technological device invented in the 1930s, or 'TV culture', or the industrial institutions of broadcasting, but rather in that of Marshall McLuhan's notion of *tele*-vision as the technological extension of human visual capacity. McLuhan thinks of electric media collectively as 'extensions of the senses' and argues that with each new epochal development in communications technology there is a concomitant evolution in the nature of the human itself. He gives an account of how this process of extension has in fact been under way since the invention of writing and later the printing press, but becomes apparent with the acceleration of the process brought about by the arrival of electric media – radio, TV and film (and one may extrapolate, with the development of computer-mediated communications). To be more precise, Corman's film can be viewed as an allegory of the seductions of the television age in its expression of the profound attraction of extending sensory capacity beyond its natural limit and the deep anxiety concerning consequences of doing so. Dr Xavier is seduced by the prospect of god-like vision and an ultimate experience - to use Georges Bataille's expression, at 'the extreme limit of the possible'. But it turns into an experience of unbearable sensory hyperstimulation and overload which finally leads to his destruction.

The subject in the *tele*-vision age lives in a world in which he or she is not only able to see, but can scarcely avoid seeing, ever more of all the possibilities of human existence, piled up, concatenated and conflated. This condition and situation is not exclusive to the actual consumption of TV culture; however, it is, perhaps, nowhere more acutely experienced than in relation to it or, quite literally, in front of the TV. We now live in a culture characterised by an extreme vision of sorts. One has an intimation of this as one skims across the channels of satellite or cable television using the remote control, but what I want to consider in particular here is how the extreme, or extremity itself (just how to describe the phenomenon I'm not quite sure), has become a prevalent theme within the contemporary cultural nexus of popular, media and consumer cultures.

Of course, the cultural theorist can no more escape this condition of 'extreme vision' than anyone else. Any theory aimed at gaining a perspective on the forms of 'extreme culture' – to which I shall turn in a moment – or at exploring the possibility of seeing beyond its surface phenomena can no more distinguish itself from its objects than can Dr Xavier the images he sees from the light of which they are made. With this observation in mind, my question is: what kind of theory of the extreme/ extreme theory can elucidate the turn towards the extreme across a range of cultural forms and how, if at all, are extremes linked? Just one indication of the way in which different extremes touch upon one another, on the cultural surface of popular discourse at least, is given in a comment by the recently retired chief commissioner of police in the UK, Sir John Stevens, who suggested that the two great challenges facing policing at the beginning of the new century were binge-drinking and international terrorism. There is in his remark, if you will, both an intuition of extremity as the name of anti-rationality in any of its myriad forms, and a reflection of the currency of the extreme as a concept for thinking all manner of cultural phenomena. Now, while excess and transgression may often be deemed matters of criminality and control, they are obviously not always so restricted. At the outset I want to introduce in as simple a formula as possible an idea of Georges Bataille's that I believe can take us some way to grasping the nature of the general and unrestricted *connectivity* thought performs in the context of *tele*-visual culture.

In his short surrealist text *The Solar Anus* Bataille writes: 'It is clear that the world is purely parodic, in other words that each thing seen is the parody of another, or the same thing in a deceptive form' (1985: 5). There is, he suggests, an unlimited possibility of 'copulation' – productive connectivity – between everything which is 'visible':

> Everyone is aware that life is parodic and that it lacks interpretation.
> Thus lead is the parody of gold.
> Air is the parody of water.
> The brain is the parody of the equator.
> Coitus is the parody of crime.
>
> Gold, water, the equator or crime can be put forward as the principle of things.
> (Bataille 1985: 5)

Indeed, any of these things, or any other thing, can function as 'the principle' of 'all things', as the node of a set of connections. But the supreme principle of everything is the connective possibility of language itself:

> Ever since sentences started to *circulate* in brains devoted to reflection, an effort at total identification has been made, because with the aid of the *copula*; all things would be visibly connected if one could discover at a single glance and in its totality the tracings of an Ariadne's thread leading thought into its own labyrinth. (Bataille 1985: 5)

The 'effort at total identification' is always a matter of expenditure (*dépense*) – for instance, of energy, creativity or innovation in the service of such things as art, life, sexuality or cruelty: connectivity names this open-ended possibility. Of course, there is no (positive) possibility of transcendence as such, at least not according to Bataille; and in any case this connectivity is not in reality merely an intellectual concern or a purely theoretical matter. In the scenes of popular culture and everyday life, however, we do witness countless examples and expressions of the drive towards extreme expenditure: to live well is widely understood and measured in the West in terms of the capacity to consume extravagantly and the ability to intensify experience. I shall return to Bataille's general economics of expenditure later. However, before that I want to indicate briefly what kind of phenomena might be *connected* via a principle of extremity. These are in fact none other than the various elements of contemporary culture which provoked this reflection on the extreme in the first place.

Second image: extreme culture

There is in affluent Western societies today a widespread fascination bordering on obsession with all things extreme. This is increasingly apparent across the entire landscape of culture. What I have in mind is particularly evident in the preoccupation within various forms of popular culture, such as social and leisure-time activities and media entertainments, with experiences of extreme conditions, situations, sensations. The appetite for the vicarious consumption of 'images' of extremity is a part of the same phenomenon, I would suggest. The extreme appears to have acquired a general cultural currency: there is a whole range of cultural phenomena, practices and events which are conceptualised as extreme, and of commercial products and services that are marketed on the basis of their association with the extreme. 'X-treme' has even become a cool shorthand for this non-specific, multifaceted cultural phenomenon I am pointing to – the 'X' accurately conveying the sense of unlimited variability of what might come along next and be included within it. It's even worn as a logo or brand name on T-shirts and, more banally still, I've noticed, advertises itself on blocks of cheese: 'X-treme Cheddar' (Tesco, £6.36 per kilo). To illustrate the phenomenon further, and for the sake of brevity, I will just survey a few examples of familiar contemporary culture where 'the turn to the extreme' is to be seen. Together they provide a kind of image which illustrates the diversity and dissemination of the phenomenon I wish to identify as having gained a general prevalence in culture today.

First, I suggest it can be seen in the form of extreme sports – a familiar term, but it is not immediately obvious what qualifies: I suggest the set of all 'sports' which expose practitioners to high risk and places them at the limits of what seems to be possible. To mention just a few: activities such as base-jumping, free climbing, high diving, extreme skiing and snowboarding, extreme surfing, hang-gliding and aerobatic flying might obviously be associated with the label 'extreme sports'. Some foreground the label, some do not. Peter C. Whybrow suggests these might be listed under the rubric of 'when you screw up you die' (2005: 121). Of course older sports such as TT motorcycle racing and single-handed round-the-world sailing could be included too. Such activities are typically characterised by record-breaking stunts or feats of endurance and exposure to danger by virtue of their pushing at the perceived limits of what it is possible to do in each context. If such things as these are the pursuits of an elite minority group of extreme sports athletes and experts – as they all involve special abilities, technical skills as well as risk taking – then what could be called extreme leisure activities provide a measure of the wider 'democratisation' of extreme pursuits into the mainstream and into everyday life. So, second, there is extreme leisure – this could include all those things I just called extreme sports but done in an amateurish or lower-key kind of way: for instance, bungee-jumping, jet-ski riding, hobbyist parachute jumping, urban sports such as skate-boarding, BMX acrobatics, *pars court* and extreme 4X4 off-roading.

Extreme leisure, though, whatever one chooses to include in this category – and it is not my aim to provide a taxonomy here – indicates a wider aspect of the relation to the extreme in culture that I want to highlight. Leisure extends the reach of the extreme into the everyday such that things as different from one another as recreational drug-taking, 'getting wasted' or 'getting high' and dancing all night, performing wild driving stunts on public roads, happy-slapping, brawling, hooliganism and vandalism all become associated in relation to an excitement quotient. If leisure activity is defined as whatever people do to amuse and pleasure themselves in their free time, then extreme leisure pursuits are, unsurprisingly, often likely to bring their participants into conflict with the law, which rigidly distinguishes between what is in fact criminal transgression (crimes against the person or property or public good – such as 'the peace', which might be breached in the course of some people having their 'fun') and what are widely considered acceptable and legitimate amusements as opposed to unacceptable, illegitimate and anti-social activities. My point here is that extreme leisure pushes at the boundary of the very concept of 'leisure' and at the conventional distinctions between what is socially acceptable and unacceptable, legal and illegal. Moreover, it actually challenges and sometimes reconfigures the distinction between such things as public and private space, moral and immoral, responsible and irresponsible acts. Extremity is always related in one way or another to unbounding and transgression. Those manifestations I have just described often involve the redefinition of urban space and architecture by challenging conventional ideas of what a building, a bridge, a street corner or a shopping mall is for. Even the boundary between night and day may disintegrate as a consequence of what extreme culture contributes to producing the 24-hour, 'always on' economy.

Third image: *tele*-vision and the extreme on TV

But it is not only in the spheres of sports, leisure and social life that the extreme finds its expression in contemporary consumer culture; it is even more generally 'available' in mediatised forms. It is, I suggest, generally linked to an ethos of optimisation and the valorisation of doing everything 'to the max', and the widespread desire for 'the extreme case scenario', such that no sphere of culture remains untouched by it. Science is now conceptualised as extreme, say in genetic modification and cloning of plants, animals or humans, as is engineering in its efforts to construct the highest building, the longest bridge or the fastest plane. Medical conditions and diseases are explained through their most extreme manifestations – such as those in the recent Channel 4 series *Bodyshock*, whose titles include 'The Boy Whose Skin Fell Off' and 'The Woman with the 14 Stone Tumour'. A documentary on the evolution of human life pitches to its audience with the title 'Mutants' and with a display of nature's aberrations – monstrously deformed foetuses preserved in bell jars. Life itself on planet earth is found to be born of extreme natural conditions in the deep oceans and is lived in an ongoing struggle to survive its geological and meteorological contingencies (witness the series *Extreme Weather*). Extremity is, so to speak, both our origin and our destiny.

When we are not being edutained by such accounts, we are entertained by the likes of extreme cosmetic surgery (as in the case of the TV show *Extreme Makeovers*) and are directed (and it seems drawn) towards the most extreme examples of violence in films and computer games. Even the orgasm has been replaced by the multiple orgasm, erections are enhanced with Viagra, and the details of the worst tortures and cruelties perpetrated in some far-off gaol are 'consumed', sandwiched between any of the above. All of these are signs of the cultural preoccupation with extremity itself.

The drive for optimisation and the 'urge to excess', which is given cultural expression in cultural practices and forms of the kind I have so far described, only becomes visible as such and in its generality as a consequence of *tele*-vision; only with the technologies of image production and circulation has the cultural purview of the multitude of extremes playing out simultaneously across the cultural landscape become possible. It is through this extended power of vision, and through the exposure of the subject to the multiple and diverse instances and possibilities of extremity ('extremity in all things', as it were) in the image, that the extreme has become a general object of consumption and a value in itself. In the context of TV culture proper, just think for a moment what most people, even by the time of their teenage years, are likely to have witnessed (albeit in mediated forms): they have probably seen the extreme violence of war, executions in close-up, starvation, the suffering victims of road accidents and natural catastrophes, all manner of sexual acts, exploding manned space vehicles, people leaping to their deaths from burning buildings, as well as countless examples of spectacular consumption and the squandering of wealth. And all of this may just be in news reportage. To these scenes of 'reality' can be added all the fictionalised and highly dramatised representations of extremity that are a staple of TV and movie culture in general. One consequence of this *tele*-visuality is a concentration of the diverse possibilities of extremity in human experience. This is focused further through the lens of the TV screen, rendering the extreme visible and at the same time integrating it into everyday life. The extreme has thus become a predominant theme by virtue of *its own power to connect* disparate elements and forms of culture, to the point where it is now a discernible vector of cultural life in general.

It is perhaps telling that the word 'surreal' is so now widely used to describe that aspect of everyday experience which is the result of arbitrary sequences of disparate bits of 'cut-up' visual information striking the visual cortex. In fact, in its presentations of collated imagery, the artistic movement of Surrealism in many ways anticipated the consequences of an ever more connected world. The phenomena of what could be called the 'popular extreme' today crystallise among the involuntary collations of extremity originating in any number of contexts. Under such conditions the extreme becomes an element within the cycle of culture and hence a potential object of cultural studies.

The prevailing *tele*-visual culture we now have (whose material forms include such things as photography, film, computer games, DIY video/DVD and webcast as well as TV 'proper') gives rise to the initial intimation of a connection, no matter how ineffable this may at first seem, between such things as extreme sports and forms of extreme (often anti-) social behaviour and the production and consumption of stylised images of actual extreme violence and cruelty. Entertainment products such as the DIY video *Bumfights* and Still Movements Productions' film *Executions* (Arun Kumar, 2000) are examples of this phenomenon. Indeed, a cursory glance across mainstream TV schedules is all that is needed to get a sense of how 'extremity' figures as a key characteristic across several genres of current programme-making. There are, for example, those programmes which are varieties of 'bad behaviour reality TV': ranging from the confessional chat show format, such as the *Jerry Springer Show*, with its 'my husband slept with the baby-sitter' kind of theme, and its displays of verbal conflict and aggression bordering on 'spontaneous' mayhem, to those exhibiting actual acts of street violence, drunkenness, robberies and road accidents as captured on CCTV. Alongside these one might count shows whose primary intention appears to be to make the audience simultaneously laugh and squirm (I studiously avoid assuming these could be described simply as 'comedy'), such as *Jackass* and *Dirty Sanchez* (originally on MTV and franchised to the British terrestrial public service Channel 4), which feature young men performing ludicrous (in the original sense of the word) stunts, often resulting in physical self-injury or injury to each other. More recently the UK terrestrial, prime-time show *I'm A Celebrity Get Me Out Of Here* stands as a measure of how what was once regarded as excessive and aberrant has become a staple of mainstream popular TV. The show's participants camp in an Australian rain forest and are set tasks and trials which include having their bodies covered with snakes, rats or insects and eating live, slimy grubs or 'repulsive' animal parts such as fish eyes. The revulsion, disgust, horror and fear which these screen antics variously indulge in and solicit from audiences play to an intense sado-masochistic emotionality, which aims essentially at excitement without content or depth; at excitement as an end in itself.

There are, however, other examples of TV culture which contextualise the relation to the extreme differently and are indicative of its wider cultural scope. I will just sketch a few of these, too, to widen out the picture. For instance, *Extreme Celebrity Detox*, a recent production for Channel 4, followed groups of TV personalities as they engaged in a range of activities which could loosely be described as forms of 'alternative therapy', all supposedly aimed at 'self-discovery' and based on ideas associated with things like shamanism, Tao, Tai Chi and other 'new age' popular interpretations of non-Western ideas. At various points in the programme these included participants experiencing episodes of sensory deprivation, the use of a hallucinogenic concoction (Ayhuasca), the drinking of their own urine, the lifting of weights attached to their genitals and the downing of vast amounts of water to produce repeated vomiting. Such 'extreme exercises' are performed as part of purging therapies designed to eliminate the so-called toxic effects of life in modern society by way of pushing the minds and the bodies of the participants 'to their limits'. (Further details of 'alternative' package holidays promising viewers the opportunity of the same extreme experiences off-screen were simultaneously advertised on the channel's website.)

Not surprisingly, the codes of extremity meet with cultural enquiry itself. Consider the two recent documentary series by the Oxford University geographer Dr Nick Middleton, *Surviving Extremes* and *Going to Extremes*. Middleton's anthropological travelogues are based on his journeys to 'extreme places' – by which he means places where the weather especially, as well as the general living conditions, are very different to those in Oxford. 'This is the story', he says in his Mpeg advert on the Net, 'of four real life adventures to four unpleasant physical environments – ice, sand, jungle and swamp . . . The idea of the project is to see how people survive in these extreme physical terrains and see if I can survive.'[1] In the second series we see the surprisingly hapless traveller, Dr Middleton, trying his hand at the dangerous work tasks and other daily activities of indigenous tribal peoples (such as clambering down a vertiginous cliff face to collect honey). But it is not only in the attempt to reach popular audiences through educational TV that this turn towards the extreme is evident: anthropological cultural research within the academy is also showing signs of it. The work of the anthropologists Nancy Scheper-Hughes and Lawrence Cohen at the university of California, Berkeley, for instance, is presented and promoted by their institution under the rubric of 'Extreme Research'. The university's web page details their activities under this banner and includes an image of a surgical-gloved hand holding open a human eye, underneath which there is a caption: 'Pathologist at a public morgue in Cape Town South Africa harvests an eye from a dead young man without the consent of his family.'[2] The image heading the web page is reminiscent of the eye-cutting scene in Luis Buñuel's surrealist masterpiece, *Un Chien Andalou*, and is clearly intentionally horrific (even though the only thing which is truly scandalous or horrifying is that organ harvesting takes place without the consent of the family involved). Scheper-Hughes' and Cohen's work on what they call the 'neo-cannibalism' of illegal organ trafficking is not in itself sensationalist, of course, and I am not questioning its importance and intellectual efficacy. It is, none the less, indicative of the intersection of 'scientific' cultural enquiry with popular understandings and forms of the extreme. Even these researchers themselves are represented as affected by the extreme: they are described as 'professors who depart for places and circumstances more remote and gruelling than most of their students, colleagues and even their own families can – or wish – to fathom . . . [they] not only trek to exotic locales, but also to unsavoury, wrenching and dangerous situations'. Now, whilst on one level this is all an obvious attempt to capitalise on the currency of the extreme, my point is rather that the validity and significance of this work are tied to its investment in and pre-understanding of the 'cultural extreme' given by media culture in the first place.

What all of these examples collectively illustrate is how what has been called the 'circuit of culture' exhibits a tendency towards extremity, and that there is no prospect of theoretical transcendence of the cultural process it describes. Cultural theory, analysis or 'cultural studies' – whatever it is that books like this one are talking about – will in the future have to take into account the consequences of its own situatedness within a *televisual culture* as I have attempted to define it here. In this culture, knowledge for most people has become a matter of spectacle, and everyday experience and concerns are mediated by the images it produces of itself. When the traditional conceptual divisions between such things as nature and culture, education and entertainment or work and play have been eroded, then theory, too, needs to rethink the conditions and consequences of its own relationship to the *surfaces of the culture from which it emerges*.

Fourth image: critique

Perhaps there are only formal and superficial similarities between all extreme phenomena and therefore each ought to be examined in a strictly delimited context: for instance, by explaining sensationalist TV culture in the political-economic contexts of the TV industry and its function in society; or by understanding the subcultural *habitus* of groups whose identities are defined by participating in leisure activities; or by considering the aesthetic aspects of consumption and related consumer sensibilities. These are all possible directions for a cultural studies of the extreme. It could be pointed out that all of the examples of extreme culture given – and countless others which might have been added – only have something substantive in common in so far as they are widely disseminated throughout media culture, and what is at issue here is really nothing more than media culture's representation of a set of phenomena *as* extreme. And if this is the case, then there are several well-established discursive frameworks and a long-standing debate about the production, consumption and function of both mass media culture and popular culture that this so-called 'extreme culture' could readily be referred to. There is no space here to rehearse in detail what such analyses might conclude. I do, however, wish to consider briefly the relation of traditional critique to the extreme.

The familiar approaches would range from Marxian ideology critique, arguing perhaps that extreme culture represses and distracts its consumers, to Gramscian analyses, making of extreme popular and media culture a scene of the struggle for hegemony, through to forms of critical celebration of how its consumption is expressive of creativity and autonomy. From such beginnings it might then be argued that participants and consumers of extreme culture are either the culturally duped, or the politically combative and resistant, or the creative agents of cultural self-determination. John Fiske's accounts of popular culture, for example, typically aggregate elements of all three of these positions, but he particularly champions the producerly creativity of consumers and includes excessiveness within his definition of popular culture:

> Popular pleasures must always be those of the oppressed, they must contain elements of the oppositional, the evasive, the scandalous, the offensive, the vulgar, the resistant. Pleasures offered by ideological conformity are muted and hegemonic; they are not popular pleasures and work in opposition to them. (1989: 127)

The analyses of popular and media culture which have predominated over the last twenty or so years have used variations of these basic positions to address issues such as the structures of identity and power, youth, gender, sexuality, ethnicity and race as these are articulated by popular and media cultural forms. I remind the reader of this here only to make the point that such critical discourses of culture could clearly, easily and logically be extended to the contemporary forms and phenomena I have identified as belonging to 'extreme culture' – perhaps taking newer issues such as the infantilisation of youth, cultural 'dumbing down' or the role of celebrity as topical points of departure. Yet no matter how insightful such approaches to extreme culture might prove to be, they would not imply, let alone guarantee, that the critical account of extreme culture itself remain *open* to the extreme as such. Furthermore, can we ever anticipate and do we really want a satisfactory explanation of the extreme? Does it make sense to suppose it will ever be fully accounted for? The extreme is, after all, philosophically speaking, a figure of the supremely irrational; and theory too must, therefore, *encounter its own limit* as it goes towards it in its attempts to know it. This is precisely what Bataille accuses Hegel of doing when he says in his 'comic summary' of him: 'Hegel, I imagine, touched upon the extreme limit . . . I even imagine that he worked out the system in order to escape [it] . . . Hegel attains *satisfaction*, turns his back on the extreme limit' (Bataille 1988: 43; discussed in Derrida 1978: 251–76).

Remaining *open* to the extreme surely means recognising that there is in an important sense a greater 'proximity' to it in each of its cultural manifestations – in the 'doing', 'participating', 'watching' and 'consuming' – than there is in any sober, rational account which might be given of it. If one were to attempt to *explain* the prevalence of the extreme across culture today, for instance in purely sociological terms, then that would literally be at the *expense* of the extreme – a kind of denial and recuperative rationalisation of extremity and an explaining away. Such an understanding of the phenomenon necessarily comes at the price of reducing it to an object. Let me just attempt to illustrate this by providing a couple of examples.

Zygmunt Bauman has written lucidly on the characteristics of the subjectivity produced under conditions of consumer capitalism, the chief among which is evident in the endless quest of the contemporary social subject for new and ever more intense sensations. Consumer culture produces a subject who is a 'sensation gatherer', according to Bauman (1997: 146). Much of what can be included under the rubric of extreme culture is the result of the desire for novelty, excitement and intensity. This is a desire which consumer capitalism does not merely service by supplying cultural commodities intended to satisfy it, but actually accelerates, as anticipated eventual disappointment is a factor in the whole process. The desire for More, More, More! is by its nature both excessive and insatiable. Dissatisfaction and boredom are built into the cycle of consumption and can only be addressed by means of even more exciting and thrilling sensations which only 'new, improved' products can promise to deliver – hence we are living in an age of aestheticised hyperconsumerism. Bigger and faster cars, more violent films, new styles of porn, more exciting theme park rides, happy-hour bingeing and extreme TV shows of all genres are all part of the 'official' extreme culture which emerges in conjunction with stylised hyperconsumerism. But as some so-called transgressive cultural practices become part of the mainstream consumer culture which tracks along with changing cultural norms, values and standards, others constantly position their 'participants', as already noted above, on the wrong side of the law. Hence a substantial element of what I have called extreme culture is quite logically seen as falling within the province of cultural criminology. The recent work of cultural criminologists such as Mike Presdee (2000) and Keith J. Hayward (2004), for instance, reflects a restitution of the emotional life of the criminal subject (in criminology), in their attempts to explain how cultural life and criminality are interwoven in terms of meaning and behaviour as these are articulated by the urban environment, by popular and media culture and by consumerism per se. Crime should be understood, says Hayward on behalf of cultural criminology, as the 'existential pursuit of passion and excitement' (2004: 9).

Whilst this approach is radical within criminology and, in my view, provides a genuinely useful insight into why today youth criminality especially takes the extreme forms it does (for which Presdee, for example, suggests the rubric 'the carnival of crime'), this discourse does not reflect on *the nature of its own relationship to the extreme*. I am not suggesting that cultural criminologists (let alone Presdee or Hayward in particular) are alone in this; rather that there is a problem for *any* critical discourse at the level of its own relation to the extreme. If it is generally the case, as this cultural criminology claims, that it is the excitement of transgression which is at the heart of much criminality and that this unites it at an emotional level with the ethos of contemporary popular and consumer culture, then it is also the case that this criminological discourse is itself but *yet another image* of the relation to the extreme, which is realised in the 'thrilling' and 'exciting' act of criminal transgression itself. Criminals and criminologists are, so to speak, partners in crime.

In a comparable way, whether someone watches a documentary film 'about' porn star Annabel Chong's record-breaking 251 all-comers gang bang porn shoot with sociological detachment, 'gets off' on the porn film itself, or is one of her fans whose application to the producers to participate in the event itself was successful, such a 'consumer' is in each case located in relation to 'the extreme' the phenomenon instantiates.[3] This is an extreme thesis perhaps, pure parody even and an ugly image, but one which expresses none the less how extreme culture is always a matter of the connections which link one image of extremity to the next. It is, though, I claim, a consequence of thinking materialism through to its logical conclusion.

Fifth image: extreme theory

What I am proposing here is, precisely, a specific image of the theory of the extreme as a construction of the *connectedness* of 'extreme phenomena' evident in different cultural registers: an image of theory whose materiality is given by the connectedness of all the possible images of it. Whether we declare that all 'images' are in any case 'phenomena' or vice versa is ultimately a moot point. Theory, I have suggested, is, in any case, always a matter of reading off the surfaces of the culture; it simply has no other origin. And my own previous 'image' titled 'critique' served to show how the theoretical enterprise at some point or other – usually by arriving at a thesis or position on some bit of contemporary culture, 'X' – always comes to neglect this fundamental condition of all theoretical reflection. In some cases it does this in contradiction to the Marxist materialism it generally aligns itself with; as if theory itself were somehow not subject to Marx's materialist analysis of 'ruling ideas' as the expression of material forces at work in society. In this final section I want to suggest that Bataille's theorisation of the extreme confronts this contradiction otherwise, in so far as his thinking closes the gap between theory of the extreme and what could be called his 'extreme theory'. In other words, in his writings we get a sense of the immanence of theory in the nexus of connections comprising culture as a whole, as well as a sense of how theory may broach the 'extreme limit of the possible' as the *experience* of the impossibility of transcendence. In fact, Bataille holds faith with materialism whilst inverting Marxism's priority of production over consumption.

Bataille's writings contain a sustained meditation on extremity and its various anthropological manifestations (such as death, sacrifice, laughter, eroticism, desire and so forth). In various ways the key determinant of culture is, for him, always a matter of the *surplus* to which extremity in all its forms corresponds. However, I can at this point only draw attention to how the central ideas of Bataille's theory of the extreme might be brought to bear on the contemporary phenomena of extreme culture. Bataille himself did not write about modern 'popular' or media culture – the terms largely used in contemporary cultural studies to refer to the formations of common culture which began to emerge around the middle of the eighteenth century and which are usually associated with the migrations away from the rural life to life in industrial centres. His critical perspective on modern culture is mainly rooted in analyses of quasi-anthropological, some would say largely notional, models of varieties of pre-modern cultural phenomena and experience. However, his understanding of the transition from pre-capitalist to capitalist cultures and societies in terms of a shift from what he calls 'general economies' of expenditure (*dépense*) – of the surplus or excess of energy – to restricted economies of production and (capital) accumulation are, none the less, relevant to the attempt to understand the cultural phenomena of late capitalism, including those of *televisual* culture as I have identified it.

This all important *surplus*, as Bataille imagines it, exists not as the outcome of industrious productive labour, but rather simply as a material given, in the same way that the surplus of solar energy falling on the earth's surface does. This is, in fact, as much a cosmological thesis about the natural world as it is about the formation of cultures whose practices he understands primarily as the forms of its *expenditure*. (Bataille would thus have immediately intuited a set of connections linking 'extreme weather', sacrificial executions, 'mutants', the evolution of life itself and so on.) Life is certainly engendered by the sun's energy and Bataille argues that it is in all cases *lived* fundamentally *for the sake of* expenditure of the surplus it gives. Hence, in his famous inversion of Hegelian-Marxist thinking, the need to consume/expend is said to precede the need to produce/accumulate. According to Bataille, non-productive expenditure underwent a general repression with the rise of commodity capitalism and from then onwards came to be regarded as antithetical to the system of values the ruling bourgeois elite established in order to secure its accumulation of capital and power of reproduction. But whereas the Marxist political-economic critique of this society accepts its principal terms of reference – market exchange, need, scarcity, labour value, accumulation and especially utility – Bataille's 'solar' or 'general economics' invokes the notion of 'useless' or 'absolute' expenditure, and he claims this as the primary determinant of every culture and society. In other words, it is a society's capacity for 'waste', or more precisely 'wastage' (waste without remainder), that gives it its specific identity and structure.

This critique of rationalist political economy on the basis of a partly fabulous account of pre-modern culture and society could no doubt be subject to critique – and unfortunately there is no space for that here.[4] I only wish to note at this point that Bataille's prioritising of non-productive expenditure in the forms (to cite his own examples) of 'luxury, mourning, war, cults, the construction of sumptuary monuments, games, spectacles, arts, perverse sexual activity', such that 'as much energy as possible is squandered in order to produce a feeling of stupefaction ', seems well-primed to anticipate many of the forms and phenomena of extreme culture I have described above (1985: 118–19). And when, for example, he defines human existence in general as 'the life of "unmotivated" celebration, celebration in all meanings of the word: laughter, dancing, orgy, the rejection of subordination, and sacrifice that scornfully puts aside any consideration of ends, property and morality' (1992: xxxii), and writes 'should one desire to lose oneself completely: that is possible starting from a movement of drunken revelry' (1988: 23), then one cannot help but think of the Bacchanalian dimension of a multitude of contemporary popular cultural activities.

However, Bataille is also quite clear that the term 'expenditure' should be exclusively reserved for activities where 'the accent is placed on a *loss* that must be as great as possible' (1985: 118). Bearing this in mind, on the one hand, we could view the prevalence of the extreme in contemporary culture as a kind of blind groping to give expression to the urge to excess which consumer capitalism continues to repress (something reflected in its moral panics, its arbitrary prohibitions and condemnations and its 'incomprehension' of unruly behaviours and offensive practices). On the other hand, it is not clear that any of the instances of extreme cultural practices one might care to examine ever 'succeeds' in effectuating such *pure* loss at all. What Bataille was unable to anticipate was the ability of entrepreneurial capitalism to accommodate, even to exploit economically, commodify and develop into an industry in its own right, the very fundamental urge to excess and non-productive expenditure he identified and sought to found a critique of capitalism upon. And isn't this famous recuperative capacity of capitalism clearly evident today in its contemporary commodifications of popular culture's wildest excesses? Just think for a moment of how the recent phenomenon of 'Ecstasy culture' (whose name is already a 'parody' of a major theme in Bataille!) is commodified in a range of forms from fashion and the pop music product through to the bottled water market and the Ibizan package holiday scene – not to mention 'branded' Ecstasy pills themselves.

If Bataille was unable to anticipate this paradox surrounding non-productive expenditure in entrepreneurial capitalist society – namely, that it accommodates and yet 'fails' in the sense that its extremes are never extreme enough – he does none the less identify it as a theoretical problem and even as the specific problem of theory as such. In the preface to his great book *The Accursed Share* (1995), he draws attention to the paradox of his own analysis of 'productivity' as it might be applied to the very theoretical project he is embarked upon. Bataille says that he is unable to escape the fact that his own intellectual efforts will result in a product, namely the book or the thesis itself, whilst all along wanting to argue that energy 'can only be wasted':

> This invites distrust at the outset, *and yet*, what if it were better not to meet any expectation and to offer precisely that which repels . . .: that violent movement, sudden and shocking, which jostles the mind . . . How, without turning my back on expectations, could I have *the extreme freedom of thought* that places concepts on a level with the world's freedom of movement? (1995: 11, my emphasis)

What I have attempted to show here with reference to Bataille's thinking of the extreme is that, for theory to be truly adventurous, it must be cognisant of its own kinship with its object; it must, in Bataille's phrase, aim to become 'extreme free thought'. But what does this mean in practice? I suggest it means being open to the contingent articulations of theory with the specific excesses of the culture from which it emerges. (In my own recent work, for example, I have investigated how modern cultural theory and philosophical thought must be viewed in the context of the wider culture of drugs and intoxication within which they have been formulated.)[5] Perhaps all adventures in cultural studies should reflect on the idea that theory is not anything other than culture, and all culture is but an 'excess of energy, translated into the effervescence of life' (Bataille 1995: 10).

Notes

1 The Mpeg can be viewed at www.geog.ox.ac.uk/staff/nmiddleton.html. There are, incidentally, two accompanying books available, *Surviving Extremes* (Pan 2003) and *Going to Extremes* (Pan 2004).
2 See www.berkeley.edu/news/magazine/summer_99/feature_darkness_scheper.html.
3 I refer the reader to Gough Lewis' documentary on Chong's career, *The Annabel Chong Story* (1999).
4 For a succinct discussion, see Goux (1990: 206–24).
5 See Boothroyd (2006).

Bibliography

Bataille, Georges (1985), *Visions of Excess*, trans. Allan Stoekl, Minnesota: Minnesota University Press.
Bataille, Georges (1988), *Inner Experience*, trans. Leslie Boldt, New York: State University of New York Press.
Bataille, Georges (1992), *On Nietzsche*, trans. Bruce Boon, New York: Paragon House.
Bataille, Georges (1995), *The Accursed Share. Vol. 1*, trans. Robert Hurley, New York: Zone Books.
Bauman, Zygmunt (1997), *Postmodernity and its Discontents*, Cambridge: Polity.
Boothroyd, Dave (2006), *Culture on Drugs: Narco-Cultural Studies of High Modernity*, Manchester: Manchester University Press.
Derrida, Jacques (1978), *Writing and Difference*, trans. Alan Bass, London: Routledge.
Fiske, John (1989), *Understanding Popular Culture*, Boston: Unwin Hyman.
Goux, Jean-Joseph (1990), 'General Economics and Postmodern Capitalism', in Allan Stoekl (ed.), *On Bataille*, New Haven, CT: Yale University Press, pp. 206–24.
Hayward, Keith J. (2004), *City Limits: Crime, Consumer Culture and the Urban Experience*, London: Glasshouse Press.

Presdee, Mike (2000), *Cultural Criminology and the Carnival of Crime*, London: Routledge.
Whybrow, Peter C. (2005), *American Mania: When More Is Not Enough*, New York: Norton.

TELL US A SECRET

CHAPTER 16

Cultural Studies and the Secret

Clare Birchall

Everywhere I look these days, secrets. Is it just me, or did a chain of secrets or a climate of secrecy characterise events surrounding the second Gulf War?

- **Secret intelligence**: An informer told British intelligence that Saddam Hussein could launch weapons of mass destruction in forty-five minutes. When this proved useful to the government in its case for war, this secret found its way into a public dossier – a secret no more.
- **Passing secrets on**: Weapons inspector Dr David Kelly met with journalist Andrew Gilligan for afternoon tea at the Charing Cross Hotel on 22 May 2003. He let it slip that some people at the Defence Intelligence Staff (DIS) weren't all that convinced by the validity of some of the secret intelligence the government had decided to reveal in the dossier, particularly the 'forty-five minutes' claim.
- **More revelations**: When Gilligan broadcast this secret on BBC Radio 4's *Today* programme on 29 May 2003, he kept his source anonymous. Though under pressure from the government to do so, Gilligan refused to divulge who was behind his claim that prime minister Tony Blair's then director of communications and strategy, Alastair Campbell, had 'sexed up' the dossier in order to make an invasion of Iraq more acceptable. On 30 June, Kelly, recognising some of his own language in the story, eventually put himself forward as the possible source to his line manager at the Ministry of Defence (MoD). It was the MoD, in a highly uncharacteristic game of question and answer with journalists, which outed the name of Kelly.
- **Suspected secret**: The verdict of suicide regarding Kelly's subsequent death has been doubted in conspiracy theory circles (and beyond). A letter in the *Guardian* from three medical professionals aired doubts as to whether Kelly could have died from either a slit wrist or overdose given the evidence (Halpin et al. 2004).

- **Secret hiding spots**: On 13 December 2003, Saddam Hussein was discovered hiding in a 'spider hole' (a narrow hole, six to eight feet deep, covered with a rug, bricks and dirt) at a farmhouse ten miles outside his hometown of Tikrit. He was arrested by US marines after a tip-off from secret informants.
- **Leaking secrets**: In April 2005, the UK government's secret legal advice, given to them by the attorney general before going to war in Iraq, was leaked to the press. The advice, contrary to the version presented to Parliament a week later, was highly ambivalent about the legality of war in Iraq in the absence of a second UN security resolution.
- **Ignoring the protocols of secrecy**: George W. Bush and his cohorts became known for circumventing CIA analysis, preferring to receive raw intelligence. The secrets they received this way were more in keeping with what they needed the secrets to say than the analysed data coming out of CIA Headquarters, Langley. By the time the agents up at Langley got hold of this material, it had already been leaked to the press. Their protestations that it was unreliable got lost in the ether like most corrections and errata.
- **Most wanted**: As of mid-2006, Osama bin Laden continues to hide in secret from the most extensive surveillance and intelligence operation in history. On the FBI's 'Most Wanted' website, it lists bin Laden's occupation as 'Unknown' (although they do know that he is left-handed and walks with a cane).

Of course, we don't get to experience many of these secrets when they count as secret. We usually only hear about them when they are becoming something else – say public knowledge. We only learn of these secrets once they are revealed, which prompts the question of whether we ever really get to know or experience the secret. In addition, you may well question whether, with respect to secrecy's ubiquity, the current conjuncture is significantly different to any other. Although it sometimes seems like it, are there *really* more secrets now than ever before? That would be an absurd, unsupportable claim, not least because of the impossibility of measuring what is hidden. But in as much as we are talking about a *conjuncture* – a singular convergence of cultural and economic 'events' – we can say that it is certainly interesting to see secrecy shaping, and being shaped by, the current convergence.

Indeed, secrets and secrecy seem to have been at the heart of many events in recent years. In particular, the currency of secrets in intelligence circles has come under close scrutiny. George Tenet's resignation from the CIA in 2004 was partly made in anticipation of the commission report investigating the US acceptance of bogus intelligence regarding Iraqi weapons of mass destruction (Borger 2004). Similar shockwaves have been felt in UK intelligence circles following the less explicitly critical Butler Review. After questioning the credibility of the government's claim regarding Saddam Hussein's weapons of mass destruction in a very public affair, the British journalist Andrew Gilligan began asking why intelligence is given more validity purely for being secret (rather than accurate). In Gilligan's post-BBC enquiry – an edition of UK Channel 4's *30 Minutes* entitled 'Do Our Spies Sex it Up?' (2004) – one of his interviewees states, 'The idea that secret information is the best information is bunkum.' It shows that Gilligan continues to be concerned with the way that intelligence is used – or rather, to employ his controversial vernacular, 'sexed up' – for political ends. His documentary went on to attack British secret services that remain, unlike journalists, largely unaccountable to Parliament and the public.[1] Gilligan seriously doubts the validity of shaping hard policy according to unreliable secret intelligence.

The current chapter was conceived in this climate of secrecy and the questions of accountability and legitimacy it raises, not just for those keeping or using the secrets, but for all of us who are in some way interpolated by this economy of secrecy. Secrecy is an important 'new cultural studies' theme for it forces some crucial questions upon us about the way knowledge is presented (by others and by ourselves). The secret makes us ask not only what ideological uses revelation is put to, but also what status secret knowledge has, and what this might mean for how we decide what knowledge is in general. These questions are important because they are concerned with accountability – with what it is to be responsible in an age of secrecy. What, for example, does it mean to make a responsible decision when the knowledge that might help us to do so is kept secret from us? How can we know who is accountable when lines of responsibility are opaque? Who will decide what is and what is not legitimate, and how do we know that that decision is being made responsibly? What apparatus is available to bring to light and/or legitimise one kind of knowledge over another? What can or cannot be fully revealed?

If we are asking at every turn what knowledge is, we are also asking what cultural studies, as a form of knowledge, 'is'. Thinking about less obvious cultural studies themes like the secret (but also, for example, the figure of the extreme – as Dave Boothroyd does elsewhere in this book) is one way of keeping open the 'project' of cultural studies, for it is important that we never take for granted the kinds of cultural phenomena or texts that cultural studies is interested in (subcultures rather than theatre, Gramsci rather than Derrida). As Cary Nelson et al. admit in their influential volume, 'cultural studies can only partially and uneasily be identified by such domains of interest, since no list can contain the topics cultural studies may address in the future' (1992: 1). I think it's important to keep challenging those familiar 'domains of interest'. We cannot know in advance what are and what are not appropriate cultural studies subjects (or what is and what is not 'political', for that matter). For as Gary Hall writes in the opening chapter of this volume, our task 'involves not so much reproducing what it is to do cultural studies as performatively inventing it, each time, *without any guarantees*'.

My approach is, therefore, two-fold. As well as looking at the secret through cultural studies, I want to pursue further this book's concern with experimentation by also considering cultural studies through the secret. In contemplating both the figure of the secret in culture *and* in cultural studies, we can interrogate the question of legitimacy (and the way that the question of legitimacy is traditionally asked); an endeavour that is crucial to the future of cultural analysis and cultural studies. But rather than thinking of this as a retreat from the political questions raised by the current climate of secrecy surrounding the 'war on terror', I propose that a consideration of the secret is necessary in order to come to an understanding of the structures that enable us to analyse or comment upon any politics of secrecy in the first place. If we want cultural studies to be up to the job of understanding the politics of secrecy, it surely has to be able to interrogate its own 'secrets' too, its own 'secret economy', not least because it might only be by understanding these secrets that we can resist or counter the arrogation of power that a certain form of secrecy can assist. In an attempt to do this, I will be calling upon the resources of deconstruction, a 'field' that has theorised the notion of the secret most rigorously (see especially Derrida and Ferraris 2001; Derrida 1992b). This final chapter therefore also allows me to revisit the subject of cultural studies' relation to deconstruction – the 'theory' that has arguably had most influence on the post-Birmingham School generation of cultural studies practitioners – something that Gary Hall, Neil Badmington and others in this book have already been exploring. To return to the quotation from Stuart Hall that Gary Hall cites earlier, this influence is in part due to our being:

> in the deconstructive moment . . . That's what deconstruction means to me: that's what I understand Derrida to be saying: we have no other language in which philosophy has been conducted, and it no longer works; but we're not yet in some other language, and we may never be . . . That is exactly what the notion post means for me. So, postcolonialism is not the end of colonialism. It is after a certain kind of colonialism, after a certain moment of high

imperialism and colonial occupation – in the wake of it, in the shadow of it, inflected by it – it is what it is because something else has happened before, but it is also something new. (1998: 189)

The art of whistleblowing

I want to begin by proposing that cultural studies itself harbours a secret. I want to approach this secret in two related ways. The first fashions the secret as one that I can (at least provisionally) reveal, but this will soon give way to a kind of secret that exceeds a logic of concealment and revelation.

The secret, if I may draw you into my confidence, is that cultural studies could well be a con, a scam, a swindle. Cultural studies might produce bogus intelligence. Cultural theorists may be a bunch of charlatans. Others certainly suspect that this is the case and say as much. The suspicion others unleash upon cultural studies is that we all just 'sex up' data (recontextualise and reinterpret it, change the wording, order and emphasis) to suit our own purposes, to arrive at a conclusion we've already decided upon in advance. When cultural studies gets lambasted for being too 'speculative' (as Toby Miller and Alec McHoul do in their *Popular Culture and Everyday Life* (1998), for example), or too poststructuralist (Bruno Latour asks in *Critical Inquiry*, 'Is it really the task of the humanities to add deconstruction to destructions?' (2004: 225)), or when Alan Sokal (1993) or Jim McGuigan (1992) (albeit in very different ways) critique cultural populism, this seems to me precisely a concern over the legitimacy or proper representation of cultural 'intelligence', of how we are going to present information gathered in the field. Are we agents who have got our hands dirty? Do we have hard and fast data to back up our claims? Or have we been sitting in our 'ivory tower' (of course, it always strikes me that people who talk about 'ivory towers' and 'out-of-touch' academics are themselves horrifically out of touch with the 'reality' of the contemporary neo-liberal university (see Rutherford 2003)), merely reading a book, or maybe venturing out to interview one person, or worse, plagiarising a postgraduate student's work on the subject of our study? (All of which, incidentally, were accusations also made against the first UK government intelligence dossier, 'Iraq – its infrastructure of concealment, deception and intimidation', which was found to contain passages from an article by Ibrahim al-Marashi, a postgraduate student from Monterey in California.) Have we risked anything in order to bring our particular cultural intelligence to light?

Critics of cultural studies, of course, suspect that it *is* illegitimate because of the way it gathers intelligence. And while the secret I'm divulging here sounds only slightly different from this, it nevertheless has radically different implications: for what I want to reveal is that it is a structural possibility that cultural studies, being in the business of knowledge-production, is illegitimate.

Traditional ways of getting around the possibility of illegitimacy (of keeping this secret *secret*) entail claims to meta-narratives like Marxism or humanism; or rooting one's statements in ethnographic observation or hard political economy. We say that cultural studies is legitimate because of its political project, for example, or we try to legitimate it by having it resemble a science as closely as possible, hoping that the more respectable discipline's credibility will rub off on ours. But I don't want to patch up this risk of illegitimacy; nor do I want to keep it secret. Before I get branded a traitor or informer for breaching a cultural studies version of the Official Secrets Act, let me just quickly defend my 'experimental' revelation. In the real British Official Secrets Act, a disclosure is deemed damaging if (and I'm going to replace the references to the Crown and State here with cultural studies to make my point):

> (a) it damages the capability of . . . the armed forces of [cultural studies] to carry out their tasks or leads to loss of life or injury to members of those forces or serious damage to the equipment or installations of those forces; or
> (b) . . . it endangers the interests of [cultural studies] abroad, seriously obstructs the promotion or protection by [cultural studies] of those interests or endangers the safety of [cultural theorists] abroad.

Rather than damaging the capability of cultural studies to function as cultural studies, to carry out the important political and cultural work we often feel we are here to do, or damaging the reputation or professional life of any cultural theorist at home (i.e. within cultural studies) or abroad (i.e. in other disciplinary contexts), my disclosure of this secret is intended to support and develop the interests of (a 'new') cultural studies. This chapter, and this book as a whole, maintain that interrogating the foundations of cultural studies, its underlying assumptions and premises, is enabling rather than disabling.

So, the question of legitimacy generates much anxiety inside and outside cultural studies (though, of course, such an inside and outside cannot easily be designated – a matter that also contributes to anxieties around identity and legitimacy). As I've already mentioned, many attacks from cultural studies' critics strike at the heart of this concern – the infamous Sokal-*Social Text* incident provides a clear example. When the physicist Alan Sokal produced a parody of a cultural studies essay (published in the journal *Social Text* in 1996), he was trying to put on display the social (and scientific) constructionism and uncritical populism that he perceived to be at work in much cultural studies. Sokal focused on the methods of cultural studies, considering them illegitimate because of a distorting political agenda. His concern stemmed from the way in which cultural theory had appropriated terms from science and used them out of context; or, put a different way, Sokal was worried that scientific terms were being used by people without the authority to do so.[2] His parody obviously represented a direct attack on the legitimacy of cultural studies as a mode of enquiry (see Editors of *Lingua Franca* 2000). Rather than being purely negative, however, I want to suggest that such an incident can also be seen as *affirming* the cultural studies 'project' – as being endemic in cultural studies' openness to the question of what legitimate knowledge is (an openness that constantly gets rehearsed as a challenge to 'canonised' histories or knowledges and to disciplinarity, but rarely in terms of legitimacy per se).

Instead of excusing the Sokal incident, then, and fashioning it as an aberration in an otherwise functional discipline, what I am saying is that cultural studies should own it. The Sokal affair, that is to say, represents a moment of undecidability around the issue of legitimacy, and I see this as central to what cultural studies, in many ways, is. It forces us to question what knowledge is and therefore what cultural studies is. And because the answers to such questions and the rules according to which answers can be arrived at are unstable, the risk of being deemed an illegitimate discipline is definitive. Rather than establishing the inadequacy of cultural studies, the Sokal affair suggests that the legitimacy of any knowledge, including that produced 'within' cultural studies, cannot be decided in advance because, as I will explain further, there is an aporetic tension between legitimacy and illegitimacy at the heart of knowledge.

So the knowledge that cultural studies deals in risks illegitimacy because all knowledge is subject to this risk. How does this come about? We can answer by thinking through the classical conditions for knowledge, which deem that: the proposition has to be true; I have to believe that the proposition is true; and I have to be justified in believing the proposition. Epistemologists have debated the assumptions at the heart of these conditions for centuries, particularly concerned with definitions of truth, the nature of belief, and what constitutes adequate justification for knowledge. Indeed, what is striking about the classical formulation is that it leaves open the question of authority – of who authorises the justification for knowing something, and whether that justification can be scientific *only* or could also be ideological. 'Justification', after all, suggests both 'rational' (disinterested) and 'non-rational' (interested) motives.

And there is a more fundamental issue with the authorising of knowledge, which rests on the question of who authorises the authorisation, and so on, ad infinitum. That infinity is the space of the mystical: there is no point at which the question of justification comes to a standstill, no final ground of justification, thus keeping the question of authority open as fundamentally unknowable, or mystical. This means that knowledge can't be justified in any rational, or should I say, knowledgeable way; it can never be legitimately legitimised in the first place.

Knowledge, then, leaves itself open to a self-authorising legitimacy or justification. Jean-François Lyotard elaborates on this issue:

> Authority is not deduced. Attempts at legitimating authority lead to vicious circles (I have authority over you because you authorize me to have it), to question begging (the authorization authorizes authority), to infinite regression (x is authorized by y, who is authorized by z), and to the paradox of idiolects (God, Life, etc., designate me to exert authority, and I am the only witness of this revelation). (Lyotard 1988: 142)

Knowledge, despite its attempts to the contrary, can't do anything to stop this regress, because it just inheres in the logic of authorisation. It can seek to limit or mitigate the 'madness' that such a state of affairs implies by making sure its objects are at least as scientifically robust as possible, but it will never stop the 'madness' per se. An appeal to one's position within an institution ('Trust me, I'm a doctor' or 'Trust me, I'm the prime minister') doesn't avoid this problem, as the founding moment of an institution is also shot through with this problem of authority (who bestowed authority on the institution, and who bestowed authority on the person or institution bestowing authority, and so on). To become knowledge, therefore, knowledge has no choice but to cut 'arbitrarily' into that regressive chain, and to posit something – to posit knowledge that will contain an irreducible and ineliminable trace of the arbitrariness that affects it. Clearly, this is a regrettable set-up for knowledge, not least because it means that 'legitimate' knowledge can never finally distinguish itself from 'illegitimate' or 'non-' knowledge, from apparent subspecies of knowledge that spawn themselves precisely on arbitrary positings of 'knowledge'. On the other hand, without this arbitrary moment of a violent decision, knowledge would not exist at all. In taking its decision to cut into the infinite chain of regress, knowledge becomes itself, and ultimately part of its authority derives just from this act of decision. The cost is that knowledge is shadowed by its 'illegitimate' twin, which has the same parent. Because of the arbitrary decision at the heart of knowledge, legitimacy is irreducibly undecidable.

Of course, in one sense, we are *only* dealing with decidability (only a decision can make knowledge legitimate), but the trace of the undecidable remains. This undecidability does not disappear once the decision has been made as to the verity/credibility/import or otherwise of particular content. (Just deciding that cultural studies, say, is one hundred per cent legitimate will not eradicate the 'secret' of its illegitimacy.) Derrida tells us: 'The undecidable is not merely the oscillation or the tension between two decisions' (2002: 252). Rather, it is a structuring impossibility at the heart of the question of authority. This means that while we *can* make local decisions as to whether a singular instance of knowledge is legitimate or not, such a decision is shot through with a more radical undecidability as to this opposition. We make provisional decisions according to laws, rules and criteria all the time, but the violent establishment of any authority that assures those laws, rules and criteria renders them unstable.

The undecidability of knowledge's legitimacy remains as a trace even when knowledge functions perfectly well. The risk of illegitimacy is never far away. The ghost of undecidability between founded or unfounded knowledge, and of arbitrariness, haunts anything that can be thought of as knowledge. This means that cultural studies can attempt to make itself more legitimate in the eyes of the university by having its journals, international associations, conferences and university departments, but the 'secret' of illegitimacy still necessarily conditions it. Without it, the knowledges cultural studies produces wouldn't be able to be recognised as knowledge at all. After Derrida again (1972), we know that cultural studies' knowledge, manifested as a set of texts and discourses, is iterable: its texts can always be cited and quoted. And because they can be cited and quoted (a necessary state if we are to recognise knowledge), they are subject to misquoting, citing out of context, or, indeed, as in the case of the Sokal hoax, parody: they are open to abuse. Legitimate knowledge is always open to the possibility of 'degrading' into illegitimate knowledge, of moving further and further from the truth. But rather than the possibility of 'degradation' coming after legitimate knowledge has been secured, it is at the very beginning; knowledge cannot be carried forward without this possibility in fact, because without citation, repetition, iteration (all of the things that make knowledge vulnerable to becoming further from the truth), knowledge would not count as knowledge – no one would be able to recognise it. Thus the risk of illegitimacy, rather than being opposed to legitimate knowledge, is an integral part of it.

What this means is that cultural studies doesn't necessarily always need to keep the secret of its possible illegitimacy because it is not just our secret: it pertains to everybody who works with knowledge. But too often cultural studies does endeavour to keep this secret, associating disclosure with a threat against its validity, funding and furtherance (threats that we are usually busy fielding from elsewhere). And so we make appeals to legitimacy through a perhaps outmoded but recognisable and respected political project, or through an identity politics shot through with residual humanism (the problems of which Neil Badmington's chapter in this collection outlines). Both of these can in fact contradict the 'original' political project by being wholly conservative in the sense of maintaining the status quo (Brown 2001). To acknowledge an aporia of legitimacy and authority would, in the view of many, risk undermining cultural studies. However, what I have been suggesting is that cultural studies is vulnerable to attacks on its legitimacy not because there is something dubious about its project, but rather because there is an aporia of legitimacy and authority conditioning *all* knowledge. Addressing this could lead us to Stuart Hall's 'something new' (1998: 189) or, even, a 'new' cultural studies.

So we can now see that, in my attempt to reveal the 'secret' of cultural studies, a more radical, unconditional secrecy (about legitimacy's foundations) has come into play. While I don't have space to do credit to the cultural-politico fetishisation and reverence of the secret here, I do want to return, albeit briefly, to the examples of political secrecy I began with to trace this movement between the conditional and unconditional secret in a slightly different context.

Secret society

First, it is important to say that while I do think the incidents leading up to and following the war in Iraq are evidence of a notable culture of secrecy, it is clear that we are not dealing here with a homogeneous phenomenon. These 'secret encounters' – secret intelligence, secret hiding spots, the leaking of secrets and so on – are not all the same. In some cases, the most important element is the revelation – the point at which the secret is told. In at least one, it is the suspicion that further secrets exist even after revelation has occurred. Other examples focus on spatialised secrets – on hiding places for America's most wanted. And yet all assume a model of surface and depth: they display the enduring, commonsensical notion that, should we manage to lift the veil (if it hasn't already been lifted), perhaps through more search parties, greater investment in surveillance, or new evidence and enquiry, the secret will and can be revealed in its entirety. But revelation is always made in the realm of politics – secrets are always revealed in particular contexts. This is why we might think of them as conditional – secrets that are contextualised, situated, vulnerable to *conditions*.

What this essential conditionality obfuscates, however ('essential' because every bit of knowledge exists in different contexts, ideologies, institutions and so on), is that knowledge (even the knowledge revealed through secrets) is also subject to an unconditional secrecy. The unconditional is still subject to conditions and context (for we are not dealing with two separate secrets), but, crucially, it is not exhaustible by context. In the event of any revelation, any communication, any expression of knowledge, something is always 'held back'. The quotation marks here signify a caveat to this image: what is 'held back' is in no way held in a reserve, waiting to be discovered. As we have learnt from Derrida, there is an excess, a *restance*, that cannot fully present itself. Even in the example of his own writing, itself often denounced for employing a kind of secretive or elitist code, Derrida tries to explain the always already encrypted nature of discourse, giving us a way of thinking about secrecy beyond this surface and depth model:

> When a text appears to be crypted, it is not at all in order to calculate or to intrigue or to bar access to something that I know and that others must not know; it is a more ancient, more originary experience, if you will, of the secret. It is not a thing, some information that I am hiding or that one has to hide or dissimulate; it is rather an experience that does not make itself available to information, that resists information and knowledge, and that immediately encrypts itself. (Derrida 1992a: 201)

For Derrida, the absolute secret resides in the structural unknowability of the future (of events, meaning, texts and so on). In this sense, there will always be something secret.

What this means is that, while a secret is just knowledge in a particularly difficult-to-penetrate context (it is 'secreted' away), that knowledge which is hidden is subject in turn to unconditional secrecy – which means even when it comes to light, it can never fully reveal or present itself. The discovery of Osama bin Laden, for example, would of course reveal the man, but not all our questions would be answered. Even if Osama told us everything he knows, the lack of self-coincidence inherent in identity would ensure that there would be a radical absence accompanying his new media presence. Moreover, these two ways of thinking about the secret – the conditional and unconditional – cannot be separated. Secret knowledge is, of course, subject to conditions, it is situated, it can be revealed – but its meanings, its future meanings, the future 'events' it will be part of, can never be fully revealed because we are not dealing with absence as a modified form of presence, hidden and waiting for its day to come. (This is why I want to keep both 'concepts' of the secret in tension when thinking about cultural studies.)

What happens when secrets – say those encountered through intelligence – are presented as fully revealable? For in the realm of politics, unsurprisingly, the unconditional secret is not acknowledged. Tony Blair and George W. Bush would be unlikely to talk about the unconditional secret because dealing with pragmatic, conditional secrets has political expediency: they have to deal in an economy of revelation ('It was al-Qa'ida!', 'Afghanistan harbours terrorists!', 'Iraq has weapons of mass destruction!', and now 'Iran has been supplying weapons to Iraq!') in order to satisfy the public's need for explanations and to give the illusion of transparency. To be sure, 'acknowledging' unconditional secrecy is difficult to picture. It is not as if something called 'the unconditional secret' is waiting to be greeted. But in the current political situation, it seems to me that secrets are not being dealt with as secrets, characterised by this relation between the conditional and unconditional. If this is the case, what happens when secrets are assumed to be more robust or bounded than the unconditional allows for? This question seems central to me for any consideration of the relationship both between politics and secrecy and between abuses of power and a certain (perhaps inevitable) approach to the secret that assumes a saturated, settled revelation.

Two examples from the list I began with are especially useful here: No. 10's inclusion of the claim that Saddam Hussein could launch weapons of mass destruction (WMD) in forty-five minutes in a public dossier; and the White House's circumvention of CIA protocol regarding intelligence. Both display instances of what happens when secrets are not dealt with as secrets with all their attendant 'problems'; of what happens when the secret is presented as fully revealable, and its content as fully present; when the unconditional is played down in favour of the conditional, splitting the secret in spite of itself.

The 'forty-five minutes' claim was made in a dossier produced by the UK government in order to support its case for an invasion of Iraq in 2003. The claim had been elicited by secret services from a single source reporting a single source. In a court of law, this might be discounted as hearsay, but in intelligence circles, it is simply another unverified claim that then has to be assessed for its validity. Of course, people tell secrets for all kinds of reasons. Sometimes, they make them up. Dr Brian Jones, who managed scientists working at the DIS, admitted at the Hutton Inquiry, 'We even wondered, when discussing the issue, whether [the informant who passed on the "forty-five minutes" claim] may have been trying to influence rather than inform.'[3] In an economy which places a high premium on secrecy, the desire to produce them, to reveal them, even if they do not have basis in fact, must surely increase. The 'forty-five minutes' claim was taken out of its 'secret' context (as well as its cultural-political context), and presented as open fact. Intelligence services, in the final analysis, are usually wary of secrets like this that are at one remove, and remain uncorroborated by other sources. But in the dossier outlining the case for war, the usual caveats expected when dealing with the fragile nature of much secret intelligence had allegedly been edited out as the drafts went by. This resulted in making the secret information seem more factually based than was actually the case. When Andrew Gilligan reported the unease of intelligence workers concerning the 'forty-five minutes' claim included in the dossier, a political crisis ensued.

The US handling of pre-war intelligence on Iraq had very similar results. In the *Washington Post*, Walter Pincus and Dana Priest reported on the difference in language used by the White House to that in a report by the CIA on Saddam Hussein's weapons in the run-up to war (2004: A17). The classified CIA report was, according to then head of CIA George Tenet, full of caveats and qualifiers, whereas the White House's language was characterised by unequivocal assertions about Hussein's weapons. Bush even repeated the UK's 'forty-five minutes' claim despite the fact that, as Pincus and Priest report, 'US intelligence mistrusted the source and . . . the claim never appeared in the October 2002 U.S. estimate' (2004: A17).

In a report in the *New Yorker*, Seymour M. Hersh records a conversation with Greg Thielmann, former director of the Strategic, Proliferation and Military Affairs Office at the State Department's Intelligence Bureau. Theilmann tells Hersh what the CIA thought of this intelligence once it did reach them. ' "They'd pick apart a report and find out that the source had been wrong before, or had no access to the information provided" ' (Thielmann, quoted in Hersh 2004). The trustworthiness of Ahmed Chalabi, who led the foremost Iraqi opposition movement – the US-backed Iraqi National Congress – before the fall of Saddam Hussein was a particularly sensitive matter: the White House liked what it heard through Chalabi's defector reports even though they were discounted by the intelligence community. Theilmann tells Hersh:

> There was considerable skepticism throughout the intelligence community about the reliability of Chalabi's sources, but the defector reports were coming all the time. Knock one down and another comes along. Meanwhile, the garbage was being shoved straight to the President. A routine settled in: the Pentagon's defector reports, classified 'secret', would be funnelled to newspapers, but subsequent C.I.A. and INR analyses of the reports – invariably scathing but also classified – would remain secret. (Theilmann, quoted in Hersh 2004)

On the basis of these defector reports and uncorroborated Italian intelligence that suggested that the Iraqi ambassador to the Vatican, Wissam al-Zahawie, might have purchased uranium in Niger in 1999, the White House made a number of assumptions. Hersh writes:

> On August 7th, Vice-President Cheney, speaking in California, said of Saddam Hussein, 'What we know now, from various sources, is that he . . . continues to pursue a nuclear weapon.' On August 26th, Dick Cheney suggested that Hussein had a nuclear capability that could directly threaten 'anyone he chooses, in his own region or beyond.' He added that the Iraqis were continuing 'to pursue the nuclear program they began so many years ago.' (Hersh 2004)

US and UK foreign policy concerning the Gulf was built upon secrets that had been stripped of the caveats and qualifiers given by the intelligence community and presented to make an airtight case for war. This intelligence was apparently given credence for being secret rather than accurate.

There might be nothing particularly unusual about this situation. The forging of ambiguous into unambiguous language is the stuff of ideology, dogma and policy-making. It is also at the heart of decision-making – for a decision necessarily makes a choice and endorses one particular version of events over others – and of securing mass consent for those decisions. Still, while there might be nothing unusual about this, there is certainly something 'violent' about it. Of course, in this respect *all* decisions are 'violent' (for they posit something at the expense of something else). Nevertheless, what we can detect here is an ethically lamentable short-termism where these decisions are made for expedient political reasons. In losing the caveats that make us remember the fragility of secrets, not only in terms of their precarious verity, but also, I would argue, with respect to what they do not, or cannot, fully reveal, we find ourselves confronted with knowledge. And as I have shown, the conditions that affect knowledge are the same whether that knowledge is secret or not.

Cultural studies and the unconditional secret

Of course, I need to apply this relationship between the conditional and unconditional to my own revelation concerning cultural studies. For in trying to say that the secret of cultural studies is that it might always be illegitimate, I have come up against a different kind of secret, one which concerns the conditions of possibility and impossibility of cultural studies (and of knowledge in general). In this guise, the secret is not that which has been hidden, later to be revealed, and is in principle, fully knowable. Nor is it an enigma that remains unknowable (like God). It is not the object of knowable or unknowable knowledge at all. Rather, we are faced with the Derridean secret: that which remains outside the phenomenal event as it happens but which nevertheless conditions that event. The irreducible, non-present secret (or in fact 'non-presence') in this sense structures presence. I can name this secret 'undecidable legitimacy' or something like that, but this is really only akin to saying the secret is that no one knows the secret. The secret remains irreducible even while we try to reveal it, keeping the future open. I will not have revealed anything that will help us to decide in advance about any future encounter with knowledge – say the next time the government tries to persuade us to wage war; or, at a more local, self-reflexive level, the next time someone tells you what cultural studies is, 'new' or otherwise. Such a programmatic approach towards the decision would wrench the decision from us; it would no longer, that is, be ours; it would be made according to someone else's law. All I can say is that illegitimacy is neither present nor unpresent in cultural studies; its presence is undecidable; the risk, irreducible. Illegitimacy is a necessary possibility that enables us to say anything that has validity and force, enables us to say anything outside an already calculable realm of set responses.

This second kind of secret is, then, the first without the lure of revelation. If the first pointed towards an aporia of legitimacy at the heart of knowledge claims and 'disciplinary' authority, the second makes it clear that the secret can only ever be that nobody knows the secret. As an originally oppositional discourse that still has a precarious status within the university (despite an undeniable institutionalisation in some locations), cultural studies has a greater capacity for opening itself up to questions of legitimacy than others. Cultural studies is well placed to 'expose' rather than 'keep' the secret of undecidable legitimacy: a secret that conditions any knowledge statement, and anything that we could recognise as cultural studies. And, as the brief discussion of just some of the ways in which secrecy permeates our political culture shows, such an exposition should be important to cultural studies. We should, if our oppositional politics is still to have force, want to operate in a significantly different way to those who simplify secrecy, knowledge and legitimacy. We should be interested in thinking through the undecidability in a way that those in power can't afford to.

I have considered the secret of cultural studies not in order to discredit cultural studies, but as a way of claiming cultural studies as *the* mode able to question the very nature of legitimacy (once it has stopped trying to keep the secret that legitimacy is always in question). I am not breaching the cultural studies' version of the Official Secrets Act because nothing I have said can harm the existence of cultural studies. But it might make it more robust, more able to show that it understands the status of the intelligence it gathers and presents in various dossiers for public consumption. How, then, can we produce a cultural studies that would be able to take on board the possibility of its own illegitimacy? It means that we have to make decisions without resorting to calculated, prescribed responses every time we encounter a cultural studies text (which might involve facing up to the limitations inherent in some forms of cultural studies), or the cultural texts we want to make sense of, including the culture of secrecy I have gestured towards.

It is with an eye on the conditions of possibility and impossibility of our own legitimacy that we should analyse the place of secrets in contemporary culture. For only by understanding the instability of the knowledge through which we speak, and the non-programmable, non-systematised decision that this therefore requires, can we begin to appreciate fully the lure and complex currency of secrets in a political climate reliant upon presenting undecidable intelligence or testimony as stable knowledge.

Notes

1 In the UK, the Intelligence and Security Committee provides parliamentary oversight of the Secret Intelligence Service (MI6), Government Communications Headquarters and the Security Service (MI5). It was established by the Intelligence Services Act 1994, but has limited resources and power.
2 I should point out here that attacks on cultural studies come from different angles, partly depending on which version of cultural studies is being attacked. In the US, cultural studies is very much associated with theoretical encounters, and Sokal seemed to be more concerned with attacking the likes of Althusser, Deleuze, Latour, Lacan, Baudrillard etc. rather than the kind of speculative cultural studies Miller and McHoul talk about. However, Sokal's essay and the incident in general are linked with Andrew Ross, one of the editors of the cultural studies journal *Social Text*, who would easily be aligned with a more British version of cultural studies.
3 See Hearing Transcripts, *Hutton Inquiry*, section 89, lines 16,17,18, 3 September, 2003, available at www.the-hutton-inquiry.org.uk/content/transcripts/hearing-trans28.htm (accessed on: 10 March 2005).

Bibliography

Borger, Julian (2004), 'Under-Fire CIA Chief Resigns,' *Guardian*, 4 June, p. 1, www.guardian.co.uk/international/story/0,,1231201,00.html. Accessed on: 15 March 2005.

Brown, Wendy (2001), *Politics out of History*, Princeton, NJ, and Oxford: Princeton University Press.
Derrida, Jacques (1972), 'Signature Event Context,' in *Margins of Philosophy*, trans. Alan Bass, Chicago and London: University of Chicago Press, pp. 307–30.
Derrida, Jacques (1992a), *Points . . . Interviews, 1974–1994*, trans. Peggy Kamuf, Stanford, CA: Stanford University Press.
Derrida, Jacques (1992b), 'Passions: "An Oblique Offering"', trans. David Wood, in David Wood (ed.), *Derrida: A Critical Reader*, Oxford: Blackwell, pp. 5–35.
Derrida, Jacques (2002), 'Force of Law: The "Mystical Foundation of Authority"', trans. Mary Quaintance, in Gill Anidjar (ed.), *Acts of Religion*, London and New York: Routledge, pp. 228–98.
Derrida, Jacques and Ferraris, Maurizo (2001), *A Taste for the Secret*, trans. Giacomo Donis, Cambridge: Polity.
Editors of *Lingua Franca* (2000), *The Sokal Hoax: The Sham that Shook the Academy*, Lincoln, NE, and London: University of Nebraska Press.
Hall, Stuart (1998), 'Cultural Composition: Stuart Hall on Ethnicity and the Discursive Turn', *Journal of Composition Theory*, 18: 2, pp. 171–96.
Halpin, David, Frost, C. Stephen and Sennet, Searle (2004), 'Our Doubts about Dr Kelly's Suicide,' Letters, *Guardian*, 27 January, www.guardian.co.uk/letters/story/0,,1131833,00.html. Accessed on: 5 July 2005.
Hersh, Seymour M. (2004), 'The Annals of Security: The Stovepipe', *New Yorker*, 30 August, www.newyorker.com/fact/content/?031027fa_fact. Accessed on: 25 April 2005.
Latour, Bruno (2004), 'Why Has Critique Run out of Steam? From Matters of Fact to Matters of Concern', *Critical Inquiry*, 30:2, pp. 225–48, www.uchicago.edu/research/jnl-crit-inq/issues/v30/30n2.Latour.html. Accessed on: 20 May 2005.
Lyotard, Jean-François (1988), *The Differend: Phrases in Dispute*, trans. Georges van Den Abbeele, Manchester: Manchester University Press.
McGuigan, Jim (1992), *Cultural Populism*, London New York: Routledge.
Miller, Toby and McHoul, Alec (1998), *Popular Culture and Everyday Life*, London, Thousand Oaks and New Delhi: Sage.
Nelson, Cary, Treichler, Paula and Grossberg, Lawrence (1992), 'Cultural Studies: An Introduction', in Cary Nelson, Paula Treichler, and Lawrence Grossberg (eds), *Cultural Studies*, London: Routledge, pp. 1–16.
Pincus, Walter and Priest, Dana (2004), 'Bush Aides Ignored CIA Caveats on Iraq: Clear-Cut Assertions Were Made Before Arms Assessment Was Completed', *Washington Post*, 7 February, A17.
Rutherford, Jonathan (ed.) (2003), *Mediactive*, 'Knowledge/Culture', 1.
Sokal, Alan (1993), 'Transgressing the Boundaries: An Afterword', *Dissent*, 43:4, pp. 93–9.
UK Government (2002), 'Iraq's Weapons of Mass Destruction – The Assessment of the British Government', 24 September, www.number-10.gov.uk/output/Page271.asp. Accessed on: 3 June 2004.

Television

Gilligan, Andrew (2004), 'Do Our Spies Sex it up?', *30 Minutes*, aired Saturday 29 May, Channel 4, UK. Prod./dir.: Richard Sanders; prod. co.: Mentorn, RAW.

Bonus Section:
Free with Every Copy of this Book

New Cultural Studies Questionnaire

How new is your cultural studies? Do you know what's hot and what's not in the world of theory? Are you up on the very latest developments in culture, politics, philosophy, science, geography, architecture, new media, technology and so on?

Think you could contribute a chapter to our follow-up to this book, *Even Newer Cultural Studies*? Test yourself with our New Cultural Studies Questionnaire and find out.

Responses on a postcard please to:
  Gary Hall and Clare Birchall
  Middlesex University
  School of Arts
  Trent Park Campus
  Bramley Road
  London N14 4YZ

New cultural studies questionnaire

1. How many people wrote *A Thousand Plateaus*?
2. What was the last chance you took?
3. Tell us a (cultural studies) secret.
4. Hardt or Negri?
5. When did the Americans go to the moon? (Are you sure?)
6. Where would we find Popbitch (and why would we want to)?
7. When was the last time you did anything extreme?
8. What is your favourite listserv?
9. Which of the following are *not* recent cultural studies book titles:
    a) *Doing Research in Cultural Studies*
    b) *More Media and Cultural Studies*

c) *How to Get a 2:1 in Media, Communication and Cultural Studies*
   d) *Media and Cultural Studies for Dummies*
   e) *Cultural Studies – The Basics*
   f) *Cultural Studies – edition 5*
   g) *A Short History of Cultural Studies*
   h) *The Big Bumper Book of Cultural Studies*
10. What 'happened' on September 11?
11. Identify a global brand more effective than al-Qa'ida.
12. What is your favourite spam?
13. Provide an example of singularity.
14. Tell us some gossip.
15. Alain Badiou – really interesting and important, or just evidence of a desire for the next big thing?
16. What was the last podcast you listened to?
17. Which of the following concepts must you never, ever, ever use to end an essay on deconstruction:
    a) Responsibility?
    b) Undecidability?
    c) Aporia?
18. What is 'ficto-criticism' (and why is it always so embarrassing)?
19. How many books has Slavoj Žižek written as of . . . *now*?
20. Hot or not?
    a) Auge
    b) Bergson
    c) Bhabha
    d) Bourdieu
    e) Braidotti
    f) Brown
    g) Cixous
    h) Debord
    i) Eagleton
    j) Fiske
    k) Foucault
    l) Gilroy
    m) Gramsci
    n) Grosz
    o) Haraway
    p) Latour
    q) Levinas
    r) Lyotard
    s) Manovich

- t) Massumi
- u) Nancy
- v) Sloterdijk
- w) Stiegler
- x) Stengers
- y) Virilio
- z) Virno

21. Columns or blogs?
22. Is there really anything interesting left to say about reality television? (Really?)
23. Who do you think was aiming from the grassy knoll?
24. Are you now or have you ever been the member of a secret society?
25. Are you prepared to plagiarise yourself?
26. Do you read footnotes?[1]
27. What does 'Ya Basta!' mean?

---

[1] Just testing.

Contributors

Neil Badmington is Senior Lecturer in Cultural Criticism and English Literature at Cardiff University, Wales. He is the author of *Alien Chic: Posthumanism and the Other Within* (2004) and editor of *Posthumanism* (2000).

Caroline Bassett is Senior Lecturer in Media and Film Studies at the University of Sussex, England. She writes widely on digital culture and gender and is currently completing a book on narrative and new media.

Clare Birchall is Senior Lecturer in Media and Cultural Studies at Middlesex University, England. She is the author of *Knowledge Goes Pop: From Conspiracy Theory to Gossip* (2006). Her work has appeared in numerous books, including Peter Knight's *Conspiracy Nation* (2002), and journals, such as *New Formations* and *Continuum*.

Dave Boothroyd is Lecturer in Cultural Studies at the University of Kent, England. He is the author of *Culture on Drugs: Narco-Cultural Studies of High Modernity* (2006) and founding co-editor of the international journal *Culture Machine*, www.culturemachine.net.

Paul Bowman is Senior Lecturer in Cultural Studies at Roehampton University, England. He is the editor of *Interrogating Cultural Studies: Theory, Politics, and Practice* (2002) and author of *Post-Marxism versus Cultural Studies* (2006). He is currently co-editing a book entitled *The Truth of Žižek*.

Jeremy Gilbert teaches cultural studies at the University of East London, England. He is the co-author of *Discographies: Dance Music, Politics and the Culture of Sound* (1999) and co-editor of *Cultural Capitalism: Politics After*

New Labour (2000). He is currently writing a book on anti-capitalism and cultural theory.

Gary Hall is Senior Lecturer in Media and Cultural Studies at Middlesex University, England. He is the author of *Culture in Bits: The Monstrous Future of Theory* (2002), co-editor of *Experimenting: With Samuel Weber* (2006) and founding co-editor of the international journal *Culture Machine*, www.culturemachine.net. He is currently completing a book entitled *Digitise This!*

Julian Murphet is Senior Lecturer in English at the University of Sydney, Australia. He is the author of *Literature and Race in Los Angeles* (2001) and *Bret Easton Ellis's American Psycho: A Reader's Guide* (2002), and co-editor of *Narrative and Media* (2006) and *Literature and Visual Technologies: Writing After Cinema* (2003).

Brett Neilson is Senior Lecturer in the School of Humanities and Languages at the University of Western Sydney, where he is also a member of the Centre for Cultural Research. He is the author of *Free Trade in the Bermuda Triangle . . . and Other Tales of Counterglobalization* (2004) and co-editor of the special issue of the e-journal *Borderlands* 'On What Grounds? Sovereignty, Territoriality, and Indigenous Rights' (2002).

Gregory J. Seigworth is Associate Professor in the Communication and Theatre Department at Millersville University of Pennsylvania in the US. He is the co-editor of the special double issue of the journal *Cultural Studies* 'Re-thinking Philosophies of Everyday Life' (2004). His work has appeared in numerous journals, including *Antithesis*, *Architectural Design*, *Cultural Studies* and *Studies in Symbolic Interactionism*.

Imre Szeman is Senator William McMaster Chair of Globalization and Cultural Studies and an Associate Professor of English and Cultural Studies at McMaster University, Canada. He is the author of *Zones of Instability: Literature, Postcolonialism and the Nation* (2003), co-author of *Popular Culture: A User's Guide* (2004), and co-editor of *Pierre Bourdieu: Fieldwork in Culture* (2000) and of the second edition of *Johns Hopkins Guide to Literary Theory and Criticism* (2005).

Jeremy Valentine teaches Cultural Studies at Queen Margaret University College, Edinburgh, Scotland. He is the co-author of *Polemicization: The Contingency of the Commonplace* (1999) and co-editor of *Politics and*

Poststructuralism (2002) and the Edinburgh University book series 'Taking on the Political'.

Geoffrey Winthrop-Young is Associate Professor, Department of Central, Eastern and Northern European Studies, University of British Columbia, Canada. He is the author of *Friedrich Kittler zur Einführung* (2005), as well as co-editor of two volumes on media and materiality. His work has appeared in numerous journals, including *Diacritics*, *Critical Inquiry*, *Angelaki*, *Yale Journal of Criticism* and *New German Critique*. He is currently co-editing a special issue of the journal *Theory, Culture & Society* on Friedrich Kittler.

J. Macgregor Wise is Associate Professor and Chair of the Department of Communication Studies at Arizona State University in the US. He is the author of *Exploring Technology of Social Space* (1997), and co-author of *Culture and Technology: A Primer* (2005) and of *MediaMaking: Mass Media in a Popular Culture* (second edition, 2005). He is currently completing a book entitled *Cultural Globalization: A User's Guide*.

Joanna Zylinska is Senior Lecturer in New Media and Communications at Goldsmiths College, University of London, England. She is the author of *The Ethics of Cultural Studies* (2005) and *On Spiders, Cyborgs and Being Scared: The Feminine and the Sublime* (2001), and editor of *The Cyborg Experiments: The Extensions of the Body in the Media Age* (2002).

Index

7/7, 18, 47
9/11 (Sept. 11), 13–14, 31–2, 47, 50n, 71–3, 80, 84, 84n

Abbas, Akbar, 206–10, 249
Abu Ghraib, 13, 74, 139
Adbusters, 74
Adorno, Theodore, 116–17, 121, 154, 212
afternoon tea, 293
Agamben, Giorgio, 3, 17, 81, 128–42, 192, 201
Al-Marashi, Ibrahim, 297,
al-Qa'ida, 304, 314
Althusser, Louis, 11, 55, 57–64, 81, 108, 111, 124n, 148
AMO (Architecture Media Organization), 256n; *see also* OMA
animal, 94, 135, 262, 264–5, 267, 269
anti-capitalism, 18, 181–96
Appadurai, Arjun, 201
architecture, 242–5, 247–54, 279
Artificial Life, 100, 228
Association of Cultural Studies, 203, 205
Auschwitz, 135, 137,
'axis of evil', 71, 73, 83

Badiou, Alain, 147–58, 201, 314
Bataille, Georges, 275–7, 285, 287–90
Bauman, Zygmunt, 285
Belsey, Catherine, 162
Benjamin, Walter, 92, 113–16, 117, 118, 120, 121, 123n, 133, 134
Bennett, Tony, 22, 130–1, 142n, 154, 183
Bergson, Henri, 21, 117–20, 124n, 314

Berlant, Lauren, 154
Bérubé, Michael, 154, 155
biopolitics, 133, 140, 214
Birmingham Centre for Cultural Studies, 1–2, 80, 82, 204, 254
Birmingham School
  brand of cultural studies, 16, 22, 24n, 203, 207
  hegemony, 132
  importance of, 3
  mass communication theory and, 224
  political project of, 3
  post-Birmingham, 2, 17, 23, 30, 36–8, 49, 50, 296
Blair, Tony, 14, 18, 36, 38, 71–2, 186–7, 304
British Official Secrets Act, 298, 307
Brown, Wendy, 3–4, 13–15, 20, 25n, 72, 76, 83, 140, 314
Bush, George, W., 14, 18, 38, 71–2, 74, 136, 139, 191, 294, 304–5
Butler, Judith, 12, 25n, 81, 152

capitalism, 190
  Althusser and, 58–60
  architecture and, 248, 252
  Bataille and, 287–9
  branding and, 74
  consumption and, 285
  cosmopolitanism and, 200
  cultural studies and, 182–3
  dominance of, 3, 188,
  Empire and, 192
  identity and, 65–7, 191,

capitalism *(cont.)*
  moralism and, 71, 75, 77, 80
  post-Marxism and, 55–6
  radical democracy and, 66
  the transnational and, 201, 212
  Williams and, 122, 182–3
  Žižek and, 164–74,
Cevasco, Maria Elisa, 210
cheese, 278
Chen, Kuan-Hsing, 22, 65, 204
CIA, 14, 294, 304, 305,
city, 230, 242, 244–9, 274
class, 20–1, 57, 60–1, 65–6, 90–1, 132, 169, 171–2, 186, 188, 190, 192
Communism, 58, 63, 72, 158, 185, 187, 243, 244
community,
  Agamben and, 134, 137, 192
  'coming community', 3, 35, 133–4, 137
  of cultural studies, 36
  exclusion from, 79, 249
  Hardt and Negri and, 41–5, 50n, 192
  Jameson and, 231
  political community, 73, 75, 129
Couldry, Nick, 24n, 151, 153
criminology, 286
Critchley, Simon, 173–4
cultural economy, 37
cultural populism, 82, 297, 299,
culturalism, 107–10, 113, 118, 123n, 152
cybernetics, 221–5, 227–9, 232–3,

De Landa, Manuel, 94, 100
Debord, Guy, 212, 314
deconstruction
  cultural studies and, 31–6, 43–7, 296
  death of, 26
  the decision, 46,
  Hall on, 50, 296–7
  Hardt and Negri and, 41–3, 45–7
  humanism and, 268
  Kittler and, 98–9
  as negative critique, 34–6
  politics and, 32–3, 172–3
  the secret, 296
  socialist deconstruction, 190
  Žižek and, 163–6,

Deleuze, Gilles
  affect, 84n
  Bergson and, 118–20
  communication, 233
  cultural studies and, 107–23, 195
  'deterritorialization', 166
  empiricism, 110, 113, 121
  German Medium Theory and, 221
  Grosz on, 22, 243, 248
  Jameson on, 230
  Kant and, 114–17
  Lash on, 95
  power, 77
  'society of control', 214, 252, 256n
  structuralism and, 121
democracy
  Brown on, 4, 14
  cultural studies and, 169
  enemies of, 73
  Hardt and Negri on, 41
  hegemony and, 56, 63,
  information society and, 232
  radical democracy, 63–4, 66
  social democracy, 187–8, 190
  World Social Forum and, 190
Derrida, Jacques
  death of, 11
  decision, 46
  dialectic, 42–3, 45
  encryption, 303
  excess, 35, 303
  Hall on, 50
  the humanities, 262, 267–8,
  iterability, 49, 301
  Kittler and, 98–9
  Marxism and, 67
  Levinas and 85n,
  'new international', 3
  politics, 33, 35, 46, 172, 185
  postal principal, 98
  pragmatics, 33
  responding to, 35–6
  singularity, 45
  undecidability, 301
  university, 33–34, 267–8
  Žižek and, 164, 173
  see also deconstruction
Disneyland, 241

INDEX

During, Simon, 24n, 25n, 77–8, 148, 151–2, 153–4

Eagleton, Terry, 12, 162, 183, 220, 314
Erni, John Nguyet, 206–11
ethics, 34, 71–84, 109, 148, 152–3, 172, 201, 270
experience
  aesthetic experience, 155, 214
  antagonism as subjective experience, 61
  British, 194
  of change, 38
  cultural studies and, 25n
  culturalism and, 107, 110–13, 261
  Deleuze and, 113–23
  empiricism and, 109–10
  extreme experiences, 275, 277, 280, 282
  German, 90–3, 101n
  of resistance, 41, 44
  shopping as an essential experience, 246
extreme, 79, 89, 157, 274–90, 313
  extreme research, 282–3

Fascism, 56–7, 60, 62
feminism, 21, 169, 184, 191
Fiske, John, 25n, 284, 314
flashmob, 220–1, 234
Flusser, Vilém, 89, 220, 221, 231
Foucault, Michel, 11, 97, 123n, 124n, 128, 133–5, 138, 214, 314
Frankfurt School, 2, 88, 90, 92–3, 113, 116, 194
Freud, Sigmund, 36, 57, 60, 61, 166, 266
Fuller, Matt, 231–2

Geertz, Clifford, 265–6
Gilbert, Jeremy, 66, 191, 194
Gilligan, Andrew, 293, 295, 305
Gilroy, Paul, 22, 25n, 314
Giroux, Henry, 22, 152
globalisation, 33, 75, 140–1, 200–1, 204, 208, 213, 215, 242, 252, 254
gossip, 314
Gramsci, Antonio
  conjuncture, 50,
  cultural studies and, 36–8, 142n, 194, 205

hegemony, 37–8, 49, 56, 62, 64, 108, 132, 156, 284
  organic intellectual, 2, 137, 175n
  post-Marxism and, 55–62
Grossberg, Lawrence, 36–8, 49–50, 124n, 171, 215, 225, 250, 252–3
Grosz, Elizabeth, 22, 243, 248–52, 254, 314
Guantánamo Bay, 18, 73, 136, 139
Guattari, Félix, 124n, 193, 221

Hall, Gary, 78, 131, 174
Hall, Stuart
  Bennett and, 131, 142n
  cultural studies and/on, 1–3, 48–50, 54, 77, 82, 107–8, 123n, 130, 302
  deconstruction and, 37, 50, 296
  'Encoding/Decoding', 224–5
  institutionalisation of cultural studies, 170–1
  Policing the Crisis, 80
  politics, 19, 36–8, 48, 54, 64–5, 80, 131, 182–3, 186–8, 190, 194
  popular culture, 37
  'theoretical fluency', 255
  Williams and, 117
Hallward, Peter, 147, 154
Haraway, Donna, 152, 227, 230, 263–4, 314
Hardt, Michael, 3, 6, 38–47, 49, 50n, 81, 174n, 185, 192, 214–15, 231, 252
Hebdige, Dick, 82, 88, 157
Hegel, G. W. F., 42–3, 95, 97, 133, 162, 166–9, 285
hegemony, 56
  articulation and, 67
  cultural studies and, 36–8, 108, 132
  the decision and, 156
  Laclau and Mouffe and, 62–4
  moralism and, 13, 46, 76
  outmoded nature of, 49–50
  popular culture and, 284
  radical democracy and, 66
  Western hegemony, 205, 207, 187–8, 190–1
  Williams and, 119
Heidegger, Martin, 67, 92, 100, 132–3

Hoggart, Richard, 22, 107, 123n, 183, 196n
humanism, 15, 25n, 82, 85n, 110, 121, 262–4, 266–70, 298, 302
 anti-humanism, 8, 15
 liberal humanism, 191
 'materialist' humanism, 121
 'neohumanism', 268
 'New Humanism', 19
 see also posthumanism
Huntington, Samuel, 73
Hussein, Saddam, 293–5, 304–6

ideology, 59, 61, 65, 117, 119, 164, 166–7, 169–72, 191, 223, 244, 252, 266, 284, 306
 'Californian' ideology, 222
 Communist ideology, 244
 'Infrared' ideology, 244
 neo-liberal ideology, 169, 191
intelligence, 293–5, 297, 304–6, 308
 artificial intelligence, 100
 critical intelligence, 157
 secret intelligence, 293, 295, 302, 305, 308n
Iraq, 12–13, 18, 38, 47, 71, 73, 189, 260, 293–5, 297, 302, 304–6

Jameson, Fredric, 6, 25n, 130, 202, 207, 213–14, 223, 230–1, 233, 249–50

Kelly, Dr David, 293
Kittler, Friedrich, 17–8, 21, 89–90, 92–100, 221–3, 229, 232
Klein, Naomi, 75, 189, 191, 194
knowledge, 16, 46, 62, 67, 113, 142n, 149, 164–7, 195, 203, 234, 283, 294–5, 299–303, 306–8
 Althusser and, 59–60
 'critical' knowledge, 153, 158
 experience and, 114–16
 'knowledge economy', 8, 187, 194
 politics of, 206–9, 215
Koolhaas, Rem, 6, 22, 230, 241–58
 junkspace, 246–7, 249, 251–2, 254

Lacan, Jacques, 11–12, 17, 97–8, 120, 166–8, 174, 224, 308n

Laclau, Ernesto, 17–18, 55, 60–4, 66–7, 75, 164–6, 173, 205
Latour, Bruno, 226, 297, 308n
Lenin, Vladimir Ilich, 58, 167
Leong, Sze Tsung, 246–7, 255n, 256n
Levinas, Emmanuel, 17, 21, 79, 81–3, 85n
life, 74, 78, 81, 109, 111, 118, 124n, 128–9, 133–41, 279, 288, 290
 everyday life, 25, 78, 81, 152, 157, 162, 202, 213, 215, 225–7, 230, 243, 246, 248, 254, 263, 277–8, 280
 political life, 132, 137, 139
 see also Artificial Life
little bomb, 22, 243, 248, 254
Lovink, Geert, 88–9, 92
Luhmann, Niklas, 17–18, 89–90, 93–6, 98, 100
Lyotard, Jean-François, 11–12, 24, 266, 268, 300

Mao, Tse-Tung, 241, 244, 255n
 Maoism, 76, 158
Marcuse, Herbert, 211, 213
Marx, Karl, 33, 46, 55, 58, 66, 78, 166, 168, 182, 287
Marxism, 54–8, 60, 64–7, 120, 167–9, 173, 192, 284, 287–8, 298
 anti-capitalism and, 188–9
 British Marxism, 123n
 cultural studies and, 12, 54, 78, 132, 158, 182–4, 225
 crisis of, 7
 Italian Marxism, 131–2
 structuralism and, 108–10
 'without guarantees', 65
materialism, 54, 111, 118, 120, 286–7
 cultural materialism, 109, 113, 118, 120–1
Mato, Daniel, 209–10
McHoul, Alex, 297, 308n
McLuhan, Marshall, 91, 253, 275
McRobbie, Angela, 22, 25n, 48, 65–6, 78–80, 82, 84, 187, 194–5, 211
Menezes, Jean Charles de, 18, 139
Meyrowitz, Joshua, 224–5
Miller, J. Hillis, 7, 266
Miller, Toby, 197, 308n
Morris, Meaghan, 22, 154, 216n

moralism, 4, 13–15, 71–2, 75–8, 80, 83
  as anti-politics, 13–15, 20, 76, 83
  morality and, 12–13, 71–77, 79–81, 84, 288
  without ethics, 76, 83
Mouffe, Chantal, 17–8, 55, 60–4, 66–7
Mulhern, Francis, 110, 122, 124n, 182–3
multitude, 3, 6–7, 40, 42, 44–7, 81, 192, 231, 233, 255

Nancy, Jean-Luc, 11, 50n, 190, 192
Negri, Antonio, 3, 6, 21, 38–49, 50n, 51n, 77, 81, 129, 131–2, 141, 174–5n, 185, 192, 201–2, 214–5, 231
neo-liberalism, 3, 26n, 73, 187, 190–1, 195, 242
networks, 6–7, 12, 25n, 74, 190, 192, 212, 228, 265
  discourse networks, 90, 97, 101
  postal network, 98
  networked politics, 74, 228, 230
  networked technologies/networked media, 6, 97, 221–2, 225
new generation, 2, 4–7, 11, 15, 21–3, 25
New Left, 3, 19, 186–8, 190, 194, 228
new media, 5, 18, 21, 94, 97, 201, 203, 220–37, 303
new subjectivities, 65–7
'New Times', 19, 49
Nietzsche, Friedrich, 84, 99
North Korea, 71, 73

OMA (Office of Metropolitan Architecture), 248–9; *see also* AMO
Osama bin Laden, 294, 303

Pearl River Delta, 241, 243–4
'people, the', 57, 60, 64
performativity, 20, 22–4, 34, 36, 47, 49, 81, 101n, 188, 296
Picasso, Pablo, 149
Plant, Sadie, 228–9
political economy, 1, 13–14, 37, 47, 108, 137, 140, 154, 158, 204, 234, 288, 298
politics, 12–18, 23, 41, 44, 62, 67, 181–96, 200–2, 212–13, 215, 231–3, 245, 251–3, 255, 256n, 257n, 304, 307
  activist politics, 75

Agamben and, 129–37, 139–42
Badiou and, 151, 156
of cultural studies, 2–3, 11, 25n, 36–9, 48–9, 65, 78–9, 82–4, 130–1, 139, 151, 153–4, 165, 170, 174, 175n, 183, 186, 194, 202, 204–9, 211–13, 251, 255, 270n
cultural theory and, 20, 26n
culture and, 55–6, 64–5, 151, 156, 207–9, 211
deconstruction and, 32, 34–5, 46–8, 172
founding narratives of, 7, 25–6n
identity politics, 21, 65, 77, 172, 194, 203, 302
Marxist understanding of, 60–1
moralisation of, 71–2, 74–7, 79–80, 83, 84n
of the multitude, 46–7, 255
radical democratic, 61
of theory, 205, 212
Žižek and, 169, 172–4
see also networked politics; secret politics/politics of secrecy
populism, 60–2, 64
  'authoritarian populism', 80
  cultural populism, 82, 182, 297, 299
posthumanism, 94, 100, 263–4, 266–70
  posthuman cultural studies, 93–4, 96, 98, 100
Prada, 252–3, 256n
psychoanalysis, 26n, 57, 60, 84n, 108, 162, 167, 224–5

Rabinow, Paul, 138–9
relativism, 14, 148, 153, 166–7, 169, 172
resistance, 33, 36–7, 44, 77, 82, 84, 154, 156–7, 171, 188, 233–4, 252, 254, 256n
  to thinking, 13
responsibility, 46, 80–2, 137, 148, 270, 295
Rose Nikolas, 138–9
Rutherford, Jonathan, 142n, 175n,

Schiavo, Terri, 74
Schmitt, Carl, 33, 130, 134, 136, 140–1
Seattle, 18, 32, 41, 189
secret, 18, 21, 35, 47, 110, 130, 153, 293–310

secret *(cont.)*
  secret politics/politics of secrecy, 35, 296, 302, 304
  secret prisons, 14
shopping, 82, 241, 243, 245–7, 250–4, 255n, 256n
  ethical shopping, 75, 83
Siegert, Bernhard, 89, 94, 98
singularity, 20, 40–1, 43–6, 48–9, 51n, 121, 132, 134, 137, 156, 190
Sloterdijk, Peter, 89, 93–4, 257n
Sokal, Alan, 297–9, 301, 308n
Speer, Albert, 92
Spinoza, Baruch, 58, 84n
structuralism, 15, 107–8, 110, 121, 124n, 224
subculture, 82, 88, 254, 266, 295
subversion, 42, 61, 88, 169
systems theory, 89–90, 92, 95, 101, 221–4, 227, 233

tactical media, 223, 230–4
techno-cultural theory, 221–3, 225, 227
technology, 8, 91–2, 94, 96–7, 99–100, 120, 139, 220–3 225–7, 231, 233, 263
  information technology, 225–6, 232, 256n
  media technology, 89, 91, 224–6, 231, 275
Terranova, Tiziana, 223, 228–31, 233–4
Thacker, Eugene, 129, 140
Thatcher, Margaret, 38, 80, 188
  Thatcherism, 64, 80, 254
Theweleit, Klaus, 89, 93
torture, 13, 73–4, 280
Toynbee, Jason, 192

university, 261, 297
  corporate transformation of the, 7–10, 12, 136, 141, 175, 195
  cultural studies and, 9, 83, 129–30, 141, 154, 164, 173, 175, 187, 205, 301, 307
  disciplinarity and the, 201
  institution of the, 4, 9, 33–4, 83
  nomad university, 129
  see also Derrida

Wal-Mart, 246
weapons of mass destruction, 293, 295, 304
Weber, Samuel, 16, 223, 262
Whatmore, Sarah, 269–70
Williams, Raymond, 22, 48, 78, 88, 114, 124n, 152, 181–4, 186, 191, 193, 210, 260–1, 265–6, 270, 270n
  culturalism/cultural materialism and, 107, 109, 112–13, 118, 120–1, 123, 123n
  experience and, 110–20, 122
Willis, Paul, 261, 265
Winkler, Hartmut, 89–91
Wolfe, Cary, 94, 262, 264

x-ray vision, 274–5

Yúdice, George, 202, 214

Zapatistas, 41, 234
Žižek, Slavoj, 16, 17–18, 21, 158, 162–75, 205

HM 623 .N49 2006

New cultural studies

APR 1 9 2007